Business and Politics:
A Study of Collective Action

In the first comprehensive study of the origins, structure, membership, and resources of business interest groups in Canada, William
Coleman argues that firms have used such associations to acquire
special privileges within the policy process and to avoid wider, political responsibilities.

Based on a survey of all national business associations and on
interviews with many of their executives, *Business and Politics* outlines
the roles assumed by interest groups in the policy process. Fragmentation of business interests makes consultation with major socioeconomic producer groups highly unlikely. Instead, adjustment
takes place as a series of ad hoc bail-outs related to an electoral
calculus, rather than as a result of more reflective consideration of
the economy's longer-term evolution and the relative economic position of various Canadians. Business possesses no organizations
prompting it to take a broad look at its social responsibilities. Consequently, some policies that might redress difficulties in the economy and social welfare system are ruled out.

Coleman concludes that the business community is not sufficiently
accountable for its actions and not organized to assume the political
responsibilities that should result from its private economic power.
He argues that Canada would do well to adopt institutions of democratic corporatism similar to those in some smaller European states.

William D. Coleman is a member of the Department of Political
Science, McMaster University.

Business and Politics

A Study of Collective Action

WILLIAM D. COLEMAN

McGill-Queen's University Press
Kingston and Montreal

© McGill-Queen's University Press 1988
ISBN 0-7735-0648-9 (cloth)
ISBN 0-7735-0664-0 (paper)

Legal deposit 2nd quarter 1988
Bibliothèque nationale du Québec

Printed in Canada on acid-free paper.

This book has been published with the help of a
grant from the Social Science Federation of Canada,
using funds provided by the Social Sciences and
Humanities Research Council of Canada.

Canadian Cataloguing in Publication Data

Coleman, William D. (William Donald), 1950-
  Business and politics
  Includes index.
  ISBN 0-7735-0648-9 (bound)
  ISBN 0-7735-0664-0 (pbk.)
  1. Business and politics—Canada. I. Title.
  HF298.C64 1988   322′.3.0971   C88-090005-9

For SRC

Contents

Tables and Figures

FIGURES

Preface

This book traces its origins to a research project on interest intermediation in Canada funded by the Social Sciences and Humanities
Research Council of Canada (410-78-0716, 410-80-0280). Working
jointly with Henry Jacek of the Department of Political Science at
McMaster University, I made a preliminary attempt to trace the
emergence of economic interest associations in Canada. While we
had some idea of the complexity of the task when we began, we
certainly did not realize how many associations we would find and
the many questions they would raise about the nature of business-
government relations in Canada. Almost immediately we had to
restrict the scope of our research, which we did in two ways. First,
we decided to study only those associations that might be defined as
"nationally relevant" (for a full definition of this term, see chapter 1).
Second, we included in the study only "associations," which we defined to mean organizations with some formal organizational presence, whether constitution, staff, or permanent means for choosing
leaders. Even with these restrictions, our data set grew to contain
1,582 associations, including trade unions, a number that took some
time to research and code properly.

Accordingly, this study looks at relations between business and
politics through the prism of interest associations. Such a prism
reveals a wide spectrum of different structures, objectives, and subjects for discussion and action involving government. Consequently,
one must broaden the perspective beyond associations to consider
other ways in which business firms relate to governments, and this
I sought to do in the theoretical framework presented in part 1. Our
research strategy consisted of three components. First, we sought to
find all the associations in our universe and to code as much information as possible on their structures and activities. For associations

that are now defunct, this required us to search in various historical documents and directories. For associations that continue to exist today, we wrote them soliciting information, and many kindly responded. Second, we chose a number of sectors for more intensive study of the historical evolution of collective action, the interaction between industrial structure and government relations, and the policy arena within which they operated. Hence, we sought to add some life to the overall aggregate picture that we developed in the first phase of the project. These sectoral studies provide the basis for part II. Third, we endeavoured to place Canadian associations in a larger comparative context, by participating in an international research project on the organization of business interests.

Co-ordinated by Professor Philippe Schmitter and Dr. Wolfgang Streeck and supported by a grant from the Volkswagen Foundation, this project brought together scholars from ten countries: Austria, Canada, Denmark, Italy, the Netherlands, Spain, Sweden, Switzerland, the United Kingdom, and West Germany. We agreed on a common research design and a set of sectors to investigate and then interviewed the associations concerned and collected detailed information on industry structure, the policy environment, and relations with labour. The project continued from early 1981 until the spring of 1985, when most of the country studies were completed and an international data set was compiled. I draw frequently on this research not only for my analysis of Canadian associations but also to place them in a wider context of advanced developed industrial democracies. Consequently, the book that follows provides an aggregate picture of the collective action of business, a political economy of the relations between business and government in a range of sectors, and a critical review of the privileged position enjoyed by business in our democracy. This picture is focused largely on the year 1980, the baseline date both for our original Canadian research project and for the international project. In the sectoral studies, additional historical background is sketched and material is updated to the mid-1980s where possible.

In such a research project, it is inevitable that many personal debts are accumulated. Although our interests have now diverged somewhat, I benefited immensely from discussions with my colleague Henry Jacek, as we developed our research strategy, made the countless coding decisions, and compared notes on interviews. In the course of this process, we were served well by several research assistants: Jessica Bayne, Deborah Dunton, Rob Elliott, Clara Greco, Linda Hyslop, and Tad Kawecki. Linda Hyslop made a singular contribution in helping to organize our work in the early stages.

I wish to thank as well Virgil Duff, managing editor at the University of Toronto Press. He encouraged me at the outset when I mentioned this project and stayed with it through some difficult times. His guidance and encouragement are greatly appreciated. Philip Cercone, director of McGill-Queen's University Press, handled the manuscript with dispatch and gave me support several times when it was much needed. Patricia Kew provided the figures in chapter 2. John Parry copy-edited the manuscript. His work improved the text immensely, and I am very grateful for his efforts.

Many people gave me comments on particular parts of the text. A. Paul Pross read a first draft of the whole manuscript and made numerous suggestions for improvements that I have adopted. In addition, his detailed remarks on each chapter were invaluable, and I appreciate greatly his effort and his professionalism. An anonymous assessor also reviewed the whole manuscript in some detail. Although I ended up disagreeing with some of his/her criticisms, this person forced me to re-examine some of my premises, to correct some errors, and to clarify some points of my argument. The manuscript is improved as a consequence. My colleagues Michael Atkinson and Kim Richard Nossal looked at an early version of chapter 3. Atkinson also reviewed for me a late draft of chapter 10. I benefited greatly from other work with Professor Atkinson, where we developed the policy network concepts that form a central part of this book. Work with him has been stimulating, and I have learned much about writing and maintaining a sustained academic frame of mind from this partnership. Parts of chapter 2 were presented at the annual meeting of the Canadian Political Science Association in 1985, where I received several helpful suggestions. Later drafts of the historical portion of chapter 2 were imiproved with the help of the comments of professors Peter George and John Weaver at McMaster. Professor Grace Skogstad gave me a detailed review of chapter 6, and I have benefited from her own research in several places in this chapter and others. Stanley Coleman circulated chapter 8 to several people at the Council of Forest Industries of British Columbia, which aided this chapter significantly. Helen Sinclair of the Bank of Nova Scotia and Andrew Kniewasser and Sandy Grant of the Investment Dealers Association of Canada gave me many critical comments and suggestions on chapter 9, forcing a major revision. They probably all continue to disagree with some of my conclusions in this chapter, but it is much improved as a result of their comments. Feedback was given me by the Canadian Pulp and Paper Association for chapter 10 and by the Business Council on National Issues and the Canadian Federation of Independent Business for chapter 5. William Chandler and Herman Bakvis provided me with useful comments on chapter 12. Finally, Keith Banting was always very encouraging as I was writing this book. He gave me comments on drafts of chapters 12 and 13 that were very stimulating and useful; these chapters were much improved as a result of his advice.

A version of chapter 3 was published as an article in *Canadian Public Administration*, Volume 28, No. 3 (1985). It appears here with the permission of the Institute of Public Administration of Canada. I owe a great deal as well to many business association executives in Canada who took the time to gather material and to compose detailed letters in reply to my questions. I went back to many of these people several times. In addition, over 50 associations granted interviews to me and Professor Jacek from which I learned much. Several of these same associations then reviewed drafts of initial working papers that served eventually as the basis for several chapters in this book. I would like to thank particularly Phil Nance of the Canadian Institute of Plumbing and Heating for his comments and criticisms.

Finally, I cannot overvalue the academic experience of participating in the Organization of Business Interests project. Working with and coming to know the many excellent scholars from the other countries in this project have been an experience I will never forget and will always draw from. I have several special debts here: Hanspeter Kriesi and Peter Farago of Switzerland have always been very helpful and received me kindly when I visited their project in Zurich; Frans van Waarden of the University of Leiden was always forcing me to think carefully as we examined the actions of business firms; Bert de Vroom of the same university has written several items on quality control that have been most instructive for me; Josef Hilbert, Claus Offe, and Hajo Weber of the West German team invited me to give a seminar at Bielefeld and provided me with some particular insights into corporatism; Alberto Martinelli, Marco Maraffi, Antonio Chiesi, and Mirella Baglioni became valuable acquaintances as well.

In the context of this project, I have three very important people to thank. First, Philippe Schmitter, whom I met as a student at the University of Chicago in the early 1970s, helped to introduce me to this research in 1979 and 1980 and then arranged to invite me and Henry Jacek to participate in the international project. I learned from him constantly as the project developed, and he gave me useful comments on intermediate research papers that provided the basis for this study. Second, Wolfgang Streeck of the International Institute of Management (IIM) in West Berlin and the University of Wisconsin – Madison arranged to have me invited to stay as a guest fellow at the IIM in 1983–4, a period crucial to the development of this book. He looked at many of the papers I wrote that year and gave me useful criticism. His diligence in organizing the research project and urging us all on in the data collection and coding stages provided an example worthy of emulation and contributed greatly to whatever successes the project eventually achieves. Finally, the international project allowed me to meet Dr. Wyn Grant of the Department of Politics at the University of Warwick and director of the British team. Dr. Grant and I have collaborated on several comparative research studies that grew out of the project, in the process of which he became the kind of colleague for which every academic hopes. He read and commented on virtually every chapter in this book and has been a constant source of support and encouragement. His wit and finely attuned sensitivity to politics have stimulated me much over the past four years. I owe him a great deal.

PART ONE

Collective Action by Business

CHAPTER ONE

The Political
Responsibility of Business

The concept of responsibility has played an important role in Canadian politics since the late eighteenth century. Many of the early political struggles in the British North American colonies were over *responsible* government – the principle that those people who allocated and spent the revenues garnered by the state should be held responsible by and to those who supplied the revenues, the electorate or its representatives. In addition, inherent in the Canadian constitution is the notion of ministerial responsibility – ministers in her majesty's government are responsible for those decisions made in their names. When the decisions are bad ones – allowing the sale of tainted tuna or making decisions on subsidies to resource companies in which you own shares – then the minister in question must submit his or her resignation. In both instances, then, a person or group is politically responsible – obliged to answer to another group, usually the electorate, for conduct.

It is not usual to use the notion of responsibility in reference to members of society at large or the business community in particular. Avoiding such usage, however, is a mistake. Is Canadian business politically responsible? Failure to investigate this question has left unexplored an important set of phenomena that may affect economic development. This study begins by examining how the concept of political responsibility might be applied to the business community.

According to Ronald Manzer, the prevailing public philosophy in Canada is a variation of liberalism.[1] Implicit in such a philosophy is equality of individuals, as reflected in Canadian public policies that stress equal access to education, universal and equal access to health services, equal treatment before the law, equal opportunities to speak one of two official languages, and equal political rights.

Associated with this liberal public philosophy is also a vague notion of pluralism. Not only should individuals receive equal opportunities and equal treatment under the law, but also categories or groups of citizens should receive an equal chance to influence laws. When the government of British Columbia proposes to change the manner of collecting stumpage fees, it is expected to listen to the owners or managers of forestry companies, workers for logging companies, professional foresters, naturalist societies, recreational camping groups, aboriginal peoples, and so on. Everyone is consulted, everyone is listened to. Then the politicians stir up this big pot of opinions until it wafts forth the vapours of the general, public interest, which are translated into law for the good of everyone. Pluralism – equal opportunity for all groups to be heard and equal consideration in the development of public policies – is quite consistent with a liberal public philosophy.

Such notions of pluralism, however, are part of an ideology, which, like all ideologies, distorts and hides what actually occurs in practice. All groups and categories of citizens are not equal. Nor is it a matter of one group being favoured in this instance and another in the next. There is a systematic bias in the Canadian system, which consistently gives the business community a better hearing and considers its demands and proposals more seriously when policies are being designed. This observation can be demonstrated in virtually any instance of public policy-making. And politicians should not necessarily be rebuked for this systematic bias: nothing could be more natural in a capitalist liberal democracy.

Such behaviour follows logically from the marriage of a democratic political system and a capitalist economy. Several nineteenth-century thinkers maintained that democracy and capitalism would not mix particularly well. De Tocqueville worried that it might lead to the tyranny of mass politics, and Marx believed that it would end in the revolutionary overthrow of bourgeois society. Surprisingly, however, the mixture has worked in many instances, including that of Canada. It has worked when it involves a compromise of the following form.[2] On the one side, those who own the instruments of production – the business class – consent to political institutions that allow those who are not owners to press claims for a redistribution of the spoils, so to speak. On the other side, those who do not own the instruments of production consent to their being privately owned.

What then are the policy consequences of such private ownership? Charles Lindblom asks us to imagine a politico-economic system without money and markets.[3] In such a society decisions on the distribution of income would be political, as would be decisions on what is to be produced (steel, cars, cotton sheets), what resources are to be allocated to different lines of production, what occupations are needed (chemical engineers, social workers, political scientists), where plants should be located, and what quality standards goods should satisfy. "In all societies, these matters have to be decided. They are of momentous consequence for the welfare of any society. But in a private enterprise market system, they are in larger part decided not by government officials but by businessmen. The delegation of these decisions to the businessmen does not diminish their importance or, considering their consequences, their public aspect."[4]

In short, a range of very important decisions, with great consequences for the lives of all Canadians, for jobs, for economic growth, for prices of goods, and even for Canada's international balance of payments, are made privately in Canadian society. They are a privilege that accompanies the private ownership of capital stock.

Governments, accordingly, depend very much on business. If business makes a wrong decision, whether it be the building of an ethylene plant in Alberta or the closing of a mine in northern Ontario, governments suffer. In particular, such decisions have financial consequences. Governments need money to do what they think they have to do. They may raise the money they need through taxes or they may borrow it on capital markets. In either case, if the private sector is not doing well, governments may experience difficulties in raising revenues. The yield from taxes may be poor, or the cost of borrowing money high. Governments thus have a direct reason for being solicitous of the interests of business.

For these reasons, the liberal idea that all groups are equal and receive equal treatment is questionable. Business persons are in a special position: they will be listened to more closely, and governments will watch carefully what they do. The reverse side of the same coin, however, must be responsibility. If business's decisions have far-reaching consequences for everyone, are sometimes as important to the way we live as those taken in the legislatures, then it too should be held accountable.

However, business leaders in Canada possess what might be called an individualistic industry culture. The term *industry culture* was developed by Kenneth Dyson to refer to the set of beliefs that business people have about the respective places of government and the firm in society.[5] Individualism (as opposed to collectivism) emphasizes minimizing the extent to which business is accountable through the political system to other groups in society. Fortified by deep-seated beliefs in the virtues of free enterprise and private ownership, Canadian business people argue that markets left unfettered and unregulated will work in the longer-term interests of all. If regulations and laws force them too much to account to the public, these market mechanisms will not work properly and will yield a suboptimal set of benefits for all concerned. In short, Canadian business leaders share an ideology that draws the line sharply between public politics and private economics. Actions taken in the former arena should interfere with those in the latter as little as possible. Firms are accountable only to their boards of directors, business leaders argue, not to society more generally.

The degree to which business assumes political responsibility may be examined in three areas: relations between corporations and political parties and between corporate leaders and politicians, corporate behaviour in the wider social context, and business's use of instruments of collective action, particularly interest associations. The latter area is the one examined in this study. It provides a broad, yet somewhat unexplored path to the heart of the issue of the political responsibility of business.

The system of business interest associations in Canada is highly fragmented, consisting of many small, narrowly focused organizations. Further, these groups are isolated one from the other. There are no "peak" associations to integrate these associations or look to the longer-term evolution of the economy. Perhaps, among developed, market-oriented democracies, only the American system of interest intermediation is as poorly integrated as Canada's.

Two interrelated consequences arise from the fragmentation of Canada's business community. First, business is not easily held accountable for the exercise of its vast private power. Yet accountability for its actions surely is at the base of the "democratic compromise" about which we have spoken. Other classes and groups whose members do not possess the instruments of production must be able to press their claims effectively for a redistribution of the fruits of their labour if a democracy is to work well. Lacking encompassing, integrated peak associations, the business community in Canada is unlikely to view its place in the larger context of society as a whole. Rather, its views tend to be more narrow and tied to a particular sector or even an individual firm. There exists little capacity for speaking with representatives of workers, farmers, and consumers in a sustained dialogue about the overall needs and objectives of all Canadians. In addition, business as a whole cannot influence special-interest deals worked out between specific sectors of business and related government agencies. Policy networks in which business is a client of the state further limit business's accountability. In these networks business enjoys a monopoly on relations with the state at the expense of other interested parties. Competing interests that should be heard and responded to tend not to be involved.

Second, the decentralized and differentiated system of business representation denies Canadian decision-makers several policy options. As a middle-sized economic power, Canada has, since the end of the Second World War, experienced increasing pressures to move towards freer trade in the international market-place. The pressure has recently been particularly intense with regard to trade with the United States. Free trade has implications quite different for a large country such as the United States or Japan and a smaller country such as Canada. A large domestic market can remain more closed to the international market-place and adjust to economic change more on its own terms. Such a strategy is not available to a smaller country. It must remain more open in the world economy and adjust more on the terms of others. Accordingly, it needs mechanisms for compensating individuals and groups hurt by international shifts. These might involve policies on incomes and on training and anticipatory industrial planning. Design and implementation of these policies require intensive negotiations among major social partners at the outset and ongoing, sustained consultation. There must therefore be a willingness to work together and to collaborate if adjustment is to be managed effectively.

Existing problems in this field cannot be blamed solely on government, as many supporters of business are wont to do. Thus Beigie and Stewart write: "Above all, the most significant barrier to better business government collaboration is the absence of an effective overall guiding framework that sets out the general directions for Canada's adjustment and the principles that governments will follow in aiding this transition. The lack of a viable strategic framework means that policy is usually limited to incremental changes with excessive vulnerability to short term 'fire fighting' measures such as bailouts and new trade barriers."[6] The latter description of the Canadian approach to industrial policy is accurate, but the initial premise is mistaken. In a country that is very open to the world economy and where various groups will need to be compensated during adjustments in that economy, it is not sufficient for governments to lay out a set of priorities on their own. The priorities need to be developed in consultation with major socioeconomic producer groups and be supported by these groups. Consultation requires representative and comprehensive peak organizations able to speak for these groups. I shall argue in this book that the present organization of business interests in Canada renders such an approach highly unlikely. Instead, adjustment will continue to take the form of ad hoc bailouts very much related to an electoral calculus. More reflective consideration of the longer-term evolution of the Canadian economy and the relative economic position of Canadian classes is not possible. Governments cannot develop long-term strategy on their own.

In addition, the combination of a disaggregated system for representing business interests and a fragmented state pushes conflicts within the business community into the public sphere. A policy will favour one sector over another. A second sector will contest the gain of the first by seeking a counter-policy. Different state agencies are mobilized as a result; perhaps ministers end up clashing and the dispute acquires added intensity. The presence of policy rectangles linking competing business sectors with corresponding state agencies is a common feature of business politics in Canada.

In the section that follows, I introduce business interest associations, commenting on why they have become more and more important in relations between business and the state. Following this discussion, I describe the study upon which much of the analysis in this book draws. The chapter concludes with a summary of the various chapters.

MODES OF POLITICAL INTERVENTION

A quick survey of the political activities of business in Canada reveals a variety of instruments for political action available to the average business firm. Let us look at a fictional forest products firm, Pacific Timber Ltd. Pacific Timber could contact government by having its president meet with a senior civil servant or cabinet minister. Or its vice-president, government relations, could write the assistant deputy minister responsible for the Canadian Forestry Service. A complicated taxation issue might be handled by having a Vancouver accounting firm draw up a brief that could be delivered by the company to the federal Department of Finance. The need to raise the tariff on a special paper product might be attended to by hiring a lobbyist in Ottawa who is an expert on such things. Pacific Timber will also belong to several associations. It may be a member of broad intersectoral associations such as the Canadian Chamber of Commerce and the Business Council of British Columbia because the company wishes to collaborate with other corporations in changing 'horizontal' policies such as unemployment insurance or research and development subsidies.[7] Horizontal policies are those designed to affect the macroeconomy and are not targeted specifically to individual sectors. In sector-specific policies, such as regulations governing the amount of stumpage to be paid by forest companies to the BC government, the company can participate on the relevant committee of the Council of Forest Industries of British Columbia.

Each of these several strategies falls into one of two general modes of action: individual (firm-centred) and collective (association-centred). Of these two modes, the second, collective one is the main focus of this book.

Interventions by Firms

Typically, firms will intervene on their own in the policy process when they are concerned with an allocative or distributive policy. For example, a firm might lobby for a subsidy to modernize its plant or for a specific tariff change, for a tax write-off or for a loan guarantee. The firm may even be lobbying for government contracts. Termed "capital aggressive" firms by Wyn Grant, such businesses cultivate personal contacts with politicians, cherish their autonomy, and are often unenthusiastic if not suspicious when it comes to associations.[8] Allocative policies of this sort are normally administered firm by firm, irrespective of sector. Only the balance sheet of the firm is involved; there is no need to consult any other firms.

However, in regulatory or self-regulatory policies, the interests of other firms in the sector are not so easily put aside. The firm is likely to intervene on its own only when it enjoys a monopoly or near-monopoly. Provincial hydroelectric power corporations, for example, the only cost-bearers in the regulation of power rates, may capture or co-opt corresponding provincial regulatory agencies. Certainly a charge to this effect is often made by environmental groups. The federal crown corporation PetroCanada has, through its special status, become the principal beneficiary of government programs on Canada Lands. Consequently, it is associated closely with the government agencies that regulate the exploitation of the resources in question.

Grant suggests that firms involved in such regulatory activities be called "tripartite," to distinguish them from capital aggressive firms.[9] Tripartite firms develop relatively bureaucratized relations with government agencies rather than personal ties to politicians. They will normally rely on a government relations division rather than friendly socializing by the company president. Such firms strongly support associations rather than ignore them. They usually emphasize cooperation with government and labour – in stark contrast with the individualism of capital aggressive firms.

To argue that firm-centred intervention is restricted primarily to allocative policies appears to contradict the growing number of government relations divisions. Yet studies of such divisions in Canada indicate that they are less important than similar structures in Britain and the United States. These divisions are found almost exclusively in large firms and tend to emphasize public more than governmental relations.[10] In a survey of firms drawn from the *Financial Post*'s list of the top 500 corporations in Canada, Andrew Gollner found trade associations and personal visits by senior executives to be the preferred approaches to government.[11] Government relations divisions appeared far down the list. Similarly, in his own survey of major firms, James Gillies found that fewer than 10 per cent of the companies had a senior officer assigned full-time responsibility for government relations.[12] "In general, government-corporate affairs are handled on an almost ad hoc basis with most activity being in response to some public initiative."[13] Gillies recommends that corporations estabish a "public affairs" division headed by a senior vice-president who reports directly to the chief executive officer (CEO) and who sits as a member of the principal management committees in the corporation. This officer would assume responsibility for business-government relations, public relations, and corporate social policy. That Gillies made this suggestion indicates that government relations divisions are not yet important in Canada.

Existing government relations divisions perform a variety of functions, often peculiar to an individual corporation.[14] Large, dominant firms like Bell Canada, Ontario Hydro, and the railways create such divisions to manage ongoing contacts with government. Many large corporations, particularly as they become conglomerates, must concern themselves with a growing number of policies that span many sectors. Normally, there will be no single trade association suitable for co-ordinating all of their interests; most groups will be either too specialized or too broadly based.[15] A large group like the Canadian Chamber of Commerce might have an interest in all the sectors covered by a corporate giant, but at too general a level to be of any use. The government relations division then performs "environmental monitoring" functions. Thain points out that keeping track of events and legislation is of increasing importance to business, as it seeks to avoid reactive, ad hoc responses to government.[16] Such monitoring prepares the firm better for political intervention, whether on its own or through an association.

Government relations divisions often help as well to co-ordinate a firm's direct action with the lobbying efforts of trade associations. Such complementarity intensifies the pressure on governments. Co-ordination is not always easy, however. Grant notes that the various production divisions within a large corporation often guard jealously the responsibility for relations with associations.[17] Thus, in a massive chemical company like CIL, the division head for agricultural chemicals will deal with the agricultural chemicals association, the head of plastics with the Society of the Plastics Industry of Canada, the chief of paints with the Canadian Paint and Coatings Association, and so on. These officers may look with suspicion on a new government relations division also interested in association matters.

Although systematic studies are still lacking for Canada, firm-based intervention may also be primary when the end sought is a "non-decision" or "non-interference." In his studies of Britain and the United States, Useem describes a group of top managers who play a crucial political role.[18] Drawn from a large company, a typical member of this circle is a director of several large corporations and is active in general business associations. Both these roles help these business leaders develop an outlook and policy proposals that define the general interests of the corporate community. Its ability both to tap significant sources of funds and expertise and to speak through the most prominent associations places it well for this kind of policy development. Analyses of the Canadian corporate elite by Clement and Carroll suggest at least the possibility of such an "inner circle" in Canada.[19] However, no one has taken these findings further and asked how and where such an elite participates in the policy process.

In summary, Canadian firms are most likely to intervene directly in the political process over allocative policies. Action related to other types of policy will involve firms much less, except for large, monopoly firms in heavily regulated sectors. Further, the policy environment for larger firms is becoming so complex that academics advising business on government relations such as Gillies, Litvak, and Thain recommend creation or increased use of government relations divisions; existing divisions should be strengthened to perform sophisticated environmental monitoring and political risk analysis. This type of work will assist firms in allocative policy and in other areas where associations remain the main mode of political intervention.

Interventions by Associations

Richardson and Jordan describe modern policy-making in liberal democratic states as following a pattern of "successive limited comparisons."[20] In an incremental fashion, policies become extensions of past efforts, with the gradual introduction of minor innovations. Successive limited comparisons continue to be made time after time, and policy-making becomes more and more limited to specialized areas and sectors. Cawson writes that the targeting of decision-making to sectors is a new, almost hidden, and scarcely studied characteristic of the policy process.[21]

This mode of policy-making works on the basis of securing agreement among groups.[22] Policy-making generally involves negotiation within the nexus of government, public service, and associations. By its very nature, then, the process discourages the clarification of values and objectives, which is likely to create disharmony. The government and the public service cannot risk discord because they need expertise and information from the private-sector groups. The decisions involved are usually specific, technical, and complex. If they are to achieve their objectives, public officials must consult with the affected parties and base their programs on information provided by business and on anticipated support. In the process of consultation, a certain affinity grows between bureaucratic agencies and interest associations.[23] Both have policy specialists, deal with policy daily, and, by virtue of their formal organization, bring expertise and permanence to the policy process.

For the public service, there is a certain logic to this growth of closer relations with associations. First, it is easier to consult with an association than with all the firms in a sector, unless the sector is oligopolistic. Differences usually exist among major parties, necessitating extensive consultations if a consensus is to be found. An association can avoid this problem.

Second, dealing with an association places much of the burden of finding a consensus on the industry.[24] Sometimes no consensus is possible, or only a minimal, scarcely meaningful consensus. Then an official will need to proceed on his or her own or drop the policy initiative altogether. In most cases, however, an effective association will work out a reasonable industry position and, in doing so, enhance its utility to the official and its own influence.

Dealing with an association will often appear to officials legitimate or proper. Any selection of some firms for consultation leaves them open to charges of bias or favouritism or to insufficient knowledge of the sector. Officials can cover themselves by dealing with the legally constituted, voluntary representative of the industry, open to all firms. The association can then choose the firms most appropriate for consultation, a task that it is often better equipped to assume.

Somewhat parallel pressures push firms to make increasing use of associations. Analysts point repeatedly to the difficulties firms have had in adapting to the rationalized procedures of decision-making now used by cabinets. These procedures have multiplied the number of officials and agencies involved in a decision and, Pross notes, have formalized consultation.[25] Interested parties must make formal submissions and take systematic account of opposing points of view in their briefs. Advocates are often asked to speak before parliamentary committees, administrative tribunals, and the mass media. Most firms do not have the competence or time for these activities. The few large firms with government relations divisions find the task less daunting, but most firms delegate the bulk of advocacy to associations.

Business has its own concerns about legitimacy. Contested more and more by sophisticated public interest groups, business cannot assume that its proposals will be welcomed by officials and the public at large. Speaking of changes in the 1970s, David Vogel writes: "A loose coalition of middle-class based consumer and environmental, feminist and civil rights organizations, assisted on occasion by organized labour, aided by a sympathetic media and supported by much of the intelligentsia, were able to influence both the terms of public debate and the outcomes of government policy in a direction antithetical to the interests of business."[26] As a consequence, business has had to spend more time cultivating public opinion as well as politicians. Again, the effort required lies beyond the capability of most firms. Consequently, they have encouraged their associations to form public relations committees and to hire professionals to serve the committees and to implement the programs devised.

Officials responsible for non-allocative policy – regulatory, self-regulatory, redistributive – look askance at interventions by individual firms. The firm is viewed invariably as pleading for a narrow, selfish interest. If a firm can wrap itself in the collective drapes of an association, its proposals may be received differently. Hence even in highly oligopolistic industries – primary textiles, tire manufacturers, agricultural machinery – the giants often deal with government through associations – in these cases, the Canadian Textiles Institute, the Rubber Association of Canada, and the Canadian Institute of Farm Equipment, respectively. Their pleading may gain legitimacy it does not otherwise have.

THE STUDY

The information used in this study is drawn primarily from a three-stage research project conducted by the author and Henry Jacek and supported by grants from the Social Sciences and Humanities Research Council of Canada.[27] In stage 1, we used directories, historical studies, and government reports to draw up a list of nationally relevant economic interest associations that had operated in Canada since Confederation: any group representing a business firm, a profession, farmers, other occupational categories, or labour unions. To qualify, such associations had to have (1) an established constitutional order that specified leaders who could speak for the association as a whole; (2) permanent staff for administration of organizational activities; (3) a budgetary process for acquiring and disposing of funds; and (4) a set of criteria for defining eligible members. This definition was applied flexibly, particularly when it came to permanent staff. In some small associations, administration was carried out by volunteers, often on company time. When they satisfied the other three criteria, such associations were included.

An association was nationally relevant if it claimed to represent an economic interest (1) on a national basis; and/or (2) in a province or group of provinces that accounted for 35 per cent of the national production or employment in the sector concerned; and/or (3) in Quebec or French Canada (paralleling a national association).

By criterion 2, the Ontario Food Processors Association would be included, because Ontario accounts for about 60 per cent of the fruit and vegetable processing in Canada. However, the Association des manufacturiers de produits alimentaires du Québec would be excluded, because that province is responsible for only 15 per cent of fruit and vegetable processing in Canada. This Quebec association would be excluded also under criterion 3: it is a regional branch organization of the national Canadian Food Processors Association. However, the Association canadienne des éducateurs de la langue française would be included under criterion 3: it is based in French Canada and parallels a national group, the Canadian Education Association.

We gathered the following information (more easily, of course, for extant associations): economic sector, date of founding and site of national headquarters, number and occupations of members, publications, number of people employed, objectives, and executive structures.

In stage 2 we sought to supplement the aggregate data base of stage 1 with more qualitative information on associational emergence, structures, and activities. To these ends, we chose several sectors: dairy farming, wheat growing, forestry, metal mining, food processing, textiles, chemicals, machine tools, construction, banking, teachers, physicians, and railway transport. Existing associations in these sectors were contacted by mail and asked for detailed information on their structures and activities. In the case of no response, up to two follow-up letters were sent. We collected, in addition, information on the history of the development of these sectors and on their industrial structure.

Stage 3 saw a closer study of the actual operations of business interest associations (for firms, for senior officials, and for co-ordination ['peak' associations]). We classified an interest association as representing business if its primary membership unit were an enterprise (or branch), an official thereof, or another business association. Enterprises include services (engineering firms, accounting firms, companies running television stations, and so on) and public enterprises and co-operatives (they are integrated into capitalist relations of exchange). In some associations, members are individuals who work at senior levels in the enterprise and whose basis of organization is their position in the firm (not a shared profession). The Canadian Natural Gas Processors Association is composed of senior plant managers in gas processing firms. In contrast, the Canadian Medical Association (which is excluded) is based on a profession. In 'peak' associations, members are other associations that fall into one of the above two categories. Debate over the class position of farmers remains sufficiently undecided – business persons or independent commodity producers? – that their associations will generally be treated separately.

Research from stage 3 served also as the Canadian country study in a ten-country international comparative research project on the associative activity of business. Other countries involved were Austria, Denmark, Italy, the Netherlands, Spain, Sweden, Switzerland, the United Kingdom, and West Germany. Under the co-ordination of Philippe Schmitter and Wolfgang Streeck and with the support of the Volkswagen Foundation, the ten country teams met three times at the International Institute of Management (IIM) in West Berlin to draw up a research design and common set of variables. This design was then used as the basis for interviewing associations in five of the sectors noted above: chemicals, construction, food processing, machine tools, and textiles. Major intersectoral associations such as the Canadian Manufacturers' Association were also interviewed. The Canadian interviews were conducted in the fall of 1981 and winter of 1982 with 54 associations, of which 51 were retained for the international study.

Selected data from all three stages of this project are used in this study. In certain chapters, I draw as well from the research of my collaborators in the international project. This study, then, combines aggregate information on the characteristics of Canadian associations and more detailed qualitative research on a range of sectors, some of which are eligible for cross-national comparisons.

ORGANIZATION OF THE STUDY

Part I provides an introduction to the place and importance of business interest associations in Canada and a conceptual framework for their analysis. Chapter 2 introduces these associations by reviewing the history of their growth and development and then by providing an overview of their structures and activities today. Chapter 3 elaborates further on two roles, advocacy and policy participation, that associations of firms can play in the policy process. It discusses possible contradictions between these roles, outlines the concept of an associational system, and suggests the criteria for determining whether this system is fragmented or integrated. Drawing on chapter 3, chapter 4 defines and describes the four policy networks – pressure pluralist, clientele pluralist, co-optive pluralist, and corporatist – that serve as the basis for the analysis of associative action found in part II.

Part II begins with an examination (chapter 5) of major intersectoral associations such as the Business Council on National Issues, the Canadian Federation of Independent Business, the Canadian Chamber of Commerce, and, at the provincial level, the Conseil du patronat du Québec and the Business Council of British Columbia. Five chapters (6–10) study associative action in several major divisions of the Canadian economy: agriculture, construction, natural resources, banking and finance, and manufacturing. Each chapter looks at one sector: how its pattern of political organization is linked to its economic structure and to state structures and policies governing it.

Part III looks beyond sectors to more general explanations for the disaggregated and very specialized character of business associations in Canada. A general chapter (11) compares the findings in part II with business associations' activities in Britain (a large, relatively pluralist state) and Austria (a small and corporatist country). Possible explanations for the Canadian arrangements include the lack of a "state" tradition in Canada and the divisiveness of the federal system (the subject of chapter 12). Chapter 13 draws together the results of the empirical studies and the canvass of explanations to reflect on the implications of the patterns found. I review in particular the weak capacity to hold business politically accountable in Canada and make suggestions for the reform of both the policy process and business interest associations that might strengthen this capacity.

CHAPTER TWO

An Overview of Business Associations

Jack Walker notes the paucity of systematic global research on interest group systems: "Most descriptive accounts deal either with the history of a small group, or more often, with small clusters of groups in a single policy area. There are almost no comprehensive descriptions of the world of interest groups in America at any historical period."[1] Similarly, Paul Pross writes about the apparent proliferation "of pressure groups" in Canada in the past 20 years and regrets the scarcity of hard data.[2]

Walker notes the exception in both the Canadian and American cases – the work of Robert Presthus,[3] who took a comprehensive view of interest groups. Using a large sample, he surveyed the activities of groups with a view to piecing together the patterns of accommodation they had developed with political elites. However, Presthus was not interested in the totality of associations and did not use the concept of interest associational systems or examine the structures and processes of the *organizations* of interest groups. He treated only those aspects of organization relevant to elite accommodation.

This chapter, then, provides a comprehensive and systematic overview of selected properties of associational systems representing business firms and agricultural producers in Canada. The first, historical section surveys the emergence and growth of business and agricultural associations since Confederation. The second section restricts its focus to associations that were active in 1980, describing structures and activities common across most divisions of the economy – a backdrop for the more detailed studies of different divisions of the economy in part II.

Figure 1   Dates of Founding, Nationally Relevant Business Associations

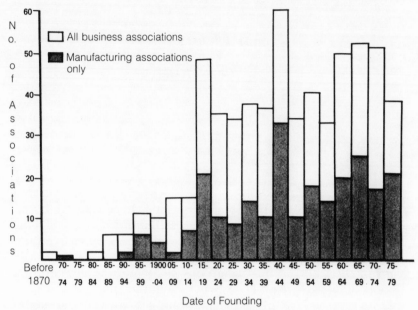

THE EMERGENCE OF
ASSOCIATIONS

Institutionalized economic interest groups active nationally are relatively recent in Canada. The number of "nationally relevant" groups at Confederation was probably under 15.[4] Prominent among these were the boards of trade in the major cities, Montreal, Toronto, and Halifax. These early groups established a pattern of working closely with government that has continued to the present.[5] Gradually, over the next 30 years, associations expanded beyond the large cities, embracing first the whole province and ultimately the nation. By 1900, there were about 70 nationally relevant groups.[6]

   In the next 80 years, this collection expanded by well over 10 times. The two world wars and the Depression spurred collective action (see Figure 1). Nonetheless, even these major events did not produce in many sectors a high level of growth like that after 1945, when virtually all sectors of business and the professions saw their greatest growth. In agriculture, the Depression and the reconstitution of many marketing systems in the late 1960s stand out as high growth periods. This section surveys the growth of business and agricultural interest associations across major economic divisions and seeks to account for the growth patterns observed.

Business Associations

It is not my purpose here to write a history of business associations in Canada. My task is more limited. I wish to examine the major factors that led to the development of *national* business associations by the turn of the century and to note the periods when some of the major associations active today were founded. Prior to Confederation, the more important business associations defined their domains based on a city rather than a colony as a whole. In speaking for the interests of Montreal, Toronto, or Halifax, these "local" associations, usually boards of trade, looked well beyond their borders to larger markets. Those associations that emerged with a broader domain – Forster cites the example of the Association for the Promotion of Canadian Industry, a protectionist group – tended to have a very short life span.[7] After Confederation, a number of developments pushed business people to look to the formation of permanent associations that organized whole industries over a broader territorial expanse: the pressure of domestic competition, the need for protection against external competition, the growing fear of the labour movement both in politics and in the work-place, and the perception that other classes, particularly agrarians and liberal professionals, were achieving political gains at the expense of business.[8]

What Michael Bliss describes as the "massive flight from domestic competition in the 1880s and 1890s" constitutes a first important pressure to form associations with broader domains. He adds: "Businessmen formed guilds, associations, pools, trusts, and mergers with the aim of restricting the free market in every form of enterprise – transportation, manufacturing, finance, and distribution ... They denied the maxim that competition was the life of trade, and justified their combinations as being in the public interest and in the reasonable interest of honest businessmen who only desired to obtain a 'living profit.' "[9] Bliss notes the existence in the late 1880s of loosely knit associations for the restraint of trade in the distribution of groceries, watch cases, binder twine, coal, oatmeal, stove, agricultural implements, and undertakers' supplies.[10] The Dominion Wholesale Grocers Guild played a leading role in such affairs and operated price-fixing agreements with manufacturers of tobacco, starch, baking powder, pickles, and sugar. Such arrangements, in turn, were reciprocated at the retail level through associative action sponsored by the Retail Merchants Guild of Canada.[11] Naylor cites restraint of trade among commercial travellers, lumber retailers, cotton manufacturers, salt producers, and foundries.[12] These early waves of association formation aimed at restrictive trade practices were to be repeated at later periods: the various sections of the Canadian

Manufacturers' Association (CMA) that grew up after 1900 concerned themselves with pricing;[13] Traves described similar attempts when business sought to deal with overcapacity in the years immediately following the First World War;[14] and Finkel writes of price-fixing during the Depression.[15]

Political demands for protection of the home market from external competition also prompted the formation of national associations. In his fine study of the protection debate between 1825 and 1879, Forster notes that the industrial structure of Canada after Confederation had become quite suited to a large-scale push for greater protection. A number of industries were now large enough to meet domestic demand: boots and shoes, agricultural implements, carriage manufacturing, cabinet ware and furniture, edge tools, refined oil, ropes and twine, starch, tanned leather, and soap and candles. Others had sufficiently promising prospects for growth that they too might be enlisted in an eventual campaign: cotton manufacturers, earthenware, and paints.[16] French-Canadian élites had become sufficiently alarmed by the migration of their countrymen to industrial New England that they too were interested in building up domestic industry. These various interests became mobilized in favour of increased protection when a depression hit Canada in the 1870s. What distinguished this protectionist campaign from earlier ones in colonial Canada was the increased role of associations. Forster writes: "The greater emphasis on association among businessmen – in order to collectively control competition, as a means of transcending petty interest and applying more effective pressure on government, and to provide a rationale for the aspirations of a business elite – was a key element of the new balance."[17]

Business people had a great deal of difficulty building and maintaining sectoral associations with national domains, even in the heat of the debate over protection in the 1870s. What did emerge over the course of this political struggle was a permanent group that was to become the CMA, one of the more important business associations in Canada's history. The Ontario Manufacturers' Association, the predecessor of the CMA, became a permanent, institutionalized entity in 1874.[18] By 1879, it had opened discussions with manufacturers in Montreal and laid the basis for a national organization. Over the next 20 years, this temporary alliance became formalized in the form of the CMA. By 1900, S.D. Clark writes, the association had hired a permanent secretary, begun to publish its own journal, *Industrial Canada*, and had moved to create a Tariff Department to help members with the technical details needed for preparing a case for protection.[19] As they emerged after the turn of the century, more specialized manufacturers' associations, many of them former sections of the CMA, took up the tariff fight on their own. This hiving off of more specialized groups made the life of the CMA easier: it reduced internal disputes between home market manufacturers and those wishing to export.[20] Relieving itself of specific fights over tariff matters was critical because the association was becoming much more active in promoting abroad the export of Canadian goods.[21]

Related to increased domestic and foreign competition was continued political struggle among various sectors of the business community. The CMA gained in importance by the turn of the century in part because of political struggles between banking and transportation interests and manufacturers. The banks had moved towards organized collective action with formation of the Canadian Bankers' Association (CBA) in 1891. The original objectives of the CBA included: considering legislation and court decisions, guarding the bank note redemption fund, and promoting the efficiency of bank officers through lectures and other educational programs.[22] J. Harvey Perry, a former executive director of the CBA, notes that the association also gained a reputation for being a rate-setting cartel for the banks.[23] Bliss amplifies on this point: "Though the CBA claimed to emphasize bankers' education and professional improvement as its primary goal, it was rightly interpreted in the business press as part of the general movement to restrict competition. There was a successful nation-wide attempt in the early years to fix the maximum rate of interest on savings deposits, and local agreements were reached regarding the handling of certain forms, bills, and special deposits."[24] All these efforts were facilitated by placing a permanent lobbyist in Ottawa in 1894.[25] Transportation interests were also a formidable political power. However, the economic pre-eminence of the Canadian Pacific Railway and its continuing strong ties to leading politicians obviated the need for a trade association.

S.D. Clark writes that the reorganization of the CMA in 1900 also represented an attempt to counter these banking and transportation interests.[26] In 1900, the CMA created a Railway and Transportation Committee, and when the federal government established a Board of Railway Commissioners in 1903, the association appointed a permanent transportation manager to represent the interests of its members before the board.[27] The CMA added a permanent lobbyist in Ottawa in 1907. For the next quarter-century, transportation was a difficult area for the CMA to maintain internal cohesion over policy. Manufacturers in British Columbia, for example, broke away from the CMA during the First World War because of disagreements with eastern firms over transportation matters.[28]

Over the quarter-century after Confederation, the labour movement too from time to time stimulated more broadly based associative action by capitalists. The Nine Hour Movement in the early 1870s, which eventually mobilized workers in Ontario and Quebec, forced employers to organize and to respond on a province-wide basis in short-lived collective organizations.[29] Canadian business people watched carefully and with growing alarm the rise of the labour movement in Europe and the United States and came to worry about the effect of such changes in Canada.[30] These worries appeared well justified when, in the mid-1880s, the Knights of Labor, a class-wide and comprehensive organization, enjoyed spectacular success in its organizing drives. Kealey and Palmer estimate that, at a minimum, between 10 and 18 per cent of all workers in cities and towns in Ontario joined the Knights.[31] In the very competitive capitalism of the time, the Knights represented an attempt, only occasionally successful, to withstand employers' efforts to reduce wages. In doing so, Palmer notes, they may have spurred employers to higher levels of associative action. "The Knights of Labor, in conjunction with the craft unions, may thus have helped to rally the individualistic and once-divided capitalists that Michael Bliss has depicted as in quest of 'a living profit' to employer combines that led out of the nineteenth century context of competitive entrepreneurship and into the age of monopoly."[32]

The CMA had difficulty with the labour issue. It could not push the conflict too far because it needed the support of labour from time to time in its battles with other business groups over tariff matters. In addition, members differed in their assessment of the importance of the struggle with labour: some industries, such as iron and steel, wanted the association to concentrate on tariff and trade questions; other sectors more susceptible to labour problems, such as clothing, wished it to pay closer attention to labour relations.[33] By the end of the First World War, the CMA essentially threw its hands up. More and more sections of the CMA broke away to form independent sectoral associations to deal with these matters. Consequently, the CMA too changed, becoming "in many ways, a body of trained functionaries paid to service individual manufacturers."[34]

Actual conflict in the work-place appeared to encourage associative action by employers, primarily in resource industries. Confrontation with labour was the precipitating force in the coal mining sector, where the Mining Association of Nova Scotia was formed in 1887 and the Coal Association of Canada in 1906. These dates correspond well to periods of intense struggle with unions in the industry. Generally speaking, however, the coming together of employers in associations jointly to repress unions occurred at the local level.[35] Bliss reports discussion in 1901–2 about the formation of a national employers' association, but the idea was set aside when the CMA refused to organize or give funds for the formation of employers' associations.[36]

The more prominent provincial and national associations in the resource industries tended to emerge gradually after the turn of the century. The first more broadly based associations to appear in the forestry industry reflected concerns with scientific management of the forest resource and with sylviculture. The Canadian Forestry Association (1900) and the Canadian Institute of Forestry (1908) were established for these purposes; provincial associations began to appear in the 1920s. The leading peak associations, the Canadian Wood Council and the Council of Forest Industries of B.C., did not arise until 1959 and 1960, respectively.

The pursuit of collective scientific interests in mining and metallurgy began early, with establishment of the Canadian Institute of Mining and Metallurgy in 1898. Most influential advocate associations appeared in the inter-war period: the problem of unstable foreign markets appears to have pushed the mining companies to collective action. Thus the Ontario Mining Association was founded in 1920, the Mining Association of British Columbia in 1921, the Quebec Asbestos Mining Association in 1924, and the Quebec Metal Mining Association in 1936.[37] The national-level lobbying group, the Mining Association of Canada, began operations in 1935. The relative latecomers in resources were in petroleum and natural gas. While varous associations were founded in Alberta between the wars the Canadian Petroleum Association (representing the large multinationals) was established in 1952, and the Independent Petroleum Association of Canada (for smaller indigenous producers) in 1960.[38]

In addition to labour, agrarians provided a direct incentive for capitalist associative action. Farmers were divided along both ethnic and religious lines. Nonetheless such organizations as the Dominion Grange and later the Patrons of Industry became sufficiently active politically, both within and outside the political parties, that business became concerned. The platforms of these organizations were perceived to be a direct challenge to some business interests in calling for free trade, government ownership of the banks to improve access to farm credit, and public control of railways, telegraph, and telephones.[39] By the end of the nineteenth century, Bliss noted, business was also becoming increasingly concerned about the privileges being gained by liberal professionals such as doctors and lawyers.[40] The Canadian Medical Association had been formed in 1871, the provincial medical associations and law societies antedated Confederation, and the Dominion (later Canadian) Education Association and the veterinarians' national association had been founded in the early 1890s. Forster summarizes well the situation at the turn of the century: "In some degree, the political system was beginning to respond to groups and classes rather than individuals and cliques: to speak reductively, policy was replacing patronage."[41]

As is evident in Figure 1, the two world wars provided fertile ground for the founding of new national associations. The conduct of war by a democratic government in a complex capitalist economy requires close collaboration with business. Cuff and Granatstein write: "The state now had to have by its side men who were sensitive to the ceremony and ritual of the business game and who could therefore persuade the holders of private economic power to support its policies."[42] Wartime planning often demands greater collective action by sectors of industry. New associations are created and, together with those already in existence, do not so much assume a traditional advocacy role as become part of the policy-making system as they join in the management of production and distribution. Thus industry and government may come into very close contact over administration of productive controls, assignment of production priorities, control of imports and exports, regulation of foreign exchange, and use of business people to run various boards and commissions.

Periods of war saw large increases in the number of manufacturing associations (Figure 1). In the First World War, the Department of Trade and Commerce adopted an explicit policy of encouraging the organization of industry-wide associations to seek out orders for their member companies, particularly from allied governments.[43] In 1915, the CMA sponsored creation of the Export Association of Canada,[44] to represent Canadian manufacturers in the markets of all the allied powers by informing buyers about what Canadian firms might be able to produce for them.

War requires the marshalling of large financial resources and the placing of these in the hands of the government. The Bond Dealers Association of Canada (now the Investment Dealers Association of Canada) was created in 1916 as a direct result of such activity. The CBA played a key intermediary role between its members and the government, as the latter sought capital. As one observer noted: "Moreover the Canadian Bankers' Association welded the individual banks into one unit, so that the Minister of Finance, if he wished to consult with the banks or put any policy into effect had only to meet the heads of that organization. Any policy decided upon was passed on immediately to the individual banks and put into execution. Practically all the business between the banks and the Canadian and British governments was done through the Canadian Bankers' Association and the executive of that association became an influential body."[45]

The federal civil service grew and became more professionalized in the inter-war period. Even so, administration of the economy during the Second World War continued to require extensive business-government collaboration. Responsibility for directing production for the war effort lay with the Department of Munitions and Supply, headed by C.D. Howe. Howe recruited a number of prominent businessmen, such as E.P. Taylor, to head up divisions within the department or crown corporations.[46] These "dollar-a-year men" had their salaries paid by their firms. A key organization within Howe's department was the Wartime Industries Control Board (WICB). It had a number of controllers, usually drawn directly from industry, for specific products: lumber, machine tools, metals, oil, power, steel, motor vehicles, and ship construction and repair.[47] These controllers had extensive authority over materials and products.

Lumber illustrates how such processes worked. The lumber controller made frequent purchases of stocks without competitive bidding for the construction of defence buildings. These purchases were co-ordinated through the offices of the Canadian Lumbermen's Association (CLA), which organized forestry manpower, production, allocations, and shipments and implemented a network of regulations. The CLA initiated new publications to communicate government orders-in-council to its members and helped the Wartime Housing Corporation prepare specifications and housing.[48]

Canadian associations assumed new roles in response not only to Canadian controls but also to American and British actions. For example, overseas exports of newsprint from Scandinavia stopped, leaving Canada and Newfoundland the only significant non-Axis exporters of pulp and paper.[49] The needs of newspapers in the "friendly" United States and Latin America were filled by various Canadian mills under the direction of the U.S. newsprint administrator, who, in turn, worked closely with the Canadian Newsprint Association in implementing allocations.[50]

Another key institution was the Wartime Prices and Trade Board (WPTB). Originally set up to watch out for exploitative pricing and for the availability of supplies of important goods, the board was called upon in 1941 to implement a total freeze on prices and wages. The board appointed administrators for commodities or services judged particularly crucial, including eventually wool, sugar, hides and leather, coal, rents, and oils.[51] Later, as its activities expanded, it grouped its commodity administrators into seven divisions: real property, pulp and paper, foods, publishing and allied industries, textiles and clothing, metal and wood products, and distributive trades.[52]

The WPTB co-ordinated its actions with the WICB; the chairman of each was a member of the board of the other. WICB controllers were also appointed administrators for the same product under the WPTB.[53] Under these agencies, industries might be called in to discuss the regulation of supply or the control of prices. Often official regulations were avoided in favour of having an industry work through its association to set up its own system of self-regulation.[54] The impetus for associative action further increased when the board requested standardization of product lines so as to free up more resources. Each industry was asked to establish its own advisory committee on standardization and simplification and to report to a new standards division of the board.[55] Designing and implementing wide-ranging price controls required the WPTB to consult regularly with wholesalers' and retailers' associations as well as with farmers and, to a more limited extent, with labour unions. Associations were drawn much more into policy formation and implementation than before the war.

The growth of manufacturing associations did not fall off very much after the war (Figure 1). The processes set in motion during the war appeared to set off a wave of organization in the business community that continued over the following three decades. These processes are investigated in some depth in part II.

Agricultural Associations

The pattern of emergence of farmers' interest associations shown in Figure 2 differs from that in Figure 1. Fewer farmer organizations are founded, and they are formed at a more constant rate. Growth was exceptional in the late 1960s. Yet even then the rates of formation are not strikingly different from those found in other periods. The constant creation of associations, however, masks the fact that agricultural associations have developed for different reasons at different times.

The agricultural associations that grew up in the quarter-century after Confederation acted as adjuncts to the very small civil service. Agriculture was the dominant sector in the economies of most provinces, particularly Ontario and Quebec. Departments of agriculture at both levels of government were embryonic, having little if any

Figure 2   Dates of Founding, Agricultural Associations

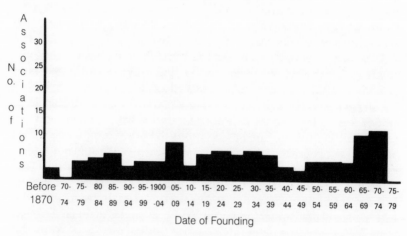

Date of Founding

expert staff and responsibilities for few regulatory tasks. Agricultural methods and research were changing farming rapidly, and governments wanted to ensure that farmers were exposed to these new developments. Lacking both in expertise and staff, departments turned to associations for promoting farm improvement.

The system of agricultural associations in place in Ontario by the early 1890s illustrates this predilection. By this time, there existed associations representing fruit growers, dairy farmers, creameries, poultry growers, beekeepers, sheep breeders, and swine breeders as well as an entomological society, specialized cattle-breeding societies (Aberdeen Angus, Shorthorn, Galloway, Holstein-Friesian, Ayrshire, Canadienne, and Herefords) and horse-breeding societies. Provincial legislation integrated these associations into a system under the auspices of the Agricultural and Arts Association (AAA) of Ontario.[56] The council of this association included ex officio the presidents of all the above-named groups. It laid down rules for the operation of the respective associations and provided them with grants to cover their operating expenses. The government charged the AAA with promoting the improvement of agriculture by every means possible, including the holding of fairs and exhibitions.[57]

Consistent with such a set of objectives, the associations became directly involved in the administration of policy in many areas. The Beekeepers Association was empowered to appoint an inspector of apiaries. The Entomological and Fruit Growers associations carried out the type of research later assumed by research divisions of agriculture departments. The Dairymen's association began a system of factory inspection, hiring and paying the inspectors. These associations also established courses of instruction for butter- and cheese-makers and directed and paid the instructors.[58] As departments of agriculture grew and faculties of agriculture expanded, associations gradually turned towards advocacy.

As associations in eastern Canada were changing away from implementing government policy, associations in western Canada representing grain growers had embarked on a new advocacy route. Feeling exploited by price-setting oligopolies running grain elevators and by the traders on the Winnipeg Grain Exchange, farmers at the turn of the century formed associations to encourage the use of co-operatives to counter the market power of private grain companies. Eventually the huge wheat pools and the United Grain Growers company were built, based on these initial efforts by the associations. In 1907, the three prairie grain growers' associations formed the Interprovincial Council of Grain Growers and Farmers Associations.[59] Three years later, the council added members from the Dominion Grange in Ontario and became the first national agricultural peak association, the Canadian Council of Agriculture.[60] Over the next decade, the council added members from Nova Scotia and New Brunswick and in 1916 four farmers' commercial companies.[61] In 1918, the council abandoned earlier practice and involved itself in direct political action, thereby setting in motion the process that led to the founding of the National Progressive party. The decision led to internal political conflicts in the council that eventually paralysed it. It ceased operations in 1932.

As Figure 2 indicates, however, the Depression did not discourage the formation of agricultural associations. Two new, lasting types of associations began to emerge: national advocacy groups for particular commodities and state-sponsored cartel managers or marketing boards at the provincial level. Virtually all areas of Canadian agriculture suffered heavily during the Depression. Prices for wheat, cheese, and butter fell sharply as income from agriculture dropped by almost 80 per cent from a peak in 1928 to a low in 1933.[62] Protectionism in world markets was rampant; the United Kingdom put restrictions on cattle imports, and the United States virtually closed its cattle market to Canada. Butter and cheese prices fell drastically in Britain, and Canadian dairy exports declined precipitously as a result. Domestic and international markets were in virtual chaos.

Farmers responded collectively by forming national advocacy organizations to put pressure on the federal government. In 1932, the Council of Canadian Beef Producers (later the Canadian Cattlemen's Association) was created, building on such organizations as the Western Stock Growers' Association, founded in 1896. Dairy producer associations and co-operatives joined together in 1934 to form the Canadian Federation of Dairy Farmers, now the Dairy Farmers of Canada. During the same period, co-operative conferences, grouping together various farm organizations in each prairie province, had begun operating.[63] Early in 1935, agricultural organizations in British Columbia joined together to form the B.C. Chamber of Agriculture. In July 1935, the BC chamber and the three prairie co-operative conferences united to form the Western Agricultural Conference, which in turn served as a catalyst to the union of dairy and various co-operative interests into a new national peak organization, the Canadian Chamber of Agriculture founded in November 1935. Renamed the Canadian Federation of Agriculture (CFA) in 1939, this organization spurred the further consolidation of provincial farmer organizations into provincial federations, a process completed by the end of the Second World War. The CFA has served since as a spokesman for farmers, particularly for their supply and marketing co-operatives. Eschewing the direct political action that scuttled its predecessor, the Canadian Council of Agriculture, it has remained an influential voice in national politics, albeit periodically challenged by the more radical farmers' union movement. Thus the most important components of the agricultural associational system were in place by 1945.

Aside from giving impetus to the formation of national pressure groups and the CFA, the Depression precipitated the transformation of provincial commodity associations into "private-interest governments." As we have seen in the case of business firms, the need to organize and control markets spurs associative action in any capitalist economy. Farmers had long engaged in this type of activity in a small way through their membership in breeding societies. Using authority delegated by the state through the Canadian National Livestock Records, livestock producers established standards and thereby rules for entry and, indirectly, prices for specified animals. Price competition in markets for particular breeds was made orderly and "fair." During the Depression, the collapse of the British market for butter and cheese led to a glut of manufacturing milk in Canada. Inevitably, the excess found its way into the retail markets for fluid milk, causing prices to fall rapidly as farmers raced to dispose of their excess. When economic collapse quickly loomed in their faces, farmers and their buyers, the processors, demanded that the state take action to restore order in the market-place.[64] Since the markets at issue were served by many small producers, it was virtually impossible to regulate them through private collusive action. Order could be restored only if the many small producers could be coerced to comply. The state was called upon to delegate its authority to private organizations composed of the producers, who would then fix prices and supply in order to bring stability to the market-place.

The first attempt during the Depression came in the form of the federal Natural Products Marketing Act. When this act was ruled ultra vires of the federal government by the courts, most provinces brought in similar legislation of their own. For example, in the Ontario dairy industry, farmer-controlled marketing boards for fluid milk, cream, concentrated milk, and cheese were created and given power to control price and supply, and entry into the industry. These state-created monopoly seller organizations have come to form the nucleus of the corporatist policy networks found in several sectors of agriculture (see chapter 6).

In summary, the contours of the associational systems representing business and agriculture were established by the end of the Second World War. Each major division of the economy had one or more institutionalized, relatively prominent associations active in Ottawa and many of the provincial capitals. Since 1945, these systems have expanded several-fold as many, rather specialized groups were founded. The section that follows surveys some of the properties of the business and agricultural systems today. Such an overview may fill some of the gaps in our knowledge of the global properties of associational systems in Canada. It will be supplemented with more specialized case studies in part II.

THE ORGANIZATION OF
ASSOCIATIONS

Schmitter and Streeck outline a useful set of categories for analysing the organization of interest associations.[65] (1) Domains are the economic, territorial, functional, and class spaces that the association purports to represent. (2) Structures are the patterns of institutionalized relationships that exist within and between associations. (3) Resources are the financial, human, and symbolic assets of the association. (4) Outputs are the public goods, selective benefits, solidarity goods, and monopoly or authoritative goods produced, by grants of state authority. Part II is devoted to the last category; hence this overview will focus on domains, structures, and resources.

These three categories are relevant to one of our key issues, namely, the degree to which interest associations have moved beyond the traditional lobbying role (policy advocacy) to direct involvement in the formulation and implementation of public policy (policy participation).[66] To the extent that associations participate in policy, there will be pressure to have more rather than less encompassing domains and for the structure of the associational system to be highly differentiated and yet strongly rather than weakly integrated. Individual associations will agree to co-ordinate formally their actions with other associations rather than to maintain complete independence. Whereas successful advocacy or participation requires resources, the advocacy group will draw these primarily from its members, while the participant group may gain additional support from the state. The general overview that follows demonstrates the tendency of Canadian business groups to be organized better for policy advocacy than for policy participation.

Domains

Since Confederation, there have emerged at least 660 nationally relevant business interest associations and another 125 farmers' associations.[67] Of this total number, 482 business groups and 95 farmers' associations were active in 1980. For business groups, Figure 3 shows that their domains range widely across all major branches of production. Associations representing manufacturing firms form by far the largest divisional bloc, 198, or 41 per cent of the total. Within manufacturing, some major sectors – food processing, texiles and clothing, chemicals, and fabricated metals – have, in turn, rather large numbers. The comparatively small number in construction is slightly deceptive: most construction associations are organized at provincial and local levels. As well, Figure 3 does not include professional associations, only associations representing business firms or farmers. Hence the totals may appear smaller than expected in education and health services.

The most striking characteristic of the domains of business associations is their product specialization. Systematic indicators of this specialization are available. First, of the 660 business groups, 481 organized firms in one sector or sub-sector only. Those associations with domains covering more than one sector tended to organize vertically in the production chain: suppliers and manufacturers, manufacturers and distributors, and so on. Second, we can use the International Standard Industrial Classification (isic) published by the United Nations. It is organized into four levels:

(1) major division, e.g. manufacturing
(2) division, e.g. fabricated metals manufacturing
(3) major group, e.g. transportation equipment manufacturing

Figure 3   Distribution in Major Sectors and Divisions of Existing
Business Interest Associations Including Agricultural Groups, 1980

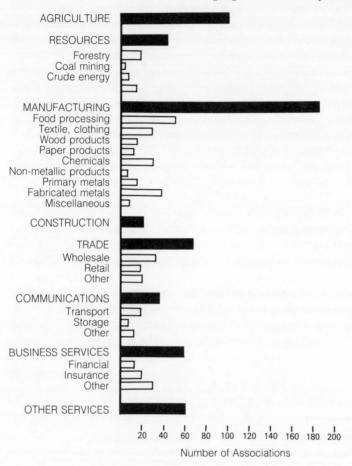

Number of Associations

(4) group, e.g. motorcycle manufacturing

The domain of each association was coded according to the level in
the ISIC code it organizes. Since the ISIC categories for construction,
wholesale trade, and retail trade are not detailed beyond the division
level, associations in these industries were set aside. Of the remaining
associations, 39.3 per cent had domains at the "group" level of the
ISIC code and 28.6 per cent at levels even more specialized than a
"group." As this study proceeds, it will become increasingly evident
that this highly specialized set of associations is also very weakly
integrated.

The number of member firms in any given association varies significantly: 50 associations have 10 members or less, while the Canadian Federation of Independent Business organized over 50,000 businesses in 1980. The typical number of members also varies, depending on the economic division. Manufacturing associations are the smallest, with an average size of 164 firms, followed by services associations (213), resource industry associations (379), and transportation groups (396). Construction associations are large, showing an average membership of 2,129 firms, a figure greater than the average size in the trade division (1,238 firms) but smaller than agricultural associations (2,726 members).

The criteria of "national relevance" defined in chapter 1 allow for inclusion of associations with territorial domains of less than national scope.[69] Among the business associations in the study, then, fully 80.9 per cent have nation-wide domains, 3.5 per cent regional domains, and 14.6 per cent provincial domains. Nation-wide domains occur less frequently among agricultural associations: 61.7 per cent, compared to 4.3 per cent regional and 34.0 per cent provincial. While integrating territorial interests may look more difficult for agricultural than for business associations, this is not the case, as will be demonstrated in part II. In fact, the large number of nation-wide business associations with varied and rather specialized economic domains poses more serious problems for integration.

Structures

Canadian business associations tend to rely on informal arrangements when appointing members to their boards of directors but show a growing degree of professionalism in their permanent officers. The usual pattern for allocating authority involves a division between policy-makers (normally drawn from the membership) and administrators (usually appointed from outside the membership). Policy-making normally is the responsibility of a board of directors, which often assigns some powers to an executive committee (elected from its members) and others to a chief executive officer (CEO) (who serves on this committee).

The board's usually central role makes the procedures followed in its selection significant. Most boards in Canada are selected informally. Although members are usually elected at the annual general meeting of the association, the elections are often ratifications of an executive already formed behind the scenes. The key consultations are usually carried out by the chief administrative officer, normally a permanent employee. Working with the chief executive officer, he or she follows a number of informal rules specific to the association. For example, the National Dairy Council, which represents dairy processing firms in Canada, seeks to balance representatives from large and medium-sized dairies, private firms and cooperatives, different regions, and fluid milk processors and manufacturers of dairy products (butter, cheese, ice cream, and so on). In many cases, the largest firms in an association's domain have a virtual right to a seat on the board. Examples would include: Du Pont Canada, Celanese Canada, and Dominion Textiles in the Canadian Textiles Institute; Canada Packers in the Canadian Meat Council; Dow Chemical, CIL, and Du Pont in the Canadian Chemical Producers Association. In addition, the association's staff endeavours to have firms represented on the board by their CEOs. To take again the Canadian Chemical Producers Association, in 1980, 12 of its 16 board members were CEOs in their firms. When these include the CEOs of Dow, Du Pont, CIL, Esso Chemical, Polysar, and so on, the lineup is impressive indeed when a politician meets with it across the table.

The use of informal procedures in forming a board suits better the task of advocating policies than that of participating in design and implementation. It is useful not so much in developing the representative structures required for participating in the policy process of a liberal democracy but for devising an instrument that will have maximal lobbying effect. Thus the most common title of chief administrative officers is "executive director" or "executive secretary." Their role is administrative: maintaining contacts in government, keeping track of issues, and preparing for political interventions by the board and its executive. Someone specialized in editing a journal or in public relations may be support staff, responsibilities one might expect to find in an advocacy association (see Table 1).

The presence of some kinds of committees often indicates an association's involvement in policy-making. These committees are composed of experts in the appropriate field drawn from the staff of the member firms of the association. Often the terms of reference parallel functional divisions in member firms: suppliers, technical operations in the plant, marketing, public relations, accounting and taxation, personnel and labour relations, and so on. Committees assigned to deal with plant operations normally work closely with regulatory agencies in developing and amending product standards and quality control procedures in the manufacturing process. The importance of such activities is illustrated by the formally stated objectives of associations, coded and summarized in Table 2.[70] While the two most common objectives speak virtually to the raison d'être

Table 1

Leading Functional Positions in Associations, 1980 (Percentage of Total Associations with a Distinct Staff Position)

Business		Agriculture	
Function ($N = 313$)	Percentage	Function ($N = 61$)	Percentage
Research	18.8	Publications	18.0
Public relations	16.3	Public relations	16.4
Accounting	14.7	Field officer	14.8
Publications	13.4	Research	11.5
Field officers	8.9	Treasurer	11.5
Treasurer	8.9	Accounting	9.8

of any association, the third shows widespread involvement in standards work.[71] Standards are often developed by committee members working in tandem with technical experts in regulatory agencies. Thus such work is possibly an indirect indicator of associations assuming roles in policy.

A final structural dimension involes the degree to which roles are differentiated along territorial lines. Truman saw high territorial differentiation to be inimical to effective lobbying.[72] Canadian business groups appear not to be notably fractured along territorial lines and hence so hampered.

Association structures were classified using a four-fold scheme.[73] (1) A unitary association has one national office and no territorial sub-units of any sort. (2) A unitary association with regional branches remains centralized, with authority concentrated in a national office. Regional branches exist as organizing points for the association but have no financial or political autonomy. (3) A federal association has national and regional/provincial offices. Powers are divided between the two levels, so that the regional/provincial offices act as independent associations at that level. Members belong to only one organization but are simultaneously members at the national and regional/provincial levels. (4) In a confederal association, the national association functions as a territorial umbrella organization: its members are regional/provincial associations sharing the same product/economic domain. Firms belong to the regional/provincial association directly and thus to the national association only indirectly. Fees are collected either independently by each level or more commonly by the regional/provincial associations, which then pay a levy to the national association.[74]

I have argued elsewhere that "confederal" decentralization may

Table 2
Formally Stated Objectives of Associations, 1980

Objective	Percentage mentions*
Provide specialized technical information to member firms	65.9
Advise governments on the needs of member firms	61.5
Development of product standards, quality control procedures	39.6
Providing information about member firms to non-members	37.1
Promoting unity and cohesion among member firms	36.0
Expanding members' share of the domestic market	26.0
Engaging in research and development on behalf of members	22.0
Promoting research and development by member firms	20.3
Providing information to other associations	19.8
Providing meetings where member firms can gather for discussions	19.2
Collecting statistics and aggregating them for member firms	18.4
Providing facilities to educate members on specialized topics	14.9
Providing selective personal benefits and services	12.7
Promoting exports of members' products	6.8
Providing a marketing service for members' products	5.4
Sponsoring shows and exhibitions of members' products	5.1

* Number of associations: 367.

pose serious problems for integration with the association, particularly where federal-provincial conflict is involved.[75] A "federal" or
"unitary" structure is better poised to maintain the balance between
differentiation and integration demanded in policy participation.

Table 3 summarizes the results of a classification of associations
according to these categories. Perhaps most striking here is the difference between agricultural and business associations. Whereas only
31.1 per cent of the former are unitary organizations, over three-
quarters of the latter assume this form. In some divisions of the

Table 3
Regional Differentiation of Associations with National Territorial Domains (Percentages), 1980

Structure	Agricultural	Total business	Resources	Manufacturing	Construction	Trade	Transport	Finance	Other services
Unitary	31.1	75.9	61.5	83.5	64.3	72.5	89.3	59.2	71.0
Unitary, with regional branches	15.6	6.7	7.7	6.5	7.1	9.8	0	6.1	9.7
Federal	22.2	9.5	23.1	4.3	21.4	3.9	3.6	26.5	9.7
Confederal	31.6	6.1	7.7	2.9	7.1	11.8	3.6	8.2	9.7
Other and mixed	0	1.8	0	2.9	0	2.0	3.6	0	0
Number of associations	45	325	13	139	14	51	28	49	31

business community – manufacturing, retail and wholesale trade, transport, services – the trend to unitary structures is strongly pronounced. In manufacturing, fully 90 per cent of the associations have essentially a unitary form. True, responsibility for agriculture is divided between the federal and provincial governments while business is more oriented to the federal government, but several divisions of business are closely tied to provincial governments: natural resources, construction, and financial/business services (particularly insurance, trust companies, credit unions, real estate, and accounting). In each of these divisions, about 30 per cent of the associations have a federal or confederal form, a figure higher than the average for all business associations yet still below that found in agriculture. Part of the remaining difference may be related to associations assuming dissimilar functions in agriculture as opposed to other divisions of the economy. Certainly, chapter 6 shows the greater development of corporatist policy networks in agriculture.

The prevalence of unitary structures among business associations is complemented by a pronounced tendency to locate head offices in central Canada. Table 4 lists the various locations of head offices for "nationally relevant" associations in 1980. Whereas only 34.4 per cent of agricultural associations are located in the Montreal-Ottawa-Toronto nexus, 80.7 per cent of all business associations have established their head offices in this area. The general pattern here favours Toronto over both Montreal and Ottawa, particularly in financial and business services. The resources division departs furthest from this pattern, since half of its associations are located in western Canada. The petroleum and natural gas associations and the Coal Association of Canada have headquarters in Alberta, with usually a branch office or lobbyist in Ottawa. Also noteworthy in Table 4 is the relatively small number of associations located in Ottawa. Admittedly, many of the larger and more important associations are included in the Ottawa contingent; also, the information is for 1980, and some associations may have moved to Ottawa since then.[76] Nevertheless the fact that so many associations are outside Ottawa, the political capital, may contribute to the "personal personnel gap" about which Litvak has spoken.[77]

To summarize, then, executive structures of business associations work on an informal basis that gives primacy to business leaders rather than association staff in the making of policy. Given the quite specialized domains of most business associations and their unitary territorial structures, they appear more adapted to advocacy than policy participation. Exceptions are found among associations involved in regulatory work pertaining to standards definition and

Table 4
Head Office Location of Nationally Relevant Associations (Percentages), 1980

Location	Agriculture	Total business	Resources	Manufacturing	Construction	Trade	Transport	Financial services	Other services
Montreal	6.5	15.4	0	17.8	5.0	21.5	15.2	7.1	22.6
Toronto*	17.2	50.6	23.8	48.8	40.0	55.3	36.3	76.8	54.9
Ottawa	10.8	14.7	7.1	17.8	30.0	7.7	27.3	8.9	11.3
Other Ontario	28.3	5.9	7.1	7.6	10.0	6.1	3.0	3.6	3.2
Other Quebec	3.2	1.9	11.9	1.5	0.0	0.0	0.0	0.0	1.6
Western Canada	31.3	10.4	50.1	5.0	15.0	7.6	18.2	0.0	4.4
Atlantic Canada	2.2	1.0	0.0	1.5	0.0	0.0	0.0	3.6	0.0
No specific city	0.0	0.1	0.0	0.0	0.0	1.8	0.0	0.0	0.0

* Includes suburbs, Mississauga, and Agincourt.

quality control and in agriculture. These associations have more developed technical committees, larger and more professional staffs, and greater capacity for voicing and integrating regional interests.

Resources

Two dimensions of resources are relevant for us: the amounts possessed, which will affect the ability to perform in either role, advocacy or participation, and the sources, which have a bearing on the autonomy of associations from their members or from the state. Most associations have relied almost completely on contributions from their members, in the form of an annual fee or set of dues paid to the association. Normally, the amount paid by a firm depends on its relative size within the group, in terms usually of sales in dollars of a given product (pesticides, potato chips, ethical drugs) or numbers of employees (more common in labour-intensive industries such as textiles). Other criteria may involve production volume directly – number of cases of canned goods (Ontario Food Processors Association), pounds of rubber produced (Rubber Association of Canada), or number of drilling rigs in operation (Canadian Association of Oil Well Drilling Contractors). The amounts contributed may vary from barely a hundred dollars to thousands of dollars. The maximum fee for the Canadian Chemical Producers Association in 1980 was $61,000, an amount probably typical for a major association organizing a somewhat oligopolistic industry.

In most cases, these fees account for between 85 and 95 per cent of an association's operating revenue. Other possible sources of income are interest on account savings, the sale of selective goods and services, and contributions from other organizations, including the state. Interest earned varies depending on rates and the association but usually counts for between 5 and 15 per cent of an association's revenue. The sale of selective benefits and services normally provides a rather small proportion of income. In the sectors (noted in chapter 1) where association finances were closely looked at, only rarely did these sales provide more than 5 per cent of revenues. These sectors included the construction industry, where associations are large and have many small firm members.

Grants and other contributions from the state virtually never appear on an association's balance books, certainly not as operating revenue. In the nineteenth century, agricultural associations in Ontario were supported by annual grants from the provincial Department of Agriculture. In the present day, some public interest groups like the Consumers Association of Canada rely to a degree on op-

Table 5

Financial Resources (Annual Expenditures) of Associations, 1980

| | *Percentages* | | | |
| | *Agricultural* | | *Business* | |
Amount in dollars (000s)	*Relative*	*Cumulative*	*Relative*	*Cumulative*
< 5	3.5	3.5	1.7	1.7
5–10	8.8	12.3	9.4	11.1
10–25	10.5	22.8	11.6	22.7
25–50	7.0	29.8	8.0	30.7
50–100	12.3	42.1	13.1	43.8
100–250	24.6	66.7	25.3	69.0
250–500	10.5	77.2	12.2	81.3
500–1,000	15.8	93.0	9.4	90.7
1,000–2,000	3.5	96.5	4.8	95.5
2,000–5,000	3.5	100.0	2.6	98.0
> 5,000	0.0	100.0	2.0	100.0
N number of cases	57		352	
Mean	409,839		576,872	
Standard deviation	694,841		2,293,479	

erating grants from government departments. Although these practices are virtually non-existent now among business and agricultural associations, state funds do pass through these associations' hands for specific programs. For example, the Foodland Ontario promotional campaign for Ontario fruits and vegetables has been run by the Ontario Food Processors Association with supporting grants from the Ontario government and from producer marketing boards. Several cases of associations implementing or administering government programs noted in part II also involve the transfer of funds from the state to the association.

There is striking variation in the financial resources possessed by Canadian business associations. Table 5 classifies agricultural and business associations into a range of expenditure categories. On the average, agricultural associations spend a little over $400,000 annually, about $175,000 less per year than the average business group. The distributions for both types of associations, however, are skewed upward by a few high-spending groups.[78] As the table shows a more typical annual budget would fall in the $100–250,000 range. The patterns of spending by the two types of associations are similar, except for the upper levels, where business associations have more cases in the upper three ranges. In 1980, the Canadian Standards Association, the Canadian Bankers' Association, and the Council of the Forest Industries of British Columbia all spent over $5 million. Within business associations, there are also variations in the respective endowments of associations across economic divisions. Conspicuously above the other divisions are those of resource extraction ($987,000 on average) and financial and business services ($1,967,000). The average expenditures in the other divisions are not only well below these but also below those of agricultural associations.[79]

Corresponding to the variation in expenditures is a similar variation in number of staff. Associations with the lowest budgets do not employ permanent staff and rely on voluntary donations of time by members, the state of affairs for 8.6 per cent of our agricultural associations and 7.2 per cent of business groups. Alternatively, an association may contract to a firm for staff services, a practice used by 14.4 per cent of the business associations but only 1.4 per cent of the farm groups. Generally, an association takes this route when its chief raison d'être is occasional lobbying. The servicing firm may provide the group with a letterhead, a mailbox, and some expertise for organizing meetings with politicians and officials when the need arises. The actual advocacy work in these meetings is done by the members themselves.[80]

The vast majority, then, of associations – 90 per cent of agricultural and 77.5 per cent of business – employ permanent staff. The number employed may vary from one to the 600 or so who work for the Canadian Standards Association. Table 6 gives a summary picture. Again, business groups tend to have more functionaries than do those representing agricultural interests. However, the average for business associations and that for financial/business services are perhaps not typical, as both are affected by a small number of extreme cases. With the exceptions again of financial/business, resources, and other services, business groups tend to be quite small, with one to two professional staff members and one to two clerical people. As staff numbers expand, personnel are added for research work, for public relations, or for editing publications. Larger associations might add their own lawyer, a technical expert (usually an engineer) for standards work, and a controller, who both manages the books of the association and advises member firms on fiscal and accounting problems.

Whether playing an advocacy or a participation role, Canadian business associations appear to be hiring more permanent professional employees. The growth of the Institute of Association Executives (IAE) reflects this change. Drawing its membership from the

Table 6
Mean Number of Employees of Associations, 1980

Economic division	Mean	Standard deviation	Maximum
Agriculture	7.6	17.4	120
Business (all)	12.9	49.5	600
Resources	15.6	30.1	
Manufacturing	4.5	9.6	
Construction	5.4	8.2	
Trade	4.4	4.4	
Transport	7.8	19.7	
Financial/business services	48.8	115.9	
Other services	12.5	40.6	

professional staffs of associations, the IAE provides a forum for discussing problems of association management and for upgrading the skills of members. Among the business associations in our study, 5.7 per cent had staff members who had completed the institute's certification and training program, and an additional 39.5 per cent had staff members belonging to the organization.[81]

An additional resource that has become important in Ottawa over the past 15 years, as well as in maintaining a membership base in Quebec, is institutional bilingualism – the degree to which an association can work in both official languages. Table 7 summarizes the amount of institutional bilingualism found among associations. The classification is conservative: an association was counted as fully bilingual only if it had a bilingual name and published its basic documents (by-laws, annual reports, and periodical publications, such as newsletters and journals) separately in French and English. An association was classified as partially bilingual if its name and only a few documents were in both languages and its periodicals were primarily in one of the official languages. If the association had no publications or there was no information on these, it was placed in one of the partial categories.[82]

A rather low number of associations (11.2 per cent of agricultural, 15.8 per cent of business groups) are fully bilingual. These figures are fairly characteristic of all the economic divisions save financial/ business services, where almost a third of the associations are fully bilingual. This finding may reflect the growing importance of French-Canadian institutions such as the Caisse de dépôt et placement, the National Bank of Canada, and the La Laurentienne group. Other-

Table 7
Bilingual Capacity of Associations (Percentages), 1980

Capacity	Agriculture	All business	Resources	Manufacturing	Construction	Trade	Transport	Financial services	Other services
English only	67.4	49.9	73.2	49.5	35.3	50.8	51.5	39.3	47.4
French only	10.0	2.4	0	2.1	0	0	3.0	0	10.5
Partially bilingual, English pre-eminent	10.1	29.5	7.3	33.3	47.1	32.3	36.4	28.6	21.0
Partially bilingual, French pre-eminent	1.1	2.4	4.8	2.5	5.9	2.5	0	0	5.3
Fully bilingual	11.2	15.8	14.7	12.5	11.8	12.5	9.1	32.2	15.8
Number of associations	89	461	41	192	17	65	33	56	57

wise, the modal organization for most economic divisions, particularly in agriculture and resources, is still one that operates in English only. Construction has a larger percentage partially bilingual, English pre-eminent. The number of totally French organizations is small, 10.1 per cent of agricultural and 2.4 per cent of business groups, as is the number of bilingual, predominantly French associations. These findings may reflect the tendency of most sections of French-Canadian business to integrate organizationally with their sectoral counterparts in English Canada.

CONCLUSIONS

On reviewing the general properties discussed in the latter half of this chapter, we note a relatively small number of associations with members that are generally large firms, operating in large oligopolistic sectors. These associations spend in excess of $1 million annually, employ a minimum of 10 to 15 people, are institutionally bilingual, and have an officer, if not their head office, in Ottawa. Associations in this category are visible to the attentive public; their leaders are quoted frequently in the business press and move freely in government circles. They are multi-functional: sophisticated pressure groups one day, competent technicians in the policy process the next. The several roles they play give them a system of comprehensive political contacts, ranging from lower and middle technical levels of the bureaucracy to senior officials, MPs, and cabinet ministers.

The majority of business associations, however, spend less than $200,000 annually and employ four or five persons, at least two of them clerical. Non-clerical staff members are jacks of all trades, who organize meetings, talk to government officials, turn the handle of the gestetner machine, and book acts for the entertainment portion of the annual convention. Unlike their larger counterparts, these associations tend to restrict themselves to one or two main activities. Many serve as half-way houses that bring together technical experts from the bureaucracy and their counterparts in member firms. Their political range is less wide and is often concentrated within the bureaucracy between the levels of director and assistant deputy minister. Contacts with politicians are less frequent and serve as symbolic, picture-taking occasions. Possessing highly specialized domains and narrowly focused interests, these groups are usually self-contained and work independent of other groups.

For reasons that will become clearer, agricultural associations operate somewhat differently. Their membership is drawn mainly from independent commodity producers, not business firms. In fact, most were formed explicitly to fight sectors of business. While many farms are in fact businesses, the historical legacy of their organizations makes them perceive themselves otherwise. The traditional need to fight capitalists continues to be reflected in their orientations and roles. In addition, the ties between farmers' groups and the state have been formed in a context that has stressed co-operation since before Confederation. Governments founded or promoted the founding of 25 per cent of the agricultural associations that existed in 1980. Among business associations, the figure is only 6 per cent. Partly as a result, agricultural associations today have special, often corporatist relationships with the state and form systems that are further integrated in terms of territory and commodity than those found for business firms.

In chapter 3, the theoretical concepts introduced in chapters 1 and 2 – policy advocacy, policy participation, and an associational system – are developed further. They then become key building blocks in the typology of policy networks presented in chapter 4, which serves, in turn, as the principal analytical device for the detailed sectoral case studies in part II.

CHAPTER THREE

Framework for Analysis

Political science research on interest groups is now de-emphasizing their pressure or lobbying activities. Groups not only pressure governments from outside but also participate in formulating and even implementing public policy. The importance of these activities was noted in the 1960s by some American pressure group theorists following case studies of American business associations.[1] The idea of groups participating formally in policy-making has been central to the literature on corporate pluralism that developed in Scandinavia following an article by Stein Rokkan in 1966.[2] Middlemas has used the term "governing institutions" to describe the policy participation of peak interest groups in Britain that has developed gradually since the turn of the century.[3] Such a role is integral to the concept of corporatism that has emerged in western Europe over the past decade.[4] Research has begun to uncover groups' involvement in the policy process not only on the macro plane, in areas like incomes policy, but also on the meso, or sectoral plane.[5]

These developments have created a need for further conceptual work on the forms of associative action. Canadian interest associations participate in policy activities, particularly at the sectoral level,[6] but most show no signs of giving up their more traditional pressure-type actions – policy advocacy, to use Salisbury's term.[7] Yet the more associations become involved in policy, the more internal tension they will feel. The roles are not completely complementary; they place competing demands on an interest association. This chapter develops concepts to help assess the extent to which groups are organized for policy participation, policy advocacy, or both. The concluding section points out where the roles are contradictory and speculates on how groups try to resolve tensions.

POLICY ADVOCACY

Policy advocacy is the attempt to influence what will or will not be a matter of public policy, the content of policies as they are being made, and the way in which they are implemented once agreed to by the government and the legislature. The key word in this definition is influence: the group is outside the policy process; it belongs to civil society and is calling upon the state, specifically those who make public policy. The guiding principle of action is competition, the capture of distributional benefits, normally at the expense of other social groups, organized or unorganized. The association pursues these benefits through exchanges with the state, providing information and pledges of political support. It manages this exchange more or less successfully depending on how well it maintains internal cohesion. The association engages in activities and creates structures that complement those needed for policy participation and engages in others that systematically undermine participation.

Pursuit of distributional benefits requires three types of information. First, an association needs detailed knowledge of the policy process, particularly within the bureaucracy.[8] It must know the course of policy proposals as they make their way from lower levels of the bureaucracy to central agencies, and finally to the cabinet. This course may differ, depending on the policy area and the departments or agencies involved.[9] The association must have sufficient political and bureaucratic contacts to be able to locate the proposals at all times and to know the details of these proposals.[10] Such information will be termed "policy process knowledge." Second, the association must be able to assess the likely political effect of policy proposals currently being considered or that it wishes the government to consider.[11] Who will benefit, and who will lose? Who will be happy enough to vote for the government or contribute to party coffers as a result? Who will be unhappy enough to mobilize votes and public opinion against the government and to donate to the opposition parties? In approaching politicians and even senior bureaucrats, who in Canada have a highly developed political sensitivity,[12] this information is often crucial. This information will be termed "political impact knowledge." Finally, the association needs to be able to generate "policy specific knowledge." It must be able to assess a given policy proposal and determine its economic and structural effects on members. This knowledge will normally be technical in character. In addition, the association may be asked to contribute technical information to bureaucrats or politicians to use in formulating policy.[13] By providing such information, associations gain indirect influence on policy and a credit note from policy-makers they can call in at a later date.

An association must be good at mobilizing political support – the expression of opinion on a policy proposal strong enough to be linked to electoral behaviour. Votes will rise or fall depending on the fate of the proposal. In mobilizing support, the association will direct itself inwards towards its own members and outwards towards the public at large.[14] Associations with many members or with firms that employ many workers will have a built-in advantage. However, numbers are in themselves not sufficient. The association must be able to mobilize its members to take political action. Members must reach bureaucratic officials, local MPs, and members of cabinet.

Increasingly, however, the mobilization of association members is insufficient in the political market-place. Associations have to involve the public at large. Their case is vastly strengthened if they can show that many voters know of and support their position. With this realization, associations have begun to use polling techniques and advocacy advertising in the mass media. An example of such an approach was the full-page advertisements taken out by the Canadian Petroleum Association and the Independent Petroleum Association of Canada during the oil industry's campaign against the federal government's National Energy Policy in 1981. In addition to using this direct, usually confrontational approach, associations will publish pamphlets, posters, and newsletters directed to narrower but politically crucial publics. These may even take the form of special publications for schools, a tactic used very successfully by the forestry and mining industries. Normally, associations use these latter methods to create a general climate of support for a sector or sub-sector, which can be drawn upon when crucial matters of policy arise.

An association's ability to generate information and to mobilize support will depend significantly on how well it maintains the cohesion of its members.[15] An association in the advocacy role wishes to maximize identification between it and its members. It strives to be its members' mouthpiece, to identify its political weight with their political strength.

Maintaining cohesion while pursuing distributional benefits is easier if the interest concerned is narrow and specialized. Political effectiveness is improved when groups define their objectives narrowly and concretely. New groups can always be formed when new objectives arise, as Bauer et al have observed.[16] Cohesion may also be strengthened by the cultivation of group ideologies.[17] The use of an explicit ideological framework often enhances the identification of members with the organization.

A narrowly defined special interest will guard cohesion and pursue distributional benefits more efficiently when the association is completely free to determine its own political strategy.[18] Small independent associations cannot worry about consistency across policy areas, even though such neglect can defeat them; rather officials and politicians must look after that. With less pressure to discipline their demands, independent associations are free to make alliances with other associations on an ad hoc basis and to dissolve them once a given political objective has been achieved.

Corresponding to information generation, support mobilization, and cohesion will be some structural differentiation within associations. First, the capable advocate group will have a political intelligence section to map the political process in selected policy areas, keep a list of contact persons, and assess the political effects of given policy proposals. Second, there will be one or more sections charged with political mobilization: maintaining internal cohesion, generating political action by members at crucial stages in the progress of a policy proposal, and cultivating public opinion. Third, one department will create and maintain technical information relevant to particular policy proposals and develop technical policy proposals. Finally, the association will have skilled lobbyists, who can use the association's resources to influence policy.[19]

POLICY PARTICIPATION

The second of the two basic roles associations may assume is policy participation – active involvement in formulating and/or implementing policy. Although this type of role is increasingly remarked upon by academics and practitioners alike, it is less well studied. Hence I will develop at greater length a schema for its analysis.

Participation in policy formulation may involve one or more of the following tasks:[20] (1) formulation of the guiding principles or general rules of the policy; (2) formulation of the actual text of a law or directive; and/or (3) formulation of the operationalization of the general rules and legal text, including the writing of regulations attached to the policy.

Similarly, participation in policy implementation may entail one or more tasks: (1) administration and implementation of a policy; (2) controlling those implicated to see that they observe the rules involved; (3) supervising others who are implementing the policy or applying controls; (4) sanctioning those who transgress the rules; and (5) handling appeals.

An association capable of playing a policy-making role will have two properties.[21] First, it will be able to order and co-ordinate the complex range of information and activity that it is asked to assume by its members and by other organizations, particularly the state. Without such a capability, the association will not be tolerated for long by others seated around the policy table. It will quickly be evident that the association has difficulties in reaching conclusions on many critical matters of policy. As a result, its positions will fail to transcend the diverse interests of its members, thereby reflecting the inconsistency and differences among them. Those policy proposals ultimately produced will be incomplete and will appear amateurish (although able staff members can often put a gloss on). To be a successful partner in policy-making, an association must reduce and manage information that it solicits and that comes voluntarily from its members and from the commercial partners of its members, including trade unions, the state bureaucracy, politicians, and the public at large.

Second, an association must be autonomous from its members and the state. As a participant in policy-making, it is more than the sum of the interests of one or the other. It takes on a life of its own and is able to rise above the short-term, particularistic interests of its members. It not only can see beyond, to the medium and longer term, it can define for its members what their interests are within this broader perspective. With this degree of autonomy, the association may even assume responsibility for directing and in some cases controlling and sanctioning the behaviour of its members.[22] When asked to help formulate public policy, it is well placed to mediate between its members and the state. If agreement is reached with the state on a policy, the association can guarantee that its members will comply. In certain circumstances, it may itself become one of the instruments used for implementing the policy. The common dismissal of associations by Canadian officials as simple "mouthpieces" for industry could not be used fairly with respect to associations that are autonomous in this sense.

Streeck and Schmitter suggest that associations with these two general properties have distinctive guiding principles compared to other social institutions.[23] The guiding principle of the market is dispersed competition, that of the community is spontaneous solidarity, and that of the public bureaucracy is hierarchical control. None of these principles adequately captures the dynamics of interaction of a system comprised of autonomous associations that co-ordinate their actions as we have described. Rather, Streeck and Schmitter suggest, the guiding principle of an associative model of social order is organizational *concertation* – "negotiation within and among a limited and fixed set of interest organizations that mutually recognize each other's status and entitlements and that are capable of reaching and implementing relatively stable compromises (*pacts*) in the pursuit of their interests."[24] This guiding principle differs from the sense of competition that motivates associations in pursuit of their policy advocacy role. These contradictory principles – *concertation* and competition – create a particular problem for associations as organizations, as we shall see in the conclusion to this chapter.

Co-ordinating and Ordering Complexity

The analysis of the capability of associations to co-ordinate complex information and demands begins with what I called in chapter 2 the domain of the association. The domain refers to the potential range of firms that, under the terms of the association's constitution or other, more informal rules, might become members. Normally the domain will be defined based on three types of factors: (1) structural: type of product or service, size of firm, ownership (public/private/ co-operative; foreign/domestic), and so on; (2) territorial: the nation as a whole, a region or group of provinces, a single province, a city, etc; and (3) functional: meets primarily with governments (trade association), bargains collectively with unions (employers' association), negotiates with marketing boards or other suppliers of materials or with customers (commercial).

For example, the Ontario Road Builders Association (ORBA) is open to those who are "actively engaged in Ontario as contractors in the construction of roads, streets, bridges, viaducts, sewers, excavations and other associated works." This domain limits the association structurally to a sub-sector of the construction industry, territorially to the province of Ontario, and functionally to being a trade association.[25] The domain also limits the information that the association might be asked to process. The ORBA would not normally speak to the Ontario government on behalf of butter manufacturers, have much contact with the government of Alberta, or have systematic ties with the Laborers' International Union of North America.

Another little-studied phenomenon that determines the complexity of an association's activity is the *associational system*. Any given business interest association is part of what will be called the business associational system – the collection of all business associations in Canada.[26] The consequences of membership in that system for an individual association fall between two extreme cases. On the one side, membership may have no effect whatsoever; the activities of the given association are completely uncoupled from other associations in the system. It operates independently from them and takes no cognizance of their activities in setting up and following its own agenda. On the other side, the association might be tightly coupled to other associations in the system. The system defines its role, draws up its agenda, and situates its actions by forcing it to take systematic account of other associations.

The associational system is a factor in reducing complexity. Let us take again the ORBA as an example. If it were completely uncoupled from all other associations, it would need, in order to represent its members, to monitor closely the activities of the federal government as well as that of Ontario and its municipalities. It would have to keep track of the burgeoning research and development in highway construction. Both of these tasks are immense. However, this workload becomes more manageable if ORBA is a member of an association devoted exclusively to monitoring the federal government (the Canadian Construction Association) and of an association specially concerned with research and development (the Roads and Transportation Association of Canada). Aggregation and organization of information are done elsewhere, and ORBA can draw upon this base when it appears useful to its membership. The structure of the associational system will determine whether individual associations are capable of participating in policy-making forums and whether that system itself is granted a systematic policy role.

In order to define what structural properties of the associational system are critical to participation, we need some terms to distinguish levels of aggregation in the economy For the purposes of this study, the economy will be divided into the general divisions shown in Table 8. Within each division, there will be a number of major sectors that correspond roughly to a two-digit grouping in the standard industrial classification (SIC) used by Statistics Canada. For example, in agriculture, these will be livestock raising, horticulture, and grains. Within each major sector, there will be a range of sectors that correspond roughly to a three-digit grouping in the SIC code. In turn, each sector will normally embrace a number of sub-sectors. Cattle raising includes sub-sectors for beef cattle, dairy cattle, and breeding cattle. In some cases, sub-sectors themselves might be subdivided. Dairy cattle can be broken down into Holstein-Friesian, Ayrshires, Brown Swiss, Canadienne, and others. Although there are associations representing these various breeds, we will not make extensive use of this very specialized level.

What then will an associational system look like if its member associations are to be prepared to assume a systematic policy-making role? Five interrelated properties summarized in Table 9 are at issue.[27] First, within a given area of the economy, there will be horizontal differentiation by product or service. This differentiation

Table 8

Classification Schema for Levels of Aggregation of the Economy

Economic division	Agriculture	Forestry	Mining	Manufacturing	Construction	Trade	Finance	Services
Major sector	Livestock	Logging	Metal mining	Food processing	Building	Retail	Monetary institutions	Recreational services
Sector	Cattle	Softwood logging	Base metals	Dairy products	Non-residential	Food retail	Banks	Motion picture producing
Sub-sector	Breeding cattle	Douglas fir logging	Nickel mining	Cheese manufacturing	Commercial	Chain store food retail	Savings banks	Animation films

Table 9
Properties Relevant to Policy-Making Capacity

Policy Capable Associations	Policy Weak Associations
PROPERTIES OF ASSOCIATIONAL SYSTEMS	
Systematic horizontal differentiation by product and by territory at each economic level	Horizontal differentiation not systematic and with gaps
Systematic vertical differentiation by different economic levels	Vertical differentiation not systematic and with gaps
Comprehensive vertical integration across product, territory, and economic level, with authority flowing down	No vertical integration; limited ad hoc horizontal alliances among associations
Concentrated in a minimal few associations	Fragmented in many associations
No competition among associations	Associations compete for members
STRUCTURES OF INDIVIDUAL ASSOCIATIONS	
Horizontal differentiation by product, territory, and function	Little, if any, horizontal differentiation
Vertical integration through coupling committee and executive structures	No vertical integration; association uses an encompassing flat structure.
No competitors for members	Competitors for members
High density of representation	Low density of representation
RESOURCE DIVERSITY	
Finances from various sources	Finances primarily from members or from selective benefits
Diverse basis of member support	Singular basis of member support
Balance between staff professionals and members' expertise	Few staff professionals; members' expertise dominant.
Balance between administrative head and elected executive	Elected executive dominates administrative head.
Generates own information base	No independent information base
State privileges	No state privileges

The right margin contains a large brace spanning the first two sections labeled vertically: COORDINATION, and a brace spanning the RESOURCE DIVERSITY section labeled vertically: AUTONOMY.

may take the form of separate associations for each product or service group, the usual case in Canada, or of separate product or service group branches within associations with larger domains. The associational system must have a place for the voicing of each relevant interest. Each interest can be taken into account. The same principle holds for territorial interests. In most cases, this will mean at a minimum that each province will have a voice in the system at higher levels of the economy. At lower levels, depending on the constitutional context of the sector or sub-sector and the amount of economic activity usually involved, it is unlikely that all provinces need have a distinct organizational presence. But the associational system must be sufficiently differentiated to be comprehensive in its representation.

Second, the associational system will be differentiated vertically by product or service group and by territory from specialized to more general levels of the economy. Separate associations or divisions within associations will exist for aggregating and speaking for the interests of each level. If, for example, the policy problem concerns all livestock (foot and mouth disease), then a policy-capable system will have an organizational unit designed for speaking at that level of generality and able to aggregate the different interests of cattle growers, sheep raisers, pig breeders, and so on. A policy-weak system will have gaps across economic levels. In this case, the state will need to deal with many associations and spend valuable time reconciling their differences. Not only is the state then likely to be reluctant to involve associations in policy formulation, it will not have an obvious partner to help implement the policy of concern.

Third, the policy-capable associational system will be vertically integrated: there will be structures that cross-cut and draw together the horizontally and vertically differentiated units noted above. Normally these structures will take the form of peak associations, which group together associations at the economic level below it.[28] For example, the association representing agriculture as a division would have as its members the associations representing the major sectors of livestock, horticulture, and grains. Each of these major sectoral associations would be an association of sectoral associations, and each sectoral association would be an association of sub-sectoral associations. The association at each level in the system would in addition be able to direct or bind its members. Hence authority would flow downwards from the peak association, representing the whole of business, to divisional associations, to major sectoral associations, and so forth.

In contrast, the policy-weak system will have little vertical integration – it will be highly fragmented. Associations existing at the different levels of aggregation will be direct member associations with no formal ties among one another. An industrial chemical manufacturing firm might then join separately an industrial chemicals association, a major sectoral association covering the whole chemical industry, and a divisional association covering all of manufacturing. These three groups would not integrate their activities. For example, in Canada, only the first (the Canadian Chemical Producers Association) and the third (the Canadian Manufacturers' Association) are available. Hence the associational system will be hard pressed to aggregate systematically or to disaggregate their activities. Policies agreed to by divisional associations will not necessarily be even known to, let alone accepted by, major-sectoral or sectoral associations in those divisions.

The fourth and fifth structural properties follow from the previous three. In a policy-capable system, at higher levels of aggregation, the representation of interests will be concentrated into a very few organizations, enabling the state to negotiate with a restricted number of associations on more general policy issues. Further, these associations will have mutually exclusive domains and thus will not compete among each other for members. In a policy-weak system, associations will be fragmented rather than concentrated, forcing the state to bargain with many rather than few groups in making policy, again the Canadian experience. These groups will have overlapping domains, making it likely that they will compete for members. The state will have difficulty in determining who speaks for what interest and which is the most representative association in a given domain.

In summary, an association operating within a policy-capable associational system will be better able to reduce and co-ordinate the complex of information that comes its way. The policy issues that it will need to deal with will be limited and relatively clear. The nature of the transactions that it needs to manage with its members – whether associations or firms – will also be circumscribed. Staff members can be hired and trained as specialists in a more limited set of tasks.

In such a systemic context, what organizational properties might we expect the individual association to have? These will tend to mirror those of the associational system (see Table 9). Within the association, branches or divisions will be created for major product or service divisions in the association's domain as well as for relevant territorial divisions or for functional tasks. This differentiation will be integrated through committees and executive structures that cross and aggregate the differences among the various product/service, territorial, and functional branches. As policy-capable associations, they will have no competitors for their members and will be highly representative of their domains. Few, if any, potential members will not belong to the association.

The policy-weak association will look somewhat different. It will not be systematically differentiated by product/service, territory, or function. Rather it will have a flat organization, with all information being channelled to a central executive structure that will deal with problems ad hoc. Pressed for time, it will be unable to develop staff expertise or a comprehensive information base for participating in policy activity. The association will be in competition with other associations for members. Its representativeness will, accordingly, be low, diminishing further its ability to play a role in policy.

Associational Autonomy

If the first component of policy-making capacity, co-ordination, is rooted in association structures, the second, organizational autonomy, rests on the association's resources. By resources we mean not just money but also the professional expertise of staff members, the degree of commitment or support from members, the capacity to generate unique information, and the privileges that the association receives from other actors, particularly the state. Following Schmitter and Streeck, resource diversity is central to organizational autonomy.[29] The more diverse the springheads from which resources flow, the greater the capability for autonomous associative action.

The first dimension of resource diversity involves sources of funds (see Table 9). A policy-capable association depends on institutionalized and stable funding methods.[30] It will not rely extensively on voluntary donations or interest, which are by nature extremely variable. It will seek to vary its sources of funds, obtaining a major portion from member dues, supplemented by sales of selected goods and services, by voluntary donations and interest, and significantly by grants from the state or other interest organizations. Such diversity helps it to take its distance from its members when necessary and preserve its autonomy from the state. In contrast, a policy-weak association may derive virtually all its revenue from members' dues, rendering it simply a mouthpiece for its members, or from the sale of goods and services, making it primarily a firm. Interest representation becomes a sideline activity. An autonomous organization must be able to take cognizance of its members' political interests.

This variation in funding relates also to the second dimension, the bases of members' support. Schmitter and Streeck identify four such bases.[31] Members may see the association as a firm, whence they can purchase needed goods and services at competitive rates;[32] as a club, providing solidarity and giving meaning to their experiences in a particular economic or class niche; as a political movement, pressing the state and society to provide them with needed public goods; or as a government with authority that permits it to make binding decisions governing their behaviour. The policy-capable association will diversify its sources of member support by cultivating and drawing upon a mix of these four motivations. In contrast, a policy-weak association will rely primarily on one motivational base of support; lacking diversity, it depends more on its members.

A third dimension of resources is professionalization of staff. An association may draw on up to three sources of professional expertise: its own professional experts in the areas most relevant to its policy capacity, technical personnel in its member firms who can be tapped for their knowledge through inclusion on association committees,[33] or experts borrowed from the state or other organizations in its environment. For example, the Society of the Plastics Industry of Canada has regularly had seconded to it someone from the National Research Council to do applied research on the uses of plastics. The policy-capable association will balance its own professional expertise with that supplied by member firms and the state. It will be able independently to reflect upon and develop positions on policy-including technical issues and therefore to engage in a dialogue with its members or with the state. In contrast, the policy-weak association will rely almost completely on its member firms, serving merely as a forum for the presentation and merging of members' expertise, invariably reflecting closely their short-term concerns.

Parallel to balance between inside and outside expertise is that between administrative head and elected executive. Generally speaking, a permanent administrative head will be responsible for running the organization day to day. A chief executive officer will be chosen by a board of directors elected by the members. In a policy-capable association, the chief elected head and the board will delegate enough authority to the permanent head that he or she can be an independent spokesperson on matters of policy for the association. This staff officer will have authority to speak for the organization on matters of public concern. In a policy-weak association, such an officer will not speak independently on policy matters – this is the responsibility of the elected executive – but will confine his or her activities to managing the organization so that it provides effective support for the elected executive in its endeavours. The policy positions of the association and of the membership are the same.

A key factor affecting the balance in the organization is the association's ability to generate information. The state may involve associations in policy-making because they have access to technical information essential for the formulation of policy but not readily available to the state. In a policy-capable association, professional staff and member firms or associations will co-operate in data collection to develop a repository of information. The association will be refined enough to complement the information and expertise of the state. A policy-weak association will not be able to generate the depth of information needed for policy development and will confine itself to aggregating and cataloguing members' policy demands.

The final component of resources is the privileges granted to the organization, usually by the state. The state may license it to produce certain goods. For example, it may grant provincial poultry marketing boards the power to determine poultry prices or give a construction association the licence to market and promote a national specification code. The state may make membership compulsory, granting the association the resource of a high density of representation. The Canadian Bankers' Association and provincial teachers' associations are examples. The state may make certain decisions taken by the association binding on non-members. For example, associations in Canada that negotiate collective agreements with trade unions are usually able to extend these to unionized firms outside the association. Each of these kinds of privileges allows the association to balance the influence of the members with that of the state. In balancing these forces, the policy-capable association achieves a measure of organizational autonomy. The policy-weak association will not receive these kinds of special privileges and, as a result, remain quite dependent on its members for resources. It will be less prepared to take an independent, responsible position in policy-making.

Summary

Drawing from Lawrence and Dyer on the nature of the firm, I noted two factors that affect an association's capacity for participating in policy-making: information complexity and resource diversity (see Figure 4).[34] The degree of information complexity – including demands by members and by actors in the association's environment – will affect the co-ordination and ordering capacity of the association. The more complex the information, the greater the problems of co-ordination. Similarly, complexity will be reduced, I have argued, by three factors: restriction of the association's domain, insertion in a differentiated yet integrated associational system, and differentiation and integration within the association itself. Lawrence and Dyer relate information complexity to the firm's capacity for innovation.[35] They argue that high complexity will overload the firm

Figure 4   Variation in Policy-Making Capacity

		Member-dependent, information-overloaded associative action	Semi-autonomous, information-overloaded associative action	Autonomous, information-overloaded associative action
Information complexity	High	1	2	3
		Co-ordinated, member-dependent associative action	Co-ordinated, semi-autonomous associative action	Co-ordinated, autonomous associative action
		4	5	6
	Low	Limited-policy range; member-dependent associative action	Limited-policy range; semi-autonomous associative action	Limited-policy range; autonomous associative action
		7	8	9
		Low		High

Resource
diversity

and inhibit innovation. Low information also inhibits innovation, because the firm lacks information needed to develop something new. Innovation becomes more likely when firms can manage relations with their environment so as to obtain information of intermediate complexity.

An analogous argument holds for associations and policy participation. Associations with complex information, whether because of broad domain, insertion in a poorly developed associational system, or weak internal organization, will be unable to co-ordinate and order well their activities. Overloaded and disorganized, they will be unable to be creative and sufficiently far-sighted to be an effective partner in policy-making. Associations with low information complexity, because of narrow domain or membership in an associational system that limits its activities, while perhaps not having co-ordination problems will be poor policy partners. Their vision and range of action will be too narrow for the more general policy issues that the state wishes to discuss. Associations with intermediate information complexity will be more policy-capable. They will be able to discuss a selected range of policy issues in depth with the government and, because they are not overloaded, will develop in-depth knowledge of these issues and take into account longer-term factors. Such associations will be the most creative policy partners of the state.

Resource diversity affects the autonomy of the organization. The key to this variable is balance: among sources of funds, bases of support from members, sources of expertise, centres of authority, and sources of information and between membership support and state privileges. The relationship is linear: the more resource diversity, and hence balance, the more autonomous the association. An autonomous association can favour the medium and longer term over the short term, control and even discipline its members, and help implement policy. In short, it is a more suitable participant in policy-making.

When we combine these two dimensions, information complexity and resource diversity, to form the grid shown in Figure 8, variations in the policy-making capacity of associations become evident. Associations with the most developed policy capacity will fall into area 6 of this grid. They are able to co-ordinate and order information of intermediate complexity, broad enough to embrace the detail and general scope needed for policy-making and yet limited enough to be processed effectively. The diverse resource base permits autonomous function.

Departure from the ideal in area 6 yields two particularly weak types, areas 1 and 7. Many Canadian associations with broad domains that span an economic division or several divisions will fall into area 1.[36] Their members are firms, not other associations; they are weakly integrated into an associational system and thus swamped with information. They find it difficult to determine where and how to develop policy expertise. As a result, the state comes to lack confidence in them and is reluctant to accord them special privileges or public status. They thus must fall back on their member firms for most of their resources, compromising their autonomy.

Related to this convergence of broad-domain associations in area 1 is that of many smaller associations in area 7. They become very narrow special-interest groups operating outside any comprehensive associational system. While they are able to co-ordinate and order information relevant to their domains, this information is of such narrow scope that it is not of much use in policy-making. Not being invited to participate in the policy process, these associations are forced to rely on their members for most of their resources, compromising their autonomy. They have become the classic "mouthpiece" of a special interest about which Olson and others have written.

POLICY PARTICIPATION V. POLICY ADVOCACY

The preceding discussion of the two major associational roles has hinted at possible overlaps on the one side and contradictions on the other. On the positive side, both roles call for a developed technical research capability, although the need is probably greater in policy participation. The knowledge about political impact and the policy process necessary for advocacy will also be of interest for those concerned about policy-making. Similarly, public support for association positions will be of as much use to representatives already at the policy table as to those pressuring the state from outside.

On the negative side, as I have suggested, the autonomy sought for policy-making may harm policy advocacy. The logic of the latter role necessitates close identity between members and the organization. Accordingly, advocacy may make associations leery of seeking resources from environments other than their members.

In addition, several of the properties that increase co-ordination capability may be counter-productive for policy advocacy. Policy participation favours widening of domains and formalization of hierarchical relationships with other associations. Advocacy is more successful when domains are narrow and the association can develop strategy and act independently of other associations. Policy participation yields better results when ideology is suppressed in favour of techo-pragmatism and when issues are not politicized.[37] However, policy advocacy will often involve ideological grandstanding (to galvanize the support of members), deliberate politicization of issues, and open, independent politicking by association members. Each of these types of behaviour, however, can undermine the atmosphere of trust and secrecy that associations and the state nurture for policy participation.

The presence of these kinds of contradictions will depend to a degree on the characteristics of the state involved and its public bureaucracy. A highly corporatist system like Austria's stresses policy-making and thereby minimizes contradictions. Membership in the agricultural and business/industry chambers is compulsory. These chambers have a comprehensive peak association structure which enables them to deal with broad macro-economic issues such as incomes policy and narrow sub-sector-specific topics such as the retail price of consumers' milk. In contrast, a highly pluralist system will encourage policy advocacy and provide few opportunities for policy participation, thereby also minimizing contradiction. Conventional analysis of the United States suggests that such a system prevails there. A third and final type of case where contradiction may be minimized is that of meso- or sectoral corporatism.[38] Corporatist relations between groups and the state may develop in certain sectors (agriculture is a common example), thereby giving primacy to policy participation. In other sectors, in the absence of corporatism, policy advocacy may be favoured. Since most business associations have domains confined to a sector or sub-sector, contradiction may be minimized. However, some strains may be placed on peak associations, which must organize under one roof associations favouring different roles.

Nonetheless, in some cases an association may have to play both roles. Economic policy-making, particularly as it affects specific sectors, is so complex that some participation by industry is needed for many policies to be properly formulated and implemented. In such cases, at least three different behavioural outcomes are possible.

(1) The association may become a "quiet lobby."[39] In order to preserve its role in policy-making, it gives up many of the techniques of advocacy in favour of using its contacts in the policy process. Less emphasis is given to waiting on politicians.

(2) Through participation in policy-making, the association may gain privileges (particularly compulsory membership) that allow it to be autonomous and still a policy advocate. When it is needed in policy-making, it can take its distance from its members, knowing that they cannot "vote with their feet."

(3) Further differentiation may lead to separate associations for each role in a policy area. We see this in the medical profession: compulsory colleges set policy on medical standards, and the Canadian Medical Association is primarily a policy advocate. Similarly, the

Canadian Construction Association acts as that industry's lobby in Ottawa, and Construction Specifications Canada, also an association, co-ordinates standard national specifications and related construction documents with the federal and provincial governments.[40]

In chapter 4, I build on these concepts of advocacy and participation to elaborate the notion of a policy network, the central analytical device in the cases studied in part II.

CHAPTER FOUR

Policy Networks and Associative Action

The study of business-government relations has been pulled into a maelstrom of theoretical debate, critique, and counter-critique over the past two decades. The storm began with an outburst against the well-established pluralist theory by American social scientists who had become impressed by the private power of business elites and business associations. The heavens opened further in the mid-1970s when the developing concept of corporatism added a new set of questions to those already posed by elite theorists. Corporatism's return to grace gave way to a rigorous theoretical critique and the unyielding test of empirical investigation. The criticisms of corporatism had much in common with earlier critiques of pluralism. Both of these competing, middle-range theories were said to have "underconceptualized" the state. They either made rather simplified assumptions about state organization and behaviour or said nothing at all.

Several conclusions from these theoretical debates are important for the study of business-government relations. The critique of pluralism demonstrates that the multiple, competing, voluntary, and relatively self-contained groups of a pluralist society may shelter a range of relationships between groups and the state. One type of relationship, commonly associated with pluralism, involves several groups competing and lobbying for the ear of a passive and neutral, relatively centralized and integrated state organization. Other types, emphasizing the diffusion of power in the state among a large number of agencies and bureaus,[1] involve groups in what we have called participant roles.

The theoretical reincarnation of corporatism under the heading of liberal, societal, or neo-corporatism in the 1970s also assumed a relatively centralized and integrated state organization.[2] Faced with the dispersal of power unearthed by the post-pluralists, corporatist scholars moved away from a macro-political focus on societal tripartism to meso-corporatism, or corporatism within sectors of the economy.[3] This new focus yielded a similarly diverse set of relationships between groups or firms and the state. Further, variations in relationship appeared to be related systematically to variations in the types of policies countenanced and ultimately attempted. Theodore Lowi anticipated well this conclusion when he wrote in 1964: "For every type of policy there is likely to be a distinctive type of political relationship."[4]

Thus the study of business-government relations cannot focus only on the instruments used by business to influence the state or the state's receptiveness to business's demands. Rather it must examine the structure of the relationship between business and government. Differences in these structures imply variations both in the actual influence of business and in the types of policies likely to succeed in a given instance. In arriving at this conclusion, Peter Katzenstein has suggested the concept of a policy network as an analytical device for characterizing such structures.[5] A policy network refers to patterns of relationships linking a social category such as business with the state. These patterns will vary according to how business and the state are organized and the degree of autonomy between these organizations.

This chapter begins with a review and specification of Katzenstein's concept. I next apply this theoretical outline to define and compare four ideal types of policy networks. Three types are pluralist: pressure pluralism, co-optive pluralism, and clientele pluralism; the fourth is corporatism. In defining these networks, I make systematic use of the contrasts of policy-weak versus policy-strong and advocacy versus participation developed in chapter 3. These ideal types become the principal organizing concepts for the closer examination of business-government interaction in part II.

POLICY NETWORKS

The "agreement" in a liberal democracy between business, the class of owners of the instruments of production, and the class of those who do not own those instruments allows the latter to press claims for resources and goods, or so I argued in chapter 1. Policy networks are the structures through which such claims are reacted to by business and responded to by governments and through which goods are eventually distributed. The conflicts involved may be intense and perceived by both sides to be fundamental. Business may argue that acceptance of claims that are too grandiose and unreasonable will lessen its ability to accumulate capital, invest, and keep the system going. Social and political chaos will result, possibly bringing on the end of democracy. Those who do not control the means of production counter that business uses its economic power to acquire more resources than it needs, depriving others, even visiting misery on the particularly disadvantaged. Variations in the structure of policy networks shape and channel this conflict, thereby influencing business's ability to control production. Some networks are more efficient in transforming economic class power into political power than are others. Of the four networks used in this study, pressure pluralism is least efficient in this respect, followed in order by corporatism, co-optive pluralism, and clientele pluralism.

The structure of a given network varies according to the configuration of three factors.[6]

(1) *The organization of the state.* Is the state strong (relatively centralized, with a definite sense of its own or the public's interest) or weak (fragmented and weakly autonomous from a range of competing interests in society)?

(2) *The organization of business.* Is business represented by a firm (or its surrogate) or by an association? If the business representative is an association, does it belong to a strongly or weakly integrated associational system? Is the business representative organized for advocacy, participation, or both?

(3) *The distance between business and the state.* Is the state or its agent particularly dependent on business for information, expertise, compliance, or support? Does the representative of business participate in the design, formulation, or administration of policy, or does it seek to influence those processes from outside? If the association does participate in any component of policy-making, does it do so on its own or does it share the privilege with other sectors of business or, even more important, with other social classes?

In addition to these three dimensions drawn from Katzenstein's work, it is useful to add a fourth. When the business representative is an association, the relationship between that association and its members becomes of interest.

(4) *The relationship between associations and their members.* Do firm members act autonomously from the association, feeling in no way bound by its agreements with state officials and governments and free to support or defect from collective action as they choose?[7] Or does the association control to some degree the behaviour of its member firms?[8]

There is little knowledge about the way in which Canadian business organizes its relationships with the state and about the range of activities at issue in these relationships. Accordingly, I draw, whenever possible, on existing research to describe the organization of the state in a given policy network. This organization, along with the structure of the industry concerned, provides the context within which I seek to delineate the dimensions of policy networks.

The components of the political structure of policy networks are summarized down the left margin of Table 10. The first of these is the organization of the state in a sector, major sector, or division of the economy. A strong organization (state) is centralized and is capable of defining its own interests and those of the public or common good. A weak state lacks these properties. The second component is the dependence of the state or its agent on the economic groups with which it is treating. If the state agency is particularly dependent on business for information, for expertise, or for support in obtaining compliance with laws or regulations, I term it high. Conversely, a state that is autonomous from business in these respects is moderate or low.

Business may involve itself in a policy network directly, as a firm or corporation, indirectly, through an association, or in both ways. In addition, the representative of business, whether firm or association, may become involved in policy in one of two ways. It may lobby or pressure the state from outside as a policy advocate, or it may work with the state on the inside as a policy participant. If it follows the latter course, the business representative may be drawn in for design and formulation of policy, for implementation of policy, or for both.

Whether a policy advocate or a participant, the representative may treat with the state one on one in a monopolistic way, it may be one of many interlocutors for a given policy area, or it may be one of a restricted smaller group of partners. Similarly, again drawing from chapter 3, the representative, when it is an association, may strive to integrate itself into a differentiated, hierarchically structured ("developed") associational system. Or the association may seek to be as independent as possible of all other groups in order to preserve maximum flexibility and autonomy for political action – in other words, to be part of an undeveloped associational system. Finally, the association may have weak authority over its members, making defection relatively easy, or its authority may be stronger, enabling it to restrict defections and even free riding.

PLURALIST NETWORKS

Common to each of the three types of policy network labelled pluralist are two properties. First, power is diffused within the state and

Table 10
Policy Networks

Components	Pressure pluralism	Co-optive pluralism	Clientele pluralism	Corporatism
Autonomy of state agencies; existence of a state tradition	Strong	Weak	Weak	Strong
Dependence of state on business for information, securing compliance	Low	High	High	Moderate
Mode of intervention by business	Firm or association	Association/monopoly firm	Association/monopoly firm	Association
Place in the policy process	Advocate	Participant primarily in design and formulation	Participant primarily in implementation	Participant in all phases
Number of groups present	Many	One	One	Several
Character of associational system	Weakly integrated	Weakly integrated	Weakly integrated	Highly integrated
Control of associations over members	Weak; defections and free riding common	Stronger; defections and free riding rare	Stronger; defections and free riding rare	Very strong; defections not permitted

throughout society. This dispersal prevents co-ordinated policy-making and invites policies focused on the short term, catering to individual centres of power in society. Pross adds that, in such a context, state agencies need the support of groups to fight their political battles with central agencies and groups need the favours of these agencies if they are to establish or maintain special privileges for their members.[9] Hence, pluralism rests on bilateral relations between business representatives (firms or associations) and the state. This is not to say that the state agency or department concerned deals with only that one business representative on a given policy issue. Rather, it deals with one representative, one on one, at any given time.

Second, pluralist networks involve business representatives, whether firms, associations, or both, that act independently one from the other rather than in concert. Independent action becomes more probable when there are many associations and firms engaged in political action rather than few, when domains of associations overlap, when associations compete among one another for members as well as for the ear of the government, and when many firms belong to no associations. When a new interest arises among firms within an association, the solution is normally to found a new association to represent this new interest rather than to absorb it within existing structures.[10] The individual firm finds itself with a number of options available and, in particular, with a variety of associations to choose from, each having a different, rather specialized purpose to which the firm's own political efforts can be joined.

The bilateral relationship in a pluralist network will involve one of the two roles for the business representative outlined in chapter 3. It may be a policy advocate, that is, exert pressure on policy-makers from outside the process wherein policies are designed, formulated, and administered. Here it is a matter of persuasion or the exertion of influence by someone outside the window trying to peer around the curtains to see what is going on within. In contrast, the policy participant is involved directly in the design, formulation, or implementation of policy. No longer peering between the folds of the curtains, the business organization is seated at the table inside.

The allocation of public goods in a pluralist policy network may involve the business representative at the start or the end of the process.[11] At one end, business may be supplying the public good. For example, in a regulatory system designed to provide consumers with safe and effective drugs, a drug manufacturing firm by itself, or through an association, is constrained to produce a good with these properties. At the other end, the business representative may receive or be the direct beneficiary of a public good. For example, when the state provides funds to automobile parts manufacturers for the creation of specialized programs to train skilled workers, those firms (or their association) that receive and administer the funds are the beneficiaries.

Pressure Pluralism

In a pressure pluralist policy network, business representatives play an advocacy role on a bilateral basis with a state agency or department. (See Table 10). The issues at stake may involve the representative as a supplier or as a beneficiary of the public good in question. Celebrated in the classics on pluralism, this type of network is what analysts and political observers call a "lobby" or "pressure group politics." In pressure pluralism, business is not the only class that interacts with the state on a given policy. It competes for the ear of those in power with other class or group advocates in an apparently open political market-place. Nevertheless this market is not as free and competitive as it might seem. Business enjoys several advantages over other social classes.[12] It has a number of instruments at hand – it can lobby as a firm, as an informal group of firms, or within an association. Its dominant place in the economy and the state's dependence on its economic performance make its demands appear normally more reasonable and more universal. More can be taken for granted by both sides. Business's organizations will be more numerous and have better resources than those of other classes. Nonetheless, the market-place, however imperfect, distinguishes pressure pluralism from other pluralist networks. Examples of pressure pluralism abound, of course, in Canada. It represents the dominant approach to government used by civil engineering construction (chapter 7), mining (chapter 8), and manufacturing (chapter 10).

Pressure pluralist networks arise when state agencies are relatively strong, with some sense of a general interest, and relatively self-sufficient in information and in securing compliance with policy directives from industry. In the absence of such strength, agencies may gain pseudo-autonomy when confronted with relatively balanced warring interests. Primarily concerned with allocative policies, these networks support interventions by both firms or associations, whichever makes the most strategic sense for the firms involved. The interlocutor will press decision-makers from outside and in competition with many other associations or firms. Since independence of action is critical to successful lobbying, ties among firms and associations remain loose and informal. Coalitions form and dissolve, depending on the politicians and competitors in the network.

Individual firms may defect freely from their associations as they pursue their particular interests.

Co-optive and Clientele Pluralism

The discovery of other types of pluralist networks took place in the mid-1960s and early 1970s. Such critics of the working of pluralism in the United States as McConnell and Lowi, those who have reflected upon pressure-group politics in Canada such as Pross, and those who have puzzled during the past two decades over the nature of group-state relations in Scandinavia have all pointed to important cases where the pressure pluralist model does not apply.[13] McConnell found groups that were not advocates but participants in the policy-making process. "More and more characteristic of American government is the conquest of formal state power by private groups and associations."[14] Pross noted that Canadian groups sometimes acted as "agents" of government.[15] Heisler borrowed the phrase "corporate pluralism" from Rokkan to distinguish between classical pressure pluralism[16] and what he observed in Scandinavia: "the continuous, structured participation of interest organizations in the policy-making (and sometimes policy implementation) process. Such organizations convey principally but not exclusively particularistic interests – in the largest number of cases dealing with economic subject matter. And, reciprocally, they are used by policy-makers to enhance the legitimacy of policies and to facilitate their implementation."[17]

Business representatives participating in policy in a bilateral relation with the state provide the core of the two additional pluralist networks ("co-optive" and "clientele") summarized in Table 10. Usually these networks are composed of a particular state agency with a limited policy mandate and a sectoral or professional association or a large, monopolistic firm. In co-optive pluralism, the business representative is a monopoly supplier of a public good, what Chubb calls the "cost bearer" in the policy process.[18] In such networks, a single sector or profession (chemical firms, meat processors, doctors) is called upon to supply a public good (clean water, uncontaminated hamburger, proper health care) and to bear most of the costs needed to produce it. However, defining the characteristics of the good may require the agency to depend heavily on the supplier for technical information, for compliance, and for good will. In exchange for these things, the supplier receives an opportunity to participate in the formulation or implementation of the policy in question. Business firms take advantage of this opportunity with mixed motives:

they gain added sway over the regulations governing their behaviour
and hence guard their control over production. They can take advantage of their more powerful position in the policy process. They
also are better placed to limit "misdirected" state intervention. Prominent examples of this type of network occur in the forestry industry
(chapter 8).

In clientele pluralism, the business representative has a "mon-
opsonistic" (the only "buyer") position as the beneficiary or recipient
of a public good.[19] The "client" gains some control over the distribution and occasionally the definition of a public good that it itself
is targeted to receive. The business representative, again usually an
association or a monopoly firm, may help formulate policies for
defining the properties of the good, share in its administration, and
even completely control its distribution. Perhaps the most developed
examples in Canada occur in the financial industries, particularly in
investment dealing (see chapter 9).

Co-optive and clientele networks are similar in most respects. They
arise when state agencies are divided and autonomous from central
co-ordinating departments, have little sense of a common or general
good, and depend heavily on business for information, expertise,
and support. Normally concerned with regulatory or self-regulatory
policies, they support more easily associations able to gather information, secure compliance, and speak generally for those who are
regulated. In particular cases, associations may be replaced by monopoly firms. In a co-optive network, where business supplies the
good at issue, the association helps the state agency formulate and
design policy. In a clientele network, in contrast, business is the
recipient of the good and is more likely to help implement the policy
developed to provide the good. In both types of network, the association works one on one with the state agency; other possible in-
tervenors, more on the outside, are restricted to advocacy. Such a
one on one relationship requires the association to have maximum
flexibility and hence independence from other associations. The
privileges it gains in the policy process facilitate the exercise of considerable suasion over members, if not outright authority. Unlike in
pressure pluralism, then, defections and free riding occur only rarely.

Observers of co-optive and clientele networks have given them
mixed reviews. Critics have suggested that their growth within various parts of the state administration loosens up government, ac-
centuates its pluralism, and further disperses its power.[20] These
developments, according to Lowi, lessen popular control over the
state. New structures of privilege develop in favour of business,
exacerbating inequalities in the distribution of power and wealth.[21]

The various networks close in on themselves, making the state inherently conservative and ill equipped to deal with social and political change.[22] As Stanbury and Hotz and others point out, the system discriminates against large groups unable to organize well, if at all, and with heterogeneous memberships that make it difficult to develop positions as coherent and well formulated as those of groups with narrow, specialized domains.[23]

Something of a counter-argument has been made by Streeck, particularly for clientele pluralist networks.[24] He suggests that in certain situations, a given sector or sub-sector will be interested in a private good (say, skilled workers) that coincides with a priority of public authorities (upgrading the skills of the labour force). Because of competition among firms in the sector, individual firms do not see to the production of this private good. Consequently, market failure occurs. At the same time, the state bureaucracy is too cumbersome, hierarchical, or inflexible to provide the given good. As a compromise solution, the state delegates authority to (usually) an association to provide the good and furnishes it with the resources it needs. Streeck argues that this solution avoids market failure and draws upon some natural strengths of the association – flexible organization and closeness to the industry – to provide a needed public good. As my analysis proceeds, we shall reflect further on this debate. In the end, we shall find it difficult to share Streeck's optimism.

CORPORATIST NETWORKS

The fourth, and only non-pluralist network type used in this study also has developed in the train of the critique of classical pluralism. The concept of corporatism has had a long and controversial life in political discourse and in political science. Over the past 70 years, it has occupied a central place in the Catholic church's philosophical response to the rise of socialism and the onset of struggle between capitalists and proletarians in Europe. The same concept provided the model, some would say smokescreen, used by such dictators as Mussolini in Italy, Franco in Spain, and Salazar in Portugal in fashioning their particular dictatorships. After the Second World War, it receded in influence in Europe as a result of the opprobrium attached to those regimes. The concept was rescued from this state of ignominy only in the early 1970s, almost simultaneously, by Lehmbruch, Pahl and Winkler, and Schmitter.[25] Reformulated into an analytic construct of social science, the concept was used to advance the critique of pluralist theory that had begun in the United States and Europe in the 1960s. In particular, the concept served as a basis for criticizing the instrumentalist view of the state and the characterization of relations between interest groups and the state found in pluralist theory.

In the rush to use the concept of corporatism in this attack on pluralism, a wide variety of phenomena came to be grouped under its byline. In particular, aspects of those pluralist networks just described, co-optive and clientele, were often labelled corporatist. What confused the matter here and led to the rather heterogeneous assemblage of strangers under the corporatist umbrella was the fact that associations participated in policy both in corporatist networks and in these two types of pluralist network. However, to see corporatism wherever groups are formally granted a say in the formulation and implementation of policy is to rob the concept of some of its theoretical power.

A corporatist policy network may arise where there is an attempt to reconcile conflicting interests, sometimes from different classes, sometimes from fractions within the same class. When this network brings together business and another class, such as workers or farmers, business is forced to take the interests of the other classes into account more than in co-optive or clientele pluralist networks. Accordingly, unlike pluralist networks, which are bilateral, corporatist networks are multilateral. "Corporatism, however, requires the three-cornered configuration of conflicting social interests and state intermediation."[26]

The state thus plays a different role in corporatism than in pluralism. It becomes less a dispenser of goods and services, with its authority open to capture as a mediator and a negotiator, and more autonomous from the interest groups involved. "State agents acquire the capacity to make an independent and significant contribution towards the negotiation of a more stable and institutionalized interest compromise and, at the same time, are empowered to extract some 'public regarding' concessions from the bargaining associations."[27] Associations gain entrée to policy-making, perhaps a say in implementing policy, and authority from the state to discipline their members and bind them to the policy.

The policies conducive to corporatism are not so much regulatory or allocative as redistributive. Redistribution generates the conflict that gives rise to the corporatist "temptation." Corporatist networks have been used on the macroeconomic plane to draw up and implement incomes policies. On the sectoral plane, they have been used for industrial policies of positive adjustment in declining sectors and to protect and stabilize farmers' incomes.[28] Examples of sectoral corporatism are presented in chapters 6 (agriculture) and 7 (construction).

The multilateral nature of the network and the relatively strong state agencies it requires place different pressures on the associational system than are found in pluralism. Associations within a sector, or across an economy in the case of macroeconomic policies, are pressed to be representative, to have mutually exclusive domains so as not to compete with one another, and to be comprehensive. As a result, the associational system for a given class in a sector or, more broadly, an economy may become more vertically integrated, culminating in strong, well-supported peak associations. The opposite occurs in pressure pluralism: broadly based peak organizations lack systematic ties to associations with more specialized domains and tend to assume policy advocacy roles only. Chapter 5 discusses the more prominent of these groups in Canada, and chapter 11 compares them to counterparts in Britain and Austria.

Summarized in Table 10, a corporatist network becomes more probable where class conflict is likely to harm business and where the state is strong enough to call the struggling parties together and act as a neutral arbiter. Associations must be the instrument for representing business interests because corporatism requires a class organization that can control or even discipline its members. Willingness and ability to provide this control gain for the association participation in policy. From the perspective of the state, the destructiveness of class conflict provokes it to invite the parties around the policy table in the first place. Corporatism requires highly representative, integrative groups that speak for a range of sectoral or broader interests. Hence the associational system feels pressure to integrate and co-ordinate the activities of its various member associations. Defections are simply not permitted.

CONCLUSIONS

In part II, these four types of policy network are the primary analytical device for describing business-government relations in each division of the economy examined. These studies will put some flesh on the conceptual skeleton developed thus far. The definitions of policy networks provided in this chapter will serve like Max Weber's ideal types – as heuristic devices. We do not expect business-government relations in any sector to fit the model exactly. To the extent that they do, we will better understand the dynamics of the relationship. However, as Weber also suggests, departures from the model are often the most interesting phenomena of all. In identifying and seeking to account for these departures, we continue both to learn and to develop further social and political theory.

PART TWO

Business
Associations

CHAPTER FIVE

General Business Associations

For many Canadians, including opinion leaders and even many business people, most of the associations referred to in chapter 2 have never before come to their attention. These associations are familiar to firms active in the sector concerned, to selected politicians and government officials, and to writers in the business press. In most municipalities, people point to the local chamber of commerce when asked which organizations represent the business community. This familiarity fosters recognition of provincial chambers of commerce in the provincial capitals and of the Canadian Chamber of Commerce in Ottawa. When television stations and newspaper reporters look for "business reaction" on budget night or following a cabinet shuffle, they normally search out the president of the Canadian Chamber and perhaps the president of the Canadian Manufacturers' Association (CMA), and so people have become accustomed to hearing from these groups. Over the past decade, the familiar insignia of the Canadian Federation of Independent Business (CFIB) has been fastened to the front doors of more and more small shops and offices across the country and the voice of its president, John Bulloch, also has become familiar to a wider public. The chambers and the CFIB are examples of general, intersectoral business associations. Together with the Business Council on National Issues, the Canadian Organization of Small Business, the Conseil du Patronat du Québec, and the Business Council of British Columbia, they form the subject matter of this chapter.

The study of these organizations will focus on their place in the systems of business associations in Canada as well as on their individual properties. What distinguishes these groups from most of those studied in subsequent chapters is their claim to represent the general interests of business. Seeking to define, articulate, or represent

the general interests of business brings an association face to face
with several challenges. Looking to distil or define what is common
to a vast array of firms and associations, these groups must integrate
and internalize three sometimes orthogonal axes of interest definition.[1] First, there are political-economic concerns, problems of production and investment, often peculiar to a given sector, that are
crucial to survival in the market-place. Second, there is a socio-political
pole of interest definition that involves primarily relations with labour and the wide sweep of issues related to employment (wage
policy, industrial relations law, occupational health and safety, etc).
Third, there is the dimension of territory, the economic and geographical space within which groups of firms interact. Business firms
define their territorial locus by location of markets, availability of
transportation and resources, custom and culture, and the governments that have the greatest impact on their activities. Consequently,
territory affects the organization of business interests irrespective of
the structure of the state.

An association wishing to speak for the general interests of business must either confine itelf to one of these poles or synthesize the
diverse political-economic, socio-political, and territorial interests of
firms. Such a task is daunting because of the tensions often existing
among these dimensions of interest definition. For example, how
does an association speak simultaneously for business interests in
Atlantic Canada concerned to maintain freight rate subsidies and
for the sectoral interests of transportation companies seeking an end
to these same subsidies? The general class association must constantly
use suasion if it is to distil a consensus on policy matters out of its
members' interests.

The creativity of business and of the state in designing these general associations has potentially significant implications for public
policy in Western democracies. In the past two decades, governments
have become disenchanted with such classical instruments of Keyne-
sianism as demand management through fiscal policy. "When such
indirect controls were eventually found to be inadequate, governments became increasingly aware that macroeconomic parameters
were also influenced by large interest organizations and might therefore be more effectively manipulated with their support."[2] Lehmbruch adds that the involvement of interest organizations in such
policies of "corporatist concertation" depends on two factors:[3] the
extent of their existing organizational links with government and
administration (policy participation) and their organizational structures (the mix of differentiation and integration in the associational
system).

This chapter will show that general business interest associations in Canada are currently organized and behave in ways that would defeat any attempt to use concertation-oriented policy instruments. Rotstein has written that Canadian business is "the missing piece of the jigsaw required for a successful policy of public diplomacy" and, he adds, "the creation of an industrial policy."[4] Canada's general business associations fit more easily into the classical mould of policy advocates, possessing neither the structures nor the will necessary for playing a more substantive role in the policy process. This argument is elaborated by reviewing, in turn, the structures and activities of the Business Council on National Issues, the small business associations, and the chambers of commerce. In the light of the analysis of these groups, the chapter concludes with a brief examination of the role of the party system in the organization and articulation of business interests and a discussion of the implications of its findings for public policy-making in Canada.

THE BCNI

The Business Council on National Issues (BCNI), founded in 1976, is a relatively new addition to the Canadian political landscape. Several factors lay behind its creation. Many corporate leaders felt that a calmer, more open business organization than the normally tough-minded and stridently anti-labour Chamber of Commerce and CMA was needed to meet and discuss with moderates in the trade unions. The increased restiveness of an already unruly labour movement after imposition of wage and price controls in 1975 reinforced this belief. At the same time, both government and business sensed that recent changes in the decision-making process had unnecessarily distanced the business community from political leaders. In particular, the formalization of cabinet committees and the introduction of collegial decision-making in the first Parliament of the Trudeau era brought home to business how much things had changed since the days of C.D. Howe in the late 1940s and early 1950s.[5] Looking for a model to follow, leading corporate executives fastened upon the Business Roundtable in the United States, an influential but scarcely visible assembly of chief executive officers of major corporations.[6]

The association that emerged now styles itself "the senior voice of business in Canada." Using other terms, Langille suggests that the BCNI is the instrument through which the "hegemonic fraction" of business in Canada – finance capital – organized the power bloc (an alliance with resource capital) to defend its interests. In the process, large corporations have come to sit in a "position of hegemony over the Canadian state."[7] Both claims are overstated. The credibility given to such arguments reflects both the very effective public relations skills of the BCNI's staff and its position as a powerful policy advocate in Ottawa. The council is largely a lobbying organization, not a policy participant. With its present structure, it is unlikely ever to be much more than one of the brighter stars in the firmament of business interest associations in Ottawa.

Who then belongs to the BCNI? According to its by-laws, general members are "firms or corporations which conduct and operate private business enterprises in Canada and who have been admitted to membership by resolution of the board."[8] The BCNI begins, therefore, by excluding all publicly owned corporations, a significant omission, as we shall see below. In practice, members are admitted through a process of invitation. Thomas d'Aquino, (permanent) president of the BCNI, states: "The criteria for membership in the Business Council is [sic] based almost exclusively on the leadership qualities of the individuals involved and of their ability to contribute to national priorities and goals."[9] In effect, members are drawn from the largest private corporations.

The Business Council, however, does not represent comprehensively big business in Canada or draw equally from all divisions of the economy. Publicly owned corporations do not belong; the top 100 companies in Canada include Canadian National, PetroCanada, Ontario Hydro, Hydro Québec, Air Canada, Canada Post, B.C. Hydro, and Alberta Government Telephones.[10] Of the largest 100 privately owned companies only 36 are members of the BCNI.[11] Twelve of the 20 biggest belong, but missing are General Motors, Chrysler Canada, George Weston, and the Hudson's Bay Company, among others.

Representation varies widely across divisions of the economy. If we look at the *Financial Post's* leading ten corporations in a division, we find the council strongest in resources, manufacturing, and finance. The roster includes five of the leading ten forestry companies and four of the first ten mining and metals companies, including the first three (Alcan Aluminum, Noranda, and Inco). Five of the top ten energy companies, including Imperial Oil, Shell, Texaco, and Gulf, belong, but with Nova Corporation, Dome Petroleum, and PetroCanada missing, BCNI represents primarily the foreign mutlinationals in this sector. In manufacturing, the council has seven of the leading ten firms (Ford, Canada Packers, Seagram, Stelco, Dofasco, John Labatt, and Genstar), and again American multinationals are strongly represented. However, none of the Japanese multinational corporations (MNCs) in the top 100 firms belongs. Canadian-owned members tend to have strong ties to the resource sectors. Finally, in finance, the BCNI includes strong direct representation from three of the four "pillars" (lending, fiduciary, insurance, securities). The six leading chartered banks belong, as do nine of the first ten life insurers, but only three of the leading property and casualty insurers. The first three investment dealers (Dominion Securities Pitfield, Wood Gundy, and Burns Fry) are also members. Missing are strong competitors to the banks: of the big seven trust companies only Royal Trust belongs, and no foreign banks are members. However, Power Corporation (which owns Montreal Trust through Power Financial Corporation), the Traders Group (Guaranty Trust), and Genstar (Canada Trustco) are members, providing indirect representation for trust companies.

The council does not represent well agriculture and transportation; none of the leading ten corporations in each group is a direct member.[12] In fact, no co-operatives, the form of economic organization predominant in agriculture, have been invited to join. Nor does the association do well in communications, real estate, and merchandising. It has two of the top ten in communications (including Bell Canada) and merchandising and one in real estate.

In short, the BCNI's strength lies in its ability to represent leading firms from resources, American-controlled manufacturing, and finance. This membership base is broader than the "staples fraction" (resources and finance) that Langille claims that the council represents.[13] Of the 128 members in 1983, the largest single group is manufacturing (54), followed by finance (31), and resources (20). Manufacturing firms had 11 members on the council's policy committee or board of directors in 1986, compared to three for resource firms and five for banking and finance, a further indication of their strong place in the association.

Such a membership structure constitutes both a handicap and an advantage. On the one hand, the BCNI is not "representative" of business in a comprehensive way, lacking a peak association structure grouping sectoral and regional associations.[14] Consequently, it cannot represent business at large through the intense internal deliberation and consensus-building required for formulation and implementation of macroeconomic policy. In food processing, neither the Canadian Food Processors' Association nor McCains is a member; in the chemical industry, neither the Canadian Chemical Producers' Association nor Dow Chemical is a member, and so on. The association has no regional divisions or branches. Its members give it a pronounced central Canadian and English-Canadian bias.

Over 66 per cent are based in Ontario (56 per cent in Toronto), with another 15 per cent having head offices in Montreal. Calgary and Vancouver firms constitute 10 per cent, with Winnipeg adding another 2 per cent. While some leading francophone firms are members – Provigo, La Laurentienne, and the National Bank of Canada – others in the top 100, including Métro Richelieu, Coopérative Fédérée, Gaz Métropolitain, Agropur, and Lavalin, do not belong.[15] In short, the council has neither the membership base nor the internal structures to integrate systematically business interests across sector and territory.

On the other hand, the association remains highly adapted for policy advocacy. Its membership roster, particularly when condensed into a policy committee, is a powerful vehicle for exercising influence and exerting pressure. The association concentrates on general policy areas and uses a task force approach to prepare polished, professional positions on critical issues in these areas.[16] These task forces draw their personnel from member firms, which donate their expertise and person hours. In 1983 they were backed up by a relatively small but professional staff, including a full-time president, two senior associates, a director of policy analysis and research, a director of administration and four staff assistants.[17] The association's budget is about $1 million per annum. In public forums, the council takes the high road, indulging in few public attacks on government or labour. It describes itself thus: "The Business Council is not a lobby group seeking to represent narrow interests that have been traditionally associated with business. Rather the Council is dedicated to the fostering of public policies that will lead to a stronger economic and social fabric within a healthy democratic society."[18]

It is one of the more difficult exercises in political science to assess the influence of a pressure group. One suspects strongly that the BCNI is listened to more than the Canadian Labour Congress, for example, and perhaps has an edge on the Canadian Chamber of Commerce and the CMA. Comparison with groups representing small business is less easily drawn. Limited evidence suggests that where a policy issue leads to the strong points in the association's roster, the council can muster considerable influence. For example, the association has the four leading multinational oil companies as members, plus their important supporters, the five strongest chartered banks. It used this unique membership base to begin discussions that led eventually to a "downscaling" of the National Energy Programme and to the signing of the Western Accord. Langille reports that the council convened secret private meetings, co-chaired by its president, Thomas d'Aquino, and the CEO of Imperial Oil, that brought together federal politicians and officials with their counterparts from Alberta.[19] So it is as a very strong pressure group that we should view the BCNI, an integrating force for big capital in Canada and contributor to the sometimes cacophonous expression of business interests when joined by several others playing a similar role.

SMALL BUSINESS GROUPS

Interest associations speaking for small businesses have both a long and a short history in Canadian politics. Early associations of manufacturers in Montreal and Toronto around the time of Confederation were small business organizations: their members employed relatively few workers. Associations of retail merchants, of druggists, of hardware store owners, and of lumber dealers, which appeared by the 1890s, were groupings of small businesses as well. Local boards of trade and chambers of commerce, particularly in smaller communities, even today might be construed as small business associations. Less common in Canadian political life have been associations that speak for all small business, regardless of sector or location. By the early 1980s, there were several: the Canadian Organization of Small Business, the Ontario Fair Enterprise Association, the Canadian Business and Professional Association, and, most notably, the Canadian Federation of Independent Business (CFIB).

The CFIB began as a protest movement in 1970 when a White Paper on tax reform published by the minister of finance, Edgar Benson, proposed raising significantly the tax rate on small business. John Bulloch, a school teacher and son of a politically outspoken Toronto tailor, paid for an advertisement in a Toronto newspaper attacking the White Paper. To his surprise and delight, hundreds of calls came into his father's shop supporting his initiative. Bulloch reports telephoning back the ten angriest callers and suggesting they get together to talk.[20] Out of this meeting was born the Canadian Council for Fair Taxation, which grew quickly into a nation-wide movement to turn back the Benson proposals. After the council succeeded in this quest, Bulloch returned to the 2,500 businesses that had contributed funds and asked whether their co-operative efforts should be continued or not. The vast majority felt that small business needed a more permanent voice and asked Bulloch to continue fighting for their interests. Encouraged, Bulloch founded the Canadian Federation of Independent Business, soon to become a very effective policy advocate.

By the mid-1980s, the CFIB was the largest direct-member business association in Canada, with over 71,000 members. Of these members,

67 per cent employ ten workers or less, and only 2 per cent employ more than 100.[21] About one-third of the members are retailers, another 27 per cent operate service businesses, and 14 per cent are manufacturers. Dues are assessed on the basis of the number of employees, with a cap of $1,000 to prevent larger firms from obtaining undue influence. The association sees itself defending the interests of small business against insensitive or ignorant governments and protecting members in opposition to big corporations, such as those represented by the BCNI. It claims to be the only small business organization that does not receive funding from major corporations, specifically the large chartered banks.[22] Accordingly, it has come to describe itself as the permanent voice of the "Canadian owner-manager, farmer and professional" and often carries a distinct nationalist bias in its literature. In a recent brochure, it wrote: "A number of associations, for example, speak for large multi-national companies whose interests are more often than not at odds with the interests of Canadian-owned independent business."

The CFIB follows a two-pronged approach to policy advocacy: it seeks to define and crystallize the interests of small businesses and then to speak to government in defence of those interests. Central to both prongs is the association's "Mandate" program. Each month, staff members draw up a list of questions on relevant issues and mail it to members. The replies received are then computer-coded and analysed in the data-processing department at head office. These monthly surveys are supplemented by special surveys of provincial issues administered in each province once a year and by an annual special national survey.

With these data, the CFIB is able to accomplish two things. First, it has in hand specialized public opinion information drawn from a large and politically active constituency. So armed, it can lobby politicians and support these sallies by drawing on information that they simply do not have. Bureaucratic officials are also sought out and provided with the data. The association seeks to increase its political capital further by offering the use of its data bank to any official or politician. The combination of being able to draw on a specialized body of public opinion data and the high media profile cultivated by Bulloch whenever he visits the political capitals gives the association maximal impact.

Second, through these surveys, Bulloch and his executive help their members define their own interests. The surveys play a role in structuring how business people view politics and what they will take action upon. The association follows up on this basic work by sending out special "Alert" bulletins when particularly crucial issues arise and massive pressure is to be placed on members of Parliament and provincial legislatures. In addition, each member is visited personally every year by a member of the association's staff and is questioned about problems specific to his or her firm. Through these means, the association increases members' attachment to the association in face of the real temptation to free ride, gets additional useful information, and reinforces members' definitions of their political interests.

Like all well-resourced advocacy groups, the CFIB supplements its lobbying with professional public relations programs. Bulloch's tours are carefully staged and use effectively both print and electronic media. The CFIB has a special education program on small business that is available to high schools, community colleges, and universities and has distributed over 300,000 copies of a pamphlet entitled "Small Business Is Good Business." About 630 community newspapers use a weekly column on small business replete with the association's editorial perspectives. In its communications with members the association plays hard on the theme that the power of small business lies in its votes. If small business can act as a cohesive political bloc and gain the support of selected "educated" publics, it will be, in the association's view, very difficult to ignore in the halls of power.

As an organization then, the CFIB looks and acts quite differently from the BCNI. Where the BCNI walks quietly and diplomatically, the CFIB trods noisily and with bluster. Where the BCNI has a few large firms for members and a small staff, the CFIB has many small firms as members and a staff of over 160. The head office of the CFIB was organized, in the early 1980s, into nine departments: provincial affairs, national affairs, research, member services, communications, planning and finance, data processing, field operations, and education. Although a unitary organization in practice, the CFIB supplemented its Toronto head office with regional offices in Halifax, Quebec City, Montreal, Winnipeg, Regina, Edmonton, and Vancouver. Its expenditures in 1981 totalled over $5 million, five times those of the BCNI.[23]

The CFIB appears to be an effective pressure group. It points to a long list of legislative changes that it claims to have secured over the past 15 years. The federal government and most provincial governments now have special offices delegated to watch over the problems of small business. Circumstantial evidence suggests that the association has overcome early difficulties organizing in Quebec; it claimed 17,000 members there in 1985. In some quarters, however, its classic approach to pressure politics, even though supported by the innovative "Mandate" program, has spawned critics.

The Canadian Organization of Small Business (cosb) was founded in the late 1970s by some former cfib personnel who wanted a more activist, grass roots organization. It has grown slowly, showing a little over 5,000 members on its rolls by 1982.[24] Over 80 per cent of its members are located either in Ontario or in Alberta. In both provinces, it has organized local "political action committees" designed to promote zealously the association's goals. More right wing, it has also worked with such organizations as the Reverend Kenneth Campbell's Renaissance Canada and the Canadian Association for Free Expression.[25] In contrast, the Ontario Fair Enterprise Association and the Canadian Business and Professional Association (located primarily in British Columbia) swing gently to the left side of the cfib. Critical of the Bulloch group's attitudes toward labour and of its weak condemnation of foreign-owned large corporations, these groups tend to have informal links to the New Democratic Party.[26]

In short, in addition to the cfib, there are several smaller yet viable organizations representing small business in Canada. Political ears are being bent regularly by each of these. The noise level increases further when the bcni and the chambers of commerce, to which we turn next, are factored in.

CHAMBERS OF COMMERCE AND REGIONAL REPRESENTATION

The representation of sectoral and broader class interests does not exhaust the needs of business firms. Invariably, companies seek a vehicle that will address a range of issues arising out of their specific territorial location. In Canada, regional and local "chambers" of commerce often fulfil this role. In some of the bigger provinces, other organizations complement the provincial chambers in this role. In particular, in two provinces where labour struggles have been particularly intense, Quebec and British Columbia, organizations with quite different structures from the chambers have evolved. These are the Conseil du Patronat du Québec and the Business Council of British Columbia.

The chamber of commerce has a three-dimensional membership structure that can be illustrated by taking as a starting point a fictional firm, Beavertail Corporation, located in Metropolitan Toronto. Since Beavertail will be assumed to be a corporation "directly or indirectly engaged in trade, commerce or the professions and in the progress and welfare of the community," it is eligible to become a member of the Board of Trade of Metropolitan Toronto.[27] In doing so, it joins over 15,000 other firms whose fees support an organization with annual expenditures of about $10 million and over 100 employees.[28] Not only would executives from Beavertail be able to dine in the splendid downtown club of the board, located in First Canadian Place, and to golf at the board's own country club, they would become part of a prominent business advocacy organization at the local, provincial, and national levels. The board of trade has all the classic attributes of an organizaton dedicated to policy advocacy. It enjoys the support of big business as well as small business: in 1980, for example, the association was headed by a vice-president from CN, and on its board of directors were the executive vice-president, international, of the Bank of Nova Scotia; the CEOs of General Mills, Imperial Optical, Tomenson Saunders Whitehead, the Toronto Stock Exchange, and Simpson Sears; and senior executives from Clarkson Gordon, Ontario Hydro, Consumer's Glass, Financial Times of Canada, CP Air, McMillan Binch, Thompson Newspapers, Bell Canada, and the T. Eaton Co.[29]

The Board of Trade of Metropolitan Toronto, like the approximately 600 other boards and chambers of commerce across Canada, itself is an "organization member" of two other bodies, the Ontario Chamber of Commerce and the Canadian Chamber of Commerce. These latter organizations, then, are "confederations" of local chambers and boards. Voting rights (selecting the executive and deciding policy positions) are vested in the local chambers. If the president of Beavertail became chairman of the Toronto board, he could become an accredited delegate of the board to meetings of the Ontario and the Canadian chambers. It is only in this capacity of a delegate that he would be able to vote at a meeting of the provincial or the national chamber. The relationship among local, provincial, and national chambers is not hierarchical; the provincial chambers are not sub-units of the national chamber but independent confederations of local chambers within a given province. What provincial chambers and the national chamber have in common are the local chambers and boards of trade as members.

There are two other avenues that Beavertail could follow if it wanted to be active in a provincial or the national chamber. It could become a "corporation member" of one of these. As a corporation member, it would not have a vote at these chambers' meetings but would enjoy otherwise all the privileges of a member, including eligibility to serve on the executive body. Corporation members attached to the provincial and national chambers are usually larger firms. Their dues, assessed on a graduated scale based on number of employees, constitute a major source of revenue for the provincial and national chambers. Thus, the money received from all 600 local chambers by the national chamber in 1982 amounted to only 2 per cent of annual revenue, while funds from corporation members accounted for 85 per cent.[30] Similarly, the provincial chamber in Quebec received 96.8 per cent of its contributions from corporation members in 1982 and only 3.2 per cent from organization members (local chambers).[31] The second avenue open to Beavertail is to belong to a trade association that affiliates with the national chamber. Like corporation members, association members do not have a vote at meetings of the Canadian chamber but enjoy otherwise full membership privileges.

What then is the significance of this rather complex structure? In the Canadian chamber, such a structure enables this organization to claim to be the business association most representative of all of Canadian business. Through the local chambers, particularly those outside the major metropolitan areas, it receives input from the small business community and independent professionals such as lawyers and accountants. Big business is well represented through the chambers in large cities and through corporation memberships. This latter device is important not only because of the revenues it yields but also because it enables the Canadian chamber to short-circuit local organizations and to bring big corporations directly onto its board of directors. The presence of senior corporate executives is essential if the chamber is to have credibility as a business lobby.

The Canadian chamber does not have an overwhelming presence in Ottawa, where it relocated from Montreal in 1982. Its annual budget is $2–3 million, and it employs 35 people in the national capital, 10 in Toronto, and 5 in Montreal.[32] Departments of public affairs and of government relations give the association expertise in political intelligence. Recently it has used this capacity to set up an "Ottawa Watch" program for a number of the smaller associations that belong to it.[33] Through this program, it briefs the smaller groups on events in the federal bureaucracy and in senior political circles. Compared to the Business Council on National Issues, the CFIB, and even the CMA, the chamber has a more traditional approach to developing policy positions. Rather than having a strong in-house policy capability, it relies heavily on committees staffed from member firms. Some of these committees work well, but others less so, rendering the chamber's performance in policy debates somewhat inconsistent and uneven. As a result, the association does not capitalize well on its rather unique membership and becomes "one of the boys" with the BCNI, the CFIB, and even the CMA as a general advocate for business.

In all provinces save Quebec and British Columbia, the picture differs significantly from the one in Ottawa. In these cases, the provincial chambers are more ascendant, suffering fewer competitors than their national counterpart. Two aspects of structure help to make this possible. The non-hierarchical, somewhat distant relationhip between provincial and national chambers provides complete autonomy within jurisdictions. In addition, possessing "corporation members" integrated into the organization separately from the local chambers allows the provincial chamber to represent the larger firms in the province directly. In fact, at the provincial level, the chamber performs more as a spokesperson for medium-sized and large firms, while sharing the small business spotlight with the CFIB and the COSB. The "blue ribbon" rosters give the chambers' voices added resonance in provincial capitals, amplified further by representation from all divisions of the economy. The unitary character of many sector-specific national trade associations means that the provincial field is less cluttered than is the case in Ottawa. The provincial chambers, accordingly, have more flexibility in arranging informal coalitions on particular policy issues and in working closely with other organizations, such as provincial divisions of the CMA, the Canadian Federation of Agriculture, or provincial branches of national trade associations, where they exist.[34]

Two provinces diverge from this pattern by having peak associations distinct from the provincial chamber and founded to deal specifically with labour relations. The Conseil du Patronat du Québec (CPQ) is in most respects a classic peak association, unique in Canada. Its voting members include 68 business associations representing most sectors of the Quebec economy. Hence its roster boasts sectors dominated by English-Canadian and foreign capital as well as sectors controlled by francophones. Its board of directors has seats for 11 elected officers from its member associations as well as for 11 association staff officials, also an uncommon provision among Canadian groups.

The CPQ is an integrating force in the Quebec business community. The CMA, the Montreal Board of Trade, and the Centre des dirigeants d'entreprise (CDE) are members and guaranteed two seats each on the board. The provincial and Montreal chambres are not members; indeed, the former is a competitor. However, the chief executive and staff officers of the two chamber organizations meet monthly with their counterparts from the CPQ, the CDE, and the Montreal Board of Trade. The meetings are used for devising common strategies and co-ordinating advocacy campaigns. The CPQ has ties, as well, into the national associational system; it is an affiliate of the BCNI.

The CPQ was founded in 1966 but became active only in 1969. Its quick rise to prominence appears to have resulted from an intensification of class struggle in the province. The former Catholic trade union central, renamed the Confederation of National Trade Unions (CNTU) in 1961, radicalized quickly throughout the 1960s. Its president, Marcel Pépin, spoke of using the trade union movement to open a "second front" of opposition to the government in power and encouraged creation of political action committees to promote workers' interests in local politics. By 1971, the CNTU and the other two major labour centrals in the province, the Fédération des travailleurs du Québec and the Centrale de l'enseignement du Québec, had issued Marxist inspired socialist manifestos. These documents were published in an explosive atmosphere of strikes and plant closings. In addition, each central was committed to political sovereignty, an option overwhelmingly opposed by business people, whether French or English.

It seems that the primary objective of the CPQ is the development of a coherent, common response to labour. The CPQ describes its mandate as one of devising "an employers' strategy compatible with the common good, of elaborating a common philosophy of action and of realizing an authentic employers' solidarity."[35] It summarizes its mission as follows: "The CPQ watches over, affirms and protects the interests of free enterprise in Quebec: by displaying concrete positions to the government, trade unions and public opinion, by transporting the perspectives of the firm into all sectors where it is active, by furnishing employers with information on the most important events happening in Quebec, in particular on the large issues in labour relations."[36] To these ends, the association has a research director on labour relations, employs two industrial relations specialists in a total staff of 16 and is formally represented on the Commission de santé et sécurité au travail and the Comité consultatif du travail et de la main d'oeuvre. The CPQ's pre-eminence in labour relations was recognized by the other groups in the province when they were asked in interviews about the division of policy responsibilities among them. The CPQ has remained an outspoken opponent of political independence.

In short, the high degree of integration of business interests, relative to other Canadian groups, found in the CPQ is best explained as a response to intense class struggle in Quebec in the late 1960s and the 1970s. The struggle was made more intense by labour's obvious interest in promoting socialism. The national question overdetermined this class struggle: organized labour tended to favour independence and employers, whether French or English, preferred remaining in Canada.

The other, rather distinctive provincial peak association is the Business Council of British Columbia (BCBC), formerly the Employers' Council of British Columbia. The BCBC, like its Quebec counterpart, was formed in 1966 as "an inter-industry organization which focussed initially on industrial relations research. The impetus for its formation was in response to a coalescing of power within the labour movement."[37] Like the CPQ, the BCBC has retained its early focus on "employee relations," but it also expanded its expertise to include finance and taxation policy and government macroeconomic management. However, while the CPQ is a classic peak organization, the BCBC grants a vote only to corporation members, with associations and public corporations being given the right to sit on selected committees and to participate in deliberations at general meetings.[38]

The BCBC has displaced the provincial chamber as the leading spokesperson for BC business interests. It might be described as an advocacy group with some capacity to participate in the formulation of general government policy. It spends close to $1 million annually, employing 17 people. On the advocacy side, it has a permanent president assisted by adjutants responsible for administration and government relations as well as a public affairs department. A carefully selected board of directors drawing CEOs from leading resource, industry, banking, and other corporations gives this president further legitimacy in his endeavours.[39] The council's policy participation capacity derives from its business economics and employee relations departments, which have their own staff expertise plus well-structured committees drawn from the membership. For example, there is a 45-person Labour Relations Committee composed of senior labour relations representatives from companies with over 1,000 employees, major employers' associations, and "smaller companies of key economic importance."[40] Other committees draw together individuals from companies currently involved in labour negotiations, safety practitioners, labour relations statisticians, and manpower planning and personnel practitioners.

In summary, then, the Canadian Chamber of Commerce at the national level joins several other associations discussed in this chapter in offering general economic advice to government from a business perspective. At the provincial level, the chamber plays a greater part in organizing and articulating the general interests of business, particularly larger firms. At the same time, capitalists feel uncomfortable working through the chamber when they perceive a need to counter a united and ideologically aggressive labour movement. The chamber's membership is too diverse and its organization too decentralized for it to respond effectively. Accordingly, when business has been challenged by a class-conscious, militant labour movement, as in British Columbia and Quebec, it has responded by creating new organizations. These organizations are more centralized in internal structure, systematically incorporate functional as opposed to territorial interests, and develop rather sophisticated policy expertise in industrial relations. Over time, these peak associations have grown in influence, partially displacing provincial chambers as the leading spokespersons for business interests.

CONCLUSIONS

The sub-system of general, sector-unspecific associations is not suited to concertation with governments on broad-range macroeconomic policy. The groups involved are best viewed as emphasizing policy advocacy. Each of the four associations studied, the BCNI, the Canadian chamber, the CFIB, and the COSB, have flat structures that are relatively undifferentiated by sector or even broader economic divisions. Explicit structural recognition of financial as opposed to resource extraction interests, of manufacturing as opposed to services, and so on is not seen to be necessary. With the exception of the Canadian Chamber of Commerce, none has any claim or right to speak generally for business interests. The BCNI represents a limited number of the largest privately owned corporations; the CFIB and COSB stand up for the interests of small firms.

On the other axis of organization, that of territory, questions of adequacy may also be raised about each of the four organizations. The BCNI and COSB are essentially unitary organizations, with members of the former based primarily in central Canada and those of the latter in Ontario and Alberta. The CFIB does represent adequately most provinces, although it does not differentiate itself to the point of having a federal structure. The Canadian chamber, again, presents more of a mixed case in that all parts of the country are represented through local chambers. Yet the linkage here is direct between the national body and the local chambers; the provincial level of organization is barely visible in the national body.

Even a casual observer then must conclude that business in Canada does not define its general class interests through broadly based, inter-sectoral associations. If such class interests are defined at all, it will be done through more sectorally specific associations or through organizations other than associations. This much is obvious. This conclusion does not necessarily carry over to the provincial level. Exceptions to this finding occur in Quebec, where the CPQ is a highly "developed" association, and in British Columbia, where the BCBC has a hybrid structure, with both individual firms and associations as members. Struggles with labour have triggered the growth of these two associations, which are better adapted for defining and articulating general class interests.

The possibility, of course, remains that business need not define for itself its own interests through associations because other institutions perform this task. The two other most obvious candidates are political parties and the state. We turn now to discuss the first of these, reserving the second for extended treatment in part III. Existing studies of the federal party system in Canada do not encourage the view that political parties organize and articulate the general class interests of business. The highly readable reflection on two decades of electoral studies in Canada entitled *Absent Mandate* by Clarke, Jenson, Leduc, and Pammett describes the federal party system using the now familiar concept of brokerage.[41] The two major federal parties, the Progressive Conservatives and the Liberals, canvass or delineate the varied interests of the electorate in a process of coalition-making or "brokering." The support bases of the two parties are not well defined and tend to change from one election to another. Rather than mobilizing against one another along a limited set of cleavages, they multiply the number of relevant political dimensions as they mine the electorate looking for new seams of support. They shy away from constructing any elaborate world views, preferring instead a series of appeals to narrow interests. Building themselves around leaders rather than ideas, they usually converge in many areas of policy.

In short, the two major parties lack an incentive to identify possible policies as solutions to problems. Pre-eminently electoral rather than policy-making organizations, they find policy simply one means among several to a given electoral end and one to be used with considerable caution. During the 1940s and 1950s, the major political parties relied, several political scientists have argued, on third parties for innovations and solutions. As time has passed, however, even this path has become overgrown as third parties ran out of ideas or became more electorally conscious themselves. Consequently, many observers argue that the primary sources of new ideas for political parties today are the federal and provincial bureaucracies.

The fact that the two major parties do not define the general class interests of business detracts in no way from the fact that they maintain close ties to business. Corporate donations remain a crucial component of the finances of the Liberals and Conservatives. Related to this dependence on business support, the two major parties also share a common, well-understood list of economic and social policies that are acceptable and another list of those that are not. They both are fundamentally committed to a private-enterprise system but are willing to intervene directly in the private sector not so as to move away from a market system but in order to shore up perceived weak areas in that system. Despite this informal policy consensus, the two major parties are not oriented towards policy formulation and program development at the federal level. As essentially electoral machines, they are less systematic and more pragmatic in these matters. In fact, in their constant brokering and juggling of positions, they often champion policies that make the business community nervous. Reactive institutions, they float on the political winds, bounce from one social group to another, trying to keep the polls high. They simply are not organized to look at the long term or even seriously at competing policy positions. It is not simply that they are incapable of defining for business firms what their general, long-term interests might be. Rather, as brokers, they are unwilling to do so.

This analysis of the federal party system may be extended with some success to many of the provincial party systems. It becomes less relevant in Quebec and British Columbia and perhaps Manitoba. In the latter two cases, the New Democratic Party is one of the two "major" parties. The NDP possesses certain properties in these provinces that distinguish its organization from that of a normal brokerage party. Its formal ties to a major social group, organized labour, hamper its flexibility in building electoral coalitions. Party members have developed and continue to design and revise a program of principles and policies to which leaders are ostensibly bound. The party is strongly critical of many actions of the business community and receives little financial support from business firms. The Parti québécois from its founding through the early 1980s shared as well in several of these properties and promoted the notion of political sovereignty, which was anathema to the business community. As a consequence, the bourgeois parties, whether Social Credit, Progessive Conservative, or the Parti libéral du Québec, have themselves reacted and changed by developing more formal programs and more explicit free enterprise ideologies.

I suspect, as well, although there is much research yet to be done, that the parties, in a more pronounced way, feed off the CPQ and the BCBC. The polarization along class lines in provincial party systems helps explain the existence of these peak associations. Informally, there appears to be considerable interchange between these organizations and the respective "bourgeois" parties. These associations, we have seen, are structured in a different way than other general business groups. They have been forced by the struggle with labour to define in a more conscious way, probably in conjunction with a "business" party, the general and longer-term interests of business.

The overall situation, however, remains fragmented at the sector-unspecific level of associative action. General business associations are ill equipped for participation in the formulation of policy dealing with the overall orientation of the Canadian economy. Theirs is an unco-ordinated choir, with members singing off-tune and striving to drown out one another in the classic pluralist style. The way they are structured and their orientation to advocacy simply rule out the pursuit of concertation-based macroeconomic strategies such as an incomes policy or an anticipatory industrial policy similar to that found in Japan. The weakness of more broadly based organizations suggests as well that the more important and stronger business organizations in Canada operate within specific divisions and sectors of the economy. The following five chapters support this preliminary conclusion by examining successively agriculture, construction, resource extraction, banking and finance, and manufacturing.

CHAPTER SIX

Agriculture and Corporatism

Save for the cod fishery and the fur trade, agriculture is Canada's oldest industry. It became the sustaining force in Quebec's economy after the Conquest and was Ontario's leading export sector until well after Confederation. Even today, the food industry is the largest single manufacturing sector in Quebec's economy and one of the largest in Ontario's. The grains and livestock industries have been leading sectors in the economies of the prairie provinces since the late nineteenth century. Canada is a major trading country, and close to 10 per cent of its exports are agricultural products.

Speaking for this large agricultural economy in Canada is an associational system that until the early 1980s was more comprehensive and highly integrated than that of any other division of the Canadian economy. Representation by such a system has enabled agricultural producers not only to influence public policies affecting them but also to participate in the design and formulation of many of these policies. Policy planning has been more systematic and long range in agriculture than in most other economic divisions, and associations have come to be integral partners in much of this activity. Compared to their counterparts in other economic divisions, agricultural associations are more frequent participants in corporatist policy networks. Such networks are found in most agricultural sectors and are singularly developed in the dairy and poultry industries.

Several factors explain the involvement in policy by agricultural associations and the prevalence of corporatist policy networks. The first is a rather unique industry structure. The predominant economic unit remains the family farm, which has become more efficient and specialized over the decades and relies only in part on the use of wage labour. Struggles with other economic groups have encouraged solidarity, co-operation, and ultimately collective action among the thousands of farmers competing to supply similar markets. Class conflict has required the repeated intervention of the state since the early 1930s. This intervention, when coupled with attempts to satisfy farmers' specialized needs for information and research, has fostered a rather unique state apparatus to serve and regulate the agricultural industry. The existence of such a state system has, in turn, contributed to the development of the associational properties about which I have spoken. Finally, although Canadian agricultural production embraces a wide range of commodities, only a subset of these is normally harvested in a particular region. Accordingly, there is less serious conflict of interest among commodity groups within a given region than might be expected.

By the early 1980s, agricultural producers had built an associational system that integrated well the various agricultural regions in Canada and to a lesser extent the many commodity groups. Certainly, compared to divisions examined in later chapters, the system came close to having the properties – centralization, concentration, hierarchy – described by Schmitter as characteristic of corporatism.[1] At the same time, it lacked several critical properties. First, it was not sufficiently comprehensive to include all commodity groups under the aegis of a single peak association, the Canadian Federation of Agriculture (CFA): the CFA did not have a representational monopoly, suffering the competition of the National Farmers Union (NFU) and increasingly that of the specialist commodity groups which were not members. Second, the CFA did not have the organizational capacity to exert authority or impose discipline on its member associations. Consequently, when a major issue arose that split the agricultural community – the rate structure for the transportation of western grain – the CFA was forced to abdicate. Two western member associations dissolved, and, like a house of cards, the system came crashing to the ground.

This chapter develops these arguments. First, I examine the industry's structure and the configuration of the state apparatus, which together provide the context for associative action. Second, I look at the pattern of organization found in the agricultural associational system in 1980, emphasizing its comprehensiveness and integration. Third, I outline two case studies: in the first, on associations in the grains sector and their involvement in the Crow debate, I show how the associational system was shaken by defections and seriously weakened in the 1980s; the second, on the dairy and poultry sectors, illustrates how corporatism has flourished in areas still strongly represented within the CFA. The chapter concludes with brief discussions of the interaction between pluralism and corporatism and of the policy style in the agricultural policy arena.

THE CONTEXT

Two factors in Canadian agriculture are crucial to the nature of associative action and policy networks in this division of the economy. First, there is a growing tendency towards specialization in production. The dominant economic unit in Canadian agriculture remains, to be sure, the family farm. Of the 318,361 farms reported in the 1981 census, 86.6 per cent were classified as family farms and another 3.4 per cent were listed as corporate farms owned by a family.[2] Since 1951, the size of farms has expanded appreciably, from an average of 80 hectares to 145 hectares in 1981. With this increase in size has come greater specialization. Certain products, such as poultry meat and eggs, potatoes, and hogs, which used to be produced as secondary commodities on dairy or cattle farms are produced more and more as primary commodities on special farms.[3]

This trend towards specialization has increased further the second factor, regionalization of agricultural production. Certain regions have become more and more identified with particular commodities. Wheat is an obvious example: 97.6 per cent of the hectares sown in 1981 were located in the three prairie provinces. Two provinces account for over 65 per cent of the production in the following commodity groups: vegetables (80.4 – Ontario and Quebec), dairy cows (71.0 – Ontario and Quebec), beef cows (65.8 – Alberta and Saskatchewan), hogs (66.9 – Ontario and Quebec), hens and chickens (70.6 – Ontario and Quebec), and tree fruits (69.2 – Ontario and British Columbia). Prairie sectors tend to have a different market orientation than those in eastern Canada and British Columbia. Prairie sectors, especially grains, are oriented more to international markets. Industries serving domestic markets, specifically dairy, fruits and vegetables, and poultry, tend to be concentrated in eastern Canada and British Columbia. Exceptionally, Maritime potatoes and fruit are exported in significant quantities to the eastern US seaboard.

This type of cleavage creates both opportunities and problems for the associational system. It lessens conflict within regional associations but creates a basis for serious conflict on the national plane both within those more general national associations that organize across several commodity groups and between associations speaking for specific commodities.

Quite distinctive to the agricultural economy is an integrated support system of co-operatives, government agencies, and university agricultural faculties. Together with the interest associations, they form a co-ordinated policy arena with a culture quite unlike that in any other division of the Canadian economy. Farmers themselves have formed co-operatives to increase their economic power in purchasing supplies, in controlling product markets, and in further processing their products. Some of these, such as the prairie wheat pools, Agropur and the Coopérative fédérée in Quebec, and the Fraser Valley Milk Producers in British Columbia, are now among the largest corporations in the country.

Following the urgings of both the state and farmers, a network of faculties of agriculture has developed. These university faculties provide training not only for future farmers but also for agricultural specialists employed by the state, co-operatives, private agri-business firms, and associations. These faculties have resisted the disciplinary fragmentation found in other parts of universities. They usually include agricultural economics, rural sociology, and various scientific specialties, ranging from chemicals and soils to animal husbandry and veterinary medicine. Specialists combine theoretical knowledge with practical understanding because of close ties with the farming community. Overall, agricultural education fosters a holistic approach to the study of the food system and its problems.

State structures also are cast along lines likely to encourage an integrated approach to farmers' problems within a given sphere of jurisdiction. Federal and provincial departments of agriculture function as clientele departments, acting as the voice of farmers in government. The federal department typically has had divisions to assist farmers in marketing products, set standards and grades to ensure "fair competition," fight animal diseases, gain access to credit and income insurance to relieve resource scarcity, and carry out research and development. It has built a far-flung network of experimental farms and work stations. Over 50 per cent of research and development is carried out by the state, and another 30 per cent by the universities. Research and development expenditures represent 1.8 per cent of gross farm income, a much better rate than in other divisions of the economy.[4] Provincial departments normally supplement federal efforts in marketing, credit provision, and grading and have extension departments that link both levels of government and their programs to the individual farmer.

The university faculties and government departments are integrated through the Canadian Agricultural Services Coordinating Committee (CASCC), which co-ordinates the total national effort for economic and social development in agriculture. Chaired by the deputy minister of the federal department, Agriculture Canada, it includes all the provincial deputy ministers of agriculture, other senior officials of Agriculture Canada, and deans of faculties of agriculture and of veterinary medicine. Under the CASCC is a network of seven provincial-regional sub-committees and seventeen "Canada Committees" set up on a problem-by-problem basis for consultation. Examples are Canada Committees on Animal Production Services, on Soil Services, on Food, and on Farm Management Services. Each Canada Committee creates expert committees for particular sub-areas. Both types of committee draw freely from the whole agricultural network for members – co-operatives and private firms, governments, universities, and associations.

Complementing the Canada Committee system is the Canadian Agricultural Research Council. This body was established in 1974 to advise CASCC on the state and needs of the national program of agricultural research and development and to vet research proposals and recommendations coming from the Canada Committees and provincial agricultural services co-ordinating committees. The CASCC system "instigates research and discussion into many of the areas where food policies evolve. It is especially important in production research ... It also acts as a vehicle of mediation and communication within and among the governments and universities; it can influence the direction of the research and it may also be one of a range of avenues used to legitimize government actions and proposals."[5] This elaborate consultative apparatus helps counter centrifugal tendencies resulting from heavy involvement by both levels of government.

The system of agricultural associations is an integral part of the agricultural institutional community and has acquired distinctive responsibilities as a result. Until the early 1980s it also had a degree of integration and co-ordination consistent with the overall institutional pattern in the industry. The structure of this system, its place in this institutional community, and its recent decline are the subjects discussed in the remaining portions of this chapter.

THE ASSOCIATIONAL SYSTEM IN 1980

In moving to discuss the structural characteristics of the agricultural associational system, it is useful to recall from chapter three the properties in which we are interested. First, we wish to examine the degree of differentiation. To what extent does the system recognize both important commodity divisions and salient territorial units? Second, we are interested in the degree of integration. Are the diverse commodity and territorial units brought together into a more comprehensive association? Our working assumption is that the more differentiated and integrated, or the more "developed," an associational system, the better will associations belonging to it perform in both advocacy and policy participation.

The associational system representing Canadian agriculture was in 1980 the most "developed" of all the systems in any division of the economy. It was distinguished by its degree of integration across both commodity groups and territories (see Table 11). At the general level, the industry has two quite different and opposed associations. The National Farmers Union (NFU) is a mass-based organization that recruits farmers directly as individual members. With long historical roots in the radical farmers' movements in the west, particularly in Saskatchewan, the NFU was most recently reorganized in 1969 in order to oppose the other general association, the Canadian Federation of Agriculture (CFA). The NFU argues that the CFA has been too attentive to the concerns of farmers' commercial organizations and thereby less attuned to the interests of individual farmers. Drawing from Skogstad's research, Forbes writes: "The predominant NFU beliefs are characterized as a feeling of lack of control over farm policy by farmers, that control is being exercised by the IPDR (inputs, processing, retailing, distribution) sector and the railways. NFU members have a radical view of class structure and prefer more government intervention and regulation in the farm sector."[6] Not surprising, the CFA, which was formed as the Canadian Chamber of Agriculture in 1935, has a different orientation and structure than the NFU. It is a peak association – its members are other agricultural associations – and its objectives correspond to this peak structure. To wit, its first objective reads as follows: "To co-ordinate the efforts of Agricultural Producer Organizations throughout Canada, for the purpose of promoting their common interest through collective action." The emphasis is on co-ordinating organizations rather than representing individuals directly.

In the three major sectors in the division (horticulture, livestock, grains), associations with domains broad enough to cover the whole of one of these are found on the national plane only. The Canadian Horticultural Council (CHC) is a peak association representing the horticulture sector. Founded in 1922, the council both plays a co-ordinating role analogous to the CFA in the horticultural industries and has had a long history working in international trade and the establishment of product standards.[7] The corresponding body in the grains sector is the Canada Grains Council (CGC), created in 1969 at the instigation of the federal government, albeit with a structure and

Table 11
National Associational System, Agriculture, 1980–5

1980	*Status in 1985*
NATIONAL/REGIONAL COMMODITY ASSOCIATIONS: CFA	
Dairy Farmers of Canada*	Unchanged
Canadian Horticultural Council*	Unchanged
United Grain Growers Ltd	Partially replaced by Prairie Pools
Canadian Egg Producers Council†	Unchanged
Canadian Pork Council†	Unchanged
PROVINCIAL GENERAL ASSOCIATIONS: CFA	
B.C. Federation of Agriculture	Unchanged
Unifarm (Alberta)	Unchanged
Saskatchewan Federation of Agriculture	Dissolved
Manitoba Farm Bureau	Mostly dissolved
Ontario Federation of Agriculture	Unchanged
Union des producteurs agricoles	Unchanged
Coopérative fédérée du Québec	Unchanged
N.B. Federation of Agriculture	Unchanged
N.S. Federation of Agriculture	Unchanged
P.E.I. Federation of Agriculture	Unchanged
NATIONAL/REGIONAL COMMODITY ASSOCIATIONS: NON-CFA	
Canadian Cattlemen's Association	
Canadian Turkey Federation	
Canadian Broiler Council	
Canadian Seed Growers Association	
Canada Grains Council*	All unchanged
Palliser Wheat Growers Association‡	
Canola Council of Canada	
Western Flax Growers Association	
Western Barley Growers Association	

* Peak associations with their own national/regional association members.
† Not formally members of the CFA but "affiliated" as "advisory committees."
‡ Name since changed to Western Canada Wheat Growers Association.

objectives somewhat different from the CFA and CHC. It is a vertical peak organization: its members are associations representing not only producers of grain but also those involved in the handling, transportation, processing, and marketing of grain and grain products. Finally, there is no peak association representing some or all of the various livestock sectors.

Within horitculture, a large number of more specialized sectoral associations exist, operating for the most part at the provincial level. Many of these double as marketing boards. Several associations representing fruit growers that were founded in the mid-nineteenth century remain today important members of the system: the Nova Scotia Fruit Growers Association and the Ontario Fruit and Vegetable Growers Association, which both antedate Confederation, and the b.c. Fruit Growers Association, founded in 1889. National sectoral associations exist only in very specialized commodities: floriculture, nursery trades, mushrooms, and honey.

The pattern in livestock differs from that in horticulture in that no peak association organizes the whole of this major sector. Instead, each of the livestock commodity groups has its own association, which is either a federation or more usually a confederation of provincial associations. The relevant national groups are the Dairy Farmers of Canada, the Canadian Cattlemen's Association, the Canadian Pork Council, the Canadian Egg Producers Council, the Canadian Broilers Council, and the Canadian Turkey Federation. These sectoral associations are the most "national" in the agricultural associational system; they have an organizational presence in most provinces. Affiliated to both the dairy and the beef cattle sectoral associations are breeding associations as well. For example, associations representing the major beef breeds (Aberdeen Angus, Charolais, Hereford, Limousin, Red Poll, and so on) are members of the Canadian Cattlemen's Association.

Like the horticultural sectors, the grains sector has a peak association. There are fewer associations than might be expected, however, because the farmers' co-operative pools in Alberta, Saskatchewan, and Manitoba and the United Grains Growers Ltd act at times as surrogate associations, a point discussed below. Representing the large wheat sector are only two associations, the Western Canada Wheat Growers Association (formerly named the Palliser Wheat Growers Association), an advocacy group based in the three prairie provinces, and the Ontario Wheat Producers Marketing Board. Affiliated to the former group are associations with similar philosophies and territorial roots representing barley and flax growers. Speaking for the rapeseed (or canola as it is now called) sector, provincial associations in Alberta, Saskatchewan, and Manitoba have their own joint council, the Prairie Rapeseed Growers Council. These associations are members of the Canola Council of Canada (formerly the

Rapeseed Association of Canada), which has a vertical structure similar to the Canada Grains Council. Hence its members are associations representing producers, crushers, processors, handlers, and marketers.

The agricultural associational system is differentiated quite systematically on the basis of territory. Each province has its own general organization analogous to the CFA except Quebec, which has two, the Union des producteurs agricoles and the Coopérative fédérée.[8] Unlike the national level, however, intermediary organizations speaking for all of horticulture or of grains are not found. Associations belonging to provincial agricultural federations have sectoral domains. Regional specialization in agriculture allows the provincial systems to avoid the intermediary step of organization at the major sectoral level. In 1980, all the provincial federations were members of the CFA. In addition, the western federations have long since formed their own group, the Western Agricultural Conference. Its objectives were to "give unity of purpose and policy to organized western agriculture" and "to reconcile the interests of the various groups of primary producers and discourage any tendencies to a sectionalism which would detract from the strength of agriculture in the national economy."[9] The Canadian Horticultural Council also integrates its sectors well in each of the relevant regions. Very few associations in its domain are not members, and those that are not remain integrated into the CFA system through membership in provincial federations of agriculture. Finally, as has been noted, the various national livestock associations all have virtually complete provincial representation, a fact that may have inhibited formation of a peak association grouping all the livestock associations.

Integration in 1980 was less comprehensive in commodity groups. Generally speaking, those sectors with associations that were part of the CFA stable of groups produce for the domestic market. These include all the horticultural sectors and the dairy sector (see Table 11). The exception is the poultry producers, which produce overwhelmingly for the domestic market and yet are outside the CFA system. Two livestock sectors, hogs and eggs, are "affiliated" to the CFA: the Canadian Pork Council and the Canadian Egg Producers Council have signed "affiliation agreements" with it. These agreements constitute the associations as commodity committees of the CFA to advise it on their respective sectors and arrange for the CFA to provide them with administrative services, although they are not CFA members. The large and powerful beef sector, headed by the Canadian Cattlemen's Association, is completely outside the CFA umbrella.

In 1980 the CFA represented the grains sectors indirectly. The Canada Grains Council was not a member of the CFA and, in fact, cannot be, because of its vertical structure. Only producers' organizations can belong to the CFA. Grain growers were represented in the CFA through the provincial federations on the prairies and the United Grain Growers Ltd, which also was a member of the CFA in 1980. However, the Western Canada Wheat Growers Association, the flax growers, and the barley growers did not belong. Alberta's rapeseed growers were members through their provincial federation, Unifarm, but not so Saskatchewan's. The national association, the Canola Council, was not a member of the CFA for the same reasons as the Canada Grains Council.

To summarize, the agricultural associational system in 1980 was well differentiated by territory. The resulting territorial units were integrated at the general divisional level by the CFA and at the sectoral level by national specialized sectoral associations. The pattern of integration was less complete for commodity groups. The CFA system integrated well the horticulture major sector and the dairy sector. Through its provincial federations and the United Grains Growers Ltd, it received input on the grains sector, but not as directly as in the horticulture and dairy cases. Some provincial federations have integrated a broader set of commodity associations than the CFA.[10] In the other livestock sectors aside from dairy, integration was weakest, with the all-important beef sector represented in the CFA only through some provincial federations.

The mixed success of the CFA in its integration of commodity groups was ripe with policy significance. The trend in agriculture since the end of the Second World War, particularly since 1960, has been, as we have noted, towards specialization. As farmers have become more specialized, the interest in and support for associations with more restricted, commodity-based domains have also increased. Consequently, the past decade has seen a series of challenges by groups such as the Canadian Cattlemen's Association to the CFA and its claim to speak for all farmers. The specialist commodity groups depart from the approach of the CFA by stressing the uniqueness of their given sectors rather than the problems farmers have in common. This disagreement is reinforced by growing ideological cleavages as well, which Skogstad has noted.[11] The commodity groups tend to be more economically conservative, preferring to rely on market mechanisms rather than on government intervention. They distrust governments generally, particularly big ones like the federal government. Given their belief that farming is a business like any other, they tend to identify more strongly with agri-business –

processors, distributors, retailers – than with their colleagues in other sectors. This belief represents a departure too from earlier philosophy that showed distrust for the ability of markets to treat farmers justly and that saw agri-business as an opponent and exploiter of farmers.

These cleavages within the agricultural community became publicly known and much deeper in the course of the debate over the Crow's Nest Pass Rate in the early 1980s. The grain transportation system in western Canada was based in 1980 on statutory rates for the movement of grain that emerged originally from a contractual agreement between the CPR and the Canadian government in 1897. By 1980, these rates bore no resemblance to the expenses incurred, and, as a result, economic distortions had developed in western agriculture. As the gap between the rates and the actual costs diverged more and more after 1960, the two sides in the agricultural community themselves divided over what changes were necessary.

ASSOCIATIONS AND GRAIN
TRANSPORT

By mid-1984, the associational system had faltered gravely as an integrating force for farmers' interests. Two members of the CFA, the Saskatchewan Federation of Agriculture (SFA) and the Manitoba Farm Bureau (MFB), had dissolved, depriving the CFA of systematic representation in those two key agricultural provinces. Also, the United Grain Growers Ltd had withdrawn. Unifarm, the CFA member from Alberta, was in serious financial trouble, having suffered a sharp decline in individual farmer members as well as the withdrawal of the Alberta Cattle Commission in 1982. In an attempt to fill the gaping hole, the three co-operative wheat pools – Alberta Wheat Pool, Saskatchewan Wheat Pool, and Manitoba Pool Elevators – had renamed their common organization Prairie Pools and become a direct member of the CFA. Needless to say, the CFA was seriously compromised as an advocate of farmers' interests in Ottawa. Its failure nonetheless is instructive for understanding the conditions for corporatism. I will begin by looking at the grain handling and transportation system in western Canada.

Grain farmers have brought this system somewhat under their control, beginning with bitter struggles against private grain trading companies at the turn of the century. In those early days, "high prices established one day, which declined dramatically as farmers hurried to deliver their grain the next, would naturally destroy one's faith in the ability of open markets to perform reliably and advantageously. Small wonder there arose an intense feeling that the private trade (multinational grain companies and monopolistic railway conglomerates alike) is not to be trusted to serve the farming community adequately."[12] In response, farmers founded their own cooperative companies to run primary elevators for storing grain prior to shipping to export terminals. The federal government also intervened, creating in 1912 the Board of Grain Commissioners, now the Canadian Grain Commission, to license the elevators and to regulate their weighing procedures. The co-operatives also have come to control many terminal elevators where grain is graded (again under the supervision of the grains commission) prior to sale. The one area in the system where farmers continue to lack a strong voice is the railways, and bottlenecks in the rail system have frustrated attempts to improve productivity.

By the late 1960s, statutory rates for transport of grain were so divergent from actual costs that pressures began to develop to revise the system. As the debate over revision developed, deep divisions emerged within the national farming community. These divisions attenuated the ability of associations to respond to the other needs of farmers. By the late 1970s, there was general recognition that the Crow rates were discouraging much-needed investment in transportation infrastructure, thereby hindering expansion of the grain economy and western livestock and meat processing.

Skogstad summarizes the debates by noting three different positions that had emerged by 1980.[13] These three positions map reasonably well onto the structure of the associational system described in Table 11. The first position was advocated by an ad hoc alliance of associations, the Prairie Farm Commodity Coalition. All the associations involved – the Western Canada Wheat Growers, the Flax Growers, the Barley Growers, the Canadian Cattlemen's Association, the Canola Council, and the Saskatchewan Stock Growers – were completely outside the CFA umbrella. Supported as well by the railways and private grain companies, the coalition advocated the payment of a "Crow Benefit." Farmers would pay a statutory compensatory rate to the railways, and the federal government would give farmers a direct payment based on crops planted to make up the difference between the new higher rate and the old Crow rate. The second position, retention of the existing system, was championed by the National Farmers' Union and the government of Saskatchewan.[14]

A third proposal emerged out of the Western Agricultural Conference (WAC), composed of CFA affiliates. The WAC proposed that farmers continue to pay the Crow rate "but that the federal government make up the difference with a compensatory payment that would cover the gap between Crow rates and the cost of transport to the railways, and that would ensure the railways a small profit."[15] This payment would go directly to the railways. Key supporters were prairie producer co-operatives: the Alberta, Saskatchewan, and Manitoba pools and the United Grain Growers. Eventually, the proposal was supported in a "straw vote" by the CFA as well.[16]

Overlaying divisions about the three proposals were also ideological beliefs about the mix of state intervention and market forces that should prevail in the grains industry. Members of the Prairie Farm Commodity Coalition sought a decrease in state intervention, particularly by the Canadian Wheat Board, and a return to more open markets in farm commodities. The NFU called for extension of public control in the industry. The pools and other CFA affiliates, except for the United Grain Growers (UGG) played pragmatic politics, hugging the middle of these debates.

The UGG, while an affiliate of the CFA, was drawn ideologically to the position of the commodity coalition. In describing itself, the company stresses that it "believes in the principles of free enterprise and capitalism," terms not used by the pools when stating their objectives.[17] Economically, the UGG was more likely to be sympathetic because of the importance of the feed industry in its internal structure; it accounted for 11 per cent of total revenues in 1983.[18] Hence the corporation had a stake in the western livestock industry. Its position in the Crow debate reflected its background: it called for the Crow benefit to be divided between farmers and railways.

In fact, the pools ended up playing a determining role in the debate. Their organization gives them a peculiar place within our usual set of institutions – firms and associations. The pools are large monopoly firms, the first two listed in the top 50 corporations in the Financial Post 500. But they act also as surrogate associations, having a policy development/government relations division and a potentially democratic membership structure. Producer members are organized into local sections, which discuss and debate policy issues and forward to the organization's board of directors recommendations which are discussed as resolutions at the annual general meeting. If passed, resolutions become the official policy stance. This "policy side" of the co-operative receives specific institutional recognition and support within the organization. For example, in the Saskatchewan Wheat Pool, which is the most developed along these lines, policy development is the responsibility of the corporate secretary, who has a research division and a corporate division to support the board in policy design and advocacy and an extension division to maintain contact with the members. The corporate secretary's operation acts as more than a government relations division because of the democratic structures linking it to members. It is, in fact, an association operating under the wing of the co-operative.

These co-operatives have traditionally been strong members of the CFA "pole" of the wheat associational system. Each was a member of its respective provincial federation, and the UGG, which had members in all three provinces, was a member of the CFA directly. In 1980, the first vice-president of the Saskatchewan pool was president of the SFA and a member of the CFA's board. Two other directors of the pool were on the advisory committee of the Canadian Wheat Board, and another was a member of the Western Grain Standards Committee of the Canadian Grain Commission. The three provincial pools also have a joint organization called the Canadian Cooperative Wheat Producers Ltd, recently renamed Prairie Pools. Composed of the CEOs of the pools, it "coordinates policy and action on matters affecting the production and marketing of grain and the level of farm income in Western Canada."[19] It lobbied in turn the provincial federations, the Western Agricultural Conference, and the CFA directly.

When the dust had cleared by the mid-1980s, the pools, working in an unholy alliance with Quebec agricultural interests, had won the latest round in the Crow debate. While farmers' freight costs would now rise as they shared future cost increases, freight rates would still be subsidized through direct payments to the railways. Here, in fact, I am simplifying a complex policy, skipping over a long debate, and avoiding further description of perhaps the most intensive lobbying campaign on a non-constitutional issue during the Trudeau years.[20] More important to this study, however, are two particular consequences of the debate. First, the CFA suffered a number of telling body blows near the end of the fight. The association early on saw that divisions among farmers were deep and feelings intense on the issue and decided not to take a formal stand or to lobby in the debate. The federation had little choice, lacking any capacity to discipline or control its member organizations. The provincial federations, in turn, particularly in Alberta and Manitoba, were hamstrung by divisions between cattlemen, who insisted on abolition of the Crow, and grain growers, most of whom demanded retention. Their inability to resolve these conflicts contributed significantly to the CFA's decision to avoid formal participation in the discussions. It also led to the reluctance of the respective Conservative provincial governments to take up positions in the debate.[21]

In the aftermath, resentment against the pools broke out into open conflict in the Saskatchewan and Manitoba affiliates of the CFA and provoked the withdrawal of the UGG from CFA membership. In

Saskatchewan, the divisions over policy were reinforced by a questioning of the dominance of the SFA in terms of both policy and finances by the Saskatchewan Wheat Pool. The CFA, in 1984, believed that it would be years before a new province-wide affiliate would emerge.[22] In Manitoba, farmers were seeking to replace the old Manitoba Farm Bureau with a new group called Keystone Agricultural Producers. This new organization was given a structure similar to that of Unifarm in having direct and organization members, with most votes reserved for the former. The CFA hoped that Keystone would join as its Manitoba affiliate.

All these developments reflect the fragility of a corporatist edifice. On the one side, the hierarchy and comprehensiveness of the associational system place the group represented in a better position to be a policy participant. On the other side, like a house of cards, if one or two of the lower cards in the structure collapses, the whole edifice comes tumbling down.

This fragility is exemplified further by the behaviour of the peak association specific to the grains sector, the Canada Grains Council, over the course of the grain transportation debate. Established in 1969 at the instigation of the federal government, the council was to provide a forum for the discussion of all segments of the grains industry and to act as a formal liaison with government. It was to have been a policy participant in a corporatist network. There were two crucial charges to the group: "Without duplicating or replacing existing functions being performed by departments or agencies of the Government of Canada to formulate recommendations which represent a consensus of the industry as a whole"; and "To report its recommendations directly to the Ministers of Agriculture, and of Industry, Trade and Commerce, and subsequently make public such findings and recommendations as are approved by the Council, except on specific matters on which those Ministers have requested the Council's confidential advice."

Thus the council was asked to develop a consensus within the industry and assured that its recommendations would be seriously considered within the policy process. If the council were to succeed, it needed to be the legitimate and only representative of the grains sector, and when it was first formed such a claim could be realistically made. However, as the years went by, like the CFA, it found it more and more difficult to hold the industry together. By 1980, of the four producer co-operatives and pools, only the UGG remained a member. The council's membership, including the railways, the private grain companies, the Western Canada Wheat Growers, and the Canola Council, was thus weighted heavily to the side of the Crow debate led by the commodity coalition. The UGG, too, as we have seen, tended to follow the commodity coalition. In 1982, Forbes et al, concluding their study of the grains industry, signalled the failure of the council: "No existing institution can fill the role of development planner for the industry."[23] The authors continued, "We recommend that the federal government in consultation with the provinces establish a Grains Industry Secretariat, composed of knowledgeable and influential individuals, reflecting a variety of individual and entrepreneurial interests and points of view in the grains industry."[24]

What better proof of the council's failure than the call for creation of an institution to do what the council was to have done? However, a key difference existed between the council and the proposed new secretariat. Forbes et al comment in a footnote that the council suffered from the withdrawal of members (such as the pools) when disagreement became particularly intense in a policy area.[25] Hence their suggestion that the new secretariat be composed of individuals, not organizations. With such a secretariat, the new body could not function in a corporatist network like its predecessor. In corporatism, associations receive some authority from the state to work on public policy in a given area in exchange for ensuring that their members comply with the policy that develops; associations exercise some control over their members.[26] In removing the organizational or associational element from the proposed structure, the authors exclude this possibility. The new secretariat becomes simply another pressure group – perhaps all that is possible in a sector so rent with conflict. The weakness of associations in this sector deprives producers of the more extensive policy participation enjoyed by the sectors to be discussed next.

DAIRY AND POULTRY CORPORATISM

In contrast to the grains sector, the pattern of relationships between associations representing dairy farmers and the federal and provincial governments reflects one of the most developed corporatist policy networks in the Canadian economy. Corporatism occurs also in the poultry sectors, but in a less elaborate form. These networks have emerged in the context of an industrial structure that is based on a highly protected domestic market and as a result of incipient conflict between farmers and the firms processing their products. By the late 1970s, both the Canadian dairy industry and the poultry industries had become highly domestic. In 1978, for example, only

2.3 per cent of the dairy market was served by imported dairy products (mostly cheeses) and the Canadian industry exported a mere 2.5 per cent of its production.[27] Import controls existed on virtually all dairy and poultry products, effectively preventing any penetration of the market except for specialty cheese products, and even there a system of quotas was in place.

The development of such a structure was in part "natural" and in part a product of public policy.[28] The dairy industry serves well to illustrate these points. Although there were some very lean periods during the Depression, the Canadian industry had been a significant exporting sector until about 1955. At that point, as western Europe recovered from the destruction of the war and re-established some traditional lines of supply, Canadian exports began to drop. By the mid-1960s, Canadian dairy farms were producing far more than the domestic market could absorb, bringing on uncomfortable declines in prices. While exports were declining, the processing industry itself was changing. Within specific regions, it was becoming more and more concentrated. (Today, for example, there is not a province where the top three processors account for less than 70 per cent of the provincial market.) With increased concentration came a new type of dairy plant, sufficiently integrated to process a wide range of dairy products. Previously, plants had been specialized according to the end use of the product (fluid milk, cheese, butter and skim milk powder, concentrated milk).

The combination of these two kinds of changes created problems for the dairy farmer. At the same time as the market was shrinking and income was failing to grow, processors wanted better milk quality and sanitation standards so the product could be used for various ends in the large integrated plants. The cash was simply not at hand to modernize sufficiently, and farmers became more active politically to protect themselves. Movement towards a solution began in 1963 when the so-called First Canadian Dairy Conference was convened in Ottawa.[29] Attending were representatives of the federal and provincial governments, of dairy farmers, and of processors. The conference set in motion a chain of political events that yielded the fundamentals of the current Canadian dairy policy.

The policy has been built around three general objectives. (1) Domestic requirements for processed dairy products and fluid milk were to be met as much as possible from Canadian sources. (2) Dairy producers were to receive a reasonable level of return for their products and to benefit from price stability. (3) Canadian consumers were to have an assured supply of "high quality" products all year round.[30] Adjoined to this policy were several other objectives to ease the political acceptance of such protectionism. Specifically, farmers were given incentives to modernize operations, upgrade product quality, and improve economic efficiency. Processing operations too were encouraged to rationalize further and to become more innovative.[31]

In these circumstances, the "corporatist temptation" arose. The state invited the opposing parties, farmers and processors, to join with it in designing and administering a policy to realize these objectives. If this sharing of responsibility were to occur, the associational system itself had to be rationalized. Farmers still tended to be organized into separate assocations depending on the market they catered to (fluid, cheese, and so on). A policy based on the integration of these end uses would require, in effect, the integration of farmers' organizations.

Beginning in Ontario and Quebec, where differentiation was greatest, integration has taken place over the past 20 years. In Ontario, there is now a single, predominant Ontario Milk Marketing Board, which absorbed four earlier organizations. In Quebec, the recent amalgamation of two federations, one for consumers and one for industrial milk, into a single marketing agency completes a similar process. Consequently, within the dairy farming sector, there is now a well-developed corporatist-style associational system. The basic unit of organization is a provincial marketing board for milk and milk products. These boards, which exist in all provinces except Newfoundland, are compulsory assocations for all dairy farmers in a given province. If farmers wish to sell milk, they must belong to a board. Each provincial organization, in turn, belongs to the national sectoral peak association, the Dairy Farmers of Canada (DFC). Thus the DFC speaks for *all* dairy farmers in Canada through an associational network that suffers no competitors in the representation of dairy farmers' interests.

The DFC and its provincial members are also fully integrated participants in the process through which Canadian dairy policy is designed and implemented. The policy is built around fixing the supply and price of milk but works differently for industrial milk (milk manufactured into dairy products) and fluid milk. In effect, authority over the dairy industry is split between federal and provincial governments, because of the division of powers and the nature of the markets in question. "Specifically, high transportation costs and perishability dictate that markets for fluid milk must be local. In most cases this means that fluid milk is produced, processed, distributed and consumed within a single province. The local nature of fluid milk markets gives constitutional authority over them to the provinces (and municipalities) ... In contrast, industrial dairy products, being less perishable and more easily transported, are subject to extensive interprovincial and (to a lesser extent) international trade. They are therefore primarily subject to federal regulation."[32]

Prices for industrial milk are fixed by a complex process overseen by a federal agency, the Canadian Dairy Commission (CDC). The CDC administers programs that identify a target return to producers, provide a subsidy to reach this target, and, through an offer-to-purchase program for butter and skim milk powder, provide a guaranteed outlet for major dairy products. The price of industrial milk is fixed by provincial marketing boards, based upon the CDC support prices for butter and skim milk powder and its target return.

Marketing boards are even more central in determining supply. The key organization, the Canadian Milk Supply Management Committee, is composed of representatives of each provincial marketing board, the DFC, and the provincial governments and is chaired by the CDC. Since the processors, through the National Dairy Council, are also attached as ex officio members, this body has a quasi-corporatist character. Based on estimates of total domestic and export requirements, it recommends for cabinet approval the total quota (market share quota) for a given year and decides how the quota is to be distributed among the provinces.[33] The CDC delegates to the marketing boards responsibility for distributing the quotas to individual farmers. In Ontario, the board also assigns quotas to individual processing plants.

For fluid milk, provincial governments delegate to provincial marketing boards power to fix the price paid to the producer and, based on a formula, the price paid by the processor. Within their jurisdictions, the boards are monopoly sellers and buyers of milk and also control supply. They assign production quotas to individual farmers and, in some cases, to processing plants. Such important decisions by marketing boards are preceded by compulsory consultations carried out with tripartite committees of producers, processors, and provincial government representatives.

While the history of the industry differs, similar developments have occurred in the poultry sector. Again responsibilities are shared between the two levels of government, with federal legislation regulating interprovincial elements of the policy and provincial laws intraprovincial elements.[34] Marketing boards exist for chickens in the eight provinces with significant production and for turkeys in the five main producing provinces.[35] In Ontario, for example, each of these boards has the power to fix minimum prices paid to producers. Supply is controlled through a national plan. Two national agencies, the Canadian Chicken Marketing Agency (CCMA) and the Canadian Turkey Marketing Agency (CTMA), regulate interprovincial and international trade. Under their auspices, national production quotas are set and allocations of this quota made among the provinces. The provincial marketing board in Ontario then allocates its quota to producers and also assigns a quota to processors. The boards also control the amount of imports under the Export and Import Permits Act administered by the Office of Special Trade Relations of the Department of External Affairs.

The poultry meat sector differs in one important respect from the dairy sector in that there is no equivalent to industrial milk inviting such strong federal government participation. Accordingly, the national farmers' organizations play a lesser role in the system than does the Dairy Farmers of Canada. The key players remain, then, the provincial marketing boards. These meet under the auspices of the respective national agencies (CCMA, CTMA) for discussions of supply and provincial allocations. Establishment of the supply-management system, in turn, has significantly affected collective action by processors. In 1974, their association, the Canadian Poultry and Egg Processors Council, was a part-time operation run by an employee of Canada Packers in his basement. Since that time, it has grown to employ five people full time. Its executive director attends all meetings of the boards of directors of the CCMA and the CTMA, is a member of their consultative committees, and is otherwise in daily contact with them.[36]

In summary, the associations representing farmers in the dairy and poultry sectors have become compulsory, monopoly organizations, as suggested in corporatist theory. They act as key intermediaries in a policy that fixes prices in order to guarantee acceptable returns to members and that matches supply to demand in the domestic market. In most instances, they join with associations representing processors (but, significantly, not consumers) and with governments in designing the policy and deciding how it is to be implemented in any given year.

CONCLUSIONS

Perhaps surprisingly, until 1980 the associational system in agriculture had integrated a wide range of quite specialized associations across both commodity groups and territory. No other division of the economy that we study in this book shows the same degree of vertical integration and hierarchical affiliation. Several factors help to account for the emergence of such an associational system. With relatively few exceptions, associations in the division began as a defensive response to attacks on farmers' economic situation by other classes and groups. Farmers quickly found that they were less in competition with one another than with sectors of business that purchased, processed, or transported their products. Like workers in trade unions, they found that they could wield power in society only as a collective force.

This initial need for solidarity was itself reinforced by other dimensions of the farmer's life. In several sectors, including even dairy in the early days, farmers were producing for international markets. They suffered from the vagaries of these markets and found that in order to protect themselves they needed a united position. The problems farmers faced in seeking to increase productivity so as to secure the domestic market and to compete internationally were common to all. The overwhelming majority having family farms of about the same size meant that needs were shared and an obvious base for collective action existed. Solidarity was reinforced further by regional concentration of production of various commodities.

The state, too, was a factor. It was involved very early in creating institutions to support and develop the agricultural economy. Gradually there evolved quite impressive and comprehensive departments of agriculture at both levels of government to speak for farmers in the halls of power. These departments have remained in close contact with other institutions that support the farmer, particularly agriculture faculties and independent state agencies. Such a well-integrated state support system encouraged further integration of associations representing the farmer.

It would appear that farmers benefited from such a developed associational system. They gained an important say in the design and administration of policy in a number of sectors, particularly dairy, poultry, and eggs. Marketing boards in several horticultural sectors also obtained policy participation responsibilities for the farmers they represent. While corporatism did not succeed in the grains sector, that it could be attempted was a testament again to the development of the agricultural associational system. As we shall see later, the underdevelopment of the associational system in other economic divisions rules out the possibility of corporatism.

As the peak of the agricultural system, the CFA enjoyed success. When the federal Department of Agriculture in the late 1970s started to develop its Agri-Food Strategy for the 1980s, the CFA was incorporated formally into the process. It has remained so as the policy was formulated, accepted by the government, and begun to be implemented. With senior officials in the department, the association is part of the formal monitoring process for the policy. However, the CFA's overall effectiveness has been increasingly circumscribed by the rising strength of commodity associations which do not want membership. Cattlemen, for example, have successfully opposed inclusion in marketing and supply-management policies and joined with other groups in the successful fight against Canagrex, the proposed federal agricultural exporting agency. The CFA, of course, supported Canagrex.[37]

Finally, the character of the associational system facilitated advocacy. It is commonplace in political circles to wonder at the success of farmers as a lobby. Perhaps now this success will appear more understandable. A system so well differentiated and yet so integrated (at least to 1980) will be prepared to exercise maximum leverage on politicians. It can speak with leaders on very specialized issues one day and have thousands in the streets the next day focusing on general issues affecting all farmers. It is often said that farmers are remarkably able to influence political decisions. To the extent that this is true, I expect it is because their organizations are sufficiently co-ordinated one with the other that all relevant politicians will realize the electoral consequences of their actions early in the decision-making process. The organizations, because of their scope, represent a socioeconomic producer group that is an important factor in scores of ridings across the country. Here it is not the individual farmer's group that is important but the system of groups.

Hence the tragedy of the 1970s and early 1980s. I argue in this book that the transformation of economic power into political power is a complex process that occurs in several forms. In particular, a given socioeconomic producer group engineers this transformation more effectively the more it controls formulation and implementation of policies affecting it. A business person owns a unit of production and appropriates value based on labour contracted with to operate that unit. For the farmer, economic power is less immediate; it is created only when many farmers work together as a solidaristic class. Without collective action, farmers are often defenceless in a capitalist system composed of large corporations. Thus it becomes crucial to independent producers like farmers to create strong collective organizations if they wish to influence policies affecting them.

In some sectors, such as dairy, farmers have succeeded admirably at this task; in other sectors they have done less well. Similarly, farmers have performed better in some provinces than in others. For example, in Quebec, the Union des producteurs agricoles has obtained a definite public status. All farmers must by law pay dues to it, and most (89 per cent) belong to it.[38] However, Canadian farmers have seriously wounded an organization they themselves created "to promote the common interests of agricultural producer organizations" – the CFA. Farmers did not see enough in common to create a peak association that represented them all. In particular, livestock and poultry interests were not well represented in its structures. When an important divisive issue arose, the absence of these interests in the CFA prevented farmers from settling their own differences. What is more, the structures in place for voicing dissent in the CFA were sufficiently underdeveloped that the disaffected felt that they had to leave instead.

In a report of a task force created to foster a dialogue of self-criticism, the CFA concluded that it had failed to reach out to the farming community and to represent all sectors. It had failed to involve the base in its deliberations. Accordingly, it removed the possibility of creating consensus, a grievous failing for a representative of small, independent commodity producers: "It is a major part of the rationale of having an organization like the Canadian Federation of Agriculture that farmers can press their interests most effectively with government if they are united on the policies which they advocate. The strength such unity adds to their representations makes the desirability very great of determining optimal positions through discussion, study and analysis, and, even where views differ reaching accommodation and negotiation of agreed positions."[39] Consequently, resolution of one of the most important issues to affect Canadian agriculture over the past quarter-century came after a pluralistic free-for-all that allowed governments full rein to pick and choose policies to maximize their own short-term electoral interests, not the longer-term interests of agriculture and perhaps the nation. If the policies work in the best long-term interests of Canadian farmers and industry, it will be only by accident. Several years will need to pass before we see if farmers in Canada organize themselves differently in order to remove the risks of future accidents and to return to a position of collective strength.

CHAPTER SEVEN

Construction

The construction entrepreneur, at first glance, appears an unlikely association member. His business is risky. Work begins with a flourish in the spring when tradesmen have to be found, equipment leased, bids made, and sub-contractors attended to. Getting started in the field often requires little capital, creating an industry usually crowded with competitors. To use common parlance, it is a "dog eat dog" world, with seemingly little time left for attending association meetings. Yet associations abound in this division of the economy that accounts for billions of dollars of economic output and employs hundreds of thousands of workers. Not only are they very much present, but associations assume an array of different tasks, many involving close participation in policy-making.

This complex pattern of associative action has its roots in differences among sectors within the industry. The construction industry is a giant, accounting for 16 per cent of the gross national product in 1977 and employing directly about 7 per cent of the labor force.[1] Canadian construction activity divides almost equally between building and civil engineering construction. The former includes residential housing and the erection of the larger structures in the institutional (hospital, schools), commercial, and industrial fields. Civil engineering includes as its larger sub-sectors construction of roads and highways, drilling of oil and gas wells, and building of hydroelectric projects. Except for some sub-sectors of civil engineering, construction firms have not followed the trend towards bigness, vertical integration, and oligopoly found in much of manufacturing.[2] Individual firms have remained small and simple operations, with little administrative overhead. Concentration is low, with the four largest firms accounting for only 1.5 per cent of output.[3] In the building sectors, 99.5 per cent of firms employ less than 100 workers; in civil engineering, about 95 per cent. This kind of flexible, unbureaucratic firm suits well the production of much of the industry's goods, invariably individual, unique, and site-bound. Each job differs for the normal builder or civil engineer. Each demands the application of different skills, usually in a different order, depending on the nature of the road, house, or dam being constructed and the setting.

The core relation in the industry involves a general contractor, who takes responsibility for completion of the job, and trades specialists, who are called upon as sub-contractors to contribute their particular skills in completing the job. Terms vary from country to country; in Canada, the relationship is maintained through the competitively bid, fixed price contract.[4] General contractors compete for jobs by submitting sealed bids fixing a price for the whole job. The same type of bid competition exists among trades contractors in their relations with general contractors.

This system places several constraints on the general contractor.[5] He must have sufficient financial reserves to pay general expenses and to maintain a core of personnel for preparing bids in slack periods. He must also be able to support capital charges for investment in the equipment he needs to take full advantage of busy periods. The need to control costs in order to remain competitive also introduces particular strains into relations with labour. By its nature, the industry is labour-intensive, and, with this need to control costs in a competitive market-place, the contractor has a particular interest in keeping labour costs down. In slack periods, he will be tempted to bid low, thereby forcing upon himself cutbacks in labour costs. He also has difficulty planning his labour requirements because he does not know how many bids will be successful at any given time. Hence the contractor looks for arrangements with labour that are as flexible as possible, which clashes directly with workers' search for job security.

This environment creates incentives for collective action for the construction entrepreneur. Collective action provides a construction firm with opportunities to increase efficiency.[6] First, relatively strong labour unions have made it difficult to control labour costs. In order to neutralize somewhat union strength, construction firms have themselves formed associations to engage in collective bargaining. Yet collaborating with competitors does not come easily to independent, aggressive entrepreneurs. Generally, employers' associations have had to receive authority from governments to coerce the unwilling to join. In some instances, the state itself has formed the association and required firms to belong. I discuss below an extreme case of such coercion in Quebec. Second, an occasional shortage of skilled labour hampers efficiency. Yet, because he either lacks the funds needed or is afraid of losing to his competitors the workers he has trained, the contractor is reluctant to train his own workers. Associations are then called upon to run vocational training programs.[7] Also often inhibiting efficiency is scarcity of capital. Forced to stretch lines of credit, firms become particularly sensitive to shifts in national monetary and interest rate policies. Accordingly they develop a strong interest in having powerful associations to advocate their point of view on these policies.

Construction firms also face important obstacles to remaining innovative. Lawrence and Dyer emphasize that innovation flourishes where firms face intermediate information complexity – sufficient information to adapt and create when required by the market, yet not so much that they are unable to react and change.[8] The normally small construction firm deals with information overload. Keeping track and taking account of competitors, of frequent advances in materials technology and in building techniques, of government regulations on materials standards and on codes of design, and of links with engineers and architects all threaten, if left unorganized, to submerge the contractor and deprive him of his capacity to innovate and thus succeed. Typically, construction firms establish associations that carry out innovative research on their behalf, or manage the ties with design professions, or develop and communicate standards for new products and materials. We consider examples of these in the fourth section of this chapter.

These competing and varied needs for collective action, particularly when they are unique to one or two sectors of the industry, help create a remarkably diverse and rather poorly integrated associational system. This tendency towards fragmentation is reinforced by the varied relations between this industry and the state. First, the state is an important customer, contracting for large portions of civil engineering work in particular. Second, the state regulates the industry, seeking to protect the health and safety of consumers and workers. Third, the state participates in the industry, constructing itself many projects using its own agencies. Finally, the state, as manager of the macroeconomy, uses this industry with its high volume of work for managing supply and demand in the economy.

Accordingly, the industry faces a variety of governmental agencies with competing needs and demands. Provincial agencies normally affecting the industry include departments of highways, labour (occupational health and safety, manpower, training, labour relations), education (implementation of training programmes) and finance and utilities (major customers). Even more federal agencies have some impact. These include: departments of National Defence (customer) and Transport, the Construction Sector Branch in the Department of Regional Industrial Expansion, the crown corporation Defence Construction Ltd (contracts for major defence construction projects), the Canadian Transport Commission (railway construction, northern roads), the Division of Building Research of the National Research Council, the Transportation Research and Development Board, the National Harbours Board, the Northern Pipeline Agency, and the Northern Canada Power Commission. However, Canada lacks departments with overall responsibility for construction at both levels of government, such as the Department of the Environment in Britain, and organizations for co-ordinating construction policy both within provincial and federal governments and between them.

In short, both the economic needs of the industry and the various demands the state places on it foster a diverse and poorly integrated associational system. Some parts of the system are well placed to assume policy participation, and others are organized to various degrees for advocacy. Some sectors of the industry, particularly non-residential building and civil engineering, meet the state in pressure pluralist networks. Residential building and special trades rely heavily on clientele pluralist networks. Finally, more limited sub-sectors or regions faced with strong labour unions or specialized training needs tend to resort to corporatist structures.

OVERVIEW

The two dominant lines of differentiation in the construction sectors are task or product and territory. The construction industry includes three major sectors by task or product.[9] (1) General contractors (building) are composed of four sectors: residential, institutional (schools, hospitals, etc), industrial (factories), and commerical (banks, stores, etc). (2) General contractors (civil engineering) are composed of roads and highways, oil and gas wells, electric power installations, waterworks and sewage, railway-telephone-telegraph, oil and gas pipelines and other petroleum-based construction, and various others. (3) Special trades contractors are composed of mechanical (plumbing), electrical, roofing, masonry, carpenters, insulation, plastering, painting, equipment operators, and various others.

General contractors subdivide along the line residential–non-residential. Non-residential builders are represented on the national plane by the Canadian Construction Association (CCA) and provincially by the general construction associations (see Table 12). In

Table 12
National Associational System, Construction, 1980

DIVISIONAL PEAK ASSOCIATION

Canadian Construction Association (CCA)

GENERAL CONTRACTORS, BUILDING

General Contractors Section of the CCA
Canadian Home Builders Association
Urban Development Institute
Industrial Developers Association of Canada
Industrial Contractors Section of the CCA

GENERAL CONTRACTORS, CIVIL ENGINEERING

Road Builders and Heavy Construction Section of the CCA
Canadian Association of Oil Well Drilling Contractors
Pipeline Contractors Association of Canada*

TRADES CONTRACTORS

Trades Contractors Section of the CCA
Canadian Acoustical Association
Canadian Automatic Sprinklers Association†
Canadian Electrical Contractors Association†
Canadian Home Insulation Contractors Association
Canadian Masonry Contractors Association
Canadian Roofing Contractors Association
Mechanical Contractors Association of Canada†
National Elevator and Escalator Association†
Terrazzo, Tile and Marble Association of Canada†
Thermal Insulation Association of Canada

ASSOCIATIONS WITH SPECIALIZED FUNCTIONAL DOMAINS

Roads and Transportation Association of Canada
Construction Specifications Canada

---

* Functions as both trade and employers' association.
† Affiliate member of the CCA.

Quebec, two associations share this charge, the Association de la construction de Montréal et du Québec and the Fédération de la construction du Québec. Residential builders are represented at both levels by the Canadian Home Builders Association. Civil engineering firms in all fields except those related to energy collect under the banners of the CCA federally and of road building associations provincially. Specific associations based in western Canada exist for oil well drilling contractors, pipeline contractors, and oilfield contractors. Finally, many of the special construction trades have their own national associations, with the most prominent representing electrical, masonry, and mechanical contractors respectively.

The division of powers in the Canadian constitution creates a basis for strong differentiation along territorial lines as well. Under section 92(10) of the Constitution Act, 1982, the provinces have jurisdiction over matters of a local nature which include by definition most construction projects.[10] This power is reinforced by judicial interpretation of the federal trade and commerce power – section 91(2) – which restricts federal jurisdiction to interprovincial or international matters. Finally these two principles, when coupled with the provinces' jurisdiction over property and civil rights, give provinces primacy over industrial relations and collective bargaining in the construction industry.

The construction associational system, accordingly, is differentiated along territorial lines in three different respects. First, the associations in the building and special trades major sectors each have provincial affiliates. Generally speaking, these affiliation arrangements are loose – "confederal" or "affiliate." The major exception is the Canadian Home Builders Association, which has a federal structure. In civil engineering, the three associations in the energy sector all have unitary structures, reflecting both the geographical concentration and the large firms in this industry. Second, a group of associations at the provincial level does not have any ties to national-level associations. Prominent here are provincial employers' associations, most of which are found in Ontario. Third, the combination of the first two dimensions yields a third: independent associational systems in the provinces. Normally, these are headed by a general provincial association affiliated to the CCA, such as the B.C. Construction Association (see Table 13). In Ontario, a provincial peak association, the Council of Ontario Contractors Associations, heads a particularly complex system.

The national and provincial systems are not as well differentiated vertically. The weak link comes at the aggregation of interests to the major sectoral level. At first glance, Table 12 appears to show that this aggregation is accomplished by two CCA sections – General Contractors, Road Builders and Heavy Construction, and Trades Contractors. Unfortunately, these sections are not suited to such a role.

Table 13
Examples of Provincial Associational Systems, Construction, 1980

QUEBEC

Divisional Peak Association:
None on the trade association side
Association des entrepreneurs en construction du Québec (AECQ),
  employers' association*

General Contractors, Building
La Fédération de la construction du Québec†
L'Association de la construction de Montréal et du Québec,* General
  Contractors Section
L'Association provinciale des constructeurs de l'habitation du Québec
Residential Construction, Industrial Construction sections, AECQ

General Contractors, Civil Engineering
L'Association des constructeurs de routes et de grands travaux du
  Québec*
L'Association québécoise des techniques de l'eau
Roads and Civil Engineering section, AECQ

Trade Contractors
L'Association de la construction de Montréal et du Québec, Trade
  Contractors Section
La Corporation des maîtres éléctriciens du Québec*
La Corporation des maîtres mécaniciens en tuyauterie du Québec

BRITISH COLUMBIA

Divisional Peak Association:
None, trade association side
Construction Labour Relations Association of B.C.,* employers side

General Contractors Building
British Columbia Construction Association†
BC division of the Canadian Home Builders Association
Pacific division of the Urban Development Institute

General Contractors, Civil Engineering
British Columbia Road Builders Association†
Utility Contractors Association of British Columbia
B.C. Water Well Drilling Association

Table 13 (continued)

Trades Contractors
Electrical Contractors Association of British Columbia*
Mechanical Contractors Association of British Columbia*
Northern Interior Woodworkers Association

---

* Affiliate member of the Canadian Construction Association (CCA).
† Integrated affiliate member of the CCA.

They were described in our interview with the CCA as discussion
forums that met only occasionally. This has not always been the case.
When the CCA was founded, it established three sections – for general
contractors, trades contractors, and manufacturers and suppliers –
which functioned as autonomous organizations, with their own executives and identities. Over time these properties have eroded, and
the sections are no longer sufficiently important to be given formal
representation on the association's board of directors.[11] Further,
their capacity to aggregate the interests of major sectors depends in
part on the CCA's ability to represent the whole construction industry.
The CCA has faltered in this respect in ways described below.

The Canadian system contrasts in this respect with that found in
Britain where distinct peak associations aggregate the interests of
each major sector.[12] Thus the Building Employers Confederation,
a peak association with 11 specialist building associations, represents
the general contractors (building) major sector. The Federation of
Civil Engineering Contractors aggregates the range of civil engineering interests. There are two peak associations for trade contractors, one for those attached to the building industry – the
Federation of Associations of Specialists and Sub-Contractors – and
one for those attached to civil engineering – the Committee of Associations of Specialist Engineering Contractors. The lack of peak
associations of this sort makes the weak vertical integration found
in the Canadian construction industry almost inevitable. The level
of integration is significantly less than that in agriculture but greater
than that in manufacturing, mining, and finance. On the national
plane then, the CCA acts as a divisional peak association, with mixed
success.

In 1984, associations affiliated with the CCA in two ways. "Integrated affiliate members" are associations with members that are
enrolled directly as firm members of the CCA. This status is open to
any "provincial mixed construction association or provincial road
builders association,"[13] and was introduced in 1965 to increase members.[14] In contrast, "affiliate association members" join without their

members being enrolled as CCA members and have one vote and hence the same weight as any individual member firm. Integrated affiliates include all the provincial road building associations, save Quebec's and Newfoundland's, and all the provincial general contractors' associations which organize non-residential building, except Quebec's. Affiliates include some trades contractors' associations, Quebec's non-residential building and civil engineering associations, and provincial labour relations associations.[15] In short, the interests of Quebec and of trades contractors are more weakly represented than those of other provinces and of general contractors. Perhaps more significant, associations representing residential building, energy-related civil engineering work, and such key trades as masonry and roofing are not represented within the CCA at all. Nowhere in western Europe can such weak vertical integration be found.

In only one province, Ontario, is there a divisional peak association concerned with all policy areas (not solely labour relations). Even the Council of Ontario Contractors Associations (COCA) has been a peculiarly reluctant peak organization. The guidelines for the council adopted on 10 March 1975 state: "We are not establishing another association but we are simply bringing together, for given reasons, the existing associations." Composed of the senior elected officer and the senior staff officer of the constituent members, the council eschews institutionalization. The guidelines state: "The Council will for an indeterminate period and until circumstances dictate otherwise, have no charter, no by-laws, no permanent staff or offices." With such an orientation, COCA is hardly suited to policy-making and is largely concerned with advocacy. Its properties are remarkably similar to the leading policy advocacy group in the British construction industry, the so-called Group of Eight.[16]

In summary, the associational system in Canadian construction is fragmented into several sub-systems of general contractors: in the non-residential and road building sectors, in the home-building sector, in civil engineering related to the oil and gas industry, and in a variety of relatively independent trades contractors' associations. These sub-systems integrate federal-provincial and trade/employer functional cleavages so that these dimensions do not fragment the industry further. However, fragmentation along product lines produces an associational system not well suited for policy participation. These sub-systems cloud the picture for federal and provincial governments, competing for their ear and often with different and competitive policy stances and variant internal organizations. Each sub-system maintains distinctive relations with government. The non-residential and road building sub-system is almost exclusively con-

cerned with policy advocacy, while the other three sub-systems are
involved in both advocacy and participation.

NON-RESIDENTIAL BUILDING AND PRESSURE POLITICS

One associational sub-system draws together the non-residential
building sectors (institutional, industrial, commerical) and the road
building and heavy construction sectors of civil engineering. The
modal type of associative action is policy advocacy. Two structural
characteristics of these sectors create the basis for heavy emphasis
on pressure group politics. First, these sectors receive much of their
work from governments. Governments contract out about 25 per
cent of the work in the institutional-industrial-commerical sectors,
close to 60 per cent in heavy engineering, and about 80 per cent in
road and bridge building.[17] This business relationship leads to lobbying on two sorts of matters, not to speak of patronage and occasionally corruption. First, the industries have a vested interest in
pressuring governments to continue allocating money for these types
of capital expenditures. As policy advocates, they argue that the
direct and indirect employment benefits from this kind of expenditure, particularly in economic downturns, outweigh the advantages
of other possible uses for government money.

Second, over time, these sectors, for various reasons, have become
more unionized, creating another impetus for policy advocacy. Malles
estimates that 70 to 90 per cent of non-residential building and 40
to 50 per cent of road and bridge building are unionized.[18] Business
and labour have struggled bitterly over the rules for collective bargaining and industrial relations as governments have groped for
arrangements appropriate to the mobile work sites, changing work-
forces, and varying skill compositions of construction work teams.
The exact character of these arrangements has long been a focal
point for lobbying.

The search for industrial relations policies specific to construction
began in earnest in the 1960s when various government inquiries
were instituted and reported. This process of study and investigation
culminated in 1968 in a report done for the CCA by Goldenberg and
Crispo entitled "Construction Labour Relations."[19] Among the many
recommendations in this report was a call for the accreditation of
employers' associations. Employers' associations had been very unstable and hard pressed to maintain discipline among their members.
"Voluntary cooperation frequently dissipated during negotiations,
particularly in the face of union pressure tactics. Because collective

bargaining was highly fragmented – by trade, area and sector – unions were able to whipsaw weak employer organizations and leap-frog wages within and across labour markets."[20] The central idea behind accreditation was the realization of unity and stability within employers' associations. Generally speaking, accreditation schemes do this by bringing non-association firms into the bargaining unit, prohibiting firms from negotiating and reaching agreement on their own, and in some cases by banning selective strikes.[21] Accreditation would be conferred, the argument went, once an association demonstrated that it was "representative" of the employers in the given sector, trade, or area.

Working out a policy centred around such a concept has been remarkably difficult and has forced business to be very vigilant. When was an association to be deemed representative? At what level should bargaining be conducted – local, regional, or provincial? Should accreditation cover one trade or many? Answers have varied from province to province because of different histories, traditions, and patterns of relationships between labour and capital. At one extreme, Quebec has virtually a compulsory state corporatist system.[22] At the other, in Alberta, New Brunswick, and Nova Scotia bargaining has remained decentralized and localized.[23] In any event, uncertainty about industrial relations and the high stakes involved for both employers and labour have intensified the need for strong advocacy associations in the sectors in this sub-system.

The CCA, the leading national advocate for firms in these sectors, was instrumental in shifting the provinces towards adoption of accreditation legislation. Industrial relations, however, is neither the exclusive policy interest of the CCA nor the interest motivating its founding. As the Association of Canadian Building and Construction Industries, it emerged in 1918 following a meeting of construction entrepreneurs in Ottawa.[24] It concerned itself immediately with the problems of reconstruction after the First World War, with the industry's public image, and with ensuring that the letting of government contracts was done in a way to stabilize the industry. The concern with stability has come to occupy a central place in its lobbying on the Rideau. It has actively lobbied the federal government over the years on matters related to taxation and to horizontal incentives to stimulate building activity. Although the CCA's structures are not well suited for policy participation, they are well adapted for policy advocacy. The public affairs department of the CCA generates useful information about the political process and political impact. It publishes a detailed guide that describes for its members the ins and outs of official Ottawa. Separate departments staffed with experts have technical knowledge for dealing with the finer details of taxation and labour relations legislation.

Relations between the CCA and its affiliate associations emphasize its political clout, another property we expect of advocate organizations. When an association becomes an "integrated affiliate" of the CCA, all its member firms become individual firm members of the CCA. The CCA also has a separate roster of usually larger construction firms that join the association directly. The structure thus emphasizes the number of firms belonging – almost 25,000 – a characteristic of an association specializing in policy advocacy. While in an ideal peak association, affiliated associations would be directly and most prominently represented on the executive or committees, in the CCA representatives of individual firms fill these positions. The CCA stresses its representation not of a broad domain, an orientation more consistent with policy participation, but of large numbers of firms, a crucial weapon in advocacy. The association seeks to draw full benefit from this large membership base by encouraging increased political awareness among its members through the activities of its public affairs department and by sponsoring a government liaison committee which holds educational sessions for members at the annual general meeting. Internal mobilization of members is complemented by the efforts of the association's public relations specialist to develop a positive image of the construction industry in the media.

In short, the decidedly weak ties between the CCA and its affiliates are an asset in policy advocacy. The looseness of the ties gives the CCA great flexibility in its lobbying and allows it to point to a membership of over 25,000 firms. The political profile of the association is emphasized while affiliates are left more or less alone. A policy participation organization would stress the size of its membership less and the representativeness of the organization more. The CCA cannot do this, however, for reasons described in the previous section.

Provincial associations in this sub-system, like the CCA, are clearly unsuited for policy participation. A typical example is the Ontario Road Builders Association. Its organization shows no internal differentiation by product, territory, or function. There is no representation of different product interests on its executive. Its elected executive clearly takes precedence over the staff. Its resource base is not diversified, with most funds coming from member firms.

On the advocacy side, the association is better prepared. Its staff has a good working knowledge of the Ontario Ministry of Transportation and Communications, its prime target. It can draw together a pool of specialized knowledge by tapping member firms to send representatives to technical committees. The association puts on social functions to introduce its member firms to MLAS. Its narrow domain facilitates cohesion among members, and its weak ties to other associations such as the CCA give it virtually free movement of action in lobbying.

In conclusion, in this sector of construction more than any other, associative action and lobbying constitute only half of the political game. Dependence on governments for contracts leads construction firms to cultivate personal ties to politicians at all levels of government. Owners of construction firms rely on these personal ties to keep them informed about possible business and, in some instances, to provide them directly with work. In return, many construction entrepreneurs become active participants in party politics, important contributors to party coffers, and even candidates themselves. Also, the particular involvement of the state in the industry, when coupled with the fragility in the market-place of many firms, creates circumstances particularly hospitable to corruption. Gaining a contract with a bribe or sharing contracts through various means of collusion and bid rigging remains endemic to the industry.

BUILDING AND PRIVATE-INTEREST GOVERNMENTS

Housebuilding

The residential building sector differs in several respects from the non-residential building and civil engineering sectors just discussed. It is dominated more by small firms. Over 93 per cent of the firms in the sector have an output of less than $1 million annually, compared to 54 per cent in non-residential building and 60 per cent in highways and bridge building.[25] This is not to say that large firms are not active in the sector. In 1980, 43 firms had an output of over $10 million and accounted for 35 per cent of production in the sector. However, in the heavy engineering sector, firms of the same size accounted for 75 per cent of the industry's output; in non-residential building, they accounted for 57 per cent.[26] The housebuilding sector is also scarcely unionized (Malles estimates 5–10 per cent), and direct government contracts account for less than 1 per cent of output.[27] The incentives for policy advocacy found prominent in the sub-system discussed above are considerably weaker in this sector.

Rather than through direct contracts, government intervenes indirectly in the sector through capital markets. Canada Mortgage and Housing Corporation (CMHC) provides mortgage insurance and some direct lending for market housing. It also has a hand in "social housing" in the north and in particular rural areas, especially where native peoples are concerned. The corporation has programs to foster renovation of housing stock and research. In these latter areas a common interest with the industry develops. Research and development in housing constitute a large sector in themselves. Innovations emerge constantly from the material supplies sector, tool and equipment manufacturers, and engineering and architectural firms. The characteristically small housebuilding firm, usually operating in a restricted area with minimal staff, cannot absorb all this information. Instead, the Canadian Home Builders Association (CHBA), formerly the Housing and Urban Development Association of Canada (HUDAC), assumes this task. Since the government too needs this same information and expertise, significant policy participation has opened up for this association. Common interests in housing standards and management training add further to this role.

The structures and operations of the CHBA differ from the primarily advocacy organizations in non-residential building. The CHBA's key structures are committees, not lobbyists. The Liaison Committee, composed of the association's officers, meets bi-monthly with senior CMHC officials to review upcoming and ongoing policy. The Technical Research Committee and its many sub-committees, supported by the association's own technical staff, conduct and promote research in housing construction. In the past decade, the committee has been especially active in research on energy conservation and has had constructed by its members a number of HUDAC Experimental Houses to study energy conservation techniques. These houses are part of a joint project with the Division of Building Research of the National Research Council. Other projects, costing several million dollars, have been carried out by the association in co-operation with CMHC, the federal department of Energy, Mines and Resources, the Ontario Ministry of Energy, the government of Alberta, and the New Brunswick Power Commission. Recently, the association agreed to manage a Super Energy Efficient Housing Program costing $6 million, with funds from the federal energy department. The CHBA participates in policy-making also in management training courses, standards for building construction, and home warranty programs.

The CHBA is well adapted to policy participation. Its diverse resource base increases its autonomy from members and the state alike. It deposits state funds as well as member dues in its revenue accounts. For members, the CHBA is like a firm, in that it provides them needed technical information; like a club, through the solidarity cultivated in its 80 local associations; like a movement, through its advocacy for the industry and its close links with the CMHC; and even like a government. For example, members joining must subscribe to the association's Code of Ethics and are expelled for failing to do so. They also must accept the direction of the association in meeting standards for home construction when they participate in its warranty programs. The association's staff of 26 is professionally qualified and generates an independent information base. The CHBA clearly enjoys a series of privileges in its relations with the state.

Structures are also well adapted for the ordering of complex information. The CHBA is differentiated by product and by territory: its 80 local branches form, in turn, provincial councils. Both product and territorial divisions are reproduced on the association's executive board through a sophisticated system of proportional representation elections. An Executive Officers Council composed of the executives of local associations discusses problems of association management, further enhancing the organization's professionalism. The CHBA's density is high, given the size of its members, about 85 per cent of industry volume. The one cloud on the horizon is a competitor for member firms, the Urban Development Institute (UDI). The UDI originally broke away from the CHBA to provide separate representation for land developers. Many of these firms have since integrated forward into the building industry, extending the domain of the UDI to the point where it overlaps with both the CHBA and the CCA.

Trades Contractors and Building Standards

Associations representing the specialized construction trades have mixed structures. They are involved in policy advocacy, albeit to a lesser extent than associations representing general contractors. They also assume some policy participation in areas critical to the conduct of their trade and the maintenance of the special, unique skills of their members; their interests dovetail with those of government agencies interested in ensuring that the end products are safe from structural failure, fire hazards, and health hazards. As Streeck has emphasized, a close link between private special interests and the state's public policy objectives is conducive to association involvement in policy-making and occasionally to the establishment of "private interest governments."[28]

Instruments of common interest to the building trades and the state are standards for materials and standard building procedures. Responsibility for devising the former is shared among four organizations: the Canadian Standards Association (electrical, plumbing, masonry construction and materials, and structural design for concrete, steel, timber, and masonry), the Canadian General Standards Board (building materials), the Canadian Gas Association (gas equipment), and the Underwriters Laboratories of Canada (fire prevention). While the Canadian General Standards Board is a government agency and the other three are private organizations, all four bodies tend to operate in the same way. Special committees, struck for particular products, are staffed by representatives from building materials manufacturers and contractors as well as general interest groups and consumers. In most instances, the construction industry's representatives are drawn from technical committees of corresponding associations. The activities of these standards organizations enter the public realm in two respects. They are recognized as "official" standards-writing organizations by the Standards Council of Canada, and their standards are incorporated directly into legislation affecting the construction industry.

The area of standard building procedures is more complex. Early in this century, provincial governments delegated to their respective municipalities authority and responsibility for promulgating and administering local building regulations. Over the years, these decisions created chaos because of the many differences that grew up among local laws. Accordingly, when the federal government passed its first Dominion Housing Act, thereby entering the mortgage field during the Depression, it also became interested in bringing some order to these laws. Gen. A.C.G. McNaughton, president of the National Research Council (NRC), proposed that a model building by-law be written.[29] Accordingly, the National Building Code was written in the form of a local by-law. Operating under the direction of the NRC's Division of Building Research, the code has been maintained since by an associate committee which, in turn, has eight standing committees.[30] These committees again are staffed largely by representatives from construction industry associations.

If we take as an example of a special trades association the Canadian Masonry Contractors Association, we see it involved in both materials standards and building standards. The association is a member of six technical committees of the Canadian Standards Association (CSA) on materials and usage, and its executive director is chairman of the CSA Committee on Mortar. The association is also represented on the Committee on Masonry Design and Construction of the National Building Code. Joined to this kind of technical work, the association has set up, in conjunction with its parallel union, the Bricklayers, and with masonry materials suppliers, programs for promoting research, which allow it to keep its members abreast of changing developments.

To summarize, the CHBA and, to a lesser extent, trades contractors associations are linked to the federal government through co-optive and clientele pluralist policy networks. A partnership develops between an association that manages a wide range of information and is autonomous from its members and an agency that too is well resourced and has its own sense of policy objectives. For efficient policy implementation, authority is delegated to the association for particular tasks. Such a policy role under these circumstances, however, is quite different from one in a corporatist system, where it is not a question of mutual interests but of social conflict, a topic I illustrate in the following section.

CLASS CONFLICT AND CORPORATISM

Earlier in this chapter, I noted several reasons why class conflict is likely in the construction industry: the pressure on general contractors to control labour costs because of the competitive-bid, fixed-cost contract; the existence of industrial relations systems poorly adapted to the mobile, ever-changing character of construction work; and the localized nature of most construction work and the variety of skills involved, which place many construction employers in a weak position vis-à-vis labour unions.

To a degree, the organization of labour in the construction industry parallels that of management. Craft unions, most American-based and separately organized into the Canadian Federation of Labour, dominate the industry. Only Quebec, with the Confederation of National Trade Unions (CNTU), has an industrial union, but it represents less than 20 per cent of unionized construction labour in the province. The strength of these craft unions vis-à-vis their employers derives first from their very special skills. They cannot be substituted for easily. Second, in a given locality, the trades have tended to negotiate by trying to leapfrog over each other. As they have improved their co-ordination at a province-wide level, the unions have also become more adept at playing one locality off against another. These factors have helped make labour relations particularly bad in the industry. Although the construction industry has about 10 per cent of Canada's union members, it has accounted for one-sixth of strike activity since 1950.[31] The effectiveness of this industrial action is illustrated by the unusually high levels of wage increases obtained. In 1950, average hourly earnings in construction were 101.9 per cent of those in manufacturing; by 1977, this figure had risen to 153.1 per cent.[32] The intensity of labour discontent has also varied among provinces, with Quebec and British Columbia far outpacing the others, a point to which we shall return below. Pronounced labour unrest in construction cannot help but be unwelcomed by governments, because they are directly responsible for about one-third of the work in the industry.[33]

Although all provinces have moved somewhat towards the use of corporatist policy networks to manage labour conflict in the construction sector, Quebec provides an extreme example, thereby highlighting especially well the nature of class tensions in the industry. It cannot be my purpose here to explain why or to describe how Quebec has arrived at its current position.[34] Rather I shall limit myself to a brief description of the policy system that prevailed until 1986. Since 1934, the system of labour relations in Quebec's construction industry has exhibited four major characteristics.[35] First, provision has existed in the law for extending a collective agreement reached by part of the industry to the whole industry. Second, bargaining has taken place at a regional and (since 1973) provincial plane that was industry-wide, i.e. multi-trade. Such bargaining was facilitated in part by a union structure where the CNTU was organized on an industrial rather than a craft basis. Third, until 1975, the administration and surveillance of the collective agreement followed liberal corporatist lines, being placed in the hands of a parity committee of workers and employers.[36] Finally, until 1969, these same parity committees were responsible for regulating and implementing the system of vocational training. In effect, then, the systems for labour relations and for manpower training were managed in corporatist networks drawing upon delegated state authority.

This liberal corporatism was largely replaced by a state corporatist system. The first step came in 1969 when the Manpower Vocational Training and Qualification Act transferred responsibility for training from the parity committees to the Manpower Branch of the Department of Labour. In 1975, this responsibility was transferred again to a new government agency, the Office de la construction du Québec (OCQ).[37] At the same time, this agency took over from the parity committees responsibility for administration and surveillance of the collective agreement negotiated for the whole industry. A new agency, the Régie de l'enterprise de construction du Québec, was added and given responsibility for evaluating qualifications for licensing contractors to do specific types of work.

Complementing this shift towards direct state control of bargaining arrangements and manpower policy was a new element of compulsion in the associational sphere. Unions were forced to meet strict representational criteria to be part of the system. Workers were

141   Construction

compelled to belong to a union that met these criteria. Employers were compelled to belong to the Association des entrepreneurs en construction du Québec (AECQ), created and designed by the state. These new organizations have fewer responsibilities than their predecessors, the parity committees. A parity advisory committee drawn from them was attached to the OCQ and given responsibility for interpreting the collective agreement. AECQ was asked to nominate five representatives to the Régie.

These changes emerged following recommendations made by a commission set up in 1974 to investigate violence in the construction industry at the end of a period of intense struggle both within and between the employers' and workers' organizations. In its report, the commission castigated the six major employers' associations in the industry: "It is without a doubt true that the employers' side is represented at the negotiating table by six extremely different associations, often even opposed to one another because of differences in their composition or their objectives."[38] It deplored the associations' inability to discipline members and lamented their lack of competence, paucity of conscience in safety and accident prevention, and poorly developed knowledge and policies in manpower planning and employment security.[39]

In short, employers had been unable to develop associations to manage their relations with workers. In the face of this manifest weakness and deteriorating conditions on worksites, the state removed delegated responsibilities from liberal corporatist bodies in an attempt to force the firms to act cohesively. It thus created for business and, to a lesser extent, labour new representative bodies and equipped them with powers that institutionalized a state-supervised, state corporatist system for handling labour relations. The new system did not work, however, and in 1986 the Liberal government moved back somewhat towards a liberal corporatist system. Admittedly, the Quebec case is somewhat atypical in the Canadian context. However, it illustrates well the dynamics of inter-class and intra-class struggle in the construction industry, how these struggles are fought through associations on the employers' side, and perhaps what steps the state is prepared to take when these associations are ineffective.

CONCLUSIONS

From the perspective of its economic structure, the construction industry would appear to present real obstacles to the acquisition of governing properties by associations. The prevalence of small firms

means that business associations will have large potential memberships, where Olson's logic of collective action and free riders looms
large.[40] The firms are very competitive with one another, generally
run by individualistic and cunning entrepreneurs who usually look
askance at any suggestion of co-operation "with the other guy." These
firms are not faced by the oligopoly buying sectors or so directly
affected by the swings in international trade that have forced farmers
to collective action. Their buyers are dispersed, and their markets
local. As a result, many construction associations, particularly in non-
residential building, have lower densities of representation than
associations in other economic divisions. They are policy advocates
rather than participants. Yet, where private business interests and
the state's view of the public or national interest coincide, such obstacles
can be overcome. Without extensive programs of selective benefits,
a number of associations in this division have achieved high densities
of representation and become directly involved in policy-making and
implementation. They have helped design energy-efficient housing,
product and building standards, and vocational training courses.[41]
In short, the needs of the modern state have drawn even such unlikely candidates as building contractors into a collaborative role.
Through collective action, builders and tradesmen have crystallized
sufficient class power to seek and obtain state power. Other possible
participants, such as consumers or construction workers, have been
largely excluded.

The level of organization of business has resulted not only from
greater government intervention. Business associations have acquired
some governing properties as a consequence of bitter struggles with
labour. The structural properties of the industry that hinder associative action by business also leave firms weaker vis-à-vis organized
labour than in most manufacturing sectors. In order to counter
labour's strength and control its demands, firms have been forced
to work together, usually with prodding and backed up by delegation
of state authority to coerce the reluctant. When the political stakes
are high and class conflict is particulary intense, the state may get
impatient and coerce firms to join employers' associations, even if it
has to create them, as the Quebec case illustrates.

As matters rest now, however, most government-business concertation takes place at the more specialized sectoral and sub-sectoral
levels. There is no single voice for the construction industry in federal or provincial governments. Likely possibilities – the CCA and its
provincial affiliates – are not candidates at all. They represent well
only part of the industry; residential building and special trades have
their own organizations. If government wants the view of the con-

struction industry on policy, it has to call in a number of organizations. Most likely, the organizations will not agree and the government must find a consensus. Governments in this situation usually go ahead on their own. The policy game of trial and error that follows may be good or bad for industry, workers, or consumers. Working with the associations is complicated further by the constant threat of corruption and presence of patronage that comes with governments being a major customer of the industry. Those making policy are not necessarily those letting the contracts. Corrupt practices invariably taint the associations, rendering policy-making arms of government suspicious and reluctant to deal with them.

An alternative scenario is the one partially evident in agriculture, particularly prior to the early 1980s. The industry peak association was broadly representative and worked hard to reach consensus and define a common interest. It then sought and obtained a formal place in the making of agricultural policy. It also benefited from the definition of more coherent and longer-term policy than has ever seen the light of day in the construction industry. The fact that farmers are recognized by most pundits as a more effective voice in Ottawa and provincial capitals than construction firms is related to differences in organization. Non-residential construction associations are tied together only very loosely and are unable to discipline their members enough to remove long-standing suspicions. Where internal discipline is exercised, as in residential building and some special trades, some associations have obtained a share of state power. These contrasts among sectors of the industry illustrate a more general point: differences in the organizational development of associational systems appear to be related directly to differences in influence and policy outcomes among sectors of Canadian business.

CHAPTER EIGHT

Resources: Forestry and Mining

Similar to agriculture, Canada's resource industries – forestry, fishing, mining, petroleum, and natural gas production – are fundamental blocks in its economic base. Each contributes on average to the positive side of Canada's international balance of payments and has important backward and forward spread effects in secondary manufacturing. For example, the forest industry, arguably the most important of these, is responsible for 15 per cent of all value added in Canadian manufacturing, fills one railroad car out of five with its products, employs directly 300,000 people, and produces more newsprint than any other country in the world.[1] Exports of crude minerals in 1982 had a value of $5,842.8 million, which placed them ahead of wheat exports.[2] Like agriculture, resource sectors are highly oriented towards and influenced by the international market-place. Politically, they occupy a similar Janus-like constitutional position in that natural resources are the responsibility of the provinces that own many of them, yet international trade brings them also within the federal government's trade and commerce power.[3] In addition, they share with agriculture an environment of economic regulation: in many cases, the price of the resource and even its supply are determined by both market forces and administrative decisions. Finally, the importance of resources to the national and provincial economies has inspired support structures in government on a scale with those in agriculture.

Resource production is directed by a different social class than agriculture. The majority of farmers are independent commodity producers; only a minority have incorporated themselves as small businesses and hired a small permanent coterie of workers. As independent, self-employed producers, farmers have engaged in collective action through associations in a series of momentous struggles with big oligopoly firms in the food processing, grain trading, and grain transportation sectors. Constituting themselves as a social class to be reckoned with, farmers have used these struggles to prompt creation of remarkably well-developed and autonomous agriculture departments to act as their voice in the cabinet rooms of the nation. In contrast to the small agricultural concern, large powerful corporations dominate forestry, mining, and petroleum. Their struggles have been of a different order, primarily with radical labour unions and occasionally with an over-zealous state.

However, one similarity is obvious. Firms in the resource sectors have organized several powerful advocacy associations whose voices in Ottawa and in selected provincial capitals are as loud and as persuasive as their agricultural counterparts. Here, however, the similarities end. The developed hierarchical structures that integrated rather diverse agricultural commodities into a system headed by the Canadian Federation of Agriculture until 1980 are not found in the separate systems representing each of the major resource sectors: forestry, fishing, and mineral production. There is substantial variation across these systems in the degree of systematic, formal integration of diverse territorial and commodity units. With the sharing of jurisdiction for resources more heavily tilted towards the provinces, territorial integration, in particular, appears less pronounced than in agriculture. Finally, the corporatist policy networks common in agriculture are relatively scarce in the resource sectors, where clientele and pressure pluralist networks are more the norm. Associations representing resource industries have captured directly more state power than those speaking for farmers because their class opponents are weaker relatively and state institutions have not developed the autonomy possessed by those overseeing agriculture. To turn the argument around, the capacity of resource capital to convert class power into state power is greater than that shown by agricultural producers.

This is not to say that sectors dominated by a few large and powerful firms do not need or are less prone to use powerful associations. The difference between these sectors and those comprised of farmers or small general contracting firms is that associations need not be the primary instrument for the defence of class interests. Corporations like MacMillan Bloedel in forestry, Esso Resources in petroleum, and Cominco in mining have the financial resources and the influence in local communities to be formidable political advocates in their own right in a way that the individual farmer or contractor cannot. At the same time, as suggested in chapter 1, participating directly in the policy process is not often seen as a legitimate activity for a single, individual firm in our democratic political system. For policies that require participation of the resource industries in formulation or administration, associations become important players. That these associations participate in clientele networks rather than corporatist ones is a tribute again to the power of the resource sectors in being able to exclude other classes from policy deliberations affecting their interests.

The development of these arguments in this chapter begins with a general discussion of the properties of the associational systems in the forestry and minerals sectors.[4] From among these sectors, two will be the subject of more intensive analysis. The forestry industry was chosen for a first case study because of its immense economic importance, its regional incidence (heavily concentrated in British Columbia, Ontario, and Quebec), and its high degree of government regulation. The vast majority of timber stands are publicly-owned, and elaborate regulatory systems exist for controlling their use by the private sector.[5] A second case, the metal mining industry, is less important economically than forestry but nevertheless significant. Its regional incidence parallels to a degree that of forestry, but the industry is not the dominant force in any one province the way the forests are in British Columbia. Nor are mineral resources public property in the same sense as the forests, partly because they are non-renewable. As a result, regulation is less comprehensive and associations are primarily advocates working in pressure pluralist networks, in contrast to those in the forest industry, which combine work as advocates with participation in clientele policy networks.

THE ASSOCIATIONAL SYSTEMS

To say that there are no linkages between the forest and the minerals major sectors would be incorrect. Several of Canada's corporate giants provide ties at the level of ownership. Brascan owns Noranda Mines Ltd, which controls, in turn, the forest giant, MacMillan Bloedel. Canadian Pacific now controls the BC firm CIP Inc., Forest Products in addition to interests in mining with Fording Coal. British Columbia Forest Products is owned in part by Alberta Energy Corporation, which has large holdings in the oil, gas, and coal industries. The British Columbia Resources Investment Corporation is active in the forestry industry and in coal mining through Westar Resources. Such major petroleum companies as Gulf Canada and Imperial Oil are increasingly important players in the coal mining sector. Despite this integration at the level of the corporation, there is no integration to date between the forest and minerals major sectors at the level of associations.

The Forest Industries

Analytically speaking, the forest industry until recently, subdivided into two sectors: the first prepared logs for the pulp and paper industry and the second for the lumber and wood manufacturing industries. To a significant extent, large integrated companies in Canada today both cut wood and manufacture it into lumber, pulp, or various kinds of paper. Operating somewhat in the shadow of these larger companies are many smaller firms, which either sign sub-contracts with the large firms to cut wood or own a private woodlot, the trees of which they log and sell to other companies. The lumber sector is perhaps a little more diverse than the pulp and paper industry. It includes large, integrated companies, particularly in British Columbia, plus a broader range of medium and smaller-sized firms operating sawmills or manufacturing furniture or other wood products.

These two groups of end products provide a key point for differentiation in the national associational system between the Canadian Wood Council and the Canadian Pulp and Paper Association (CPPA) (see Table 14). The former is a peak association, the member associations of which represent timber owners, loggers, and manufacturers and sellers of lumber and lumber products; the latter is a direct membership association grouping pulp and paper companies. I discuss the CPPA at greater length in chapter 10. These two associations, in turn, join the Canadian Lumbermen's Association and most provincial associations in an overarching peak association for the industry formed in 1983, the Canadian Forest Industries Council (CFIC).

Reflecting the divided constitutional jurisdiction in this industry are the strong and plentiful associations at the provincial level. Forest industry associations representing at a minimum the primary extraction components of the sector are found in all provinces except Newfoundland and Prince Edward Island. The closest analogue to the CFIC at this level is the Council of Forest Industries of British Columbia (COFI), which represents lumber, plywood, shingles and shakes, and pulp and paper companies. The remaining western associations listed in Table 14 are oriented primarily to the lumber markets. The provincial associations in eastern Canada represent companies producing for the pulp and paper markets.[6] Picked up at the provincial level but not at the national level is the division in the industry between the small, independent logging companies and the large integrated firms. For example, the Truck Loggers Association and the B.C. Independent Loggers' Association represent the former and COFI the latter in British Columbia.

Table 14
Associational System, Forest Industry, 1985

GENERAL ASSOCIATIONS

National/International
Canadian Forest Industries Council
Canadian Wood Council*
Canadian Pulp and Paper Association*

Provincial
Council of Forest Industries of British Columbia*†
  Cariboo Lumber Manufacturers' Association*†‡
  Interior Lumber Manufacturers Association*†‡
  Northern Interior Lumber Sector*†‡
British Columbia Independent Loggers Association
Truck Loggers' Association (BC)
North West Loggers' Association (BC)
Alberta Forest Products Association*†
Central Forest Products Association*†
Ontario Forest Industries Association*
L'Association des industries forestières du Québec*
New Brunswick Forest Products Association*
Nova Scotia Forest Products Association*
Nova Scotia Woodlot Owners and Operators Association

FUNCTIONALLY SPECIALIZED ASSOCIATIONS

Safety
Forest Products Accident Prevention Association (Ontario)
L'Association de sécurité des industriels forestiers du Québec
Quebec Logging Safety Association
New Brunswick Forest Industries Safety Association

Industrial Relations
Forest Industrial Relations Ltd
Interior Forest Labour Relations Association
North Cariboo Forest Labour Relations Association (CONIFER)

Conservation
Canadian Forestry Association (a confederation of provincial associations
   from all provinces except Prince Edward Island)
Poplar Council of Canada

Table 14 (continued)

Professionals
Canadian Institute of Forestry (formerly Canadian Society of Forest
   Engineers)
Association of B.C. Professional Foresters
Association of Registered Professional Foresters of New Brunswick
L'Ordre des ingénieurs forestiers du Québec
Ontario Professional Foresters Association
Canadian Pulp and Paper Association, Technical Section

Research
Pulp and Paper Research Institute of Canada
Forest Engineering Research Institute of Canada
FORINTEK

---

* Member of the Canadian Forest Industries Council.
† Member of the Canadian Wood Council.
‡ Member of the Council of Forest Industries of British Columbia.

The division of powers also creates a place for some functionally
specialized associations at the provincial level. In Ontario, Quebec,
and New Brunswick, associations founded with the charge to educate
woodsmen in accident prevention exist to implement many sections
of the occupational health and safety and workmen's compensation
laws. In British Columbia, the Occupational Health and Safety departments of COFI and its member associations (see Table 14) assume
this function. A second functional division arises in British Columbia
where labour relations law has encouraged the growth of the employers' associations listed in Table 14. Very much players in the
associational system as well are the provincial associations grouping
professional foresters in New Brunswick, Quebec, Ontario, and British Columbia. Many of these same foresters also belong to a separate
national organization, the Canadian Institute of Forestry. The fourth
functional division in the associational system relates to forest conservation, the raison d'être of the Canadian Forestry Association and
its provincial associations. This conservation wing is tied to other
parts of the system through the large forestry companies, which not
only are members but also contribute the largest block of funds.

The associational system is completed by three research institutes,
funded jointly by government and industry, which are tied closely
to provincial and national associations in the industry but are not,
strictly speaking, associations themselves. Of these two, the Forest
Engineering Research Institute of Canada (FERIC) is the more important to the primary forestry industry per se. The Pulp and Paper

Research Institute devotes most of its program to topics related to pulp and paper manufacturing and will be discussed in more detail in chapter 10. It is listed here only because a small part of its program is directed to the investigation of the raw material properties of wood. Forintek Canada Corp. serves the solid wood product sectors by providing technical support to codes and standards committees as well as conducting basic and applied research.

The forest industries associational system differs from those found in other resource sectors as well as in secondary manufacturing principally in its high degree of vertical integration across sector and territory. The CFIC brings together the primary extractive, the lumber, and the pulp and paper sectors of the industry on the national plane as well as all the relevant provincial associations. The Canadian Wood Council includes most of the lumber-oriented provincial forestry associations as its members. The eastern-based forest industry associations, more oriented to the pulp and paper sector, belong neither to the Wood Council nor to the CPPA. The Woodlands Section of the CPPA, which deals with the problems of the primary (logging) industry, has "section branches" for the Maritimes, northeastern Quebec, the Ottawa Valley, and central Ontario, but none for western Canada.[7] The CPPA then does not have a developed structure for integrating regional interests. Perhaps in an industry dominated by large, national firms, such a structure is less necessary. The absence of formal links between the national association and its provincial counterparts also characterizes professional foresters' associations. The provincial associations keep in touch informally with the Canadian Institute of Forestry but are not directly affiliated to it in any way. We shall see that this type of informal, weak affiliate relationship between a national association and provincial counterparts, a legacy in all probability of constitutional arrangements, occurs also in metal mining.

The most notable example of vertical integration at the provincial level occurs, not surprisingly, in British Columbia. The COFI was formed in 1960 following the amalgamation of the following groups: the B.C. Lumber Manufacturers' Association, the B.C. Loggers' Association, the Northern Interior Lumbermen's Association, the Consolidated Red Shingle Association, the B.C. Division of the Canadian Pulp and Paper Association, and the Plywood Manufacturers' Association. BC pulp and paper companies have retained as well their membership in the CPPA. Similar developments have not occurred in other provinces. Vertical integration, however, does not extend to include organic links between the general industry associations listed in the first half of Table 14 and those in the second half that are functionally specialized.

The Mineral Industries

Each sector of the mineral industries – coal, petroleum and natural gas, other minerals – has its own associations which are, in turn, relatively autonomous from those in other minerals sectors. Table 15 indicates that distinct national-level associations exist in each of these three sectors (the original name of the Mining Association of Canada was the Canadian Metal Mining Association). The special institutes for gold, silver, and zinc have domains that are North America–wide, and these groups are somewhat separate from the others. Provincial-level associations subdivide less along commodity lines, given that production in each group tends to be regionally concentrated, except in Quebec, which has separate associations for metallic minerals and asbestos.[8] The petroleum and metal mining sectors follow the pattern observed in the forest industry, where small and large firms congregate in separate associations. The Canadian Petroleum Association (CPA) represents the large multinational oil companies; the Independent Petroleum Association of Canada (IPAC) speaks on behalf of "independent" and smaller Canadian firms. Whereas the Prospectors and Developers Association represents any or all small mining operators, the Mining Association of Canada (MAC) retains only the larger mining companies on its rolls. Differentiation on the basis of firm size occurs also in British Columbia, where the Mining Association of British Columbia represents the larger companies and the two BC chambers listed in Table 15 the smaller ones. The table shows also that the associational system for minerals has some of the functional divisions found in the forest industry, including safety groups, professional societies, and research bodies. Missing from the minerals system are conservation groups and industrial relations associations.

Differentiation by territory is as pronounced for minerals as for the forest industries. With the exception of petroleum, provincial organizations have only weak, informal ties with their national equivalent groups. The CPA has semi-autonomous regional sub-units in British Columbia and Saskatchewan. The Arctic and Eastcoast Petroleum Operators groups enter into ad hoc alliances with the CPA. The Mining Association of British Columbia and the Alberta Chamber of Resources both profess to represent coal companies (among others) but have no formal ties with the Coal Association of Canada. The MAC (metals) has no provincial branches but places presidents of provincial associations ex officio on its board of directors: "There are in Canada a series of provincial mining associations, chambers of mines etc. and since those organizations are pretty well-supported by the same companies as are members of the MAC, it can be said

Table 15
Associational Systems, Mining, 1980

COAL

Coal Association of Canada
Mining Association of British Columbia
Alberta Chamber of Resources
Mining Association of Nova Scotia

PETROLEUM AND NATURAL GAS

Canadian Petroleum Association (divisions in British Columbia and
    Saskatchewan as well as Alberta)
Independent Petroleum Association of Canada
Alberta Chamber of Resources
Arctic Petroleum Operators Association
Eastcoast Petroleum Operators Association
Canadian Oil Scouts Association

OTHER MINERALS

Mining Association of Canada
Prospectors and Developers Association of Canada
Mining Association of British Columbia
B.C. and Yukon Chamber of Mines
Chamber of Mines of Eastern British Columbia
Northwest Territories Chamber of Mines
Yukon Chamber of Mines
Alberta Chamber of Resources
Saskatchewan Mining Association
Manitoba Mining Association
Ontario Mining Association
Quebec Metal Mining Association
Quebec Asbestos Mining Association
The Gold Institute
The Silver Institute
The Zinc Institute

SPECIALIZED ASSOCIATIONS

Safety
Mines Accident Prevention Association of Ontario

Table 15 (continued)

Professional

Canadian Institute of Mining and Metallurgy
Canadian Well Logging Society
Canadian Society of Petroleum Geologists
Canadian Society of Exploration Geophysicists
Canadian Mineral Analysts
Mineralogical Association of Canada
Canadian Geoscience Council

Research

Petroleum Recovery Institute
Institute of Occupational and Environmental Health
Coal Mining Research Centre
Mining Industry Research Organization of Canada
Petroleum Research Communication Foundation

---

there is a loose affiliation of companies."9 As in the pulp and paper industry, dominance by large companies appears to relieve associations somewhat of the need for formal structures for territorial integration.

Integration across commodity sectors is also ad hoc at best on the national level. Associations invite one another to their annual meetings, and they get together yearly at the meetings of the provincial ministers of mines. Provincial associations are more integrating: some organize more than one sector. The Alberta Chamber of Resources, for example, claims to represent coal, energy, and metal producers. Ties with the professional groups vary by sector. The MAC has traditionally maintained very close links with the Canadian Institute of Mining and Metallurgy, but ties between the CPA and IPAC and the several petroleum industry professional groups are less developed.

In summary, associational systems in the resource industries are distinguished by two properties. First, although well differentiated by commodity and by territory, these various units, in turn, are not integrated through formal structures. Instead, relations are informal and unstructured. Co-ordination appears to be accomplished through the large companies that dominate these sectors. The companies are the glue: they belong simultaneously to national and provincial associations as well as to general and more functionally specialized associations. Second, as in the forest industry, the associational system embraces not only firms but also associations of professionals working in technical areas or in research and development. Similarly, industry-sponsored research organizations work closely with both the general business associations and the professionals' groups.

THE BC FOREST INDUSTRY

The first of two case studies in this chapter describes interest intermediation in the forest industry in British Columbia. This case shows well how the system of forest associations outlined in Table 14 works on behalf of the industry and provides, in addition, unique Canadian examples of clientele pluralist networks. Approximately 10 per cent of the BC labour force is employed directly in the industry, which accounts for over 45 per cent of the province's manufacturing shipments.[10] British Columbia is the leading province in two sub-sectors – logging and manufactured wood products, including lumber – and trails Quebec and Ontario in pulp and paper products.

First, one characteristic of the industry that shapes associative action is its activity in international markets. In 1984, the industry exported goods valued at $15.6 billion, over 15 per cent of all Canadian exports.[11] (The agriculture and food industries exported $7 billion of products, and the crude petroleum sector, $2.9 billion.) Even more important, the industry generated net foreign exchange earnings in 1984 of $14.1 billion, more than any other single major sector.[12] Sixty per cent of BC exports come from the industry. In 1980, Canada contributed 10.1 per cent of the value of world exports of forest products; British Columbia by itself was responsible for 8.7 per cent of the world total.[13] The pre-eminent market for these exports was the United States, which received 63 per cent of the Canadian total in 1980, followed by Japan at 9 per cent and the United Kingdom at 7 per cent.[14] The largest Canadian suppler of the US market for all forest products save newsprint was British Columbia. The province shipped 56 per cent of its softwood lumber to the United States in 1984, and 14 per cent to the rest of Canada.[15]

This international trade is dominated by large, vertically integrated companies. Marchak estimates that 70 to 90 per cent of BC timber licences were held by the 10 largest companies in the late 1970s.[16] The same companies accounted for 35 per cent of the lumber, 74 per cent of the plywood and veneer, and 90 per cent of the pulp facilities.[17] Four of the five largest companies, based on "committed allowable cut" (MacMillan Bloedel, Westar Timber, Canadian Forest Products, and Northwood), are Canadian-owned, but the next ten or so on the list were foreign-owned.[18]

Second, because the sector is an international industry, another characteristic affecting business-government relations is a growing

shortage of wood.[19] Each government agency that has examined the
forest sector recently and the industry itself, agree that unless coun-
termeasures are taken soon, harvests will not meet demand. Several
developments have led to this problem. The amount of reasonably
accessible virgin forest left for logging is declining. In some areas,
forest management practices in logged areas have not been sufficiently intensive, while many programs to fight disease and pests
have been too small to be effective. Cutting practices have not promoted the highest use of existing timber stands, particularly small
ones.[20] Seed orchard and nursery capacity lag well behind what is
required for the interior forests, although progress has been made.
In 1960 in British Columbia, 6 million seedlings were planted; in
1984, 120 million.[21]

Coinciding with a shortage of wood supply is poor deployment of
qualified personnel. Canada has about 4,400 qualified professional
foresters; only 500 or so are engaged in forest management on the
ground.[22] The resulting average of one forester to every 43,000
productive hectares of forest pales in comparison with 1 per 15,000
hectares in the United States and even larger ratios in Scandinavia.[23]

The shortage of raw materials arises while the international market-place is becoming more complex and competitive. World demand for forest products has been levelling off as new sources of
timber supplies from New Zealand and from tree plantations in
Africa and South America become available. In the major US market,
production has been expanding rapidly in the south. In addition,
US producers have mounted a series of campaigns against imports
of Canadian softwood lumber, arguing that these are subsidized
through Canadian pricing regulations. These challenges have arisen
while Canadian firms faced the need to market more "second growth"
timber, less saleable than virgin timber and with higher production
costs.[24] International competitiveness also depends heavily on sustained research and development (R&D). There, too, Canada is beginning to fall behind its competitors. In 1980, Canadian R&D were
valued at 0.7 per cent of forest products sales, compared to 1.5 per
cent in the United States and even more in Scandinavia, New Zealand, and Japan.[25]

Third, there is a changed socio-political context. The forest is
valued not only for its economic wealth but also as a habitat for
wildlife, as a wilderness for aesthetic reasons, and as a total ecological
system. The purity of its water, the erosion of its soil, and the amount
of debris that it contains are only some of the factors considered in
this systemic view. Public interest groups have risen over the past
two decades to challenge the BC industry over its plans and practices

in such areas as the Queen Charlotte Islands and Meares Island. Encountering, addressing, and fighting in the wider public domain over matters once discussed quietly with public servants, if anyone at all, have made the environment of forest industry firms considerably more complex.

These three problem areas – promoting and sustaining international markets, managing the wood supply, and balancing diverse uses of the forests – have been addressed by governments directly and in co-operation with industry groups. Traditionally, the role of the federal government in the industry has been to facilitate international trade and to promote longer-term R&D. As in agriculture, federal involvement in forest research goes back almost to the turn of the century. The agency currently responsible, the Canadian Forestry Service (CFS), began to assume its present form in 1960 with the merger of the Forestry Branch of the former Department of Northern Affairs and Natural Resources and the Forest Biology Division of the Department of Agriculture. The CFS began recently to operate again under the aegis of the Department of Agriculture following a decade in the Environment Department. The Mulroney government appointed a minister of state for forests, who works with an assistant deputy minister who heads the CFS. The service manages eight research centres spread across the country and is the agency mainly responsible for overseeing the federal government's 38 per cent share of R&D expenditure in the industry.[26]

Some of these expenditures are directed to institutes funded jointly with industry. Thus the Western Forest Products Laboratory, formerly run by the Canadian Forestry Service, is now operated by a private corporation, FORINTEK, funded jointly by the federal government and industry. Similarly, the Forest Engineering Research Institute of Canada (FERIC) emerged as the successor to the Woodlands Research Division of the Pulp and Paper Research Institute and the Logging Research Program of the Forest Management Institute run by the Canadian Forestry Service. Slightly over 50 per cent of FERIC's 1984 budget of $3.4 million came from industry. The Western Division of the Institute employed a manager, a research director, ten researchers, and four forestry technologists in 1981. In total, industry was responsible for 39 per cent of R&D in Canada at this time.[27]

The involvement of the BC provincial government arises directly from its ownership of over 93 per cent of the productive forests. In exercising the rights of ownership, the basic policy of the government has been to ensure "a sustained yield of timber" from the forest base. As owner of this forest base, the government has assumed primary responsibility for its maintenance. In order to exercise this responsibility, it has favoured the growth of large, integrated firms in the belief that such firms will have a greater interest in the long-term maintenance of the resource and hence be more reliable and more responsible in its harvest.[28] It has granted these companies long-term timber licences and public expenditures in the infrastructure needed for transportation and for services in company towns. Working mainly through the BC Forest Service, the government has elaborated forest management, reforestation, and protection programs. Unfortunately, chronic understaffing and dependence on unpredictable annual budget allocations have hampered the effectiveness of the service.[29] The principal site for educating the professional foresters who staff the service has been the Faculty of Forestry at the University of British Columbia. The Science Council of Canada has noted that this faculty, and the five others like it across the country, have suffered as well from underfunding by provincial governments and are too small to meet the need for trained personnel.[30]

The provincial government seeks to manage the resource as well through the regulation of harvesting rights, annual allowable cuts, and pricing. The key instrument for the latter is stumpage, the payment of a royalty or rent for the use of the resource. Calculated by the BC Forest Service separately for interior and coastal logging, stumpage in the former region is defined as the selling price of lumber and chips in a relevant area minus the mill operating costs for an operator of average efficiency plus an allowance for profit and various risks. The service can administer such a system only if it maintains clear communication lines to industry in order to obtain the relevant technical information and secures industry's co-operation over time.

In light of industry structure and the configuration of state policies and institutions, industry associations play several key roles in the policy system. First, they constitute an important line of defence for large integrated companies wishing to maintain significant influence over forest management policy. Three associations play complementary roles in this defensive system. An examination of these roles begins with the Forest Act, which sets out the regulatory framework for the use of the resource and reflects the approach favoured by these large firms. Like many laws attempting to regulate economic activity, it is vague. "Unfortunately while the legislation sets out the goals and framework of regulation, it does not contain precise criteria for setting harvest rates or determining the value of standing timber. In large part, the criteria are determined administratively."[31]

The specification of the regulations, then, requires close co-operation among the forests department bureaucracy, the BC Forest Service, and the industry. Working primarily through the Council of the Forest Industries of British Columbia (COFI), the industry participates actively in the formulation and administration of the policies that govern its access to the forest. In our terms, policy is made within a clientele pluralist framework. COFI has a Forests and Environment Department, staffed by professional foresters, that works actively with government agencies on forestry regulations, stumpage appraisals, land use, environmental protection, and the like. This department works under the vice-president, forests and environment, in the association's executive structure.

COFI's capacity to apply influence and to exercise power on behalf of its members is complemented by the behaviour of a second group, the Association of B.C. Professional Foresters (ABCPF). Generally speaking, this group has not spoken out for the public interest but has remained relatively inward-looking and self-protective, as is often the case with professional associations. Formally, this group has three objectives: (1) ensuring that the forests are managed by professionally qualified foresters; (2) promoting policies of integrated use of forest lands to provide the greatest social and economic returns to society; and (3) advising governments and the public of the implications of policies affecting the use of forest lands.[32] In practice, until at least 1980, the association restricted itself to the first objective. Using the standard tools of a professional association – a board of examiners, a registrar, a code of ethics, and a discipline and standards committee – the association confers the title of registered professional forester (RPF) on its members, using authority delegated from the provincial government. Forestry companies and the BC Forest Service collaborate by hiring primarily RPFs for forestry jobs. As a result, instead of being a neutral objective proponent of planned, integrated forest use and a defender of the resource, the ABCPF has been a largely silent participant in the management system run by the companies, COFI, and the government. The tension between these two possible roles has plagued the association in recent years. The president's 1979 report illustrates this division well:

I believe that in stressing registration as our main function, we reinforce the public's image of professional associations as being mainly self protective. Until we acknowledge and execute our *duty* in guiding the public and government towards the level of forestry on which our Province depends, we will not be given *responsibility* for management. It is small wonder that a recent government publication, in discussing timber shortages, contains the questions: "Where were the professional foresters when this sorry record was being written?" ... Will the public soon echo these questions? How long will it be before the public and the government hear what foresters have to say? For certain, it will not be before we speak.³³

Maintaining influence and a grasp on state power requires, as well, cultivation of a positive view of the industry among the public. Such support becomes crucial when the industry is challenged by environmentalist and other public interest groups. COFI is particularly well adapted for this type of advocacy role. The association has created a vice-president's position specifically for Government and Public Affairs and placed under this officer Government Relations and Public Relations departments for support. Complementing the efforts of these departments are those of a powerful board of directors. The eight active members of the association who pay the largest dues have the right to appoint their own director. This practice ensures that executives from large companies such as MacMillan Bloedel and BC Forest Products are available when needed for lobbying senior political leaders.

In addition to COFI, the industry also has the British Columbia Forestry Association (BCFA) available for these purposes. This association is tied closely to the companies in that 77 per cent of its revenue from fees comes from them, 10 per cent from the general public, and 13 per cent from a government grant.³⁴ The large companies pay proportionately more of these fees because dues are assessed on the basis of a percentage of the hourly payroll of the company member. The primary objective of the BCFA – to educate the public on "full development" and "utilization" of forest resources and on their protection – converges well with the objectives of industry. The association puts on seminars explaining government forestry legislation and promoting fire management and control. Its staff of 25 runs a "Project Learning Tree" for the use of teachers and their pupils wishing to learn about forest programs, operates five environmental centres with programs and camping facilities, and manages Junior Forest Warden Clubs and summer camps. The association also administers in British Columbia such national Canadian Forestry Association (CFA) programs as National Forest Week, the Smokey Bear Campaign, and the National Forest Fire Prevention Poster Contest.

Government responsibility for management of the resource has led to a history of involvement with such associations. In 1900, following years of agitation by fruit growers, lumber interests, and a few forestry academics, federal government officials founded the

national parent body, the CFA.[35] Its first meeting took place in the
Railway Committee Room of the House of Commons, the King's
Printer published its first annual report in 1902, and for a number
of years the federal Department of the Interior managed the association.[36] Even today, the governor-general is the patron of the BCFA,
the prime minister its honorary president, and the premier and
ministers of forests, education, recreation and tourism, and environment are ex officio directors. In short, the BCFA joins COFI and
the ABCPF in working *within* the existing policy system as a participant
and supporter of existing policies. It is not, therefore, to be confused
with naturalist societies, which tend to be more critical of the fundamental principles of existing policy.

Complementing this first defensive role is a more offensive one
focused on the problem of access to international markets. Of primary importance here is the part played by COFI, a part quite unlike
that performed by any other Canadian association. After the Canadian
Standards Association and the Canadian Bankers Association, COFI
is the third largest business association in Canada, with a staff of 110
and a budget, in 1985, of $10.5 million.[37] The association directs 45
per cent of this budget, almost $4 million, towards promoting BC
forest products in international markets. Its Product Promotion Department, headed by the senior vice-president, wood products, works
to create acceptance and demand for forest products in Canada and
abroad. With offices in the United Kingdom, West Germany, Hol-
land, Japan, and soon Shanghai, the association's fieldmen implement programs funded by COFI and by the federal and provincial
governments. Thus, the association oversees the implementation of
plans developed under the tripartite (federal-provincial-industry)
Cooperative Overseas Market Development Program designed to
find markets outside the United States. Here again there are elements of clientele pluralism – an association is participating in making policy that involves the delivery of goods to its own members.

Working somewhat parallel to COFI on securing international markets, specifically the US market, is the Canadian Wood Council (CWC).
COFI itself along with two lumber manufacturing associations, represents the BC forest industry on the council. The CWC operates in
a fashion analogous to the Masonry Contractors Association described in the previous chapter. Working in co-optive pluralist networks, the council serves on an Associate Committee of the National
Building Code and provides the secretariat to Canadian Standards
Association Committee 086, the wood design code. In both committees it seeks to develop building codes, fire regulations, and product standards. Drawing upon a special set of dues levied on its members

based on their North American lumber shipments, the Wood Council holds membership in the American Wood Council, a promotional body that busies itself with increasing consumer awareness of the benefits of wood-based construction. The council also furnishes 10 per cent of the budget of the National Forest Products Association, which works to ensure that Canadian wood species and technical data are included in the design of US building codes and to provide technical assistance to US agencies on matters pertaining to both US and Canadian lumber.[38]

The Wood Council has recently followed the lead of COFI in founding the Canadian Forest Industries Council. This new overarching peak association for the industry has assumed responsibility for monitoring the actions of American agencies likely to make decisions affecting Canadian lumber imports, particularly the erection of non-tariff barriers. A second strategy employed by the BC industry in its fight against non-tariff barriers involves ensuring that lumber is graded so as to be suitable for both the Canadian and American markets. Thus an autonomous BC division belongs to the Pacific Lumber Inspection Bureau, an American association responsible for enforcing standards for sorting, selecting, grading, inspecting, measuring, and tallying timber and timber products. This bureau in turn belongs to the Canadian Lumber Standards Committee and its American counterpart and employs in British Columbia eight field superivsors and 100 field inspectors.

In summary, in British Columbia the combination of public ownership of the resource and its leasing to private firms for development creates a context for close industry-government collaboration. The regulatory system requires intensive industry participation and has fostered clientele pluralist networks. The partnership spills over into trade promotion, with COFI, in particular, playing a key administrative role. In most respects, government organizations are sympathetic to industry and supportive of private as opposed to public enterprise. Associations do not have their origins in class conflict nor have government agencies been spawned to contain class struggles, the situation we found in agriculture.

METAL MINING

Like the logging of the forests, the mining, preparation, and sale of metals constitute one of Canada's great resource industries. In 1980, the metal mining industry employed directly 89,000 Canadians and supported the existence of over 100 small and medium-sized communities.[39] The leading metals in descending order by dollar value in 1981 were iron ore, copper, nickel, zinc, gold, uranium, and silver.[40] Approximately 80 per cent of the metals produced are exported. In 1980, the United States received 34 per cent of crude metals (ores and concentrates), the European Community (EC) 22 percent, and Japan 18 per cent.[41] Semi-processed metals (smelted and refined) travelled at an even higher rate to the United States – 60 per cent – compared to 20 per cent to the EC and 4 per cent to Japan.[42] Exports easily exceed imports in this sector, making it a major contributor to the positive side of Canada's balance of trade. Ontario, British Columbia, and Quebec are the leading producers but do not dominate as completely as they do forestry, since Saskatchewan, Newfoundland, and the Northwest Territories are also significant producers.

Competing in international markets has forced the industry to emphasize large-scale production. As a result, the total number of active mining operations is not large. Excluding uranium, 113 mines were producing ore in Canada in January 1983.[43] Five corporations dominate non-ferrous metal mining, accounting for about 75 per cent of the output – International Nickel (Inco), Noranda, McIntyre-Falconbridge, Kidd Creek, and Cominco.[44] Concentration is even higher in ferrous mining, where the top four producers are responsible for slightly over three-quarters of the output.[45] Adjoined to this concentrated corporate sector running large producing mines is a "junior mining" industry composed of smaller, independent exploration and development companies. Predominantly Canadian owned, the "juniors" have a remarkable record in mineral exploration: "Although [their] share of total mineral production expenditures fell from approximately 50 per cent in 1969 to 10 per cent in 1979, this segment of the industry was responsible for 40 per cent of all new discoveries and about one third of the *major* mineral discoveries in the 1970s."[46] These junior companies have a range of problems quite different from their "senior" colleagues.

The context for the associative action of the big companies centres on the following problem: the size of markets for metals is shrinking while competition is becoming more intense.[47] Shrinkage is occurring for several reasons, beginning with the dramatic decline in world economic growth over the past decade and a half. In addition, the arrival of new, more sophisticated alloys and other substitutes such as plastics together with the energy crisis has encouraged downsizing of vehicles of transport and contributed generally to the declining intensity of metal use on a per capita basis in the developed countries. At the same time, less developed countries have expanded production capacity by working primarily through state-owned corporations and drawing upon international funding bodies like the World Bank. A compelling need to obtain foreign exchange and to maintain domestic employment levels makes these countries reluctant to reduce their production, forcing privately owned companies in developed countries to pull back. Other newly developing countries specializing in manufacturing have copied their developed cousins by maintaining high tariffs and non-tariff barriers against smelter and refined products, preferring to import ores and concentrates. As a result, Canadian smelting and refining mills are plagued by serious overcapacity.

In order to remain competitive internationally, Canadian mining companies have turned their attention to costs. Two groups of factors are relevant here. The first pertains to the ore deposits themselves: their size, grade, the type of ore, the depth of the deposits, and their remoteness. The second embraces a host of "external" factors: costs of labour, energy, materials, and capital; environmental protection; level of productivity; access to technology; level of taxation; and exchange rate. The second group of costs is less fixed than the first, and it is here that the major mining companies have directed much of their associative action.

The problems of the junior mining companies are somewhat different. Increased environmental regulation, stricter taxation rules, and revised securities legislation have hampered their growth. Questionable share promotion, unfairly high grading, unsafe working conditions, and environmental damage have brought costs to the industry.[48] As well, technological changes have increased exploration costs. Such technological developments, coupled with more and more impenetrable environmental, securities, and taxation rules, have complicated the juniors' information environment several-fold. Their relative decline over the past decade reflects difficulties in adapting to a much changed environment.

Evidently, relations with governments will be frequent and highly significant for both components of the mining industry. Actions by the federal government have a direct bearing on the costs of energy and environmental protection, on the level of taxes, and on the exchange rate. The Mineral Policy Sector in the Department of Energy, Mines and Resources (EMR) acts occasionally as the industry's advocate for pressuring the relevant sister departments on these issues. Yudelman notes, however, that its willingness to play this role has ebbed and flowed since 1970.[49] The very technical nature of environmental and fiscal policy in mining creates for this agency a certain dependence on the industry for information and advice. Provincial governments set regulations for extraction and the terms for royalty payments. They also control policy in labour relations, occupational health and safety, and environmental protection. Co-ordination among all governments is sought through the annual meetings of ministers of mines, a major event in the industry's calendar.

Perhaps less well known is the large public R&D development system, on the scale of that found in agriculture, which supports the industry in its efforts to improve productivity and efficiency. The Geological Survey of Canada is a major scientific branch of EMR, employing 750 people, about half of whom are scientists.[50] Organized into nine divisions, the survey seeks to provide a comprehensive inventory and set of studies of the country's geological framework and related processes. For both junior and senior mining firms, such information is fundamental to all mineral exploration, assessment, and development. Complementing the Geological Survey is the Canada Centre for Mineral and Energy Technology (CANMET). Founded in 1907 as the federal Mines Branch, CANMET conducts fundamental and applied research on mining and process technologies, properties of materials, metals fabrication, and work related to mineral and energy management, environmental impact, and worker health and safety.[51] The centre employs about 700 scientists, engineers, technicians, and support staff in its work.[52]

Despite quite striking similarities between the forest and the metal mining sectors in having problems maintaining international markets, the industries manage their relations with governments through associations quite differently. The playing of an advocacy role is more pronounced in mining and the availability of clientele or co-optive pluralist policy networks more restricted. Three factors help account for these differences. First, mineral resources are non-renewable. Ownership of the resource does not remain in the hands of the state nor does the public power have the same interest in how the resource is extracted. In mining, as compared to forests, governments have not so much stressed use of the tax system to stimulate and control development and have been less concerned to regulate directly extraction and pricing of the resource. Regulation, it will be remembered, was a major reason for clientele pluralism in the forest industry.

Second, the minerals sector includes a diverse range of products. Each has its own peculiarities in the extraction and refining process, its own markets, and its distinctive end uses. As a result, marketing cannot be handled by a sector-wide organization like COFI and thus tends to be much more of a company function.[53] This product diversity also mandates a different division of responsibilities in R&D. Federal and provincial governments concern themselves with general issues of extraction, processing, and utilization technology, and the large corporations focus on applications research. Lacking a common product base, they have little room for large, joint forestry-style industry-government institutes.

As a consequence of these differences, the industry has created an associational system geared to compete with other interests in pressure pluralist networks on taxation, environmental protection, occupational health and safety, and monetary policy. Clientele and co-optive networks are less developed than in forestry, occurring in some provinces in occupational health and safety and at the federal level for policy formulation related to international markets. Finally, the associational system provides a co-ordinating forum for bringing together government and industry research efforts. Following is a brief illustration of each of these roles.

The Mining Association of Canada and the three provincial associations most concerned with metals – Ontario, Quebec, and British Columbia – have the kinds of structures typical of an advocacy group. Their boards of directors draw upon senior company executives for meetings with influential politicians. Supporting the boards are normally a department and a committee devoted to public relations. The structure outlined for the Ontario Mining Association in Table 16 is typical. Inco and Falconbridge have two senior executives and Kidd Creek one serving on the board. A series of committees deals with subjects for lobbying: labour relations, environmental protection, taxation, mining rules, and occupational health. The committees mirror functional divisions within larger corporations in the industry. Accordingly, when the association goes to Queen's Park in Toronto to discuss environmental legislation, the senior environmental managers of Inco, Falconbridge, and Kidd Creek go as well. The combined effect of collective action, major corporate power, and professional expertise enhances greatly the likelihood of success. The OMA's structure illustrates well how associations representing very concentrated sectors with powerful individual firms can channel and target that power for utmost effect.

Like the other associations, and analogous to the forestry case, the OMA runs a large public relations operation in support of its lobbying efforts. Hence, in 1980, it placed advertisements on the industry's behalf in more than 50 daily and weekly newspapers and in *Time* magazine and distributed brochures to educational institutions and tourism outlets. Interested secondary school geography and geology teachers were provided with a tour of mines and processing operations and given a package of slides on the subject appropriate for classroom use. The Association put on a "Meet the Miners" dinner

Table 16

Company Representation on Ontario Mining Association, 1980

Association	Inco	Falconbridge	Texasgulf‡
BOARD OF DIRECTORS	Senior VP, President, OD*	VP, Planning, President, CND†	Senior VP, Production
COMMITTEES			
Labour Relations	Manager of Industrial Relations, OD	Manager, Employee and Community Relations	VP, Employee Relations
Wire Rope	Senior Specialist on Hoisting, Mining & Milling Section, OD	Mechanical Super- intendent	Assistant Maintenance Super- intendent
Public Relations	Director of Public Relations, OD	Community Relations Manager	VP, Public Relations
Energy	Manager of Utilities, OD	Supervising Electrical Engineer	Chief Engineer, Technical Services
Industrial Employment Standards	Assistant VP, Mining & Milling, OD	Manager, Employee & Community Relations	Assistant Mine Super- intendent
Ground Control	Chief Mines Engineer, OD	Director of Mining Engineering & Research	–
Operating Engineers	Manager of Utilities, OD	–	–
Environmental	Supervisor, Environmental Control OD	Manager, Environmental Control	Senior Environmental Engineer
Taxation	Manager, Canadian Taxes	Manager of Taxation	Senior Counsel and Assistant Secretary
Retail Sales Tax	Senior Tax Representative	Manager, Purchasing & Sales Taxes	Purchasing Agent

Table 16 (continued)

Association	Inco	Falconbridge	Texasgulf‡
Mining Rules	Assistant to the President, OD	Manager, Mines, CND	VP, Mining
Occupational Health	Medical Director, OD	Executive Assistant to VP	Safety Supervisor
Property Tax	Senior Tax Representative	Assessment and Municipal Tax Manager	Controller

SOURCE: Ontario Mining Association.
* Ontario Division.
† Canadian Nickel Division.
‡ Now Kidd Creek Mines.

for politicians and officials and distributed a facts and comments sheet to all attending. It also ran a speakers program in conjunction with the MAC. Public relations was thus oriented towards building public support, which presumably could be drawn upon in times of crisis.

Associations such as the Prospectors and Developers Association and the B.C. and Yukon Chamber of Mines representing junior companies have slightly different structures. In addition to the types of committees found in the OMA, they have committees on securities legislation and technical geological information. Supplementing these are selective benefits such as the following offered by the BC and Yukon chamber: an Annual Placer Mining School, a journal (the *Mining Exploration and Development Review*), annual publication of a location map of mining properties, a mineral identification service, and short courses on geophysics, ore petrology, and outcome estimates.

The mining industry, then, is able to use these associations, its corporate muscle, and the political strength it draws from being the backbone of many small communities to work effectively in pressure pluralist networks. The very loose informal ties between the MAC and the provincial groups multiply the independent points of pressure vis-à-vis political leaders.[54] When there is consensus on action across the industry, the effect can be very telling indeed. However, weak integration can redound against the industry when it is divided. I have argued elsewhere that as ties between federal and provincial associations become weaker, an industry becomes more susceptible to being whipsawed by governments when these governments are in conflict.[55] This sorry fate becomes even more likely in this industry, where the differences between small and large companies rest only slightly below the surface. As Yudelman concludes, the chances for developing long-term policy and a stable domestic environment are small: "These internal divisions, within both government and industry, are important. Both appear unable to speak for themselves with a united voice. And if neither government nor industry can decide within themselves on a mineral policy, how can they get together to formulate something lasting and coherent?"[56]

Such a failing becomes even more crucial in the current policy environment. With governments more reluctant to intervene and to "manage" sectors in the 1980s than they were in the 1970s, a partial vaccuum is created for the industry in the policy-making process: "This withdrawal, however partial, provides an opportunity for the private sector to get more involved in the policy-making process. It needs to aim at being more pro-active, participating in the setting of strategy, rather than confining itself to the traditional reactive response, limiting its contribution merely to making special interest representations."[57] Does the industry have the organizational capacity to participate more in policy? Its well-honed advocacy organizations and their weakly integrated associational system inhibit a more proactive role.

Complementing these advocacy activities in pressure pluralist networks is a series of clientele pluralist networks that the industry has been strong enough to create in selected issue areas. At the federal level, the MAC has come to work in such a network with EMR for the design of various policies. A notable recent example is the MAC/EMR Subgroup on International Mineral and Metal Markets. Formed late in 1982, the sub-group was created for the exchange of views and information on short- and long-term international market problems. The hope is that the work of the group will yield an inventory of market access problems for selected major commodities and from there provide a basis for policy development. The sub-group is chaired jointly by the president of the MAC and the assistant deputy minister (minerals) of EMR. Its members included senior executives from Canada's largest mining companies.[58] It follows in a line of "task forces" or "committees" that the MAC has been asked to join for policy development since the late 1970s.[59]

At the provincial level, clientele pluralist networks have been even further developed in occupational health and safety, although the pattern differs by province. In British Columbia, the Mining Association has a regular committee for safety and compensation supported by three professional specialists. The Quebec Metal Mining Association has an Accident Prevention Committee, with its own director, professional staff, and budget, which regularly inspects mining sites of members seeking to identify problems. In Ontario, clientele pluralism is advanced further under the auspices of a separate assocation, the Mines Accident Prevention Association of Ontario (MAPAO). This association grew out of the Accident Prevention Committee of the Ontario Mining Association and was recognized as a separate association under the Workmen's Compensation Board Act in 1930. Under this act, employers in given industries, with the approval and under the control of the board, may form themselves into an association for the purpose of education in accident prevention. If the board judges the association sufficiently representative, the association's rules of operation become binding on all firms in the industry.

The MAPAO is a well-resourced organization to which the government delegates responsibility for developing and implementing policies on accident prevention. With a budget of slightly over $800,000 in 1980, it employed 20 people, including engineers, visual aids technicians, an industrial hygienist, and a training co-ordinator. The association offers supervisory personnel courses on safety and on control of ventilation and dust, of noise, and of hazardous materials. It has also developed silica- and asbestos-dust monitoring guidelines and provides a dust measuring service. Over the years, the association has fought steadfastly to keep control over these matters and not to share them with labour or the "people," in short, to keep the network clientele rather than corporatist. To date the kind of argument made by its sister organization in the forest industry has held sway with the government: "Accident prevention work is as much a 'tool of management' as production facilities, financial management or personnel relations. Safety and health are an integral part of the production process."[60] Whether the argument will continue to stand in the way of ever-increasing demands from labour for a role in this area is unclear.

Finally, the associational system provides a clearing-house and centre for co-ordination in research. As we have seen, research related to this industry is carried out in federal government laboratories, provincial research institutes, universities, and the companies themselves. The Canadian Institute of Mining and Metallurgy (CIM), established in 1898, links these centres. The CIM has seven autonomous product divisions: coal, geology, industrial minerals, mechanical-electrical, the Metallurgical Society of the CIM, metal mining, and the Petroleum Society. The institute's staff of 30, with a $1-million budget, publishes a range of scientific and applied research journals. The 62 regional branches of the CIM bring together technical specialists for further discussion of research and scientific papers. Ties to industry and government are close. In 1980 the president of the CIM was a vice-president at Noranda, and the past president was manager of exploration properties for Cominco. The president and the executive director attend ex officio the annual conferences of the ministers of mines.

CONCLUSIONS

In order to compare business-government relations in resource industries to those in agriculture and construction, we make a conceptual distinction between political influence and the exercise of state power. Political influence refers to the ability of a given group to persuade politicians to act in response to its demands. In the exercise of state power, the group is delegated state authority to respond autonomously to its own demands, and the group's demands change from inputs to "withinputs," to use Easton's term.[61]

Obviously, a group that can trade influence for the exercise of state power is more likely to succeed on its members' behalf. In comparing agriculture, construction, and resources, we find that associations representing agriculture and resources enjoy more political influence than those representing construction. The influence of agricultural groups arises from sheer numbers. Of course, there are more construction employers than farmers, but farmers tend to be geographically concentrated in a number of ridings across the country. Through the process of class struggles, Canadian farmers have created associations well adapted to advocacy and policy participation, which represent a very high proportion of farmers and, until recently, have been integrated into hierarchical systems encompassing most commodities and all provinces. Construction associations do not represent anywhere near such a proportion of their domains and are not integrated into so encompassing an associational system.

Numbers play a more indirect role in gaining influence for associations representing forests and metals. The big resource firms employ many workers and indirectly create jobs for thousands of others. Their effect on the lives of so many voters was bound to give them influence, particularly since these jobs are geographically concentrated. The resource sectors, unlike construction, are concentrated. Economic power accumulates in a few firms. The associations concretize this concentration by putting together boards of directors and committees from virtually all these large firms. Accordingly, the association speaks to politicians with more force than a construction group ever can.

Policy participation takes political influence a step further in that an association shares in the exercise of state power itself, increasing the probability that a group will see its demands realized. Associations in farming and in the resource sectors studied thus far participate in policy-making, but those in the former were active in corporatist networks, while those in the latter worked in clientele pluralist networks. In clientelism the sharing in state power by an association is less public and needs take less account of other interests than in corporatism. Manzer's distinction between practical reasoning and prudential reasoning in decision-making is useful here.[62] In the former, the party making the decision takes into account the interests of all other actors. Decision-making is thus "other-regarding." In the latter, the party taking the decision takes account of its own interests only. Decision-making then is more "self-regarding." These concepts summarize well the difference in decision-making in corporatist and clientele pluralist networks. Practical reasoning predominates in corporatist networks, prudential reasoning in clientelist ones.

That the resource sectors, particularly the BC forest sector, work through clientele networks reflects a more successful translation of economic into political power than that found in agriculture or construction. Resource sectors have sufficient economic importance in particular regions and can concentrate their forces so that they claim and receive a more exclusive say over policies affecting them. They can largely exclude other classes and groups that might demand a say. Farmers have gained a share of state power following a different road – class-based struggle with fractions of the business community. As a class, farmers have been troublesome politically and socially. Corporatist networks may channel and control their demands by tempering them with the views of the state and their opponents. Because they must share their power more broadly, farmers are unlikely to be as politically successful as the resource industries.

CHAPTER NINE

Finance: Clientelism and Self-Regulation

Writing in the mid-1980s about business-government relations in the Canadian financial industry is a delicate enterprise. The financial sector world-wide has undergone sweeping changes over the past decade, and Canada has not been spared. When coupled with the recent deep recession, these changes have contributed to some casualties in the industry. Small, regional banks and trust companies, which sought to establish themselves on the basis of similarly small and risky business loans, have had immense difficulties keeping afloat. In fact, Canada has experienced its first two bank failures since the demise of the Home Bank in 1923 – the Canadian Commercial Bank and the Northland Bank. Some smaller banks have merged with larger institutions. The list of failed trust companies since 1980 is even longer.

These recent, rather spectacular failures tend to distract attention from some more fundamental pressures for change. The Canadian financial system shares with US and British systems an important property: financial and market intermediation have been segregated. Financial intermediaries are those institutions that take the savings of their customers, issue claims upon themselves, and invest these funds for their own account.[1] Traditionally, public policy has further segregated these intermediaries, distinguishing those that take deposits (chartered banks), administer trusts and estates (trust companies), and underwrite life insurance and issue life-contingent annuities (insurance companies). These three functions form the core of three of the four "pillars" of the financial industry. The fourth draws on market intermediaries, those that accept monies "for the purchase of the debt or equity of another corporate entity."[2] Normally investment dealers or stockbrokers, these intermediaries facilitate direct financing – the immediate transaction of business between borrower and lender. In primary markets, they design financial instruments that are attractive to users of capital and investors and engineer their sale from users to investors.[3] They participate in secondary markets by facilitating the sale of financial instruments between investors. Market intermediaries lead investors to direct investment in a business, government, or other user of capital.[4] They are used primarily by governments and large corporations that seek to issue securities, including stocks, bonds, and short-term money market instruments.[5]

In the Canadian financial system there is a certain separation between the finance sector and the "real" sector – industrial and commercial operations. Legislation and accompanying regulations "have prevented, in large part, the intermingling of financial businesses with other commerical and industrial operations."[6] Those who wish to use others' savings have to approach financial or market intermediaries and convince them of the soundness of their investment plans. This requirement, it is assumed, further enhances the soundness of the financial system.

The increased intensity of debate on financial policy centres on challenges to both defining characteristics of the system. Within the industry, the distinctions between the four pillars are becoming more and more blurred as institutions associated with one of the four core functions involve themselves in other functions. Governments have sought thereby to increase competition and efficiency. Also, institutions in the respective pillars have interpreted broadly the powers given to them in legislation. The intermingling of formerly distinct sets of institutions is particularly pronounced among financial intermediaries. Their ability to jump into the domain of market intermediaries or vice versa is much more limited, with important consequences for public policy.

The breaking down of barriers between the pillars brings into question the distinction between financial and real sectors. Over the past decade, there have developed in Canada large financial "supermarkets," corporations that have accumulated companies in several of the four pillars. The two most prominent examples are Power Financial Corporation and Trilon Financial Corporation. Power Financial is controlled by Paul Desmarais and his family. Its assets include Montreal Trust Company and several associated trust companies, the Great West Life Assurance Company, the Investors Group, and Pargesa Holding s.a., an international financial holding company. Trilon is part of the business empire of Edward and Peter Bronfman. Its holdings include Royal Trustco Ltd, Royal Lepage Ltd (real estate and brokerage), London Life Insurance, Wellington

Insurance, and CVL Inc. (vehicle leasing and fleet management). Both
companies have interests in three of the four pillars, lacking only
entry into banking. Both are part of business empires heavily involved in the "real" sector. The Bronfman group includes Brascade
Resources, Noranda, John Labatt Ltd, and Westmin Resources. The
Desmarais holdings include Consolidated Bathurst, publishing and
transportation interests, and CB Pak (packaging).

Debates over these several issues provide the backdrop to business-
government relations in this industry in the 1980s. Associations representing financial intermediaries must act as strong advocates for
their members, seeking legislative changes that would expand their
market opportunities and countering proposals that might deprive
their members of market share. Two brief discussions provide background information on the institutional properties of the four pillars
and on the associational system for the financial industry. In the
discussion that follows, I will examine first the Canadian Bankers
Association (CBA) as an example of a group that plays this role particularly well. The less scalable barrier between market and financial
intermediaries leaves a different role for the principal association
representing the former, the Investment Dealers Association of Canada (IDAC), our second case. Drawing upon a delegation of authority
from the state, the IDAC oversees one of the most sophisticated self-
regulatory policy systems in Canadian politics. This case illustrates
well a highly developed clientele pluralist policy network.

THE FOUR PILLARS

The traditional four-pillar structure of the Canadian financial industry is fast disappearing because of changes in government regulations and the globalization of financial markets. However, the
associational system in the industry has changed much less and continues to mirror the long-standing four-pillar arrangements. In order
to understand well this system, we must begin by reviewing salient
dimensions of each of the four pillars. A historical glance back over
the development of this quadrilateral structure reveals the banking
pillar to be the first that was solidly embedded. The chartered banks
had a series of struggles against other financial intermediaries, resulting usually in a pyrrhic victory, producing ever-increasing concentration of banking capital but diffusion of financial assets. In
1870, the chartered banks had 73 per cent of the assets of all financial
intermediaries; close to 100 years later the ratio stood at 29 per
cent.[7] In the past decade, the banks have improved this ratio to 37
per cent.[8] In 1900 there were close to 200 private banks and over

30 chartered banks in Canada; today, no private banks and only a few chartered (schedule A) banks remain. These divide into three groups: the dominant five (Royal Bank of Canada, Canadian Imperial Bank of Commerce, Bank of Montreal, Bank of Nova Scotia, and Toronto Dominion Bank), the rising sixth, the National Bank of Canada, and (at time of writing) two smaller institutions. The top six account for over 95 per cent of domestic bank assets. The leading five banks are among the largest in North America, the Royal Bank, for example, being the fourth largest.[9]

Since passage of the 1980 Bank Act, foreign banks have become more visible. If a foreign bank can convince the minister of finance that it can make a contribution to competitive banking in Canada and that Canadian banks will receive similar opportunities in its home country, it may be granted letters patent as a schedule B bank and a licence to operate in Canada.[10] It must appoint Canadians to half of its directorships, and its combined domestic assets are limited to a percentage of the total domestic assets of all banks. The chartered banks remain today the major suppliers of commerical credit in Canada. Business loans continue to be the largest component in their assets, with mortgage loans rising rapidly into second place since this market was opened fully to the banks by the 1967 Bank Act.[11]

The chartered banks have followed Canadian traders and resource companies into the international market-place, earning a strong position in the United States, Latin America, and the Caribbean and a major presence in western Europe and in certain Far Eastern countries.[12] In June 1982, Canadian banks possessed 6.1 per cent of the international financial market; the Canadian gross domestic product accounted for 2 per cent of world production.[13] International assets amounted to as little as 34 per cent of total assets for Montreal and the Commerce and as much as 46 per cent for Nova Scotia.[14] These figures are lower than those of such prominent American banks as Citicorp (61 per cent) and Chase Manhattan (59 per cent).[15]

Most institutions in the remaining three pillars share at least one important property with the banks – domestic control. Canada's first trust company, Toronto General Trust Company, was incorporated in Toronto in 1872. Since provincial governments have responsibility for property and civil rights and thus contract law, the emphasis on estates, trusts, and legacies encouraged some, usually smaller trust companies to incorporate themselves with provincial charters. However, 59 of the larger trust companies controlling 66 per cent of the assets come under federal legislation.[16] Some of these bigger concerns have enjoyed close historical associations with the chartered banks: Royal Trust with the Bank of Montreal, Montreal Trust with the Royal Bank, and a provincially chartered company, National Trust (since merged with Victoria and Grey Trust) with the Commerce. These ties have been tempered, however, because the revisions to the Bank Act of 1967 forbade interlocking directorships with the banks and limited bank holdings in trust companies to 10 per cent.

Unlike the schedule A chartered banks, trust companies can be "closely held," i.e. controlled by one individual or group. In fact, of the seven leading companies, only one, Canada Trustco Mortgage Co., was not closely held in 1980; it was taken over by Genstar and subsequently merged with Canada Permanent in 1985. Closely held ownership has been controversial because of the temptation for "self-dealing" – a financial intermediary using funds at its disposal for its own benefit rather than seeking the optimal return for its trustees or depositors.[17] While the trust companies' principal asset is still mortgage loans, their role in business finance has increased significantly since 1970.[18]

The business of companies in insurance is relatively well known and understood. The same cannot be said for investment dealers. Generally speaking, investment dealers occupy themselves with three functions:[19] stock brokering (buying and selling common and preferred stocks on a commission basis), secondary distribution (trading among one another in fixed-interest securities such as bonds, debentures, notes, and bills), and primary distribution (marketing new issues of municipal, provincial, and corporation securities). Recently the industry has seen several big mergers, the most spectacular involving Dominion Securities Ames (itself the product of an earlier merger) and Pitfield Mackay Ross. The new Dominion Securities Pitfield is now challenging Wood Gundy and MacLeod, Young Weir for industry leadership. Another newly formed firm, Gordon Capital Corp., has engineered a rapid rise by diverging from normal industry practices in corporate underwriting.[20] Usually, a group of dealers shares the underwriting of a securities issue with an "out clause" that allows the syndicate to withdraw if market conditions are unfavourable. In contrast, Gordon Capital has used "bought deals": one dealer buys the whole issue outright (thereby requiring a higher capital base), making timing and commitment tighter and faster. If "bought deals" continue to proliferate, they promise to change both the structures of and working relations among existing dealers.

Recent moves to ease the segmentation of the financial community around these four core functions represent a shift away from long-standing government policies. The 1967 Bank Act forced banks to relinquish much of their ownership of trust companies, and the 1980 act restricted, for the first time, the banks' ability to engage in securities dealing.[21] Other regulations have worked in a similar fashion to prevent the blurring of the pillars: investment dealers and members of stock exchanges were ineligible to serve as bank directors;[22] only trust companies could act in a fiduciary capacity, but they were also heavily restricted when it came to diversifying into commerical and personal lending; insurance companies were not allowed to hold more than 30 per cent ownership in any company and were prevented thereby from setting up subsidiaries that would allow them to compete with banks, trust companies, and investment dealers.

Governments have sought to keep ties distant between financial institutions and other sectors of the economy. Banks, for example, may not own more than 10 per cent of the voting shares in other companies. No more than one-fifth of the members of a board of directors of any Canadian corporation may act as the directors of any one bank.[23] Bank and trust company officers are also restricted in their directorships. The report of the Ontario Task Force on Financial Institutions perhaps summarizes the current situation best: "The picture that emerges from such an analysis is that of a financial services industry not organized into discrete sectors in which institutions perform and are required by legislation to perform only their core function, but rather an industry organized into discrete markets for specific financial products or services offered by a wide range of financial institutions."[24]

Federal and provincial governments take a strong interest in the finance industry. The behaviour of financial institutions significantly affects the ability of political leaders to realize broad economic objectives.[25] Certainly in fighting inflation in the 1970s, governments intervened in finance in order to control the supply of money. They have also sought to influence the cost and supply of credit so as to alter consumer spending and reduce perceived instabilities in prices and economic growth. The principal intermediary between the Canadian government and the banks in these broad policy areas is the Bank of Canada.[26] Founded in the midst of the Depression in 1934 (initially as a private institution), it has emerged as a key policy-making institution and has developed and maintained a certain independence from departments of governments. The bank monitors closely the activities of banks and financial markets, publishing weekly statistics used widely in the industry. It participates actively in capital markets, buying and selling government Treasury bills and bonds to influence their price and the level of interest rates. Traders working for the bank also buy and sell foreign currencies in order to control the rate of exchange of the Canadian dollar. The bank operates its own econometric model of the Canadian economy, which it uses to analyse trends and likely consequences of longer-term policies.

Governments regulate financial institutions in order to control self-dealing, avoid conflicts of interest, ensure greater competition and hence efficiency, maintain public confidence in the system, and guard against excessive concentration of ownership. Authorities have also intervened in financial markets to remove rigidities perceived to be blocking the realization of certain social goals.[27] They have sought to redirect the flow of funds using guaranteed loan schemes and industrial development agencies and have even operated their own financial intermediaries (Federal Business Development Bank, Alberta Heritage Savings and Trust Fund, the Caisse de dépôt et placement du Québec, and so on).

THE ASSOCIATIONAL SYSTEM

The associational system in the finance industries summarized in Table 17 shows little integration and much differentiation, particularly in lending and insurance. Most striking is the conformity of their domains with the traditional four-pillar industry structure. One major association dominates each pillar, except insurance, where there are three. Predominant in finance and lending is the Canadian Bankers' Association (CBA), which employs 100 people. Joining it in this sub-sector are the Association of Canadian Financial Corporations, which represents consumers sales finance companies, consumer loans companies, and industrial and commerical loans companies; the Association of Canadian Venture Capital Companies; and associations representing factoring finance companies and chartered customs brokers. Credit unions are listed here although they do not have their own national association; like the co-operative wheat pools, their overarching co-operative organizations act both as commerical companies and as associations. For example, the Fédération de Québec des Caisses populaires Desjardins, which groups many of the local credit unions in Quebec, both services these organizations with inspection staff and other personnel and represents them and their interests before governments.

The structure in the trust pillar is somewhat simple. The Trust Companies Association of Canada (TCA), the only group representing this sub-sector, is the smallest of the major pillar organizations, with ten employees and a budget of a little over $500,000 in 1980. The

Table 17
Associational System, Finance, 1980

Banking and lending	Fiduciary	Securities	Insurance
Canadian Bankers Association (100, n.s.)* └ Institute of Canadian Bankers (50, n.s.)	Trust Companies Association of Canada (10,0.550)† └ Trust Companies Institute (8)	Investment Dealers Association of Canada (30,1.1) └ Canadian Securities Institute Investment Funds Institute of Canada (7,0.225)	GENERAL Insurance Bureau of Canada (150,6) └ Insurance Institute of Canada (30,0.950) Canadian Life and Health Association (50,4.4) └ Life Insurance Institute of Canada Life Underwriters Association of Canada (62,2.7)‡ └ Institute of Chartered Life Underwriters (11) Canadian Boiler and Machinery Underwriters Association Canadian Board of Marine Underwriters Canadian Federation of Insurance Agents and Brokers Associations (4,0.230) Canadian Industrial Risks Insurers Canadian Ship owners Mutual Insurance Association Nuclear Insurance Association of Canada
Association of Canadian Financial Corporations (8,0.3)			
Association of Canadian Venture Capital Companies (0,0.014)			
Factoring and Commercial Financing Conference of Canada (1, n.s.)			
Dominion Chartered Customs House Brokers Association (2, n.s.)			
Credit Union organizations			
SERVICES			
Canadian Payments Association (10)			
Canadian Insolvency Association (1,0.041)			
USERS			
Financial Executives Institute of Canada (3,0.175)			

Table 17 (continued)

Banking-and lending	Fiduciary	Securities	Insurance
Canadian Credit Institute (5,0.22) Canadian Association of Financial Planners			SPECIALIZED GROUPS Canadian Institute of Actuaries (3,0.150) Canadian Independent Adjusters Conference (2,0.085) Canadian Federation of Insurance Claimsmen INDUSTRY SERVICES Association of Independent Insurers Insurers Advisory Organization of Canada (450,10) Insurance Crime Prevention Bureaux (95, n.s.) Society of Fellows of the Insurance Institute of Canada (0,0.003) OTHER Association of Canadian Pension Fund Management (3,0.200)

* Number of employees and annual expenditures in millions of dollars; n.s.: information not supplied.
† Includes expenditures for the Trust Companies Institute.
‡ Includes expenditures for the Institute of Chartered Life Underwriters.

dominant group in the securities sub-sector is the Investment Dealers Association of Canada (IDAC), with a budget in 1980 of over $3 million; the Investment Funds Institute represents open investment and mutual funds companies.

Insurance is the most differentiated of the four sub-sectors. The three dominant national associations are the Insurance Bureau of Canada, representing general and casualty insurance companies; the Canadian Life and Health Association, the voice of life insurance companies; and the Life Underwriters Association of Canada, the members of which are life insurance brokers. Brokers in the general and casualty fields have strong provincial organizations, which belong to a national confederal body, the Canadian Federation of Insurance Agents and Brokers Associations. As in the resource sectors, small business (brokers) is organized separately from big business (major insurance companies). A number of smaller associations represent rather specialized insurance companies: boiler and machinery, marine, shipowners, nuclear disaster, and industrial risks. Some functions, such as actuaries, claimsmen, and adjusters, have their own associational representatives as well.

Although the two levels of government share responsibility for the financial industry, territorial differentiation is not pronounced. The federal government regulates the banks; both levels intervene in trust and loan and in insurance, where companies can be incorporated through provincial or federal charter. Credit unions and caisses populaires come primarily under provincial legislation. Not surprisingly, the CBA is a strictly unitary organization; but so are the Canadian Life and Health Association and the Insurance Bureau, though the latter has regional "offices" in Montreal, Halifax, Edmonton, and Vancouver. The TCA and the IDAC are slightly more differentiated, with branches in all provinces. While the IDAC's branches have sufficient autonomy that the association might be said to have a federal structure, the TCA's branches are less autonomous and administered by head office.[28] The more centralized structures in this industry are perhaps best explained by the nation-wide markets of the dominant companies in each pillar.

The one exception involves insurance brokers, who are licensed by provincial governments. The life underwriters are organized into 83 local associations, grouped, in turn, into five regional councils. Only in Quebec is there an autonomous provincial association, which has been federated with the national life underwriters association. Recent disputes between the Quebec and national associations over training programs may lead to the secession of the Quebec group. The property and casualty underwriters, regulated by provincial legislation, are all organized into provincial associations, which form a nation-wide confederation.[29]

The associational system is differentiated along several functional dimensions as well. First, and perhaps most important, is the educational affiliates created by the dominant associations in each pillar (see Table 17). These affiliates vary in size from the Institute of Canadian Bankers, with 50 employees, to the Life Insurance Institute, which has fewer than 5. These educational organizations serve different roles in different sub-sectors. For the banks and trust companies, they help staff upgrade their professional skills. In property and casualty insurance, the institute introduces employees to the complexities of the industry. The Canadian Securities Institute (CSI) plays an integral part in the self-regulatory system in securities. Its parent group, the IDAC, has assumed responsibility for standards, ethics, and professional practice, and the CSI helps to fulfill this charge by training employees of its members and any others wishing to enter the securities industry. Graduates in all four sub-sectors obtain certificates and the right to indicate this in their signature. These certificates presumably carry status in the sub-sector and facilitate promotions. Examples are FICB (fellow of the Institute of Canadian Bankers), FIIC (fellow of the Insurance Institute of Canada), and FCSI (fellow of the Canadian Securities Institute). The insurance "fellows" even have their own association, the Society of Fellows of the Insurance Institute of Canada.

Second, another functional division in the associational system relates to services to the respective industries. In the finance and lending sector, the more important is the Canadian Payments Association (to be discussed in the section on the CBA); and in the insurance sector, these are the Insurers Advisory Organization (IAO) and the Insurance Crime Prevention Bureaux. The IAO traces its roots as far back as 1855, and it is the successor to the Canadian Underwriters Association, the Dominion Board of Insurance Underwriters, and the Canadian Fire Underwriters Association. It acts to provide general insurance companies "with the information they need to make intelligent decisions with respect to the acceptability and pricing of various insurance risks."[30] The organization employs 450 people as loss control engineers and inspectors, actuaries, and insurance rating specialists and publishes pamphlets related to fire protection standards and loss control engineering. The IAO also works closely with the Underwriters Laboratories of Canada, an official standards-writing body in fire protection analogous to the Canadian Standards Association and the Canadian General Standards Board. Finally, the IAO joins construction associations on advisory committees of governmental building code agencies. The Insurance Crime Prevention Bureaux were founded in 1923 to help combat the high incidence of arson and fraud fires. Serving again the general property section of the industry, they provide inspection services for insurance crimes such as arson and insurance-related crimes like motor vehicle thefts.[31]

The final important functional division pertains to user associations in banking and lending. The Financial Executives Institute (FEI) represents senior financial officers in major Canadian corporations. For example, in 1980, the chairman of FEI was the treasurer of United Grain Growers, and the three vice-presidents were the vice-presidents – finance – for Simpson Sears, MacMillan Bloedel, and Dominion Textile. The FEI provides a forum for discussing problems common to financial officers and gains additional importance through advocacy. The very large corporations represented on its executive and board give the institute considerable influence when it speaks out, which it has done forcefully, attacking the four-pillar structure and particularly the investment dealers.[32] The Canadian Credit Institute, in contrast, has a much lower profile, primarily offering courses for credit officers in firms or in credit bureaux.

The reverse side to differentiation in an associational system is integration, not especially notable in Canada's financial industry. There are no formal or informal ties between the dominant associations in the four pillars and no vertical peak association analogous to the Canadian Federation of Agriculture or the Canadian Construction Association grouping together the financial sectors. Perhaps the market instability in the industry discourages common action. The strict line between financial and market intermediaries discourages common action by the investment dealers and the other three groups. Government structures reinforce differentiation further. At the federal level, regulatory responsibilities are divided among the Office of the Inspector General of Banks, the Department of Insurance, and the Canada Deposit Insurance Corporation. In Ontario, to illustrate the provincial case, there are separate superintendents of insurance and of deposit institutions, who report through the assistant deputy minister of the Financial Institutions Division of the Ministry of Consumer and Corporate Relations. But the Ontario Securities Commission, the Ontario Share and Deposit Insurance Corporation, and the Pension Commission of Ontario have separate mandates, with no formal or informal reporting relationship with this division.[33] Consequently, each sector of the industry remains somewhat self-contained in the policy arena and seeks to influence its companion agency to promote its interests in government.

THE CBA

In 1887, Canadian bankers started on the road towards their own association when they founded a bankers' section under the Toronto Board of Trade. Four years later, they moved out of the board's offices and established the Canadian Bankers' Association (CBA). By 1894, the new association had hired a permanent lobbyist in Ottawa. In 1900, Parliament incorporated the association. The CBA emerged for several purposes stated in chapter two: promoting mutual interests in the political sphere, educating officers, and protecting the interests of members contributing to a central redemption fund. In its early years, some saw the association as a kind of cartel, acting to restrict competition.

The state's regulation of Canadian banking has been based on the maintenance of trust between the two parties and the use of moral suasion. The federal apparatus was traditionally very small and relied on the banks' internal auditors and inspectors for much of its information. Accordingly, the CBA has had two primary functions: to advocate continued minimal intervention and to counter claims of other financial intermediaries for a share of the banking pie. Ironically, the CBA's success may have helped make the banks less efficient and innovative. Rich in resources and lulled into inefficient performances,[34] the banks have had difficulty responding to a series of recent challenges mounted by leaner, more aggressive financial intermediaries. Each challenge has attacked part of the banks' lending markets, forcing the CBA more and more into the open and competitive political arena, hence into pressure pluralist policy networks.

Decennial revisions of the Bank Act have come to involve a wide range of special interests, making it more difficult for the banks to defend their interests. Perhaps the best symbol of this change was the appointment in 1980 of R.M. MacIntosh, a former executive vice-president of the Bank of Nova Scotia, as the first permanent president of the CBA. Previously, the president had been a leading bank executive who handled the job on a part-time basis with the help of a permanent "executive director." The change was presented as "recognition that the industry's involvement in federal and provincial government relations activities had become too time-consuming to be handled on a part-time basis by a banker with heavy responsibilities in his own bank."[35] The fact that the revision of the Bank Act due in 1977 was not completed until late 1980 also weighed on the association. Part-time, low-profile discussions by senior bankers in clientele networks no longer worked and had to be replaced, at least partially, by full-time, high-profile lobbying by a senior banker in a pressure pluralist network.

The CBA nonetheless remains one of the more formidable associations representing Canadian business. Its influence derives not only from having one of the largest staffs of any association outside standards writing organization but also from its internal structures. It is not an interest group in the normal sense because membership is not voluntary – by its act of incorporation, all schedule A chartered banks must belong. Further, a bank's representative must be its chief executive officer.[36] The executive council includes also two representatives of foreign banks. This council will thus always include the CEOs of the six largest banks as well as of all the smaller ones. The CBA will thus be perfectly representative of its domain with the support of the most senior officers of its members. Underneath this executive structure are 32 committees, 25 task forces, and 9 provincial committees, all composed of relevant experts from lower executive levels of the banks.

The chartered banks, through the CBA and through direct representations, co-operate closely with the Bank of Canada. Twice yearly, the governor of the Bank convenes a meeting in Ottawa with the CEOs of the domestic chartered banks, where general policies are discussed and observations on trends made and examined.[37] To determine the money supply, set the value of the Canadian dollar, and keep track of financial transactions, the Bank needs systematic and comprehensive information. The CBA's Statistics, Taxation and Property Division[38] maintains a confidential data base for the banking industry, covering virtually all aspects of banking touched by law.[39] The association reports itself as being in very frequent contact with the Bank of Canada at all levels, as it is with the Department of Finance. Expert personnel from the banks go to Finance for various stints of service.[40] Too little information on relations among the banks, the CBA, the Bank of Canada, and Finance exists for us to assess in any more detail the types of policy networks in operation.

The CBA has developed structures highly adapted for policy advocacy. The permanent president is supported in turn by a Public Affairs division and a Legislation and Government group. The former seeks to maintain and develop a favourable business climate for the industry, through regular monitoring of public perceptions about banking and bank-related issues and the design of public relations programs directed at "correcting" erroneous or harmful views. Legislation and Government monitors all federal and provincial legislation and regulations, advises members and the president on their likely effects, and follows foreign legislation. When required by the president or the executive council, this division prepares industry briefs for presentation to government departments, agencies, and commissions. Robert MacIntosh, the CBA's president, summarized well the association's task when it acts as a policy advocate: "Business, the banks, have to communicate to the people out there. That's where it's at. This is true of all business. People in jobs like mine and the senior officers of the banks and other business firms have to communicate constantly to sell their position, to respond to criticism in a constructive way. You have to beat down unfair criticism every time it comes up; and we do that a lot. It's an unremitting process. I spend a tremendous amount of time trying to communicate with the public on any issue that comes up. Because that's what makes the politicians move."[41]

The CBA also provides important services to its members. It operates a Foreign Exchange Brokerage Service: voice communication and computerized video-display terminals relay foreign exchange market information simultaneously to participants' terminals throughout the country. Operations are overseen by the Foreign Exchange Committee of the CBA, composed of the senior international representatives from each chartered bank and the chief of the Foreign Exchange Department of the Bank of Canada (note the close working relationship).[42] The CBA's standards work is tied into a continuing concern with the operational aspects of banking. Many areas of the industry require a high level of co-operation and co-ordination: the systems for transferring funds and securities, the use of bank cards, security procedures, telecommunications networks, and money market procedures. Where these areas extend beyond the chartered banks themselves, either domestically or internationally, the CBA speaks for the banks on such bodies as the Standards Council of Canada and the International Standards Organization.

Finally, when the CBA was incorporated in 1900, it was delegated the authority to operate a clearing-house for the banks.[43] This facility aided the banks as they sought to improve chequing services to their customers. In order to work the system, the CBA established over the years standards for cheque size and magnetic encoding and then set the rights and obligations of drawer and drawee banks. Again, however, competition has intervened. Credit unions began issuing cheques, as did trust companies, as they both became more and more like deposit-taking institutions. Following the 1980 revision to the Bank Act, the clearing-house system was transferred to a new governing group, the Canadian Payments Association (CPA). The new system was intended to make "near banks" better able to compete for savings deposit business.[44] The CPA's board is composed of representatives of the four types of deposit-taking institutions (banks, trust companies, savings banks, credit unions), with the banks appointing half the directors. All chartered banks must by law belong, but membership is voluntary for the other institutions. Supervision of the CPA's affairs is given over to the inspector general of banks.[45] The CBA plays the largest role in the CPA, if only because the banks are responsible for close to 90 per cent of the traffic in the clearing system. The CBA co-ordinates the banks' participation in the system through three committees, the CPA National Clearings Committee (composed of banking industry representatives), the CPA Senior Planning Committee, and the CPA Bank Directors Committee.[46]

THE IDAC

In a self-regulatory policy, an industry-level organization, as opposed to a governmental one, sets and enforces rules and standards for firms and individuals in the industry. Such an industry-level organization shields its members from government interference and, with its powers and status, may even control entry to the industry. The politics of self-regulation are also clear. The organization must walk a tightrope, protecting the private interests of its members and the public interest. If it leans too much towards its members' private interests, or is even perceived to be doing so, other interested publics will challenge its privileges. If it is too strict with its members, it may lose their support. One Canadian organization successfully balancing its responsibilities is the Investment Dealers Association of Canada (IDAC).

The policy arena of the securities sector is more complex than that found in banking. The industry is governed partially by federal companies law but even more by provincial securities laws. The system of laws is administered by a compendium of institutions: provincial securities commissions (among which the Ontario Securities Commission plays a leading role), the stock exchanges (Montreal, Toronto, Vancouver, and Alberta), and industry associations (the IDAC and the Montreal and Toronto bond dealers' associations). Within this compendium, the IDAC is delegated responsibility for maintaining a high standard of business conduct. As we shall see, the association, in pursuit of this objective, has developed structures and disciplinary procedures unusual for a voluntary interest association.

Like the CBA, the IDAC began as a section of the Toronto Board of Trade. During the First World War, the federal government became very interested in the securities market as it sought to float bonds and debentures in order to pay for the huge costs of war participation. It thus in 1916 suggested creation of the Bond Dealers Association of Canada as a means to co-ordinate better the sale of government securities. After the war, the association continued, but as a traditional lobby group, changing its name to the Investment Bankers Association of Canada in 1925 and assuming its present name in 1934.[47] The association has assumed a self-regulatory role only gradually since the end of the First World War.[48]

In the early 1980s the provincial securities commissions set down the preconditions for business transactions such as disclosure rules and the structure of prospectuses, and the IDAC monitored the business conduct of securities firms. These activities of the association are tied in closely with provincial securities law. For example, in Ontario, regulations under the Securities Act specify that a person registered as an investment dealer must be a member of the Ontario district of the IDAC. Once a member of the IDAC, a securities firm comes under its "audit jurisdiction" unless it opts for the jurisdiction of one of the stock exchanges. In the mid-1980s, most large, national dealer firms were regulated by the IDAC.[49]

The IDAC's self-regulatory system has four components. First, the association defines strictly the conditions for entry to the industry, including capital requirements and partners' experience in the securities business.

Second, the association monitors the business practices of its members, ensuring that they are ethical and proper. To these ends, the association prescribes safeguards designed to "ensure the solvency of [its] ... members, including audit procedures, minimum record keeping requirements, financial reporting and disclosure rules, margin rules, and minimum net free capital and insurance requirements that are generally much higher than those prescribed by the regulations under the Securities Acts."[50] Complex regulations govern the conduct of the business itself. For example, section 19 of the Securities Act directs the Ontario district of the IDAC to select a panel of auditors and to employ its own auditors.[51] Each member in the association's jurisdiction must be audited every year by someone from the panel chosen according to IDAC procedures. These statements are then reviewed by the auditors employed by the association. In addition, each member must file with the IDAC's director of compliance one surprise audit, one annual audit, and monthly and annual reports. The association has detailed regulations also on minimum records to be kept, minimum insurance, trading and delivery practices, disclosures of financial condition to clients, money market operations, and so on.

The IDAC, unlike most voluntary business associations in Canada, has a mechanism for receiving complaints, investigating them, and disciplining rule-breakers.[52] Complaints are referred to an appropriate disciplinary panel, which investigates and may require the member to furnish information or open its books to the association's auditor. If the committee concludes that the member may have committed an offence, it summons the dealer to answer the charges. If it finds the member guilty, it may issue a reprimand; levy a fine not exceeding $100,000 per offence; suspend the member's rights and privileges including dealing with the public; or expel the member from the association – and hence the industry. A penalized member may appeal to the board of directors and ultimately to the securities commission.

Third, the Canadian Securities Institute is a component of the self-regulatory system. Set up by the association in 1948, it developed a series of courses and a reputation for competence. In 1969, the IDAC agreed to share responsibility for the institute with the four stock exchanges. Anyone wanting to become a partner in a securities firm or act as a registered dealer must complete the institute's Canadian Securities Course, which examines the industry, the ethics of business practice, and dealers' responsibilities to clients and the public at large.

Fourth, the self-regulatory system contains a trust fund, the National Contingency Fund, set up in 1969. Sponsored by the IDAC and the four stock exchanges, this fund (with resources of some $9 million) protects individual investors in the event of a member firm's insolvency. The sponsoring organization must reimburse the fund for amounts paid out for the insolvency of a member and so seeks to ensure that its members follow the rules strictly. The association concludes: "The real strength of the self-regulatory process lies in the fact that it is member money that is at risk. That the Fund has only had to pay out $2.1 million in 16 years is a testament to this strength. No other industry in Canada accepts an unlimited contingent liability for the consequences of a Member firm's financial difficulties."[53]

The IDAC's structures diverge significantly from those of most interest associations in Canada. There is a Member Regulation Department with three divisions: compliance, investigation, and registration. The Compliance Division monitors the financial and operational activities of member firms for conformity to the association's by-laws and regulations. The Investigation Division looks into complaints relating to firms under the prime audit jurisdiction of the association and most other claims received by the Toronto Stock Exchange. Finally, the Registration Division guides prospective members through the various requirements for becoming a registered dealer and a member of the association. The board of directors includes representation from member firms and from the four stock exchanges and, an uncommon feature, four "public" directors, usually prominent business people from outside the securities industry.

In chapter 3, I discussed briefly the likely responses of a group with well-developed policy participation, like the IDAC, that has to play an advocacy role. It can become a "quiet lobby," working through the more established channels to which it has access. This appears to be the IDAC's approach. It presents high-quality, detailed submissions to government. "We would never sign a submission to government or engage a Minister or an official in a subject that had not been painstakingly prepared well in advance and that did not meet the test of the public interest. We spend most of our time working out within the investment industry, with the best minds we can find, measures which will improve the savings and investment process in Canada and in Ontario."[54] The president of the IDAC has stated:

We are making progress in shifting the balance in Canada's economic strategy from government to business and we have, as a result, made some real economic progress in this country. Further progress along this path is certainly possible and desirable. It will happen if we perform better, as businessmen, in the national interest, and if we improve the quality and acceptability of the advice we communicate to governments and, of course, to the public. Lobbying does little to improve things and, in fact, is nearly always counterproductive and a serious disservice to business credibility. Thinking, participating in industry affairs, and communicating to government and to the public intelligent, honest, practical advice in the public interest is clearly our challenge and our responsiblity.[55]

The ideas of conflict and of "beat[ing] down unfair criticism" found in the statement by the president of the CBA (p. 186) are simply not present here. Rational discussion and the supplying of technical advice to reasonable governments and publics seem more appropriate for a group with extensive policy participation.

CONCLUSION

At the end of the previous chapter, I asked how economic power, measured in terms of such factors as productive capacity, assets, or sales, is related to political power – the capacity of a business sector to have its political demands consummated and to frustrate the demands of others that might oppose its interests. I argued that clientele and co-optive pluralist networks indicated greater political power than a pressure pluralist network. In the former types, the voices of competing interests are muted. The state is sufficiently dependent upon the business group for information, expertise, or support that it surrenders substantial power – control over demands. The economically powerful mining and forestry sectors have more access to clientele and co-optive networks than construction and agriculture, with less economic weight.

The largest chartered banks, trust companies, and insurance companies rank easily with the big resource conglomerates in assets and influence over corporations in other sectors. They, too, have translated economic power into political power, as evidenced by their access to clientele pluralist networks. Investment dealers have amassed even more power than the resource industry: note the multitude of self-regulatory (as opposed to regulatory) policies in their networks. In a clientele pluralist network, political demands change from inputs from outside the political system to "withinputs." In a self-regulatory policy in a clientele network, the change in status is even more pronounced. Wants and needs need not even be expressed as political demands; they can be acted upon in a private forum which benefits from formal state sanction.

The analysis in this chapter shows also that maintaining a grip on self-regulatory policy-making in a clientele pluralist network is difficult. A business sector must preserve autonomy and separation from related sectors (labour, suppliers of raw materials, consumers, and cohabitants in the same environment) while acting prudently to avoid mobilization by one or more of these related sectors against its powers. Of the divisions of the economy studied thus far, the financial industries would appear to be best placed for "keeping their distance." They do not pollute the environment. Their customers are diffuse and unlikely to organize themselves well (except for large corporate customers, as illustrated by the Financial Executives Institute of Canada). Their branch structures, laws on industrial relations designed primarily for manufacturing, and insurance companies' practice of working through independent agents and brokers make confrontation with organized labour less likely. Nor do they have raw materials suppliers in the usual sense. The most serious threat to their autonomy comes from other financial sectors. If a related sector begins to encroach, creating and maintaining a self-regulatory apparatus becomes more difficult. Such a system requires an identifiable domain of firms, with no obvious outsiders sufficiently strong to press for admission.

An excluded group with some economic power can always try politically to force its opponent out of the latter's area of activity.

However, pursuit of this goal pushes both challenger and self-regulator towards pressure group politics. In the hurly-burly world of lobbying, the self-regulated group becomes particularly vulnerable, asked to show that it does not place private interests above the public interest or earn profits by exploiting consumers rather than by maintining efficient operations. The IDAC, accordingly, has consistently sought to consider the public interest and control its members. It maintains that its trained personnel are able to identify problems at an early stage, relieving the strain on already over-burdened governments and providing substantial investor protection at lower cost to the taxpayer. The National Contingency Fund has built-in incentives for compliance with the rules. At the time of writing, however, the IDAC appeared to be losing its argument, as governments moved to open the industry up to financial intermediaries.

In short, the relation between economic and political power is strong but neither simple nor direct. Chapter 8 showed the importance of industry structure – concentration and geographical dispersion; chapter 9 has highlighted the significance of the relative other sectors. If clientele or co-optive pluralism indicates political power, self-regulation in such networks indicates even greater political power.

Manufacturing: A Divided Community

The institutional structures of national economies vary considerably among the developed states. No economy approximates the mythical ideal of balanced, self-sufficient economic development across all divisions – primary resources and agriculture, manufacturing, transportation and utilities, construction, and financial services. Specialization occurs: the United States and Japan are the most advanced technological centres, West Germany is strong in heavy industry, England and Switzerland have financial services, and Canada, the United States, and Australia are agricultural surplus centres.[1] The Canadian economy sees faster capital accumulation in raw materials production and in transportaion and utilities than in manufacturing.[2] Canadian manufacturing is stronger in the initial transformation of raw materials into basic products and in the production of intermediate goods, weaker in the manufacture of end products. Since the First World War at least, Canada has usually imported far more finished goods than it exports. The large deficit in end products continues to characterize Canadian manufacturing today. However, contrary to the reports of some analysts, this deficit has not worsened but remained relatively stable.[3]

Also distinctive to the Canadian manufacturing economy is a relatively high proportion of foreign ownership, and with it foreign control, which reached its apogee immediately after 1945. Since that time, the proportion of Canadian manufacturing under foreign control has declined somewhat, but, at 50.76 per cent in 1982, it remains well above that found in other developed economies.[4] Foreign control also remains higher in this part of the economy than any other major division. Critics of government policy on foreign investment argue that foreign firms do less research and development and import more capital goods than do domestically controlled firms. In fact, studies advance evidence for both sides of the debate. More important to our analysis of business-government relations is the effect of branch-plant status on firms' involvement in collective action.

I show in this chapter that this status varies with the sector involved. In a sector like chemicals, where foreign-controlled firms dominate, ownership has only an indirect influence on associative action. Similarly, in sectors like pulp and paper, where Canadian firms now dominate, and where all firms tend to serve the same us markets, the locus of control is largely irrelevant. Only in our case study of food processing do we find foreign control directly associated with fragmentation in associative action. There the interaction of foreign control with other economic and political factors creates some deep divisions.

These two characteristics of Canadian manufacturing – emphasis on basic and intermediate products rather than end products, and significant foreign control – help us to understand associative action in this division of the economy. A long-established comprehensive association represents secondary industry, the Canadian Manufacturers' Association (CMA). It is not a peak association like the Canadian Federation of Agriculture, the Canadian Construction Association, or the Canadian Forest Industries Council. Rather it has direct membership: firms affiliate to it directly rather than through another association. In addition to the CMA, there exist over 140 more specialized associations that have no formal ties to this comprehensive association. There are few intermediate peak associations representing major sectors of manufacturing like those that constitute comprehensive peak associations in many western European countries.

In Canada, patterns of organization vary from one sector to another and are usually competitive, divided, or organized. (1) In competitive systems, no peak organization exists for the sector, and several associations compete openly for members and over the guiding principles of public policy. Examples are food processing and electronics. (2) In divided systems, perhaps the most common pattern, numerous associations have narrowly defined, mutually exclusive domains. No systematic arrangements exist for aggregating the sector's various interests. Examples are the chemicals, machinery, primary metals, and clothing sectors. (3) In organized systems, collective action in a sector is integrated through either a sectoral peak association or a single, comprehensive direct-membership association. An example of the former is the Canadian Textiles Institute (primary textiles and knitting mills); of the latter, the Canadian Pulp and Paper Association.

The argument that Canadian manufacturing is weakly organized begins in this chapter with a general discussion of the structures and activities of the most well-known and broadly based association, the CMA. Following in succession are analyses of food processing, a competitive sector; chemicals, a divided sector; and pulp and paper, an organized sector. Comparison of the three types aids in isolating properties of industrial structure and state structure that favour one pattern over another. The chapter concludes by drawing together the analyses of the CMA and the three sectoral types in order to explain the low level of organizational development in Canadian manufacturing.

THE CMA

As we saw in chapter 2, the CMA arose in the midst of Canadian manufacturers' struggle for greater tariff protection which culminated in the National Policy of 1879. In the early years, it was preoccupied with defending industrialists against banks, railways, and eventually organized labour. In each of these campaigns, the CMA played an advocacy role. Rather than participating directly in the formulation of policy, the association sought to influence policymakers from the outside. The CMA has always favoured this approach to collective action. In remaining an advocacy group, it has developed many of the properties predicted by Mancur Olson's theory: a wide range of selective benefits and services to attract members, which have grown to prominence in the association's life. As an advocacy group and a dispenser of services, the CMA has avoided systematic policy participation and, with this, any integrating role on behalf of more specialized associations representing manufacturing interests. The relative absence of these two roles distinguishes the CMA from most comparable manufacturing organizations in western Europe.

The first property pointing to advocacy rather than participation is the CMA's membership structure. An advocacy group seeks to enhance its political clout by enrolling large numbers of firms employing many workers. "Any business that gives employment in its manufacturing department to not less than five employees" is eligible to join the CMA.[5] Member firms, in turn, may sponsor more than one individual member on the association's roster. In 1986, approximately 3,800 firms belonged to the association and were responsible, in turn, for close to 10,000 "members." Generally speaking, these firms participated in the association at three levels. The CMA has 33 local branches in medium-sized and large manufacturing centres around the country. For example, in Ontario, it had in 1980 local branches in Toronto, Hamilton, St Catharines, Barrie, Grand Valley, Peterborough, and Ottawa. Normally, these branches are not very active politically; their primary purpose appears to be social, cultivating the solidarity and cohesion required for advocacy. The association also possesses a federal structure, with seven divisions organized at the provincial level. While these divisions have autonomy in policy matters dealt with by provincial governments, they do not have their own independent financial resources, and their staff is allocated by and subject to administrative policy established at head office in Toronto. Each division has its own vice-president as a permanent employee who takes day-to-day direction from a divisional chairman and board of directors. Although the CMA has members from every province, Ontario accounts for 61.8 per cent of member firms and Quebec 18.1 per cent: 80 per cent of the association's members come from the two central provinces.[6] Thus the association can put concentrated pressure on the Ontario and Quebec caucuses of the national parties and on the two provincial governments.

Playing pressure group politics requires resources. The CMA employs about 100 people and in 1980 spent $3.6 million. Its major sources of revenue were membership fees (72 per cent) and a specialized, widely used trade catalogue, the *Canadian Trade Index* (11 per cent). About 30 per cent of staff members were assigned to managing divisional offices; the rest worked in head office operations. The CMA also maintains an office in Ottawa for lobbying.

Head office staff are organized, under executive vice-presidents, into two divisions, one to deliver services, and the other to support policy advocacy. The association's services are extensive. It operates a "Servicecentre" with a telephone "hotline" that provides members with information on export development and promotion and on problems with customs, among other things. It publishes periodical bulletins covering such topics as taxation, export, customs, and consumer and corporate legislation. More specialized publications include: *Positive Employee Relations* (for union-free employers), *On Strike* (a discussion of steps employers can take to protect themselves), *Understanding Export* (a 106-page step-by-step guide), and *Inside Government* (a manual explaining the workings of the federal government). An association services division sets up and manages associations for a fee on behalf of specific industries – usually small, very specialized sectors that need only one or two staff members to manage their interests. Examples in 1980 were die casters and manufacturers of grinding wheels, of water heaters, and of water conditioners.

Advocacy support is organized into a series of departments which work in tandem with standing and special committees composed of

individuals drawn from the membership. The association lobbies in
a number of policy areas that cut horizontally across the manufacturing sectors. The most important have standing committees, whose
chairpersons sit automatically on the board of directors: business
environment, customs, export, industrial relations, legislation (corporate, commercial, and consumer law), taxation, and transportation. Standing committees for membership and public affairs also
are represented on the board but are not involved in policy formulation. In an interview, the association's former president emphasized the importance and strength of the standing policy
committees, pointing to chairpersons who were "tops in their field"
in the country.[7] (At the provincial level, the usual committees are
workmen's compensation, industrial relations, and transportation.)
Overall policy direction for all these committees comes from the
board of directors, composed normally of chief executive officers
from major firms. With significant staff support for each standing
committee, the association can produce the technical knowledge
needed for effective advocacy. This knowledge is then fed to the
association's permanent president, to the board of directors, and to
the public affairs department, for transmission to the mass media.

Also consistent with an emphasis on policy advocacy is the relative
absence of formalized, ongoing policy forums involving the association and government officials. Rather, the association works more
informally, largely on an issue-by-issue basis. In most cases, the contact will be intense but short-lived. In a few cases, contact may be
ongoing for a long period. Contact over the reform of competition
policy, for example, was sustained at varying intensities for 15 years.
The association is represented on advisory committees for the Employment and Immigration Department, the Canadian Commercial
Corporation, and the Standards Council of Canada. But nowhere
do we see the intensive clientele pluralist policy networks described
in finance or the clientele networks discovered in forestry and mining.

The CMA has been less successful in transforming the economic
power of its member firms into political power than many of the
groups described in previous chapters. It resembles, in this respect,
the general business associations discussed in chapter 5. It operates
reactively, responding to government plans and questions from outside the policy-making machinery. Occasionally, in recent years, it
has been more proactive, publishing documents that look to the
future and make suggestions about longer-term government policy.[8]
To be involved legitimately in policy-making, an association with a
domain as comprehensive as the CMA almost certainly would need a
peak association format. Then, like the Canadian Federation of Ag-

riculture for example, it could offer its own offices in arranging a consensus on policy among the various sectoral associations in exchange for a role in formulating and implementing policy. Certainly, this has been the role of many associations analogous to the CMA in western Europe. The association could then claim to be broadly and systematically representative of the manufacturing industries in a way that it cannot do now.

The importance of having a viable peak association for Canadian manufacturing will vary with the policies that politicians wish to pursue. Certainly, the absence of such an association may prevent the informed state intervention associated with a planned industrial policy, a point to which I return in the concluding chapter. The CMA appears ill-equipped for concerted long-term policy discussion with governments, when compared with other peak associations in its class such as the Confederation of British Industry or the Federation of German Industry.[9]

FOOD PROCESSING

When people think about Canada's manufacturing industries, visions of the steel mills on Burlington Bay, or rows of automobiles on vast parking lots in Oshawa, or of the "Canadarm" on the space shuttle plucking a satellite out of space seem to come to mind. The butter sitting on the table, or the french fry speared on a fork, or the frozen strawberries poured over ice cream for dessert are seldom given a second thought, except when prices go up. Yet of all the major sectors of Canadian manufacturing – textiles, clothing, wood products, primary metals, and so on – food processing is the largest. It produces more goods and employs more workers than any other. With 39 "nationally relevant" business interest associations representing its many firms, the sector also has the highest number of associations of any manufacturing sector. These associations' narrowly defined domains, competition with one another in several instances, and weak integration do not appear to be the consequence of the sector's size, however. The narrowly focused and sometimes competitive associative action appears to result from differences in orientation between foreign and domestic firms or between sectors close to the farm gate and those further away, and from differences in perishability of products and in market structures. Also, mandates of governmental agencies regulating the sectors occasionally overlap, thereby encouraging bureaucratic competition.

The distinction between use of raw materials and use of processed inputs is useful for explaining some aspects of collective action.[10] In

terms of value added, the five most important primary sectors in
Canada are meat slaughtering and processing, the manufacture of
dairy products, the canning and preserving of fruits and vegetables,
fish processing, and grain mill products. The manufacture of vegetable oils, of wines, and of prepared animal feeds and the distilling
and blending of spirits are smaller primary sectors. All these differ
in key respects from such secondary processing sectors as bakery
products, sugar refineries, chocolate and confectionery manufacturers, and malt liquor and soft drink manufacturers.

This distinction between primary and secondary sectors is significant because components of the primary sectors operate in rather
controlled markets: poultry meat, dairy, fruits and vegetables, and
grains. We saw in chapter 6 how supply management works in the
dairy and poultry sectors. In the fruit and vegetables sector, prices
are managed but supply is not. There are 22 vegetable marketing
boards and 12 fruit marketing boards in Canada, all at the provincial
level.[11] These boards license producers, monitor their farming practices, and are monopoly buyers and sellers of their products. Some
can fix prices while others negotiate prices with processors. In the
grains industry as well, price but not supply is controlled. The domestic prices of major western grains excluding canola are negotiated under the aegis of the Canadian Wheat Board; the price of
Ontario wheat is negotiated by the Ontario Wheat Growers' Marketing Board.

Of all the larger primary sectors, then, only fish processing and
the beef and pork components of the meat industry operate in free
markets.[12] Consequently, each of the five major primary sectors
operates in a separate market. There is little that is common from
one to another. Rather than developing working relations across the
food processing sectors, each primary sector tends to develop close
working relations with its corresponding farm groups (or fishermen).
Similarly, the problems and experiences of controlled markets make
collective action quite different from that of secondary processing
sectors, which operate in less structured markets.

Reinforcing this cleavage is the division between foreign and domestic firms. Two sectors affected by supply management, poultry
and dairy, are Canadian controlled, as are the red meat, fish, feed,
and alcoholic beverage sectors.[13] The two sectors with price setting
but not supply management, grain mills and fruit and vegetable
processing, are controlled by American firms. American firms also
dominate the biscuits, confectionery, soft drinks, and various miscellaneous foods sub-sectors. Within the foreign-controlled sectors,
ownership follows divisions in firm size: most larger firms are foreign

controlled and smaller firms domestically owned. In short, the large, American-controlled, food multinationals are especially prominent in sectors engaged in secondary processing or not governed by supply management marketing régimes.

The associational system summarized in Table 18 illustrates an important property of the food processing industry: associations have narrow, product-based domains. Virtually all the associations have a domain equal to or narrower than a standard industrial classification category.[14] Only two have broader product domains, the Canadian Frozen Food Association (CFFA) and the Grocery Products Manufacturers of Canada (GPMC), but both build in limitations. The CFFA includes firms using freezing methods for preserving food: meat, dairy, fish, fruits and vegetables, and miscellaneous. The domain of the GPMC includes firms "who, regardless of size, are engaged in the manufacture of branded, packaged products distributed and generally available through grocery outlets."[15] Since branded products are sold in virtually all sectors of this industry, the GPMC draws firms from all of these.

When the GPMC's definition of its domain is mapped on to the structure of the industry, particular types of firms select themselves onto its roster. Branded products are devices used by large firms, in particular, to cultivate stable markets for generic products. For example, since all firms in the jam industry may sell strawberry jam, firms seek to foster consumer identification with Kraft or Malkins or ... strawberry jam. In Canada, these large firms tend to be disproportionately American multinational corporations. Consequently, the GPMC's membership list is dominated by firms of this type. To illustrate, its 20-member board in 1980–1 included the CEOs of the following subsidiaries of mainly American companies: Warner Lambert Canada, Club House Foods, Quaker Oats, Kraft, Pepsi Cola Canada, Imasco Foods, General Foods, Canadian Canners (owned by Del Monte), Nabob Foods, Catelli, Ralston Purina, and Colgate-Palmolive Canada.

The GPMC's ability to speak for the large, primarily American firms in the industry is accentuated by another aspect of its structure. The GPMC "services" a number of smaller associations by providing staff support and policy advice on a contractual basis. Table 18 signals these groups – all of them in American-controlled sectors. By servicing them directly, using its own professional staff rather than creating an autonomous "association services" section like the CMA, the GPMC gains more influence over their behaviour. Hence these associations act from time to time like association members of the GPMC, reflecting closely its point of view.

Table 18
National Food Processing Associations by Sector, 1980

Sector	Association
Beef and pork meat	Canadian Meat Council
Poultry meat	Canadian Poultry and Egg Processors Council
Fish processing	Fisheries Council of Canada
Canning and preserving of fruits and vegetables	Canadian Food Processors Association
Dairy products	National Dairy Council
Flour mills	Canadian National Millers Association
Feed industry	Canadian Feed Manufacturers Association
	Pet Food Manufacturers Association of Canada*
Biscuit products	Association of Canadian Biscuit Manufacturers*
Bakeries	Bakery Council of Canada
Confectionery products	Confectionery Manufacturers Association of Canada*
Sugar	Canadian Sugar Institute
Vegetable oil mills	Institute of Edible Oil Foods*
Soft drink manufacturers	Canadian Soft Drink Association
Distilleries	Association of Canadian Distillers
Breweries	Brewers Association of Canada
Wines	Canadian Wine Institute
Miscellaneous food manufacturers	Canadian Potato Chip Association
	Coffee Council of Canada*
	Edible Nut Processors*
	Tea and Coffee Association of Canada*
	Canadian Honey Packers Association
	Canadian Pasta Manufacturers Association
	International Maple Sugar Institute
	Canadian Spice Association
Inter-sectoral	Grocery Products Manufacturers of Canada
	Canadian Frozen Food Association

* Serviced by the Grocery Products Manufacturers of Canada.

The GPMC states that its objective is to become the spokesperson for the whole food processing industry. It possesses significant resources for the pursuit of this role. It employs more people (16) and spends 100 per cent more (about $800,00 in 1980) than any other association in the system. It also displays the classic attributes of an advocacy organization: a full-time president paid amply for lobbying (over $100,000 per year), a corporate secretary who relieves the president of most of the administrative components of running an association, and public relations specialists to support the president's lobbying campaigns. Using an aggressive, high-profile style, the association actively competes with other associations in the system for members and for the ear of governments. Not surprisingly, its recruitment drives show most success in fruit and vegetable processing, which is heavily American controlled, moderate success in the meat sectors, and least success in the dairy industry (the GPMC has strongly opposed and has fought strenuously against marketing boards and supply management).[16]

The highly differentiated and competitive properties of associative action in the food processing industry are reinforced further by interactions with the state. Since the industry's products are consumed directly by individual citizens, their composition, quality, and safety have come to be highly regulated by the state. As the regulatory régimes have evolved, primary sectors, close to the farm gate or to the sea, have come to be regulated by the Food Production and Inspection Branch of the Department of Agriculture or the Department of Fisheries and Oceans. The secondary sectors, in contrast, have their regulatory touchstone in the Health Protection Branch (HPB) of the Department of Health and Welfare. Accordingly, normally through co-optive pluralist networks,[17] the Canadian Meat Council, the National Dairy Council, and the Canadian Food Processors Association work closely with Agriculture Canada, and the Fisheries Council of Canada with Fisheries and Oceans. The GPMC and its "serviced" groups, which represent secondary sectors, interact much more commonly with the HPB. The GPMC's opposition to supply management often makes it persona non grata in the Agriculture Department; the minister traditionally has defended such policies in the government. Thus divisions in the state administration reinforce primary-secondary divisions and competition between the GPMC and the primary-sector associations.

The Food Production and Inspection Branch and the HPB have themselves been in competition. In the late 1970s, Agriculture Canada proposed the creation of a single food agency which it would oversee and which would absorb the HPB's Food Directorate. This proposal was resisted strongly by HPB officials, who argued that Agriculture Canada was tied too closely to the food industry and hence might place the interests of food consumers second to those of producers and processors. The HPB succeeded, but the department's ambitions and the HPB's suspicions remain.

Tension between Agriculture and Industry/Trade reinforces divisions between the GPMC and primary-sector associations. In recent years, Agriculture Canada has strengthened considerably its Marketing and Economics Branch, which searches out foreign markets for commodities and then looks for firms to serve those markets. In contrast, Industry/Trade officials are less interventionist, arguing that firms should seek export markets themselves and that the government should support those firms only when they need help. Consistent with this laissez-faire approach is decided hostility towards supply management in particular and marketing boards in general. The GPMC has developed closer ties with these officials than have the primary-sector associations. In short, when a sector has a "competitive" pattern of organization, conflicts within the state often reinforce conflicts among associations, and vice versa.

The absence of an effective peak association in the food processing industry now becomes less mysterious. In effect, several types of associations are active in the system. The GPMC, its "serviced" groups, and the Canadian Meat Council work primarily in pressure pluralist policy networks, emphasizing policy advocacy. They help make some regulatory policies, but only incidentally. Associations like the Canadian Food Processors, the Fisheries Council, the Millers, and the Feed Manufacturers are about equally advocates and participants. This balance, however, renders their lobbying more "quiet" as they seek to maintain their policy participation. Finally, the dairy and poultry associations stress policy participation and are actively involved in the corporatist policy networks that oversee supply management in their respective industries.

CHEMICALS

The manufacture of chemicals and of chemical products occupies a prominent place among Canada's manufacturing sectors, with shipments totalling over $11 billion in 1980. Economists normally divide the industry into three parts: basic chemicals (industrial organic and inorganic chemicals); chemical materials, formed from these basic chemicals (synthetic resins, fertilizer chemicals such as potassium); and chemical products, manufactured, in turn, out of the intermediary materials (drugs, paints, perfumes, plastics, and so on). The industry services many other manufacturing sectors by providing them with key inputs – goods numbering in the thousands.[18] These goods are changed and refashioned, frequently as a result of the intensive research and development that characterize the industry. Since survival in the industry has come to rest on research capacity, large, usually multinational corporations capable of sustaining such activity have come to dominate, engendering oligopolies in many sub-groups of the sector. Yet high industrial concentration coexists with high competition among firms as each seeks further production innovation. Firms have sought to protect themselves against the rigours of competition by integrating forward: large basic chemicals manufacturers such as British-owned Imperial Chemical Industries (ICI), American companies like Du Pont, Dow, and Union Carbide, and the West German firms of Bayer, Hoechst, and BASF are all important players in the chemical materials and chemical products sectors.

Within Canada, therefore, several properties distinguish the industry from food processing and favour a different pattern of business associability. Foreign ownership is less divisive because the sector is so highly foreign controlled. Thus the sub-sector of the chemical industry least under foreign control is printing ink manufacturing, where foreign firms account for 73.9 per cent of production. The other sectors range between this figure and 93.5 per cent, the amount of production accounted for by foreign firms in the plastics materials and synthetic resins sub-sector.[19] The more prominent division is a more usual one in manufacturing, producing for international or domestic markets. A group of large, vertically integrated firms spanning the basic chemicals and chemical materials sectors is active in export markets: Canadian Industries Limited (CIL), Esso Chemicals (Exxon), Du Pont Canada, and Polysar. In chemical products like pharmaceuticals, paints, household chemicals, and cosmetics and toiletries, the more conventional branch plant structures prevail, with firms oriented to the home market. This division between basic chemicals and chemical materials on the one side and chemical products on the other distinguishes the Canadian from the British and West German cases, where all sectors export. It may also help explain why overarching peak associations dominate associative action in the latter two cases but have not developed in Canada.

The system of associations summarized in Table 19 is "divided." Associations have highly specialized, mutually exclusive product domains. Hence there are no players like the Grocery Products Manufacturers of Canada, competing with other associations for members. Since the presence of a divided pattern may be less than apparent, I will briefly review the sectors.[20] The Canadian Chemical Producers Association (CCPA) represents the basic industrial chemicals firms save those that manufacture compressed gasses. These firms, vir-

Table 19
National Chemical Manufacturers' Associations by Sector, 1980

Sector	Association
Basic industrial chemicals	Canadian Chemical Producers Association (CCPA)
	Sulphur Development Institute of Canada (SUDIC)
	Compressed Gas Association, Canadian Division
Fertilizers and pesticides	Canadian Fertilizer Institute (CFI)
	Potash and Phosphate Institute of Canada
	Crop Protection Institute of Canada
	Canadian Manufacturers of Chemical Specialties Association (CMCSA)
Plastics resins	Society of the Plastics Industry of Canada (SPI)
	Rubber Association of Canada
Paints, varnishes, lacquers	Canadian Paint and Coatings Associatioin
Drugs and medicines	Pharmaceutical Manufacturers Association of Canada (PMAC)
	Proprietary Association of Canada
	Canadian Drug Manufacturers Association
Soaps, perfumes, toiletries	Soap and Detergent Association of Canada
	Canadian Cosmetics, Toiletry and Fragrance Association
	CMCSA
Plastics products	Society of the Plastics Industry of Canada
Miscellaneous chemicals	CMCSA
	Canadian Printing Ink Manufacturers Association
	Adhesives and Sealants Manufacturers Association of Canada

tually all American, form a regional "Canadian" division within the (US) Compressed Gas Association. The Sulphur Development Institute is supported by sulphur-producing firms and government grants and carries out research into industrial applications for sulphur. In the fertilizers and pesticides sector, the Potash and Phosphate Institute, a somewhat autonomous branch of another American group, carries out and sponsors research on fertilizer development, while the Canadian Fertilizer Institute performs more usual trade association functions for the industry. Pesticides used for agricultural purposes are manufactured by firms represented by the Crop Protection Institute of Canada (formerly the Canadian Agricultural Chemicals Association), and those used in the household are produced by firms under the purview of the Canadian Manufacturers of Chemical Specialties Association. The drugs and medicines industry subdivides among three associations: the Pharmaceutical Manufacturers Association of Canada (PMAC), which speaks for prescription drug manufacturers; the Proprietary Association, which represents producers of drugs sold over the counter; and the Canadian Drug Manufacturers Association, which looks after the interests of generic drug manufacturers. Finally, Table 19 indicates that the Society of the Plastics Industry of Canada (SPI Canada), itself originally a subdivision of the Society of the Plastics Industry, represents two sub-sectors: manufacturers of primary plastics materials (polyethylene, polypropylene, and so on,) and the buyers of these materials – plastics processors.

Canada has no peak association like the Chemical Industries Association in Britain or the Verband der chemischen Industrie in West Germany to integrate the many sectors of the industry and speak for them as a whole. There are virtually no formal arrangements integrating the activities of the associations horizontally one with another.[21] Informally, however, a scarcely visible process ("association deference") integrates some association activities. In interviews, the executive officers of the Canadian Fertilizer Institute and the Crop Protection Institute of Canada reported that on policy matters of general concern to the industry they deferred to the Canadian Chemical Producers Association and let it take the lead. Similarly, the president of SPI Canada reported that his association and the CCPA co-operated on more general matters. The CCPA speaks for the basic chemicals and chemical materials sections of the industry on more general issues, not surprising in the light of the overall dominance of the industry by the large basic chemicals manufacturers.

This ad hoc role is rooted in the arrangements joining the industry to the associations involved. Table 20 looks at major associations in the industry for which I have information and shows the extent to which the same firm sits on different boards of associations. For example, the table suggests that seven firms have seats on the CCPA's board and on the board of SPI Canada. The CCPA enjoys the greatest number of interlocking members, and these interlocks are strongest with the chemical materials sectors. The firms involved are the larger ones – CIL, Esso Chemicals, Dow Chemical, Cyanamid, and Du Pont. More senior executives sit on the CCPA's board; its 16 members in-

Table 20
Interlocks among Boards, Selected Chemical Associations, 1980–1

Association	CCPA	CFI	SPI	CPIC	CPCA	PMAC	CCTFA	CMCS
Canadian Chemical Producers	–							
Canadian Fertilizer Institute	3	–						
Society of the Plastics Industry	7	2	–					
Crop Protection Institute	5	1	1	–				
Canadian Paint and Coatings Association	2	1	2	1	–			
Pharmaceuticals Manufacturers Association	1	1	0	0	0	–		
Canadian Cosmetics, Toiletry, & Fragrance Association	0	0	0	1	1	0	–	
Canadian Manufacturers of Chemical Specialties Association	3	0	1	1	0	1	1	–
Totals	21	8	13	10	7	3	3	7

clude 12 CEOs and 4 vice-presidents, while boards of other associations (excluding the PMAC) have a wider range of ranks. For example,
the president and CEO of Du Pont Canada sits on the CCPA's board,
and the vice-president, plastics and films, sits on the board of SPI
Canada. The executive structures of chemicals associations foster
deference to the CCPA. At a minimum, there will be a voice on each
board interested in such an arrangement. In foreign-controlled and
oligopolistic industries like chemicals, such quiet arrangements may
constitute a "Canadian way" of doing things.

In the food processing industry, state structures reinforced competition in the associational system. In chemicals, they appear more
neutral, except in drugs and medicines. Protection of consumer health
against pesticides is the responsibility of the federal Department of
Agriculture; protection against environmental hazards is a focus of
both Environment and Transport at the federal level and of pro-

vincial environment departments. Industry development has traditionally been the responsibility of the Chemicals Branch of the Department of Regional Industrial Expansion, which has been sufficiently close to associations like the CCPA to have officials sit on their committees.[22]

The only exception to this rather placid picture comes in the contradiction between compulsory licensing for drugs and encouraging development of pharmaceuticals. Compulsory licensing is administered by the Department of Consumer and Corporate Affairs. The department has supported the domestic generic drugs industry in the hope of forcing reductions in drug prices and developing the drugs industry. In contrast, Regional Industrial Expansion is linked more closely to the multinational ethical drugs industry. Its officials are sympathetic to the argument that compulsory licensing has discouraged R&D and expansion of the ethical drugs industry. They favour encouragement of the ethical drug manufacturers without compulsory licensing.

The closing of several research operations during the late 1970s and early 1980s and their transfer abroad have placed the future of the drug industry higher on the political agenda. In competing for the ear of the cabinet, each department has enlisted the relevant association (the Canadian Drug Manufacturers Association, generics; Pharmaceutical Manufacturers Association of Canada, ethicals), among others. Such politicking helps maintain the divisions in drugs and medicine.

In chemicals, firms are often large and have their own government relations departments; products are diverse, making R&D firm-specific; and most firms are subsidiaries of foreign corporations. Why are there strong and well-resourced associations? Their activities suggest several reasons. First, virtually all sectors are subject to regulation, most often, to ensure fair competition and protect workers or consumers. The state needs industry-wide information, advice in drafting the rules, and support in ensuring compliance. Given the importance of such regulations to the life of a firm, entrepreneurs want a say. The state needs "input" from the industry but has neither the time nor the personnel to hear out each party that may be affected. The association then becomes a logical intermediary.

The extent of association involvement depends on the type of regulation. In the chemical industry, two types may be distinguished. In the first case, the state seeks to regulate chemicals intended to act directly on human biological systems (pharmaceuticals). Regulations normally involve extensive pre-market testing, close quality control in production, and examination of every new product. Such a system requires detailed information and certainty of compliance. Industry-wide questions arise in the process, about the properties of a valid test, sufficiency of evidence, and guidelines for quality control. The state agency concerned may involve the industry in the formulation of policy on these matters. Co-optive pluralist networks link the Department of Health and Welfare and the PMAC and the Proprietary Association of Canada.[23] Responsibility for implementation may also be delegated to the industry concerned.[24] Most notably, the Pharmaceutical Manufacturers Association of Canada shares in the regulation of marketing and advertising practices in the prescription drug industry. Greater legitimacy for the regulations encourages compliance.

In the second instance, the state regulates chemicals that affect human biological systems through their presence in the environment. Extensive pre-market testing does not normally take place; rather firms are asked to do some assessment and to provide the state with this information when they put the product into the market-place. Production is not usually regulated, but the environment around the plant is monitored. The state is more reactive. When evidence of a problem appears, regulations are developed to control potential environmental hazards.

Reactive regulation draws associations into policy formulation, but less regularly than in the first case. As a result, associations like the Canadian Chemical Producers Association have not become institutionally involved in regulatory policy-making. Further, regulation usually involves the testing of public spaces and of air and water tangential to the plant. The public character of the effects makes it more seemly for the state to conduct the tests itself.

In short, developed co-optive pluralist networks like those in pharmaceuticals do not emerge as strongly in other regulated areas such as the manufacture of industrial chemicals. However, most Canadian regulatory policy-making in chemicals follows co-optive pluralist patterns rather than US-style pressure pluralism, emphasizing, according to Ilgen, the formation of "consensus through informal negotiations among affected parties."[25] "The intent in all cases is to devise a regulatory bargain that engenders widespread acceptance and support, thereby diminishing the emphasis on monitoring and enforcement and reducing the administrative costs to the state."[26]

Associations in this sector exist also to perform industry-wide functions related to customers and suppliers. Examples are the development of product standards in the plastics processing industry and the negotiation of transportation rates with the railways on behalf of the fertilizer industry. Associations are also logical places for sophisticated and detailed statistics programs. In several highly capital-intensive chemical sectors, unused capacity can have disastrous consequences. Firms need detailed market intelligence on production and are provided frequently with figures on industry-wide inventories. Programs of this sort are managed for industrial chemicals by the Canadian Chemical Manufacturers Association, for fertilizers by the Canadian Fertilizer Institute, for plastics resins and other plastic products by SPI Canada, for rubber and rubber products by the Rubber Association of Canada, and for ethical drugs by the PMAC.

Finally, associations cultivate public opinion and support politicians in response to campaigns by other interest groups for and against regulatory policies. Public interest groups and single-issue environmental movements use mass media more and more effectively in putting pressure on politicians. In response, the industry may want to convince the public of the value of a chemical industry or of plastics or of pesticides. Such campaigns appear self-serving when centred on a firm. Rather than saying that x set of regulations is harmful to Dow Chemical, one says that it is harmful to a chemical industry that employs y number of Canadians or that it threatens the industry's ability to provide Canadians with wormless apples or with bright interior paints for apartments and homes. Associations like the CCPA have professional public relations experts and the classic lobbying structure of a permanent "president," who is relieved of administrative responsibilities in order to concentrate on "politics." In short, a mixture of involvement in regulatory policies, of treating with customers and suppliers, of providing extensive market intelligence, and of conducting lobbying and public relations campaigns fills the day-to-day agenda of most chemical industry associations.

PULP AND PAPER

In terms of value of shipments, pulp and paper mills are ranked by Statistics Canada as Canada's second leading industry.[27] Paper industries employed over 130,000 workers in 1981.[28] The industry has an especial importance in certain regions: it is the first or second industry in the Atlantic provinces, Quebec, and British Columbia and the fifth in Ontario.[29] Many communities owe their existence to the industry (Prince George in British Columbia, Dryden, Kapuskasing, and Iroquois Falls in Ontario, Matane and Buckingham in Quebec, and so on), heightening its social and economic importance.[30]

Several aspects of the industry's structure provide a framework for collective action. Product diversity is minimal: newsprint and wood pulp account for close to three-quarters of the industry's shipments. This property encourages collective action in R&D, unlike in the chemical industry, where R&D are much more firm-specific. A majority of pulp and paper production comes from Canadian-owned and -controlled firms, but a significant minority emerges from foreign firms. Since both types of firms aim heavily for American markets, this division appears meaningless in terms of common collective action, unlike in food processing. In short, the industry shares a range of economic interests that does not occur in other sectors: large integrated companies manufacture relatively homogeneous products and ship primarily to the same market.

Interest representation in the sector approximates the "organized" model. Business interests work heavily through a single group, the Canadian Pulp and Paper Association (CPPA). Founded in 1913, the CPPA is a large organization, employing over 80 people in 1983. It is a highly "developed" association, well prepared for both policy advocacy and participation. Its full-time president is freed for lobbying tasks by the support of a vice-president responsible for administration. The president draws on an executive board composed, by statute, of CEOs and on six policy committees composed of members of the board or their alternates. Accordingly, CEOs are directly and intimately involved in the making and presentation of policy by the industry. The now-familiar public affairs division provides support both for communications directed to the general public and for "government affairs."

Less common among manufacturing associations in Canada is the extensive organization found in the CPPA for policy participation. It involves systematic differentiation along several dimensions. First, the association has separate product sections: newsprint, wood pulp, absorbent products, book writing and coated papers, kraft and specialty papers, paperboard and boxboard, paperboard and container board, and sanitary papers. It represents over 90 per cent of production in the first two categories and only slightly less in the others. In the food processing and chemical sectors, product "sections" took the form of independent associations, scarcely integrated if not competitive.

Second, differentiation within the association follows the vertical functional division between harvesting and processing wood. Harvesting techniques are the special concern of the Woodlands Section of the association and processing techniques of the Technical Section. Both sections are semi-autonomous, with individuals from member companies rather than firms themselves filling their rosters, which are organized into chapters and sub-sections. Thus the Technical Section in 1981, for example, had 22 standing committees of its own, drawing from 4,500 individual members organized into 10 regional branches.[31] It enjoyed an annual budget of $500,000 and employed 13 people. The section describes itself as "a membership organization of technically-oriented individuals whose main objectives are to improve their own technical and scientific competence and to raise the technology of the Canadian pulp and paper industry." It publishes various papers and articles written by members on problems and improvements in production.

Third, the CPPA has a line of differentiation sometimes found in associations with domains dominated by large, integrated companies – differentiation by function within the firm. Hence it has sections for company officers responsible for finance, industry development, trade, tax, insurance, computer systems, transportation, purchasing services, and human resources. Finally, it has an extensive statistics and economic services program, essential to policy participation. These divisions and sections of the association are integrated in two ways. The executive board is composed of the CEOs from each major firm and gives overall policy direction. The extensive (by Canadian standards) bureaucracy keeps track of the activities of the divisions and sections under the general co-ordination of the permanent president.

The various sections and divisions of the CPPA make distinctive contributions to its participation in the policy process. Let us take, for example, the central policy problem facing the pulp and paper industry – water pollution. "The production processes commonly used in the industry involve enormous quantities of water: for transporting wood within the mill, as an input in the cooking and grinding processes, and for carrying the separated fibres through the bleaching, refining and sheet forming phases of manufacture. Ultimately, after various forms of treatment, the water is returned to the environment carrying large quantities of wastes, usually in a very dilute form."[32] Water pollution is regulated by provincial environment departments and by the Environmental Protection Agency of the federal environment department, working primarily through the Fisheries Act. The companies work at the provincial level through both the CPPA and the provincial forestry associations discussed in chapter 8 and at the federal level through the CPPA alone.

The evidence is strong that the CPPA operates at both levels in co-optive pluralist networks, formed because of heavy dependence by government on the association for information. Thus the CPPA participated in a federal-provincial task force that defined the approach to regulation adopted by the federal government in 1971.[33] The task force has since been reconstituted occasionally to discuss changes in the regulations. Public interest groups were not represented, and decisions were made on a consensual basis following discussion. Effective regulation in this area requires information on company expenditures, pollution abatement, financial status of the mills and firms involved (so as to take account of economic and social effects), and amount and type of effluents discharged.[34] Government agencies also need the expertise required to assess these various types of information. To date, information has been collected from the companies by the economics and statistics section of the CPPA and supplied confidentially to government agencies.[35] By entrusting these data to the CPPA, members of the association have gained a significant role in the formulation of environmental policy. They participate in the process through the various divisions and sections of the association. Thus committees from the Woodlands Section work on water problems associated with transporting harvested logs. Others from the Technical Section and the newsprint and wood pulp divisions study issues related to the discharge of effluents. Finally, the section for financial officers considers the financial implications of various regulatory approaches.

The partnership with the federal government extends to R&D. In 1925, the CPPA signed an agreement with the federal government to help support and manage an industry program of pulp and paper research. The fruit of this early collaboration exists today in the form of the Pulp and Paper Research Institute of Canada (PPRIC). Located in Pointe Claire, Quebec, in facilities built to the industry's specifications by the federal government, the PPRIC employs 320 scientific and supervisory staff. A second, western laboratory has recently been opened in Vancouver, also drawing on federal financial support. The institute supplements and complements technical efforts of individual firms by supplying them with basic research data and technology that they can use to become more competitive. "The industry looks to the Institute for research that no single company could normally justify carrying out alone."[36] When a company joins the CPPA, it automatically becomes a member of the institute and must help pay for its support. The institute spent over $19 million in 1980.[37]

The existence of the institute follows the pattern of government-industry collaboration in research in the forestry industry that we saw in chapter 8. Both it and the comprehensive character of the CPPA contrast strongly with the patterns of collective action found in the food processing and chemical industries. Industry structure appears crucial in accounting for these differences. The pulp and paper industry is owned and controlled to a significant extent in

Canada; its large, integrated companies produce for and compete on world markets; and their products are relatively homogeneous. These factors, combined with a need to respond collectively to governmental regulation, foster uncommonly well integrated associative action.

CONCLUSIONS

Compared to other divisions of the Canadian economy, manufacturing firms have undeveloped associational instruments. The CMA, which speaks for the division as a whole, is primarily a policy advocate and enjoys little of the share in policy-making enjoyed by corresponding associations of its size and scope in the other divisions of the economy we have examined. It also has not sought to differentiate itself formally to represent the various sectors of manufacturing, something commonly done by western European associations of its kind (see chapter 11). Organization within sectors is either "competitive" or "divided," with few exceptions. The overall picture that emerges emphasizes fragmentation and little likelihood of joint collective action. Narrow, special-interest politics dominates manufacturing in Canada.

There is no simple or obvious explanation for this pattern. Even several relevant factors must be treated cautiously. Canadian manufacturing is stronger in the primary transformation of raw materials and in intermediate products. In several sectors, notably forest products, some metallic minerals, petroleum, and natural gas, the dominant companies are vertically integrated. Thus the companies that cut timber, mine metals, or extract petroleum also produce lumber or pulp, smelt and refine metals, and manufacture basic petrochemicals. The associations representing these sectors concern themselves with problems of resource extraction and manufacturing. Several basic and intermediate goods producers in secondary sectors have stronger ties to primary producers than those manufacturing finished goods in their own sectors. Producers of finished goods are oriented less to export markets than producers of basic and intermediate goods in sectors like chemicals and food processing, making formation of comprehensive sectoral peak associations difficult, as we have seen. In western Europe, such associations have been important building blocks in (primary and secondary) industry-wide peak associations.

This has not been the case in Canada, however. The powerful sectoral associations that join primary with secondary sectors could not become members of the CMA because their firms are not engaged only in manufacturing. Forestry and mining companies can join the

Confederation of British Industry and the Federation of German Industry, but not the CMA. Why has the CMA chosen a somewhat restricted domain? Perhaps its historical origins in the fight of home-market manufacturers for protection and its early preoccupation with this issue provide part of the explanation. Export-oriented industries established their own associations outside the CMA to deal with their problems. Even today the CMA is split between domestic and export orientation. Exporting firms even have the Canadian Export Association, and the major resource sectors have associations that deal with trade issues, as we saw in chapter 8. Accordingly, primary-sector firms devote greater energy to their own associations and support the CMA only tangentially. There was probably not much internal pressure on the CMA to make its domain more comprehensive.

The CMA's restricted domain deprives it of some of the stronger, more politically active Canadian companies. Also, these companies are not available to counter the more politically inert branch plant members. Both parent-company priorities and Canadian political culture lead many of these latter companies to keep their heads low. In addition, in a large firm divisional managers have less freedom for political involvement than CEOs. Hence, in a recent interview, the deputy minister of Ontario's Treasury noted that the CMA often held back in the political process because its branch plant members were more diffident than Canadian-owned firms.[38] Carroll shows that these branch plant companies are not interlocked with Canadian financial institutions and the large resource and transportation corporations.[39]

Fragmentation is accentuated by the organization of the state. Both levels of government take an active interest in manufacturing through subsidy and R&D programs. In Ottawa, there has never been a touchstone for manfacturing, except perhaps the Department of Industry (1963–9). Prior to 1963, Trade and Commerce had some sector branches for manufacturing, but its mandate included also agriculture and resources. In 1969, Industry was merged with Trade and Commerce to form Industry, Trade and Commerce, blurring again its mandate. A further reorganization in 1982 combined Industry with Regional Economic Expansion; manufacturing firms did not know whether the new department was to promote industrial growth or encourage regional equalization. The two objectives are not necessarily compatible. In addition, Agriculture, Energy, Mines and Resources, and Fisheries and Oceans had a strong interest in particular manufacturing sectors. At a minimum, horizontal and vertical diffusion of responsibility for manufacturing discourages more integrated associative action.

A conventional explanation for the weak integration of associative action in Canadian manufacturing would take the following form. Since the manufacturing economy is populated by a large number of firms, producing a diverse range of goods, and occupying myriad different markets, integrated collective action is highly unlikely. However, such an explanation is inadequate. As we shall see in the next chapter, some countries with manufacturing at least as diverse and complex have strong, vertically integrated peak associations representing both key sectors of industry and the whole of industry. Specialization in primary and intermediate goods, the presence of a strong foreign-controlled component, and decentralized state organization all may help explain Canada's peculiarities.

PART THREE

Business and Society

CHAPTER ELEVEN

Fragmentation: Two Foreign Comparisons

A review of the previous six chapters suggests that it is incorrect to speak of a single business community in Canada. There is rather a series of autonomous communities, joined often only by the tenuous ties of large conglomerate firms. Fragmentation begins at the top, where we found no overarching peak associations but a series of competing, sometimes influential lobby groups. This picture was mirrored below in various divisions of the economy. Patterns of organization varied significantly from one division to another – hierarchical, somewhat integrated associational systems in agriculture and the forest industries; flat, highly differentiated, unintegrated systems in construction and manufacturing. Within sectors wide variation in patterns of organization occurs, suggesting further fragmentation. Horticulture was organized quite differently from cattle growing, housebuilding from road building, banking from investment dealing, and food processing from chemicals. In short, business does not organize itself well on a class-wide basis in Canada, preferring narrower organizations looking to class interests within particular sectors of the economy.

The absence of class-wide organization does not imply that business in Canada lacks political influence and political power. Rather, the labour movement has been so weak and social democratic parties so inconsequential that some of the incentive for overarching class organizations has been removed. The lack of integration in the Canadian economic structure itself makes it unlikely that the whole of Canadian business can feel threatened at once. Business in Canada is left free to pursue its class interests in struggles within less encompassing divisions of the economy.

Our case studies indicate variation among different fragments of the business community in political influence and the exercise of

Table 21
Business Concentration and Political Power

	High industrial concentration	Low industrial concentration
Geographically concentrated	Very high political power Resource extraction Pulp and paper	Somewhat high political power Agriculture
Geographically dispersed	High political power Finance	Weak political power Construction

political power. The transformation of economic power – share of national production, control over capital, or level of employment – into political power is by no means straightforward. Two factors that emerged from our discussion as affecting this process are degree of geographical concentration – whether a sector is dispersed across most electoral constituencies or concentrated in fewer – and industrial concentration – whether a sector is dominated by a few large firms. Table 21 shows how these factors interact for several economic divisions already examined. Construction (chapter 7) had the least political influence and fewest opportunities to exercise political power in co-optive pluralist, clientele pluralist, or corporatist networks. Although it was responsible for a greater share of the gross national product and had a greater number of firms employing more workers than any other economic division we examined, it remained significantly handicapped in translating these properties into political influence and power. Its firms are dispersed across most constituencies and are uniformly very small. Contrast it to the resource sectors (chapter 8). These were concentrated into fewer constituencies, where they had sufficient importance that politicians could not ignore them. Further, they were dominated by a relatively small number of large firms that were able to concentrate their economic power even further through their interest associations. For the forest industries, these properties gained access to many areas in the policy process. In mining, access was more restricted, but the mining associations also were effective in warding off much state intervention. Keeping the state out of its affairs is as important to a sector of business as gaining a place in the policy-making process.

Geographical and industrial concentration was not the only element of economic structure affecting the transformation of economic into political power. The comparison of food processing, chemicals, and pulp and paper manufacturing (chapter 10) highlighted the importance of divisions between foreign-controlled and domestic firms and of the products of the sector. Divergent interests between foreign and domestic firms were largely responsible for the competitive system of interests found in food processing. The relatively homogeneous product mix of the pulp and paper sector and the highly divergent mix in the chemical sector led to highly "organized" associative action in pulp and paper and a "divided" pattern in chemicals. The presence of conflict with other classes also was a critical factor, leading to the development of corporatist networks in several agricultural sectors. The absence of effective class opponents in the finance sector permitted the development of self-regulatory and clientelist networks.

The most important consequence of this fragmentation of Canadian business and the resulting pursuit of narrower, sectoral interests is that business's power and influence are not matched by political responsibility. The dispersal of political power among various fractions of Canadian business makes it especially difficult for the state and other classes of society to hold business accountable for the exercise of its private power. I argued in chapter 1 and have amplified further in subsequent chapters the hypothesis that an inability to hold business politically responsible has important consequences for policy-making. Some kinds of policies, particularly those that require *concertation* among major socioeconomic producer groups in society, simply are not possible. These very kinds of policies are becoming more necessary in Canada with each passing year.

Two tasks remain for us before we can address this argument. First, in this chapter, I will seek to clarify further how fragmented the Canadian business community is by comparing its organization to others with different patterns of organization. Such a comparison also helps us to isolate further the factors responsible for Canadian fragmentation. Second, in chapter 12, I will place this fragmented business community in the broader context of state organization in Canada, specifically federalism and the British parliamentary tradition; both factors make their own independent contribution to the fragmentation we have found.

A CORPORATIST TYPOLOGY

Over the past decade, scholars have argued that the structure of systems of economic interest associations bears directly on choices of policies in a given democratic polity and on their success. Their preliminary conclusions about relations between economic performance and interest group systems suggest further investigation of the differences between Canadian and European associational structures. If indeed the institutions for interest representation differ between western Europe and Canada, and these differences very much matter in policy-making, then it becomes important to know precisely what these differences are. Several scholars, most notably Cameron, Lehmbruch, and Schmitter, have devised typologies that speak to these differences.[1] The schema that conforms best to the concepts used in this book is the most recent one, proposed by Lehmbruch.[2] He presents a descriptive scale of "corporatism" based on four categories.[3] (1) In *pluralism* (e.g. Canada), pressure group politics predominates; fragmented and competing interest groups lobby government agencies and parliament. (2) In *weak corporatism*, (e.g. the United Kingdom, Italy) labour participates in the formation and implementation of policies only within certain restricted policy areas or at certain stages of consultation. Together with decentralized collective bargaining, these make incomes policies difficult to implement. (3) In *medium corporatism* (e.g. Switzerland, West Germany), collective bargaining takes place at a plane broader than the firm; incomes policies enjoy temporary success. (4) In *strong corporatism* (Austria, Sweden, the Netherlands), organized labour and business participate effectively in policy formulation and implementation across those interdependent policy areas crucial for management of the economy.

As one moves along the scale from pluralist to strong corporatist, both the organization of business interests and the character of interaction among major socioeconomic producer groups change. At each step, the associational system becomes more "developed." It assumes a tighter pyramidal form, with sectoral associations becoming integrated into more general peak associations and these, in turn, becoming members of a single peak association representing all of business. To use Lehmbruch's term, vertical integration becomes more "formalized." Means are built into the system to minimize breakaways and to ensure compliance. Similar structures emerge for other classes such as labour and farmers. As vertical relationships *within* classes become more formalized in corporatist systems, horizontal relationships *between* classes become more informal and conducive to serious negotiation and bargaining.[4] Conversely, in pluralist systems, where relations among associations within classes are informal, relations between classes are formal and ritualistic.

From a macropolitical perspective, Lehmbruch's classification of Canada as pluralist is consistent with my findings. The associational system representing business described here has virtually the opposite set of properties to that found in strong corporatist systems.

Vertical relations among associations within classes are informal and ad hoc, except in several agricultural sectors. Horizontal relations between class peak associations, particularly between business and labour, are formalized, relatively infrequent and often highly stylized and symbolic. However, we found that within different divisions of the economy, associational systems vary as to type. We have found corporatism in agriculture and, to a limited extent, in construction, clientele pluralism in banking and finance, co-optive pluralism in resources, pressure pluralism in manufacturing, and so on. The overall pluralist character of Canadian associational life does not mean that pressure pluralist policy networks are the dominant form in all divisions of the economy.

In this chapter, I shall complete my characterization of the associational systems representing Canadian business by placing them in a broader comparative context. First, the Canadian systems are set off against their counterpart in a strong corporatist system, Austria, with emphasis given in the analysis not only to differences in structure but also to the range of roles assumed in the policy process. Second, a comparison is made between Canada and a weak corporatist state, the United Kingdom, with the additional dimension of a matching of sector-level associations. Here again, particular attention is paid to differences in the roles played by associations in the policy system.

AUSTRIA: STRONG CORPORATISM

In the outpouring of comment on and analysis of the Japanese economic record since 1960, other successful economic performances by industrialized democracies such as Austria are often ignored. Throughout the 1970s, unemployment stood at around 2 per cent in this small central European democracy, and in the late 1970s youth unemployment rested at 0.8 per cent, less than one-tenth the OECD average.[5] Only Switzerland and West Germany among industrialized states had a lower inflation rate. Austria had with Norway the highest growth rate in Europe in the 1970s[6] and surpassed the OECD average in total exports, investment, productivity, and so on. Politically, the country has been a remarkable success in the post-war period, its stability belying its misfortune in the 1920s and 1930s.[7] Almost all explanations of its remarkable economic and political record invoke its corporatist system of governance as a crucial factor.

At the core of this system lie two important phenomena. First, there is a well-developed ideology of social partnership among busi-

ness, labour, and farmers. Developed as a response to the series of
crises in Austrian society between 1935 and 1955, this ideology emphasizes the need of the major social partners to co-operate with,
and to listen to, one another. There is a commitment to allow class
conflict to grow only so far before it is internalized and addressed
in ways judged a "fair" compromise. The process of internalization
of conflict takes place within the second basic component of the
Austrian system – the long-established chambers. There are two such
bodies at the federal level, the Federal Economic Chamber (Bun-
deswirtschaftskammer), representing business, and the Chamber of
Labour (Arbeiterkammertag), and these are normally joined by the
Presidents' Conference of the regional agricultural chambers.

The only commonality between these organizations and the Chamber of Commerce in Canada is the word "chamber." The Austrian
organizations are all-encompassing, compulsory associations to which
business firms, workers, and farmers must belong.[8] According to
their public law status, they are obliged to represent common and
legitimate members' interests only and to take account of the "general interest" in making their representations. The law states that
they must arbitrate internally between conflicting member interests
before confronting the state. To these ends, they are expected to
organize themselves according to democratic principles. In exchange
for meeting these conditions, the chambers must be consulted by
government about legislative proposals and about fulfilling advisory
functions in the state, and they receive other governing responsibilities noted below.

In Canada, those few compulsory associations are almost invariably
mirrored by voluntary associations (the Colleges of Physicians and
Surgeons by the Canadian Medical Association, the Association des
entrepreneurs en construction du Québec by the "traditional six"
construction associations). The same pattern occurs in Austria. The
Austrian Trade Union Federation (ÖGB), which is voluntary and
represents about 60 per cent of Austria's workers, plays the key role
on the labour side. A highly centralized organization, it in effect
controls the Chamber of Labour and is closely tied to the Austrian
Social Democratic Party (SPÖ). On the business side, the Federal
Economic Chamber is weakened by a system giving large and small
firms alike one vote, thereby failing to give big business its due, and
by a prohibition against engaging in market or cartel functions.[9]
Alongside the chamber, there has grown a voluntary association, the
Federation of Austrian Industrialists, which represents primarily the
larger industrial firms. As Katzenstein notes: "Since it faces fewer
internal restraints, the federation is more flexible, maneuverable,

and outspoken on controversial issues than the chamber is in normal practice. Even so, the federation maintains intimate contacts with the chamber and, in particular, with its industry section."[10]

However, while the ÖGB, a voluntary association, is the key organization on the labour side, the reverse is true for business. The Federal Economic Chamber takes precedence over voluntary business interest associations. Marin writes that, to succeed, the functional self-government of business appears to require compulsory structures of *intra*-organizational interest intermediation.[11] Business interests are simply too diverse and competitive to coalesce otherwise. At the same time, these compulsory associations must be supplemented by voluntary ones if business people are to grant them legitimacy. This difference between business and labour reflects well Offe and Wiesenthal's argument that separate logics of collective action govern these two social categories.[12]

Consequently, the size and structure of the business chamber organization depart widely from those found among Canadian business associations. It employs 4,610 persons, compared to 10 for the Business Council on National Issues and about 30 for the Canadian Chamber of Commerce.[13] In 1984, its budget was approximately $357 million, which dwarfs the budgets of even the largest Canadian groups.[14] The typical Canadian association executive is a jack-of-all-trades, speaking with officials and politicians at one moment and arranging with caterers for the annual meeting the next. His or her Austrian counterpart resembles most closely a professional administrator in a large bureaucratic organization. He or she lives in a technocratic, rationalized world performing a restricted number of specialized functions.

The overall structure of the business chamber differs also in its pattern of internal differentiation. Charged with representing all of business and mediating disputes between sectors of business, it is highly differentiated along sectoral lines. These sectoral divisions, whether they represent machine tools or industrial chemicals, perform analogous functions to Canadian sectoral associations, with one important difference. They perform these in the context of a set of overall policy positions promoted by the chamber, they remain bound by these, and they are subject to the authority of the chamber's leaders. Austria's sectoral representatives are vertically integrated into a single representative body, whereas Canadian groups are not vertically integrated at all into any of the competing associations claiming to speak for all of business.

As was noted in chapter 5, the worlds of business interest associations and of political parties are quite autonomous in Canada.

The opposite is the case in Austria. Co-ordination between the Austrian Trade Union Federation and the Social Democratic Party on the one side and between the Federal Economic Chamber and the Austrian People's Party (conservative) on the other is regularized and intensive. Parties and associations commonly share and trade staff, particularly on the left side of the spectrum.[15] Drawing on such relationships, policy-making begins at a very crucial pre-parliamentary stage. Positions on issues are hammered out first in the peak associations of the social partners and then discussed in informal meetings which include association officials, party and government leaders, and bureaucratic officials. Decisions are taken in forums organized on a double-parity basis, reflecting the social partnership ideology – business versus labour, conservatives versus social democrats – and governed by a unanimity principle.[16] Consequently, Marin estimates, 85 per cent of all legislative proposals related to economic and social policy end up being passed unanimously.[17] Lehmbruch adds that such a system does not mean that parliament and parties have lost power at the expense of interest groups. On the contrary, he argues, and Katzenstein concurs, these links render Austrian corporatism democratic (as opposed to authoritarian).[18] Parties and associations retain some autonomy from one another. "Too much autonomy from political parties would not only risk the democratic character of Austria's corporatism, but make for explosive conflict among interest groups and political parties. Too much dependence on political parties would tie interest groups directly to the competitive relations among parties and thus risk the consensual bargaining that now occurs."[19]

How has this corporatist system of interest representation affected Austria's impressive economic record? Fritz Scharpf notes that analysts of economic policy often neglect two rather crucial points.[20] First, in any economic policy, there is an element of strategic choice: different countries choose to pursue different strategies by different means. Second, once a strategy is chosen, it will fit more or less well, depending on the structure and state of the economy. The Austrians made a strategic choice to pursue full employment in a Keynesian fashion in the 1970s. This policy succeeded partially because their corporatist system was well adapted for its implementation. In addition, there was a good fit between this strategic choice and the structure of the economy.

In general terms, Austria pursued throughout the 1970s a classic Keynesian macroeconomic policy.[21] The government sought to stimulate demand by deficit financing and to use this means to maintain close to full employment. At the same time, it encouraged wage restraint and sought to keep prices under control. The emphasis then was on macroeconomic policy instruments, with considerably less effort devoted to such microeconomic instruments as labour market policies, industry restructuring, and promotion of R&D. The key to successful implementaion of such a policy is control over prices and wages, something accomplished through a remarkable institution called the Paritätische Kommission für Preis- und Lohnfragen (PKfPL). Established in 1957, the commission includes five bodies under its wings. One of these, the Subcommittee on Prices (Unterausschuß für Preisfragen) reviews and recommends requests for price increases.[22] These recommendations are voluntary yet invariably followed. A second subcommittee, for wage questions (Unterausschuß für Lohnfragen), approves the initiation of negotiations for collective agreements and authorizes, from time to time, certain details of contracts, particularly as they relate to duration.[23] Negotiations are overseen by the ÖGB, which, being strongly centralized, also directs and approves any agreement. The other organs of the PKfPL supervise and direct not only this incomes policy, but also economic forecasting and labour market, agricultural, social, regional, and industrial policy.[24]

The double-parity rule governs all meetings of the commission's organs. Labour is represented by its chamber and the ÖGB, business by its chamber and by the presidents' conference of the regional agricultural chambers. The state is present almost ex officio, observing negotiations among the social partners but not arbitrating among them. In the PKfPL organ entitled the Präsidentenvorbesprechen, which makes recommendations in times of crisis on crucial issues of social and economic policy, only the social partners are represented.[25] Lehmbruch, it will be remembered, remarked that in corporatist decision-making very formal vertical organization within social classes is complemented by informal, horizontal relationships between them. This property certainly prevails in the Austrian system. "The *Paritätische Kommission* has also no fixed places for meeting, and no address under which it can be reached. There is no telephone connection, no letterhead paper, no particular or uniform office staff ... Sessions of the Commission, with the exception of the Subcommittee on Wages, follow no set agenda ... There are no fixed orders, statutes, written and fixed duties and laws."[26] Key decisions are often made in head-to-head sessions between the presidents of the Federal Economic Chamber and of the ÖGB.

Not only was the corporatist system well adapted for the type of informal negotiations crucial to an incomes policy, it fit well with the Austrian economic structure. A basic structural prerequisite of such

228 Business and Society

a policy system is a relative balance of power between business and labour. Labour's power base in Austria rests upon its success in organizing a high proportion of the labour force, its strongly centralized trade union structure, and direct organizational linkages between trade unions and the Social Democratic Party. The usually dominant voice of business in capitalist economies is more muted in Austria. In an attempt to maintain independence following the Second World War, the government nationalized a significant number of firms. Today, the country's transportation, communications, and power industries are virtually completely publicly owned. There are a number of state monopolies, including the salt and tobacco industries. The two largest commercial banks and seven of the largest eight joint stock companies are state-controlled.[27] Consequently, public-sector firms have a prominent place in the basic materials industries and in semi-finished products. Heavily tilted towards large firms, public enterprises produce about one-fifth of total gross industrial output and about one-third of exports.[28] When one adds to this public sector a sizeable number of foreign firms, it becomes apparent that the Austrian-controlled private sector has a lesser position than the private indigenous business class in most capitalist countries.[29] Oriented to domestic markets, these private-sector firms play a much more subdued role in national politics than do business communities elsewhere. In addition, the presence of a significant publicly owned sector in which the trade unions have invested heavily and have some equity shares creates an important base for interchange between business and labour. Each social partner is tied sufficiently to these nationalized industries to sense a need to co-operate on matters of general policy.

The organization of business interests in Austria thus differs significantly from what we have seen in Canada. First, Canada lacks the commitment by major socioeconomic producer groups to an ideology of social partnership, an ideology that energizes and governs behaviour in the elaborate Austrian system of interest representation. Second, the fragmented associational system in Canada contrasts with that in Austria, where business firms are represented by a centralized, vertically integrated, compulsory association which is complemented by a limited number of voluntary associations. This system of associations is tied to the central governing institutions of the Austrian state through a symbiotic relationship with the conservative Austrian People's Party. Third, the Austrian peak association for business participates in the making of economic and social policy much more directly than its Canadian counterparts. Working through a series of informal policy structures that bring it face to face with a powerful labour foe, business participates in the implementation of an incomes policy as well as in the making and delivery of other macro-social policies. Business then initiates and participates directly in the formulation or amendment of policies in these areas to a degree unknown in Canada.

Perhaps the most obvious advantage of this network of structures has been Austria's successful pursuit of Keynesian demand management in the 1970s. The crucial additions of an incomes policy and controls on wages supervised by unions were not possible in Canada because business and labour were not committed to internalizing their differences through notions of co-responsibility or organized to implement such policies. Canada has been left to follow the kind of liberal policy course found in large countries, which pays little attention to the quality of inter-class relations. I argue in chapter 13 that European countries with small, open economies and liberal trade policies anchored in the concerted action of social partners may provide a more suitable model for Canada.

At the same time, the Austrian policy system has its disadvantages. In the face of increasing pressures of international competition, it is not yet clear whether Austrian corporatism is flexible enough to implement the microeconomic policies required to facilitate industrial rationalization and adjustment. In addition, the system by definition excludes certain categories of people. Socialist farmers and business people and conservative trade unionists are not well accommodated. Unorganized labour and third parties such as the ecologically minded Greens are frozen out as well. At present, these categories represent a very small proportion of the population; pressure remains strong in the country to tie oneself to one of the two Lagers, or camps. If conditions change, particularly in the economy, these disenfranchised groups may grow in size, precipitating a crisis in the system, since it will not represent them well. Yet the analysis in this book shows that many of the same groups in Canada are effectively disenfranchised by co-optive or clientele pluralist networks in many sectors. What is more, organized labour finds itself on the margins of the policy system in Canada. In Austria, labour is a central player in policy-making.

BRITAIN: WEAK CORPORATISM

The interest in a comparison between Canada and Austria arises from some intriguing economic similarities. Both countries have small, open economies. Both lie close to a big industrial country with which each shares cultural traditions and a language. Both have a relatively strong cohort of foreign-controlled firms. On the same dimensions, the comparison between Canada and the United Kingdom is less compelling. Britain remains one of the larger industrial nations in the world. Its economy is not dominated by foreign capital; it is not "dependent" on another economy in the way in which Canada is dependent on the United States. In Britain the manufacturing sectors are heavy traders in international markets, while in Canada the resource sectors carry this load.

The reasons for comparing Britain and Canada relate more to political institutions and culture. The two countries share a parliamentary tradition, and Britain and English Canada share certain cultural traits. They partake of an "Anglo-American" political tradition that emphasizes the autonomy and voluntary self-regulation of civil society, including business.[30] The cultural tradition of the "self-sufficient" firm is thought by some to discourage collective action by business.[31] Market-based financial systems favour "company-led" as opposed to "state-led" industrial adjustment and encourage business to maintain a certain distance from government, in contrast to the closeness found in states like Japan and France where adjustment is negotiated.[32]

Somewhat puzzling is the greater organizational integration in Britain than in Canada. Despite Britain's larger and more diversified economy, its business associational systems are more developed. First, British business coalesces better as a class through the medium of inter-sectoral associations than does Canadian business. Second, major British manufacturing sectors such as chemicals, food processing, and machinery organize themselves into sectoral peak associations much more than Canadian manufacturing. British business thus has a more institutionalized and systematic place in policy-making than Canadian business.

For the interests of business as a class, the relevant comparison lies between the British peak association, the Confederation of British Industry (CBI), and the associations discussed in chapter 5 plus the CMA. The CBI differs from these Canadian groups in several telling respects. The CBI occupies a middle ground between western Europe and North America. It is more tightly joined to sectoral associations than the Canadian equivalents but lacks the more closely knit, vertical hierarchical structures of such groups as the Federal Economic Chamber in Austria, the Vorort in Switzerland, and the Federation of German Industry. The CBI is a "mixed association," having both individual companies and associations as members. In fact, the association has four categories of members: industrial companies, trade associations and employer associations, public-sector (nationalized) companies, and commercial companies.[33] Individual industrial companies contributed 73.7 per cent of membership revenue in 1979, commercial companies 14.1 per cent, associations 7.7 per cent, and public corporations 4.5 per cent.[34] Associations figure prominently on the CBI's governing council, the "parliament of British business," with about half of the 400 seats.[35] They are less well represented, however, on the key CBI President's Committee. The CBI, unlike its Canadian counterparts, can aggregate systematically the interests of the various sectors of the economy, define (sometimes successfully, sometimes not) the longer, common class interest of these sectors, and press this interest, all the while claiming with justification to represent the nation's industry.

By British "industry," I mean the resource (mining, petroleum production), manufacturing, construction, and transportation and communications divisions of the British economy. In this respect, the CBI is more broadly based than the CMA, which does not include even resource extraction sectors. All the clearing banks, 20 merchant banks, and 10 major insurance companies also belong, and so the CBI's domain is as broad horizontally as that of the Business Council on National Issues (BCNI).[36] The CBI's scope of representation exceeds the BCNI's in two respects, however. Since 1969, all the major nationalized industries have been enrolled as full members of the association, while they are excluded by the BCNI. In addition, its many sectoral associations give the CBI greater "depth" in its representation of business. The position of financial firms in both the CBI and the BCNI is similar. Grant and Marsh caution that financial institutions value the CBI less as their spokesperson than as a means for maintaining contacts with "industry."[37] Finance in Britain continues to have its own associational system, as it does in Canada.[38]

Finally, the CBI also speaks for small business. Although some small firms split away from the association in 1965 and established what is called today the Association of Independent Businesses, many have been effectively integrated in what is now called the Smaller Firms Council of the CBI.[39] Thus the Association of Independent Businesses has less than half as many member companies as the Canadian Federation of Independent Business. In short, the CBI possesses greater vertical representation and a broader definition of "industry" than its Canadian analogues.

The CBI thus has a greater claim to be the single legitimate representative of business as a class than any British or Canadian association that we have studied. Other British associations have general, inter-sectoral domains, but distinctly less prominent than the CBI. Such arrangements contrast with the Canadian case, where there is not a distinct primus inter pares. The Institute of Directors is the first of these other British groups, composed of individual business people (not firms) drawn from many of the larger outfits. This group has enjoyed some recent prominence because its views are more right-wing than those of the CBI and hence more pleasing to the ears of the Thatcher government.[40] The Association of British Chambers of Commerce is another possibility but remains very weak at the national level, with its strongest units being based in the cities.[41]

The CBI's activities provide a contrast to the Canadian case. Middlemas describes the CBI as one of a limited number of "governing institutions," "a body which assumes functions devolved upon it by government, shares some or all of the assumptions about national interests held by government and accepts aims similar to those laid down by government."[42] Until 1979, major changes in economic policy were pursued only after intensive consultations with such governing institutions as the CBI. Middlemas notes that the formal, representative, and broadly inclusive domain of an organization like the CBI relieved the government of the difficult task of dealing with and harmonizing the clashes of wills of large numbers of heterogeneous groups.[43] Under the Conservative governments of Margaret Thatcher, interest in consultation has been less. The CBI, accordingly, has found itself forced to work more frequently through pressure pluralist networks. In contrast, none of the associations in Canada with domains as general as the CBI could be classified as "governing institutions." They are rather, as was suggested in chapter 5, strong and not so strong advocacy groups working outside the policy process through pressure pluralist policy networks.

Similar conclusions emerge at the major sectoral plane, particularly within manufacturing. These can be illustrated by comparing British and Canadian associations in two manufacturing sectors discussed in chapter 10, chemicals and food processing. The associational system in the British chemical industry differs from the Canadian system in two respects.[44] First, the British system is more complex: there are many more associations, some with domains considerably narrower than those found in Canada (e.g. the British Fluoropolymer Processors Association). Second, despite its larger size and diversity, the British associational system is more integrated than Canada's. Most British associations belong to a sectoral peak association, the Chemical Industries Association (CIA), a phenomenon not found in Canada. The CIA operates with revenues more than seven and one half times that of the largest Canadian group, the Canadian Chemical Producers Association (CCPA).[45] It employs 111 people (to the CCPA's 11) and has been relatively successful in defining and articulating the common interests of this large and varied industry.[46] In contrast, the Canadian system was described in chapter 10 as "organized": a series of discrete, non-overlapping but scarcely integrated sectoral associations. A similar contrast may be drawn between the British and Canadian food processing sectors. In Britain, a broad sectoral peak association, the Food and Drink Federation, while not as successful perhaps as the CIA, has fostered integration of collective action far surpassing that found in the "competitive" Canadian system described in chapter 10.

Activities of the associations in these sectors differ in the two countries.[47] The CIA has assumed responsibility for implementing a program of occupational training for the whole of the chemical industry, a major role with long-term consequences for the sector. Designing and implementing a policy of this kind are scarcely feasible in Canada, where sectoral associational systems are populated by very loosely coupled specialist associations and no peak associations. Another difference pertains to the conversion of economic power into political power. While Canadian chemical associations (except for prescription drugs) work primarily through pressure pluralist networks, British groups have more frequent recourse to co-optive pluralist networks, most notably the Association of the British Pharmaceutical Industry, the British Agrochemicals Association, and the British Aerosol Manufacturers Association.[48] Similar differences emerge in food processing.[49]

Several explanations exist for these differences. The existence of a unitary state and greater cultural homogeneity in Britain are not as useful as might be expected.[50] Rather, differences in industrial structure and British membership in the European Community (EC) are more promising avenues to explore.[51] Since joining the EC in 1973, directives and regulations from the Community on health and safety in the work-place and environmental pollution have become increasingly important for the British chemical industry. While individual firms might cope with these issues on their own at the national level, they find the task too complex at the European level and resort heavily to associative action. However, it is not simply a matter of volume of work and new, difficult-to-understand political institutions. Community membership has required a more sophisticated strategic response from each national unit and a longer-range view of issues. Consequently, staff members have become more professionalized in British chemical industry associations as these have been called upon to function as policy "think tanks" and to produce well-researched policy reviews. The industry-wide nature of many of the problems has fostered greater unity in the industry and with it greater integration in the sectoral associational system.

Differences in industry culture and firm "philosophy," partially related to the foreign-ownership question in Canada, provide a second route for explanation. The "industry culture" in Britain tends to be more co-operative than that in Canada. The British chemical industry is dominated by indigenously owned firms, particularly Imperial Chemical Industries (ICI). This firm operates very closely to what Grant has called a tripartite firm.[52] It supports associative action enthusiastically and is concerned that the associations to which it belongs are effective and well organized. This co-operative style is not uncommon among firms in the sector and has stimulated the continued development of chemical industry associations in Britain.

The Canadian chemical industry possesses a different structure, being dominated by a group of large American firms rather than by a single, indigenously controlled one. These firms direct associative action along different lines than those cultivated by the ICI. American firms see associations as "lobbies primarily, organisations that can be mobilised to fight political battles that are derived from the need to preserve or expand markets. Associations are not countenanced as interlocutors with labour nor are they seen as potential partners with labour and the state in managing the socio-political order."[53] Canadian associations often represent primarily branch plants, not totally independent firms. Their more limited tasks appear to reflect the limited autonomy of a branch plant. Associations, in short, must behave as an extension of the firm. Firms in the sector in Canada display more individualism, restricting their co-operation with the state and with labour. Associations, accordingly, are not pushed to cultivate the autonomy and expertise required for longer-range policy development that are found in the British case.

CONCLUSIONS

This chapter has sought to clarify further the properties of the associational systems representing Canadian business by placing them in a broader comparative context. In previous chapters, I have assessed associations by comparing them to the theoretical schema outlined in chapters 3 and 4. While this ideal-type approach to analysis reveals associational characteristics considered essential for the study of policy-making, it is useful to supplement it with comparisons among actual alternative systems. Capitalists in other advanced industrial democracies have fashioned divergent systems for collective action. Business communities elsewhere are not necessarily organized in the disintegrated, classically pluralist Canadian manner. There are advantages and disadvantages to any system, and it is a complex question whether advantages outweigh disadvantages in any one case. I shall turn to this question in chapter 13.

In chapters 5 through 10, I considered two sets of factors that shape the organization of business interests in Canada. The analysis of business associations in each division of the economy sought to relate their structures and activities to an economic context. The approach was to look, for example, at the farmer as an economic actor or the building firm and its economic plight and, from this perspective, to ask what would motivate the farmer or contractor to engage in collective action. In addition, specific state structures and policies oriented to a given economic sector or sectors and addressing the economic problems identified for the actors concerned were studied as to their likely effect on the collective action of business. In this respect, then, I have carried out a study of the "political economy" of associative action: "The analysis of political economy aims to explain political strategies and, so far as possible, economic and political outcomes by showing how these strategies and outcomes result from the self-defined interests of actors."[54]

However, aspects of economic structure more general than sectoral properties may fragment business interest associations. All the advanced capitalist countries share several impediments to an integrated organization of business interests. Business firms in different sectors, say chocolate bars and machine tools, have a difficult time seeing what problems they have in common. Similarly, firms located in Sackville, New Brunswick, may not be easily persuaded that they have some interests in common with those in Penticton, British Columbia. In all capitalist economies subject to liberal democratic polities, sectoral and territorial differences make the unification of capitalist interests trying. Two other obstacles to class unity are perhaps less central but important. Firms producing primarily for export markets have quite different interests and concerns than those oriented towards the national domestic market. Finally, most capitalist firms divide on the basis of size: small firms do not see readily a set of mutual interests with large firms, and vice versa.

Do these general factors pose problems that make integrated associative action unlikely in Canada? There is no apparent reason why the usual divisions between small and large firms are any deeper in Canada than in other countries. However, when the other three factors are examined, as a combination, they may present higher barriers than usual to capitalist unity.

Turning first to sectoral differences, Canada is distinguished from Britain and most of western Europe by the relative strength of its raw materials sectors. These are large, and active in the international market-place, and vary in their dependence on indigenous manufacturers for survival. Most export more goods than are used in the domestic market. Hence the ties, for example, between the Canadian metal mining industry and manufacturing sectors using metals are not as strong and as mutually reinforcing as those between comparable sectors in most European countries. In short, with significantly larger resource sectors less dependent on domestic manufacturing sectors for survival, Canada may have less of an economic basis for integrated collective action than Europe.

The relative autonomy of primary sectors from secondary ones is reinforced further by territorial differences. Raw material industries tend to be located in northern Ontario and Quebec and in the other provinces, whereas manufacturing remains highly concentrated in the Windsor-to-Quebec City corridor in central Canada. Geographic divisions coincide with sectoral divisions, further inhibiting integrated associative action. In such western European countries as West Germany, Switzerland, and Spain, territorial business interest associations have domains that cross-cut sectoral divisions and become an integrating force in the associational system.[55]

Finally, the dimension of market orientation – home or export – reinforces sectoral divisions as well to a limited extent. In western Europe, more manufacturing sectors, particularly those producing finished goods, are export oriented than in Canada. There is a common interest across manufacturing in export trade, hardly countered by primary sectors tied closely to the manufacturing economy. These common goals provide an important basis for unity in such comprehensive associations as the CBI in Britain, the Federation of German Industry (BDI), the Swedish Federation of Industry (SI), and the Vorort in Switzerland. They also encourage primary-sector associations to join these peak associations. The Canadian manufacturing economy has always been much more divided between home- and export-market industries. Some export industries, such as pulp and paper and petrochemicals, are tied much more closely to primary sectors than to other manufacturing sectors. Significant components of the primary sectors have no ties to Canadian manufacturers at all. Such a set of economic linkages has encouraged a comprehensive association in manufacturing, the CMA, which excludes primary sectors from its domain and is continually handicapped by divisions between export and domestic orientations. It also fosters divisions within some sectors, such as chemicals, between producers of basic and intermediate goods, usually more export oriented, and manufacturers of finished goods, which concentrate on the domestic market. Such intra-sectoral divisions discourage, in turn, the formation of sectoral peak associations which are the basic components of comprehensive peak associations in most western European countries.

These impediments to class formation created by these general properties of the economy are not countered by the Canadian state. Lacking a strong centre and prone to diffusing power, the state reinforces divisions among business that have their roots in economic structures. The diffusion of state power has two institutional sources – federalism and the British parliamentary tradition. These two institutions perhaps pose two different problems for the organization of business interests. In the case of federalism, territorial decentralization in government may foster territorial fragmentation in business associative action. In the case of parliamentarism, the emphasis on representation and its tendency to invite "bureaucratic pluralism" may reinforce the already strong divisions among sectors that result from the Canadian economic structure. Upon considering these questions in the following chapter, I conclude that both characteristics interact with economic structure in encouraging the fragmentation of business interests in Canada.

CHAPTER TWELVE

State Institutions and Business Associations

My examination of the Canadian state so far has been confined to a series of snapshots of particular components as they relate to different divisions of the economy. Yet not only the patterns of relations between state agencies and civil society vary, but so do the very institutional forms of the state across a range of countries. This chapter investigates whether two basic institutions of Canadian government, federalism and a British parliamentary tradition, are important contributing factors to the fragmentation of business interests in Canada found in earlier chapters.

With respect to federalism, the argument suggesting that it fosters fragmentation (discussed in the first section of this chapter) may be summarized as follows. Federal and provincial sharing of jurisdiction over large areas of the economy, including agriculture, natural resource production, construction, transportation, and finance and other business services, divides business within itself. Caught in a vise between the federal government and growing provincial governments, business associations are highly decentralized, squeezed dry of initiative and innovation, and often reduced to passive observers. My investigation of this argument draws, first, upon a systematic comparison of association structures among sectors under federal, shared, and provincial jurisdiction. Second, it places Canadian associations in selected sectors side by side with their counterparts in three western European countries: the United Kingdom, a "union" state; West Germany, a functional federation; and Switzerland, a jurisdictional federation. These two sets of comparisons yield a perhaps surprising conclusion: Canada's federal system favours decentralization in some business associations, but not nearly to the degree that writers in this field have led us to expect.

A corollary of this argument (analysed in the second section) relates specifically to Quebec. The combination of decentralized federalism and a movement to increase the powers of the provincial government fosters the growth in most sectors of society of separate associational systems that parallel the existing "national" systems. This proposition, however, does not reflect accurately the relations between francophone, Quebec-based business and the rest of the Canadian business community. In sectors most likely to engage in autonomous collective action, we find integration into the existing national associational system. Federalism, I conclude, does not encourage the fragmentation of individual business associations but reinforces divisions in the associational system that arise from the institutional properties of the economy noted in chapter 11.

The third section of the chapter turns to an argument centred on parliamentary government. In the British parliamentary tradition, the emphasis on representation and on bargaining among actors in a political "arena" as the means to define public or general interest begets an organization in civil society that places self-interest and division over common interests and unity. Investigating such consequences of parliamentary government is an elusive task. Recent analysis of interest group politics in Canada, when coupled to the studies in this book, suggests that, at a minimum, such a system does not counter the impetus towards fragmentation arising from the institutional structure of the economy and federalism. The workings of parliamentary government appear, if anything, to reinforce fragmentation.

FEDERALISM AND BUSINESS INTERESTS

The "Vise" of Federalism

Alan Cairns has vigorously and eloquently argued that the very workings of the Canadian federal system divide Canadians among themselves.[1] Lamenting the tendency in Canadian social science to explain patterns of Canadian government by peeering upwards through the lenses of societal cleavages, he pleads for more attention to the effects governments themselves have on divisions in society. Noting the growth of provincial governments, with larger and larger bureaucracies, and the federal government's response in kind, he sees this mutual self-aggrandizement to be reinforcing fragmentation in Canada. "Possessed of tenacious instincts for their own preservation and growth, the governments of Canadian federalism have endowed the cleavages between provinces, and between provinces and nation which attended their birth, with an ever more comprehensive political meaning."[2] The pursuit of governmental self-interest, Cairns adds, leads political and bureaucratic élites to structure society itself in ways that will serve their ends. "Governing elites view their task as the injection of provincial or federal meaning into society, giving it a degree of coherence and a pattern of interdependence more suited for government purposes than what would emerge from the unhindered working of social and market forces."[3]

As key interlocutors between society and government, interest groups are affected by such behaviour and structure their associational life to take account of the vicissitudes of predatory élites. The normal response, Cairns argues, reflecting the conclusions of David Truman and the findings of Helen Dawson and David Kwavnick, is for a group to take on a federal structure itself.[4] It immediately limits its own effectiveness. Units with local authority become competing sub-centres of power,[5] straining the cohesion of the membership and lessening the effectiveness of the organization.

Dawson elaborates on this argument for the Canadian case. She writes that most national groups are weak federations where regional units dominate the national headquarters.[6] Tension-riddled federal-provincial arenas place groups in a double bind. Members belong to provincial organizations first. "If a provincial organization permits its policies to be too profoundly influenced by national as opposed to local considerations, it will lose support among its local clientele, and this, in turn, will diminish the national organization's political impact; whereas if the provincial organizations adhere too rigidly to policies approved at the local level, it may be impossible to achieve any kind of national policy at all."[7] Such problems intensify when the national office comes to identify with the federal government and the provincial offices with provincial governments. In a policy arena filled by federal-provincial conflict, a group may be torn apart.[8]

Life becomes even more complicated when different levels of government seek to enlist a group on one side or another.[9] Not wishing to be caught in such a trap, a group may end up being frozen out of policy-making completely, to the detriment of its members. This is not a result any group relishes, yet it remains very much an occupational hazard of interest associations in Canada, so it is argued.[10] Considerable policy discussion and informal decision-making take place in meetings between federal politicians, officials, and provincial counterparts. With no access to such processes, groups find their effectiveness further limited.

Cairns's thesis, with the various supporting case studies, is powerful and has had a great effect on studies of Canadian federalism.

His generalizations and those of Helen Dawson cast a wide net, embracing all interest groups. Perhaps their nets have been cast too widely – individual business interest groups appear to resist somewhat the pressures they have identified. Chapter 2, it will be remembered, presented a scheme for classifying associations according to territorial centralization, with categories ranging from unitary associations at one extreme to independent regional associations on the other. Such structural data, admittedly, are limited, because they reflect only indirectly the actual behaviour of groups. Nevertheless, they do provide some indication of the applicability of Cairns's arguments because of his own consideration of interest group structures. Somewhat in contradiction to his propositions, the aggregate data furnished in chapter 2 revealed that most Canadian business associations possessed unitary structures. Such aggregate analysis, however, treats associations of varying importance equally, possibly distorting the picture of group life. While the vast majority of groups may have unitary structures, a smaller set of important associations may have structures that differ from the general pattern.

In order to reflect upon the applicability of Cairns's argument to business groups, while compensating for the possible weaknesses of the aggregate analysis in chapter 2, this chapter concentrates on a restricted group of more influential associations. I looked at each three-digit category of the Canadian Standard Industrial Classification and chose the dominant association in that category.[11] In most cases, the choice is obvious; in the remaining cases, I relied on my own knowledge and evaluation of relative performance. The sectors represented by groups in the sample were then sorted into three types of jurisdiction. The first type, "primarily federal jurisdiction," includes most of manufacturing and banking and selected sectors of the distribution trades. The second category, "shared jurisdiction," contains the resource sectors oriented to international markets, manufacturing sectors tied to resource industries or agriculture, nuclear and gas utilities, housing construction, cultural industries, and trust and insurance companies. Under the third, "primarily provincial" heading are placed hydroelectric utilities, the remaining construction sectors, retail trade, restaurants and food services, trucking, urban transit, investment dealers, and real estate companies.

Table 22 outlines the relationship between territorial decentralization and constitutional jurisdiction. Of these more influential business groups, over half fall under federal jurisdiction and under 20 per cent are in sectors primarily regulated by provincial governments. In practice, the line distinguishing associations that are "weak" in terms of territorial concentration from those that are "strong"

Table 22
Association Structures and Federalism

Structural type	Primarily federal jurisdiction	Shared jurisdiction	Primarily provincial jurisdiction	Total
Unitary	41 (87%)	11 (44%)	6 (37%)	58 (66%)
Unitary with regional sub-units	4 (9%)	1 (4%)	2 (13%)	7 (8%)
Federal	1 (2%)	5 (20%)	5 (31%)	11 (13%)
Confederal	0	3 (12%)	2 (13%)	5 (6%)
Affiliate	1 (2%)	2 (8%)	1 (6%)	4 (4%)
Informal affiliate	0	2 (8%)	0	2 (2%)
Independent regional associations only	0	1 (4%)	0	1 (1%)
Total	47	25	16	88

should be drawn between "federal" and "confederal" structures. In a federal association, members belong simultaneously to federal and provincial units, paying one set of dues. In the confederal case, firms belong to provincial/regional associations only, and these, in turn, join a national "umbrella" group. Problems of co-ordination and integration are more intractable for confederations than for federations. The data thus suggest caution in any attempt to apply Cairns's thesis to business interest groups. Rather than most associations being "weak federations," close to two-thirds have unitary structures. If "strong" groups include all those with federal structures, then over three-quarters of our sample are relatively well integrated over territory.

However, the predisposition towards centralized arrangements is most pronounced among "primarily federal" associations. Only one associational system – for clothing industries – is highly decentralized; only one – for bakeries – has federal arrangements. In order to understand these two cases of decentralization, it is useful to think of two forces on an association.[12] On the one side, the constitutional division of powers pushes associations either towards decentralized arrangements, as their domains are shared or primarily provincial, or towards centralized ones, with more exclusively federal jurisdiction. On the other side, the number of firms and their size come into play. The greater the number of firms, particularly when these are small or medium-sized, the greater the pressure for relatively autonomous branches to service members on location and thereby cultivate solidarity. In 1980, there were close to 1,500 bakeries in Canada and perhaps twice as many clothing manufacturers. In both cases, the firms were widely dispersed geographically. Decentralized arrangements help these associations to keep attuned to the needs of these many members.

In sectors under shared jurisdiction, the modal structure remains unitary: 44 per cent of the associations possess such a structure. The unitary associations under this category represent the nuclear power industry, gas utilities, coal mines, petroleum and natural gas producers, canola processors, pulp and paper manufacturers, and life insurance companies. Of the five associations in the federal category, three represent food sectors dominated by large national firms (a centralizing factor) with raw inputs subject to provincial regulatory régimes (decentralizing). The two others, representing housing construction and fertilizer manufacturing, have more of a mix of small and large firms and would be confederal but for strong federal government involvement. Confederal arrangements serve the poultry, fish, and wine processing sectors, and affiliate structures the dairy and publishing industries. In each case, the need to accommodate smaller firms serving local/regional markets, coupled with strong regulatory régimes at both levels of government, explains decentralization. Informal weak affiliate ties have developed in the metal mining and lumber industries. Independent regional associations are found in the primary forestry industry. These latter two cases were discussed at some length in chapter 8.

If the division between federal and confederal types is retained as the line between centralized and decentralized structures, then the primarily provincial category contains more centralized associations than even the shared category. The unitary associations here include those speaking for the electrical utilities, urban transit corporations, real estate companies, and three branches of retailing. Construction associations account for three of five of the federal structures, one of two confederal structures, and the affiliate arrangement. The remaining federal associations are in the retail and restaurant sectors respectively; the other confederal group is the Canadian Trucking Association.

The predominance of unitary associations in Table 22 suggests the following tentative hypothesis: while both factors affect the degree of territorial fragmentation, industry structure has a greater effect than constitutional arrangements. One simple approach to assessing this hypothesis follows: association structures in a constant set of sectors are compared across a group of countries that vary in political centralization. Data are available for three countries in addition to Canada: the United Kingdom, West Germany, and Switzerland. The United Kingdom is the most centralized of these. Described by Rokkan and Urwin as a "union state," its centralized state structure retains certain areas of decentralized administration as a historical legacy of its formation.[13] Overall responsibility for economic development and international trade lies with the central government. Yet Scotland retains its own legal system and administers its own regulatory programs in the building and parts of the food processing industries, among others, guaranteeing some pressures towards decentralized associations in relevant sectors.[14]

The federal system in West Germany falls between the more decentralized federations of Canada and Switzerland and Britain's union state. Termed by some authors "functional federalism," the West German system assigns primary responsibility for policy-making to the federal government and administration and implementation of policy to the Land or state governments. The latter have most of their legislative competence concentrated in three areas – education, police, and local government – but have also defined and carried out industrial policy.[15] We would expect West German interest associations to have strong federal-level organizations, even more so because federal ministries must attend to the interests affected by any proposed measures.[16] Yet associations may want a strong regional presence as well, because the powers of the Länder over administration give them an important discretionary influence on the content of policy.

The Swiss and Canadian systems conform to the concept of jurisdictional federalism. The cantons and provinces respectively have significant areas of legislative competence and proceed in those areas much more autonomously from the national government than one finds in West Germany or Britain. From the perspective of business, the Swiss system is more centralized than the Canadian. The Swiss central government has wider powers over commerce and, important for our discussion, over the regulation of food and drugs than the federal government in Canada.[17] In addition, article 32 of the federal constitution states that "the appropriate economic organizations" are to be heard before federal laws are made, thereby giving the same stimulus to a strong federal presence in associations as we found in West Germany.[18] In short, the constitutional inducement to decentralization in associations should be greatest in Canada, followed in order by Switzerland, West Germany, and Britain.

This incentive will be reinforced or cross-cut by industrial structures. The more firms in a sector serving national and international markets, or the more firms that are large and fewer rather than

Table 23
Classification of Sectors by Firm and Market Size

	Large firms predominate	*Smaller firms predominate*
National/ international markets	Red meat (CDN, GB) Fruit and vegetable processing Industrial chemicals Pharmaceuticals	Machine tools
Local/regional markets	Dairy processing	Construction (excluding civil engineering) Red meat (CH, D)

NOTE: CDN = Canada; CH = Switzerland; D = West Germany; GB = Britain.

small and plentiful, the greater the pressure for a more unitary structure. In order to add this dimension to our analysis, seven sectors where comparative data are available are studied. These are classified in Table 23 along two dimensions of industrial structure: size of firm and market orientation. Based on this classification, decentralized structures should be most pronounced in construction and in meat processing in West Germany and Switzerland, which continue to have a strong artisanal component. In these sectors, small firms serving local or regional markets predominate. Conversely, unitary structures would be most likely in sectors dominated by large firms serving national or international markets: fruit and vegetables processing, industrial chemicals and pharmaceuticals, and the red meat industries in Britain and Canada.

Structural data on associations in these seven sectors were collected in our international comparative research project on the organization of business interests (see chapter 1). Using the data set and published and unpublished reports in the project, I selected the leading association(s) in each sector for each country and classified its internal structure (see Table 24).[19] Generally speaking, decentralization along territorial lines seems more responsive to industrial structure than to constitutional arrangements. Looking first at the sectors where unitary structures would be expected based on industrial organization (the four listed in the upper-left-hand cell of Table 23), unitary structures, in fact, prevail. The red meat industries in Britain and in Canada and the pharmaceutical industries in all countries are represented by unitary groups. Unitary arrangements also dominate in fruit and vegetable processing and industrial chemicals in all countries except Canada. The two Canadian exceptions,

Table 24

Four-Country Comparison of Association Decentralization within Sectors

Sector	United Kingdom	West Germany	Switzerland	Canada
LARGE; NATIONAL/INTERNATIONAL MARKETS				
Red meat (CDN. GB)	U	–	–	U
Fruit and vegetable	U	U	U	F
Industrial chemical	U + R	U + R	U	2U, U + R. F
Pharmaceuticals	U	U	U	U
SMALL; NATIONAL/INTERNATIONAL MARKETS				
Machine tools	3(U + R). F	F. CF	U	U
LARGE; LOCAL/REGIONAL MARKETS				
Dairy processing	A	U. 2(U + R). F. CF. A	F	A
SMALL; LOCAL/REGIONAL MARKETS				
Construction (excl. civil engineering)	F. F[A]. U + R	2CF	2CF	F. CF(A)
Red meat (D. CH)	–	F/CF	F	–

SOURCES: Organization of Business Interests Data Bank; Hanspeter Kriesi and Peter Farago, "The Regional Differentiation of Business Interest Associations in Switzerland," Paper presented to Conference on the Regional Organization of Business Interests and Public Policy, McMaster University, May 1985; W. Coleman and W. Grant, "Regional Differentiation of Business Interest Associations: A Comparison of Canada and the United Kingdom," *Canadian Journal of Political Science* 18, No. 1 (1985) 3–29.

NOTE: U = unitary; U + R = unitary with regional subunits; F = federal; CF = confederal; and A = affiliate.

fertilizers in industrial chemicals, and fruits and vegetables, are explained partly by concurrent jurisdiction over agriculture and by the regional character of Canadian markets. This latter factor may be more important, because red meat processing also should be affected by shared jurisdiction yet is represented by a unitary association. Further, even though the provinces have an important voice in drug pricing and in regulation of pollution and occupational health and safety in industrial chemicals, the Canadian associations have unitary structures.

The sectors with industrial organization most likely to predispose associations to decentralized arrangements – construction in all countries and red meat in West Germany and Switzerland – behave as expected. All countries have federal or confederal associations, except Britain. There, the most important construction group, the Building Employers Confederation, has a federal structure combined with an affiliate relationship with the Scottish Building Employers Association. The association representing sub-contractors has a more unitary structure, but again with special arrangements for Scotland. In Canada, the Canadian Construction Association is a confederation combined with affiliate relationships with Quebec groups (see chapter 7). As expected, the artisanal red meat sectors in West Germany and Switzerland also possess federal or confederal associations. In both construction and red meat, then, constitutional differences appear to have no systematic impact.

The machine tools sector adds to this impression, since the two more centralized states have the more decentralized associations. Britain and West Germany have much larger and more developed machine tool industries than Canada and Switzerland and need regional associations to service and maintain the memberships of the many smaller firms. A small industry in a small state like Switzerland does not invite decentralization; the same holds for a small industry geographically concentrated in southern Ontario in Canada, a larger state. Industrial organization is certainly the important determinant here, not constitutional structures.

Finally, the dairy industry is the most complex. The West German system is fragmented between associations representing private firms and co-operatives and associations speaking for different sub-sectors (fluid milk, manufactured dairy products). These, as shown in Table 24, have a range of different territorial structures. The presence of regional units may be traced to three factors: regional differences in West Germany in the structure and size of firms, the structure of regional agricultural co-operatives, and the importance of Land governments in the implementation of quality control and price regulation. In the Canadian and British systems, provincial/regional marketing boards have significant pricing responsibilities, while central government agencies maintain overall responsibility for quality control regulation. Associations adapt to this political division of labour by choosing an affiliate-type structure. In Switzerland, however, the federal government possesses primary responsibility for the industry, including quality control. The federal structure of the Swiss dairy association then is explained better by the presence of regional dairy co-operatives and artisanal cheese factories than by constitutional factors.

Summarizing the analysis of Table 24, industry structure largely determines the degree to which an association has centralized structures. Only in fruit and vegetable processing and in fertilizer manufacturing did the Canadian constitutional structure have a singular impact, and even there regional marketing practices were also important. Nowhere in the rows of the table does one find the pattern one would expect, based on constitutional centralization. In these particular sectors, at least, Canadian associations are no more fragmented along territorial lines than are those found in the three other countries.

I have argued elsewhere that the decentralization inherent in jurisdictional federalism has its major effect in regional inter-sectoral associational systems[20] – distinct sub-national systems embracing the range of sectors active in the given region. Such associational systems are found in Canada and Switzerland but not in Britain and West Germany. Thus in Switzerland, in a canton like Zürich, regional associations or units of national associations of building contractors, meat processors, and so on belong to the regional units of national peak associations, like Vorort (representing industry) and the Association of Small Businesses and Trade. Consequently, miniaturized replicas of the national-level associational system are reproduced at the cantonal level. Chapter 5 described examples of such systems in Canada, with the most developed occurring in Quebec under the aegis of the Conseil du Patronat du Québec. Nonetheless, as I argued in that chapter and as Kriesi and Farago have shown for Switzerland, these regional systems do not fragment the associational system further.[21] On the contrary, they work to integrate business interests and to counter-balance constitutional pressures towards fragmentation.

In conclusion, contrary to the expectations of Cairns and Dawson, a federal régime does not fragment unduly the individual associations through which Canadian business interacts with Canadian governments. In fact, fragmentation was not significantly greater than in two more centralized states, Britain and West Germany. Many business associations in Canada are relatively centralized and show considerable capability for defining and pursuing members' interests, with both provincial and federal governments. There are exceptions, of course, and occasionally business associations get caught in an intense fight between the two levels of government. However, these cases are by no means the norm. Federalism facilitates fragmentation of business interests, I shall suggest in the conclusion to this chapter, at the associational system level, through its interaction with the properties of the economy noted in chapter 11.

Quebec Nationalism

Speaking generally about interest groups, Thorburn summarizes the common understanding of the interaction between the self-assertion of the francophone Québécois and group life: "To counter the tendency of the 'national' associations to claim to speak for the whole country, and also to make their own, often different, positions heard, the francophones have gone a long way in setting up parallel francophone associations."[22] He writes that such a phenomenon covers much of associational life in Quebec, including that of business. He cites as examples, incorrectly in my view, the Conseil du Patronat du Québec and the Chambre de Commerce du Québec.[23] In an argument that parallels that of Alan Cairns, Thorburn postulates that the parallel francophone groups identify primarily with the provincial government: "Once in place, these francophone groups are inclined to develop closer relationships with the Quebec government than with Ottawa. This is especially true in areas where the relevant jurisdiction is provincial. This pressure on the Quebec government is inclined to push it further along the road to autonomy."[24]

Daily observation of the political action of French-speaking business in Quebec suggests caution: most French-speaking business owners have strongly opposed independence and favoured revitalization of the existing federal system. Even in the sensitive and acrimonious area of language usage, francophone business representatives have been closer to the positions of non-French-speaking members of their own social class than to those of other Québécois classes.[25] My own interpretation of the Quiet Revolution emphasizes the desire of French-speaking firms for rattrapage – catching up to and integrating into the mainstream of North American capitalism.[26] Since the early 1970s, successive Quebec governments have supported these objectives.

Information on the structures of business associational systems plus more limited knowledge of associational behaviour suggests that language has not been a disintegrating factor in the collective action of business in Canada. Supporting evidence may be drawn from the collective action of a segment of the business community in Quebec most likely to behave in the way that Thorburn postulates. This segment, called the bourgeoisie québécoise by Pierre Fournier, is described as a growing, dynamic, primarily French-speaking business class which, with provincial support, has challenged traditional anglophone economic dominance in key economic sectors.[27] Fournier identifies three components to this new class: private firms from

selected sectors, several provincial public corporations, created after
1960, and the Mouvement Desjardins financial group. Yet the associative action of this class is well-integrated into national associational systems.

Turning first to the private firms, recent work by Raynauld and
Vaillancourt shows that since the start of the Quiet Revolution, enterprises owned by French Canadians have advanced in all sectors
of manufacturing (save leather goods), in construction, in resource
development, and in services.[28] Francophone-controlled firms in these
areas differ structurally from those controlled by English Canadians
or by foreign firms. They are smaller, with about one-fifth the average value added per establishment shown by the foreign firms.[29]
Whereas the francophone firms export 31 per cent of their output
on average, Anglo-Canadian firms ship 56 per cent of their products
abroad, and foreign firms 51 per cent.[30] Raynauld and Vaillancourt
conclude: "With respect to francophone enterprises, it is still the case
that they are those whose establishments are the smallest, whose
productivity is the poorest, whose wages are the lowest, but on the
other hand whose labour costs are the highest, finally those who
serve principally the local market."[31]

This first component, the francophone private sector, is too large
to survey comprehensively. Accordingly, three significant sectors only
will be examined: construction, which is highly francophone-controlled and regulated primarily by the provincial government; wood
products manufacturing, also highly francophone-controlled but attuned relatively equally to both the federal and provincial governments; and dairy products, a francophone industry more highly
oriented to the federal than the provincial government.

The detailed survey of the manufacturing sectors in Quebec by
Raynauld and Vaillancourt revealed that in 1978 francophone-owned
firms accounted for 79 per cent of production in the wood products
industry and 51.6 per cent in the furniture industry.[32] Normally the
wood products industry subdivides into several sub-sectors: sawmills
and planing mills, veneer and plywood mills, window-sash-door manufacturers, kitchen cabinet manufacturers, and particle board manufacturers. The character of associational representation in these
sub-sectors is summarized in Table 25 and may be illustrated well
by looking at the first two of these and the furniture sector. The
Association des manufacturiers de bois de sciage du Québec (AMBSQ)
represents the diverse sawmilling industry of which the 396 establishments in Quebec include a host of smaller firms and a number
of well-known larger ones – Domtar, Donohue St-Félicien, J.H. Nor-
mick, Les produits forestiers Saucier, and so on.[33] By Canadian

Table 25
Associative Action of Quebec-based Bourgeoisie

Sector	Association
WOOD PRODUCTS	
Sawmills, planing mills	L'Association des manufacturiers de bois de sciage du Québec; Canadian Lumbermen's Association
Furniture	Quebec Furniture Manufacturers Association
Plywood, veneer mills	Canadian Hardwood Plywood Association*
Window-sash-door mills	Canadian Window and Door Manufacturers Association*
Particleboard	Canadian Particleboard Association*
Kitchen cabinet manufacturers	Canadian Kitchen Cabinet Association*
CONSTRUCTION	
General contractors	La Fédération de la construction du Québec L'Association de construction de Montréal et du Québec
Housebuilders	L'Association provinciale de l'habitation du Québec
Civil engineering	L'Association des constructeurs de routes et de grands travaux du Québec
Electrical contractors	La Corporation des maîtres éléctriciens du Québec
Mechanical contractors	La Corporation des maîtres mécaniciens en tuyauterie du Québec
DAIRY PRODUCTS	
	Le Conseil de la coopération laitière Le Conseil de l'industrie laitière du Québec National Dairy Council of Canada

* Managed by the Canadian Lumbermen's Association.

standards, the association is well resourced, spending $1.3 million in 1980 and employing between 25 and 30 people.[34] Aside from participating in pressure pluralist policy networks, the association runs the quality control and lumber-grading system in Quebec and a purchasing organization for its smaller members.

Like its provincial counterparts in Ontario (the Ontario Lumber Manufacturers Association) and British Columbia (Council of the Forest Industries of B.C.), the AMBSQ is integrated into the national forest/wood products associational system. The AMBSQ, like the other two, is a member of the national peak organization, the Canadian Wood Council, which does extensive work on grading and standards, particularly as these are applicable in the United States. The AMBSQ co-ordinates certain activities with the federal-level wood manufacturers organization, the Canadian Lumbermen's Association (CLA): it participates as a member of the Council of Eastern Forest Products Associations organized by the CLA and joins with the CLA and the other provincial associations in supporting the National Lumber Grading Authority. Many of the larger members of the AMBSQ are also direct members of the CLA.

The pattern of organization in furniture manufacturing resembles that in the sawmill sub-sector. There are 615 establishments active in Quebec, a good proportion of them of small and medium size.[35] They have their own association, the Quebec Furniture Manufacturers Association, which is close to the Canadian average in size, with an annual budget of about $300,000 and staff of 12.[36] This association is very active in marketing, putting on large furniture shows annually in Montreal and Toronto. It also maintains a permanent office in Toronto, Decor-Action, with a full-time promotion manager. The association's interest in opening up wider national markets for its members is complemented by its joining together with the two other associations in the industry from Ontario and western Canada to form the Canadian Council of Furniture Manufacturers.

Integration into the national associational system is even more direct in the remaining sub-sectors of the wood industry. The Canadian Lumbermen's Association operates four product-specific associations: the Canadian Hardwood Plywood Association, the Canadian Kitchen Cabinet Association, the Canadian Particleboard Association, and the Canadian Window and Door Manufacturers Association. Firms operating in the corresponding sub-sectors in Quebec belong directly to these associations. For example, 13 of the 18 veneer and plywood mills in Quebec, which account for 89.9 per cent of the employment in the sub-sector, are members of the Canadian Hardwood Plywood Association.[37]

The degree of integration into a national system is less pronounced in our second chosen sector, construction. As indicated in Table 25, six main associations represent this industry on a provincial plane in Quebec.[38] Road builders and heavy engineering firms are represented by the Association des constructeurs de routes et grands travaux du Québec, electrical and mechanical contractors by the Corporation des maîtres éléctriciens du Québec and the Corporation des maîtres mécaniciens en tuyauterie du Québec respectively, house builders by the Association provinciale de l'habitation du Québec, and general and other trades contractors by the Fédération de la construction du Québec and the Association de la construction de Montréal et du Québec.

General contractors, road builders, and other civil engineering firms are represented on the national plane by the mixed association, the Canadian Construction Association (CCA).[39] It will be recalled from chapter 7 that the CCA has had two categories of members.[40] Integrated affiliate associations enter into an agreement with the CCA whereby all their member firms become direct member firms in the CCA; affiliate associations join the CCA, but their member firms are not given direct member status. The prevalent pattern shows provincial general contractors' and road builders' associations becoming integrated affiliates of the CCA. Quebec departs from this pattern: none of the three relevant associations – the AGRGTQ, the FCQ, or the ACMQ – is an integrated affiliate, but instead all hold simple affiliate membership in the CCA.

Quebec is not alone in departing from the national pattern, however. The situation has been very unsettled in Ontario. The Ontario Road Builders Association and the Ontario General Contractors Association (OGCA) are integrated affiliates of the CCA, but the provincial peak organization, the Council of Ontario Contractors Associations (COCA), has no relationship with the CCA whatsoever. In addition, several powerful regional associations in Ontario, which belong to COCA but not to the OGCA (Grand Valley, Hamilton, Niagara, Orillia, Sudbury, and Windsor), retain simple affiliate membership; the influential Toronto Construction Association is listed in the CCA directory with double asterisks and the words "partial integration only." In my interviews with Quebec and Ontario associations, officers sometimes questioned the efficacy and value of the CCA. These interviews and the pattern of integration found in Ontario suggest that the weak integration of the three Quebec associations in the CCA may have more to do with the performance of the CCA than with nationalism. Several large Quebec construction firms, including Hydro-Québec (a leading light in Fournier's bourgeoisie), are direct "national" members of the CCA.

Integration arrangements compare favourably to those found in other provinces in the remaining sectors of the industry. The electrical contractors' and the mechanical contractors' "corporations," like other provincial groups, are members of their respective national associations, the Canadian Electrical Contractors Association and the Mechanical Contractors Association of Canada. The local units of the housebuilding association are members of the Canadian Home Builders Association (CHBA), as is the case in other provinces. However, the Association provinciale de l'habitation du Québec appears more autonomous from the CHBA national office than the CHBA provincial councils elsewhere. However, in an interview with the CHBA, it was stressed that Quebec firms participated more than those from most other provinces.

The third industry drawn from the "private-sector" component of the Quebec-based bourgeoisie – the manufacture of dairy products – also supports the general trend whereby Quebec business organizations follow an integrative approach to collective action on the national plane. The dairy products industry in Quebec subdivides between co-operatives (Agropur, Coopérative Fédérée, etc.), which are responsible for 80 per cent of volume, and private firms, generally smaller, responsible for the remainder. The co-operatives do have a very informal association, the Conseil de la coopération laitière. However, when co-operatives negotiate with the Quebec government on matters related to marketing, a large co-operative firm, the Coopérative fédérée, acts as their representative. On the federal plane, all the co-operatives are members of the National Dairy Council (NDC), which represents the whole of the dairy processing industry. The private firms also have their own provincial association, the Conseil de l'industrie laitière du Québec (CILQ), which is directly analogous to the Ontario Dairy Council and other provincial associations. The CILQ, like the Ontario group, has a weak affiliation with the NDC. Generally speaking, however, the NDC is an association of firms, not a peak association, and hence dairy firms in Quebec join it directly. By my estimate, firms accounting for 72 per cent of Quebec production belong to the NDC, comparable to the 74 per cent for Ontario. Again, then, Quebec business appears to participate actively in national associational structures at a level quite homologous to business firms in other provinces.

The integrative behaviour of the private-sector component of the Quebec-based bourgeoisie should be duplicated by the public-sector component. Public corporations have co-operated in many investment projects with English-Canadian and American capital since the early 1970s.[41] The public holding company La Société générale du financement (SGF) has joined in projects with British Columbia Forest Products, with Gulf Canada and Union Carbide Canada, and with the Noranda Group. Soquem, the government's mining exploration company, has worked with Noranda, the Hollinger Group, and Rio Tinto Exploration. Sidbec, the government-owned steel company, has concluded agreements with British Steel and the American company Quebec Cartier Mining.

Associative action by Quebec's public-sector corporations follows more integrative lines. The flagship of the public fleet, Hydro-Québec, belongs to the Canadian Electrical Association, which represents public and private electricity-generating companies in Canada. Hydro occupies virtually a permanent position on this association's board of directors, and its officers have served several times as chairman. Hydro-Québec is also a member and an occasional director of the Canadian Nuclear Association, which embraces the nuclear power industry.

Sidbec joins Canada's other three large integrated steel firms, Algoma Steel, Dofasco, and Stelco, as a member of the Canadian Steel Producers Association and the Canadian Steel Construction Council. The council is a mixed umbrella group that includes such associations as the Canadian Institute of Steel Construction, the Canadian Sheet Steel Building Institute, and the Canadian Welding Bureau.[42] A mining subsidiary of the company, Sidbec-Normines, holds membership in the Quebec Metal Mining Association, which represents the primarily English-Canadian- and American-controlled mining sector in Quebec.

The third star in the pantheon of public corporations, Soquem, has two producing subsidiaries, Louvem (zinc and copper) and Niobec (columbium), which are members of the metal mining association as well. Relative to other mining concerns, these firms are rather small, probably why Soquem is not a member of the Mining Association of Canada, which represents the large national mining companies. The government's representative in the petroleum industry, Soquip (Société québécoise d'initiatives pétrolières), belongs to the Independent Petroleum Association of Canada, which represents the independent, predominantly Canadian-controlled firms active in the sector. Finally, the corporations controlled by SGF do not shy away either from joining pan-Canadian groups. For example, both Domtar and Donohue St-Félicien are members of the Canadian Pulp and Paper Association.

Integration with English-Canadian firms in associations is less pronounced for the third component of the class defined by Fournier, the Mouvement Desjardins. More than the previous two components, the financial co-operatives work within a Quebec-based network and probably finance primarily francophone businesses. Over the past 15 years, the Mouvement Desjardins has centralized its operations, drawing together a significant pool of capital. It has created two subsidiaries, the Société d'investissement Desjardins (SID) and the Crédit industriel Desjardins, in order to expand investment in industry. The former, for example, now controls the food manufacturing firm Culinar, which has expanded rapidly into Ontario and the northeastern United States. The Mouvement Desjardins also has close ties with the two other major francophone-controlled financial groups, the National Bank of Canada and the Caisse de dépôt et placement du Québec. It is the largest shareholder in the National Bank. The Caisse has acquired 15 per cent of the SID and is also a large shareholder in the National Bank. This trinity of institutions is now developed sufficiently to service the provincial government and francophone businesses to a point where both are far less dependent on English-Canadian finance capital than they were 20 years ago.

The Mouvement Desjardins also participates in national business associations. The National Bank of Canada belongs to the Canadian Bankers' Association (CBA). With the establishment of a new clearing system managed by the Canadian Payments Association (CPA) rather than the CBA following passage of the 1980 Bank Act, the Desjardins Caisses populaires, through their caisse centrale, joined with the chartered banks and many trust companies for the first time. In fact, they moved faster than English-Canadian credit unions; of the eight units of the Canadian Cooperative Credit Society, only three have so far joined the CPA. The Desjardins Group has moved gradually into two other areas of the financial services sector, trust companies and insurance, and gained an increased presence outside Quebec. With this expansion have also come memberships in national associations. Its trust subsidiary, La Fiducie du Québec, is a member of the Trust Companies Association of Canada. In life insurance, it owns two companies, L'Assurance Vie Desjardins, which now serves most provinces, and La Sauvegarde, which works primarily in Quebec. Both companies, however, are active members of the Canadian Life and Health Association. The movement's two general assurance companies, La Société d'Assurance des Caisses populaires and General Security, have recently been merged to form La Groupe Desjardins, which is active in all provinces except Saskatchewan. This new company holds membership in the Insurance Bureau of Canada, which speaks for the general insurance sector, and in its educational arm, the Insurance Institute of Canada.

In summary, associational involvement in national associations by three components of the Quebec-based bourgeoisie indicates that language or cultural differences between French and English do not contribute significantly to the fragmentation in the associational systems of Canadian business. Both membership patterns and interviews support the conclusion that francophone firms from Quebec participate in national associations on a par with firms in other provinces. This is not to say, of course, that no forums exist for francophone firms to coalesce against non-francophone firms in the province. Class fractions may be organized through the actions of political parties or through involvement in nationalist associations open to all and not just business firms. Yet there is also little evidence that francophone business firms use either of these vehicles to confront Anglo-Canadian firms in the province. Finally, the survey of general business associations in chapter 5 indicated that these too were an integrating force in the business community rather than a disruptive one.

THE PARLIAMENTARY TRADITION

Kenneth Dyson recently has examined the state as a social, cultural, and philosophical phenomenon in western Europe.[43] The distinctive, some might say aberrant, state coincident with the British parliamentary system of government, Dyson argues, begets a pattern of interest group behaviour that is competitive and relatively unordered – to wit, pluralist in character. The emphasis in the British system is placed on representation, not integration, as it is in Continental Europe. Such a system, with a fragmented group of departments, agencies, regional and local authorities, public corporations, and various ad hoc advisory boards, creates an "unstructured" pluralism of government.[44] The emphasis is on arms-length relationships; authorities worry whether public corporations, for example, are "independent" rather than whether they are acting as a coherent organ of state policy. Reform tends to be piecemeal, the centre of power difficult to locate. The political executive does not represent interests; this task remains the responsibility of the legislature and private interest groups. The executive acts as a broker between contending interests. Such a system encourages the perception of politics as an arena, "a fluid, competitive pluralistic politics of bargaining in which a complex of groups emerges in a self-determining fashion on the model of market place relations and the establishment of stable tripartite arrangements between government and both sides of industry proves an elusive quest."[45]

Most business associations presented in this book were active not at the political centre but in the middle and upper levels of the line departments and of the quasi-independent agencies hovering under the protective umbrellas of these departments. Viewing politics through the lenses of interest associations revealed a state divided within itself and lacking integration and focus. In a recent survey of changes in the policy process since the Second World War, Pross confirms this conclusion.[46] He argues that power has been increasingly diffused throughout the administrative arm of government, leaving the political executive with reduced capacity to control both policy development and implementation.

Pross uses the term "bureaucratic pluralism" to describe changes in the Canadian federal government that began in the 1960s.[47] Rapid expansion of the policy agenda to include environmental, consumer, and social welfare problems invited the government to parcel out tasks to a variety of new agencies and departments. These agencies and departments (and, as Pross notes, branches of departments) developed close ties with special interest groups that also proliferated at this time, an observation partially confirmed by the data presented in chapter 2. Initially, Pross writes, the new government agencies maintained the upper hand with these groups, but then changes at the political centre gradually altered this situation. Faced with a rapid multiplication of departments and agencies, the prime minister and his senior officials became more and more concerned with co-ordinating policy-making and avoiding duplication. The late 1960s and the 1970s saw a range of reforms of cabinet decision-making and of the financial management system aimed at addressing these problems. These reforms, in turn, accentuated pluralism in the bureaucracy. Line departments and quasi-independent agencies sought to guard their autonomy from the new central agencies and, in addition, found themselves in increasing competition with one another for the ears of these agencies. Interest groups had increased difficulty in locating the centre of decision-making for their sector and expanded their physical presence and lobbying activities.[48] Pross adds that this expansion was encouraged by the line departments and agencies, which were increasingly inclined to work through these groups to lobby their own bureaucratic masters or to use the groups to speak on their behalf before parliamentary committees.[49] Members of Parliament might then be enlisted to pressure central agencies and ultimately the cabinet.

Pross's analysis implies that the decision-making centre in the federal government is embattled and lacks the strength one would expect to find in a society with a developed state tradition. Campbell has described in detail some of the failings of the Canadian central agencies.[50] Other evidence, as well, points to a political centre that is somewhat isolated from line departments and civil society. Senior bureaucratic officials in Canada have less contact with interest groups than their counterparts in other Western countries. About 52 per cent of Canadian officials report "regular" contact with interest groups, compared to 93 per cent in the United States, 74 per cent in West Germany, and 67 per cent in Britain.[51] Asked whether they agree or disagree with the following statement: "The general welfare of the country is seriously endangered by the continual clash of particularistic interest groups," 50 per cent of senior Canadian officials agreed with the statement, compared to 18 per cent in Britain, 19 per cent in West Germany, and 23 per cent in Sweden.[52] Only officials in the Netherlands were close to the Canadians, with 57 per cent agreeing.

In short, there are interesting parallels in Canada between the structures of the federal administration and those of the national business associational system. The central agencies resemble the broad inter-sectoral associations, somewhat detached from the line departments, as the latter are from the more specialized sectoral associations. Many question the effectiveness of central agencies in co-ordinating government policy just as I have pointed to the ineffectiveness of the broadly based associations in integrating the diverse interests of business. Within the federal administration, there are problems of co-ordination among departments and even within departments. Mandates are not always clearly defined, leading to overlapping responsibilities, inter-departmental competition, and narrowly focused policy outlooks. Similarly, we have found associations in most divisions of the economy to be weakly integrated with one another, sometimes in competition with one another for members, and too often solicitous only of a very narrow special interest. Natural linkages between these special interest groups and their counterparts occur in line departments, often branches or even sub-branches within these departments. These linkages, in turn, inhibit integration and co-ordination within both the public service and the business associational systems. To conclude, it looks as if a weak Canadian state begets a weak associational system.

CONCLUSIONS

The political forces identified by Cairns and others that reinforce existing cleavages and fragment Canadian society even further have a weaker effect upon the integration of individual business associations. A significant majority of individual associations have unitary structures, a minority have well-integrated federal organizations, and only a smaller minority have weaker confederal or affiliate arrangements. Yet we should not be hasty to conclude that federalism does not fragment business's collective action. Its effects are felt, in my view, at the level of associational systems. The conclusion to the previous chapter discussed how reinforcing sectoral, geographic, and market-orientation cleavages may erect special barriers to the integration of business collective action. These same divisions at the level of economic structure are sustained, if not exacerbated, by the constitutional division of powers. Provincial governments share with the federal government responsibility for business and are especially prominent in primary sectors. Hence some provincial governments line up more strongly on the raw materials, export-oriented side; others, notably Ontario and Quebec, have a particular interest in the finished goods, home market-oriented side. When disputes along these lines arise, the federal government often finds itself caught in the cross-fire, with insufficient power to stop the fighting. In short, the federal system does not encourage the bridging of the structural divisions already present in the Canadian business community.

The fragmentation of the Canadian business community has its roots in the microeconomic factors identified in chapters 5 through 10 and in the broader economic cleavages noted in the conclusion to chapter 11. The divisions along sectoral lines are reinforced by state structures that diffuse power and frustrate the co-ordination of public policy. In moving to discuss possible changes and reforms of group structures and the policy process in the next chapter, we do so under no illusions. The benefits of these reforms may be realized only when the Canadian economy has become better integrated in itself.

CHAPTER THIRTEEN

Business and Democracy

Capitalists possess ambivalent feelings about democracy. On the one side, democratic politics provides the mechanism for divorcing the role of entrepreneur, profit-maker, and employer from that of political decision-maker. The logic of the interaction between a market economy and liberal democracy produces, by definition, a privileged position for business.[1] On the surface, business can appear to be one group among many, when, in practice, it is often the only group that is consulted and whose interests are considered. On the other side, capitalists have a small number of votes. The danger always exists that the majority may overcome its divisions, find unity in a common opposition to capital, and press claims that would remove the rights and privileges that come with private ownership.

In playing the democratic game, then, capitalists are always tempted to draw on their superior resources. They seek to secure better their influence over politicians in order to protect themselves from the possibility of a focused opposition. Canadian business behaves no differently in this respect than any other national business community. The survey of collective action in this study leads us to question, however, whether business's success in enhancing its influence and power harms the political community at large. First, the structures of business interest associations and associational systems may restrict the policy options available to decision-makers as they face the economic crises of the 1980s. Specifically, business has not developed the "encompassing" organizations that would allow it to take a broad view of society as a whole,[2] organizations that might check special interest bargaining and might at least speak to the claims and demands of other classes. Second, the accumulation of privileges by business associations in clientele and co-optive policy networks undermines democratic practice in Canada, necessitating further reforms to Parliament, the electoral system, bureaucratic procedures, and the interest organizations of other classes and groups.

This chapter examines both of these consequences of business organization in Canada. In order to do so, it reviews first the political responsibility of business as defined in chapter 1. Second, the position of the Canadian economy relative to others in the advanced capitalist world is surveyed to provide a context for the analysis of the reforms presented in the third and fourth sections of the chapter. These reforms pertain to the basic structures of interest representation and party politics. Structures are emphasized because, as John Zysman has stated, "a structure creates an enduring set of penalties and rewards that mold action independent of the motivation or purposes of the actors. The constraints of the situation or the channels of action determine which choices are expensive and which are cheap."[3] Existing institutional arrangements in Canada limit which policies might be appropriately attempted.

POLITICAL RESPONSIBILITY

Since the mid-1970s, a sense of economic crisis has settled into the consciousness of many Canadians. To be sure, such a perception exists in other Western countries as well, and in each country the components of the crisis vary. In Canada, the crisis is marked by high levels of unemployment. No Western country has had a higher average rate of unemployment than Canada since 1960.[4] In the mid-1980s, the national rate remained stubbornly close to 10 per cent; some provinces – British Columbia, Quebec, and Newfoundland – have had rates consistently well above that figure. Sadly, there appears to be no trend away from this pattern. High unemployment corresponds, in part, to serious structural problems in the economy, which have gradually revealed themselves over the past half-century. At the turn of the twentieth century, some analysts argue, Canadian prospects looked very good indeed. "Canadian exports had the greatest proportion of finished to primary manufactures of any industrial nation."[5] Manufactured exports included agricultural implements, wood products, iron and steel, musical instruments, and chemicals.[6] Canada placed well in comparison with other late industrializing nations such as Japan, Sweden, and Italy. Sixty years later, this promising start had failed to turn out as well as might have been expected. Imports of finished goods were five times the value of exports. In fact, Canada had the highest per capita level of imports of finished goods of any industrialized nation. In the mid-1980s, Canadians were still paying their way in the international market-place in the traditional way, relying on the export of resource staples and much, much less on finished manufactured goods.

As we saw in chapters 6 and 8, such an approach remains risky. Droughts, poor weather, and "Green Revolutions" in the Third World play havoc with agricultural markets. The fishery is dangerously over-exploited. The disappearance of accessible virgin timber, poor reforestation practices, and acid rain threaten another vital renewable resource, the forests. Other common exports such as metallic minerals and natural gas are non-renewable resources. They will run out some day, and as their costs rise successful substitutes are being found. In the face of these worries, Canadian manufacturing has been standing still. While the past 25 years have not seen a worsening of the poor ratio of finished-goods exports to imports, they have not shown an improvement, either.[7] Some evidence suggests that performance in the high-technology electronics sectors has fallen off dramatically.[8] Faced by these various problems, governments have reacted in different ways: Quebec and Alberta have looked somewhat towards anticipatory planning, British Columbia has attempted to drive down labour costs in the name of a search for the elusive pure and unfettered market, and Ontario has looked to classical incremental policy-making involving ad hoc supports to industry. The federal government has tried a little bit of everything: devising an industrial strategy, cutting back government expenditures, pursuing economically liberal policies, and following a nationalist program.[9] In the mid-1980s, it placed its hopes in the negotiation of a bilateral free-trade agreement with the United States.

The business class must figure prominently in any consideration of solutions to these economic problems. The principles of a capitalist market economy assign wide-ranging decision powers to the managers or owners of private firms. They decide where and how capital will be invested, what technology will be used, how many workers are needed and with what skills; how big a plant should be, and so on. Taken together, these decisions have vast consequences for other classes and strata in society. The principles undergirding a liberal democratic political system provide that those other classes and strata, which do not own the instruments of production, consent to the private ownership and private disposition of capital stock. In exchange, business people, the owners of the productive instruments, consent to political institutions that permit these other classes and strata to press claims for a certain redistribution of output. Implicit in this relationship, then, between the business class and other classes is a certain political responsibility. Since their decisions affect fundamentally the basic conditions of life of so many members of society, business people and their firms must give a rendering for these same decisions. Business must be accountable, that is, it must be willing to give reasons and provide motives for what it does and be subject to censure when these are inadequate or inappropriate.

Chapter 1 noted that the individualist business culture in Canada resisted such notions of accountability. Rather, business people believe in the virtues of markets, arguing that if those markets are left to operate freely, all members of society will be better off in the long run. Yet it remains open to debate whether a system anchored on the private appropriation of profits coupled with the sought-after laissez-faire state optimizes the realization of the very different needs of other classes and strata. Certainly this assumption has been questioned by social democratic and socialist parties since the early nineteenth century. The often large disparity between the economic power of business and that of other classes makes it very difficult for the latter to accept the resistance of business to a redistribution of wealth. The concentration of economic power in a few large firms in many sectors has proceeded apace since the beginning of the twentieth century. We have seen in this book, particularly in chapters 8 and 9, that as a magnifying glass densifies the rays of the sun, associations can organize and concentrate this power further. We have observed, as well, that business associations in a range of sectors have facilitated business people stepping inside and assuming places of various importance in the calmer halls of policy-making while their opponents are left outside jostling in the hurly-burly world of pressure group politics. I have recounted how individual sectors of business enjoy a number of special, privileged relations with government through a series of clientele and co-optive pluralist policy networks. These privileges and exceptional relationships with the state occur as a "natural" outcome of the working of the economic system. Business is not simply one special interest among others but a class that privately makes a number of decisions that affect critically the well-being of the whole of society. The extraordinary place of business is reflected in its constant demands to be consulted on most matters of economic policy and in the seriousness with which these demands are greeted by the state.

With power, privileges, and special relationships must also come responsibility and accountability. A democratic system of governance provides a means to classes other than business as well as to competing sectors of business to question the private decisions taken by firms and to ensure the proper sharing of private gains accumulated as a consequence of the logic of capitalism. On the basis of the evidence in this book, the functioning of the democratic system in

Canada needs some reform because the Canadian business class is not held sufficiently accountable for its actions.

APPROPRIATE MODELS

Among the more advanced capitalist states, Canada occupies an awkward middle position. On the one hand, the Canadian prime minister stands proudly with the US and French presidents, the West German chancellor, and the prime ministers of Japan, Britain, and Italy at the annual summits of the major economic powers. On the other hand, Canada had to beg to be let into this select company and made it only with helpful assistance from the United States. This ambiguous status on the world summit stage correponds to the peculiar middle position of the Canadian economy. With a domestic market of 25 million people, it has half as many people as the smaller major industrial powers: Italy, France, Britain, and West Germany. Yet it has at least twice as many people as most of the smaller European capitalist democracies: Sweden, Norway, Denmark, Belgium, the Netherlands, Austria, and Switzerland. Moreover, the physical size of Canada splinters the population into smaller regional markets that come quite close in size to the smaller European states.

When Canadian economists and others talk about Canada's economy and compare it to others, they usually refer to the United States, Britain, France, and so on. In doing so, they ignore another kind of comparison, namely with the smaller European states just mentioned. Like Canada, these states are virtually forced to be open trading nations. The ratio of their exports to the size of their GNP is almost double that of the large states.[10] The same ratio calculated for Canada places it in the middle, more trade-oriented than the large states but less so than the small states. Small states, by necessity, borrow technology and innovations – while one out of two patents taken up in large countries is foreign, four of five are foreign in smaller states.[11] Canada follows the smaller states' pattern, showing nine of ten patents as foreign in the 1970s.[12] Smaller countries usually run deficits in their trade balances, while large countries have surpluses.[13] Here, too, Canada looks more like a small country, except that resource exports account for its occasional surpluses, while the smaller European countries draw more on exports of manufactured goods. Small countries absorb more direct foreign investment than larger ones, as does Canada. Larger countries are less dependent on imports of energy than are smaller countries; here Canada matches a larger country.

Corresponding to the distinction between small and large countries are different approaches to industrial and trade policy. A large state can sometimes export the costs of change and adjustment – make the citizens in other countries pay.[14] Since a large domestic market may facilitate protection for a large state, such a state will sometimes be able to engage in forward planning, including the identification and promotion of strategic sectors. Critical to this option are centralized, strongly autonomous state structures and a financial system where prices are administered through state intervention.[15] Japan and France have, from time to time, followed this approach.

The small state can seldom afford to be protectionist.[16] Protection threatens to raise the price of its intermediate goods and thereby to undermine the competitiveness of its manufactured goods on world markets. The small state is less able to pay domestically for a protectionist concession to one or more sectors. It is particularly vulnerable to retaliation by larger states for protectionist measures as well. Open to international markets, small states find it difficult to engage in long-term planning. Instead, they seek to realize economic objectives by promoting free trade and a liberal international economic order and by arranging compensation for those victimized by changes in world markets.[17] This kind of economic strategy and the management of domestic politics become feasible with democratic corporatist arrangements.

Democratic corporatism, as practised in the smaller European democracies, involves three things.[18] First, an ideology of social partnership provides the backdrop to discussions of economic and social policy. Such an ideology emphasizes the need to iron out differences among major economic groups like business, labour, and farmers through pragmatic political discussions and political compromise, rather than through political conflict. Second, there must be a system of relatively centralized and concentrated interest groups, to speak on behalf of these major interests, particularly business. These groups must be highly representative of their respective communities and expert in policy matters. All of the smaller European states have strong peak associations representing business and possessing such properties.[19] In some cases, these are matched by comparable labour organizations; in others, labour was more weakly organized, and special arrangements had to be devised to compensate for these weaknesses. Some political debate takes place within these peak associations, freeing up time on the public agenda. These centralized interest groups, in turn, make possible the third defining property of democratic corporatism: a style of bargaining that is voluntary, informal, and continuous. "Victory or defeat on any given issue does not lead to an escalating spiral of conflict because a continuous sequence of political bargains makes all actors aware that victory today can easily turn into defeat tomorrow."[20]

Complementing these arrangements in interest representation are specific properties of the party and electoral systems. All of the small European states have proportional representation, providing some political voice to a broad range of interests. Such a system encourages accommodation and compromise. In addition, ties are relatively close between parties and interest groups, particularly on the left-labour side. The parties and interest groups are distinct organizations, yet linked in a mutually supportive way by common political goals and shared élites.[21] The division of political labour leaves economic and some social policy questions to the interest groups and other questions to the parties. The parties act as a safety valve when deadlock develops among the interest organizations. Put together, these two properties help compensate for labour's natural weakness in the face of business and ensure that labour is somewhat integrated into policy-making.

Such corporatist arrangements are critical if the smaller states are to compensate victims of changes in world markets on both sides of the class barrier. The cultivated sense of partnership encourages the articulation of national interests and continued commitment to free trade as the best guarantee of future economic success.

Protection becomes less and less viable for the Canadian economy with each passing day. Canada has felt the pressure of the international trading community for a lowering of tariffs and has done so, albeit gradually, over the past 20 years. While Canadian tariffs are still high relative to other Western capitalist states, the gap has declined over the past decade, and tariffs are now much lower in absolute terms.[22] The logic of protection has changed considerably as well, because of the entry of newly industrializing countries into Western markets, particularly Taiwan, Singapore, Hong Kong, and South Korea. These countries can remain competitive in price even against very high tariffs. Canada has reacted to this competition like many other developed countries by introducing quantitative restrictions on trade in several key sectors. However, these policies have been essentially a rearguard action, will probably fail in the longer term, and have incurred the increasing wrath of consumers and the powerful retailers' lobby.

These pressures against protectionism are coupled to growing unease about dependence on resource exports, and policy-makers have looked to improve the viability of Canadian manufactures in the world economy and, in particular, reverse the large trade deficit in finished manufactured goods. Beginning to think in this way brings Canadians closer and closer to the smaller European states.

In short, Canada should look for inspiration from the smaller European states when it comes to fashioning trade and industrial policy and, even more important, reforming the political process to make the new policies viable. Because Canada is not a large state like the United States or Japan, these countries provide less appropriate models. Inevitably, like the small countries, Canada is being forced towards greater trade liberalization and producing finished manufactured goods for export. The Canadian domestic market is not large enough to permit the planned adjustment and limited protection practised across a broad range of sectors by such countries as France and Japan. Canadians cannot normally compete fully in sectors that function with long production runs of mass consumer goods. Canada's lot in manufacturing lies with more specialized production for smaller, yet often lucrative markets. Selective state intervention may be critical for firms seeking such niches. Accordingly, Canada must maintain the political flexibility that might be useful in such cases. Solutions to the country's problems lie more with internal political reforms than with the panacea of free trade with the United States, which may restrict the range of policies that might be used.

A glance at the small states, then, is merited partially because of their economic performance. In a useful summary of the literature, Banting writes that these states managed in the 1970s to keep inflation and unemployment in check.[23] Entering the 1980s, some of their corporatist arrangements have broken down, and they have not been spared the economic dislocation of the recession. While their economic performance draws some of our interest, it is not their only attraction. Contrary to some expectations, the presence of encompassing organizations in policy discussions checks the tendency to protect at all costs in times of crisis. Other solutions are at least canvassed. Even more important, in my view, the political process confronts business with its responsibility and asks for an accounting. More holding of business to account would be salutary in the Canadian context.

THE POLITICS OF ECONOMIC MANAGEMENT

In moving to discuss alternative arrangements for the organization of business interests, my objective is not to champion these arrangements but to emphasize that there must be a fit between policies and structures. Many policies being proposed to resolve problems in the Canadian economy, whether anticipatory planning, wage and price controls, or positive adjustment, cannot be implemented willy-nilly, whatever the institutional context. Policy options are constrained by institutional arrangements. Particular structural arrangements are suitable for some kinds of policies and unsuitable for others. As they stand, Canadian political institutions favour company-led growth rather than state direction, horizontal economic policies rather than sectoral planning, and autonomy of the firm rather than *concertation* among business, labour, and government. If political leaders are to look to implementing different kinds of policies, particularly those inspired by the smaller European states, then they should consider whether the institutional context is appropriate. Without some changes to institutions, significant changes in policy direction are likely to founder.

While looking to the smaller European states for some inspiration, Canadians must, at the same time, avoid what Lehmbruch calls the "techno-sociological fallacy."[24] They cannot simply transport institutions and processes from very specific socio-cultural contexts and put them into Canada's own rather different context. Yet, there are several guiding principles common across these rather diverse countries that merit the attention and consideration of those considering major changes in policy directions.

(1) Business must be accountable to the political community at large through a very few organizations that can give voice to the diversity of interests resulting from territorial and sectoral factors. At the same time they must be centralized enough to integrate those diverse interests through constructive debates. They must also be highly representative, so as to justify claims that the resulting opinions are legitimate.

(2) Labour must be recognized as a legitimate social partner to business and given an equal voice in the policy process. In view of the evident weakness of labour organizations in Canada, political institutions must be reformed so as to compensate for these difficulties.

(3) Given the continued importance of agriculture to the Canadian economy, particularly in export markets, steps must be taken to end the isolation of farmers' organizations from those of business and labour.

Let us now examine each of these principles in turn.

The Organization of Business Interests

The studies in this book reveal that Canadian business is not organized for the consensual discussion of policy required in the management of a small, open economy. The need for such discussion was recognized recently by the Royal Commission on the Economic Union and Development Prospects for Canada (Macdonald Commission):

In all modern industrial societies, the representation of private-sector interests in public decision-making has become an important issue. Pervasive interdependence between the public and private sectors has created a situation in which what major economic interests can achieve depends not only on their own initiatives, but also on the sensitivity of the state to their concerns. Conversely, the success of government policies depends heavily on the response of private interests to them. This fundamental interdependence has produced intense pressures for new mechanisms for consultation between the public and private sectors, inevitably involving business and labour, but extending, to an even greater degree, to other organizations in the social and voluntary fields.[25]

This general point is amplified in a recent book by James Gillies.[26] Three advantages derive from such a consensual approach to policy. (1) In the appropriate place in the business cycle, co-operation among major socioeconomic producer groups facilitates control over inflation and levels of employment. At the same time, as Banting notes, performance may not necessarily be better in growth, profits and rates of return, investment, productivity, and income distribution.[27] (2) Planning for industrial adjustment and rationalization is enhanced because of the increased capacity to co-ordinate industrial, social and manpower, and employment policies. (3) The usual lack of understanding and knowledge of the other's position, which creates frustration and mutual alienation, is more easily remedied.

Unfortunately, the Macdonald Commission rejects "elaborate consultation" involving "formal co-operative decision-making."[28] It argues that such an approach would circumvent parliamentary institutions and would lead to the protection of weak industries. Such conclusions are hasty and premature. Not all the small European democracies studied by Katzenstein had the formalized tripartite structures that left the commission "ambivalent."[29] The commission outlines an approach for "elaborate consultation" that would be quite compatible with the Canadian system of government. A permanent Economic Policy Committee formed by the House of Commons would hold annual pre-budget hearings, take testimony about the nation's economic prospects from relevant government departments, and gather the views of major groups, including business and labour.[30] Special investigative committees on comprehensive policy matters would encourage interest groups to present their demands and justify them in terms of the "broader interests in national policy development."[31] The Special Committee on Reform of the House of Commons added that committees should become places for consultation before legislation is introduced.[32]

Such reforms will have minimal effect on economic performance, however, unless accompanied by changes in the organization of business interests in Canada. As the commission notes: "Yet while Parliament exists to hold the executive to account, there are no formal institutional arrangements or governing principles to hold accountable the private interests, which are major beneficiaries of the national tax and expenditure system."[33] The problem of increasing the accountability of private interests therefore is two-fold, involving reforms to both the political process and the structures speaking for interests. If the process is reshaped following the suggestions of the Macdonald Commission and the Special Committee, it will hold groups accountable only if the groups are themselves adapted for consultation. Skogstad, in her study of parliamentary committees, has demonstrated that consultation may exacerbate conflict if a given sector of the economy is itself divided and not organized into encompassing organizations.[34] The mixture of conflict in the sector and partisan divisions in the committee creates a highly explosive political experience. Consultation becomes more effective when an association has to find a consensus, which depends on the organizational capacity of the association involved.

Without some change in group structures, the new committees will become another forum for the traditional self-serving pleading to which Canadians are already too well accustomed – and will be ignored by the government. If business gains access to specialized forums for pre-formulation discussion of economic policy, it becomes an "official" part of the policy-making process. At this point, political leaders and the public at large should query whether the structures of business organizations conform to expectations about official participation in a parliamentary democracy. As Charles Anderson argues: "The internal government of the interest organization must be itself democratic."[35]

The system of associations representing business in Canada falls down seriously in this regard. There are no umbrella or general associations speaking for business that are acceptable by this criterion. While the Business Council on National Issues from time to time evinces an openness to labour, it speaks for an élite group of large corporations. The criteria for membership are anything but transparent, making it difficult to determine whom the association speaks for. The remaining three organizations, the Canadian Chamber of Commerce, the Canadian Federation of Independent Business, and the Canadian Organization of Small Business, are all extremely hostile to labour. They are unlikely to contribute to consensus-building and partnership, which the small European states have shown to be necessary. In addition, each has major flaws in its organizational structure in the light of democratic principles.

The existing system of business interest associations does provide for expression of a wide range of sectoral and territorial interests. Almost every sector and region has an association to speak for it. Lacking are structures to tie these assorted voices together. The peak association, an association of associations, is rare in Canada. Yet it would appear to be necessary. A well-articulated peak association would be built systematically from the most specialized sectoral association, from sectors, from groups of sectors, and finally from whole divisions of the economy – manufacturing, resource extraction, transportation, and so on. It would be scrupulous to ensure each of these interests a voice in its deliberations. It would represent most of the firms accounting for most of the productive capacity of the economy. Most important, it could give vent to conflicts among different fractions of the business class and build a consensus from these debates. It would not always succeed, nor should this be expected. A consensus could be presented to politicians and other major socioeconomic producer groups, examined in the light of competing proposals, and acted upon. Business then becomes accountable for the vast private power it wields in the Canadian economic system and at the same time probably gains influence over policy that it did not have before.

How feasible is such reform? Certainly, as noted in the conclusions to chapters 11 and 12, obstacles remain in the institutional structure of the Canadian economy. The manufacturing group remains bifurcated between most of the finished goods sectors, content (for over a century in some cases) with the home market, and basic goods sectors as well as the primary raw materials industries, oriented towards world competition. Reinforcing this cleavage is a division of powers that invites governments to exacerbate rather than soften conflict and a parliamentary system that itself diffuses power. However, business interests in Quebec have shown some creativity in getting around these obstacles in the establishment and relative success of their Conseil du Patronat.

Despite their institutional constraints, governments in Canada need not sit idly by waiting for reform. They can become more sensitive to the organizational properties of business associations. They might ask specifically about which interests are being represented, what the density of representation is, how a given position was arrived at, and whether it was formed using democratic procedures. Governments can become more transparent in their allocation of policy-making privileges to associations, giving them only to groups organized in light of democratic principles and public accountability. Governments might even ask that business improve its capacity to speak for the class as a whole and make this a condition for further systematic consultation. Such an idea has been thought about by business representatives in Canada. The Canadian Manufacturers' Association, in its forward-looking document entitled *A Future That Works*, notes: "An intriguing question remains: will the exigencies of international competition require Canada to develop some sort of private sector umbrella organization which would be able to mobilize opinion and action in support of goals agreed upon with government? We think this should be seriously addressed."[36] At the same time, governments cannot coerce business to change its ways – an Austrian chamber–type system simply goes too much against the tradition of voluntary collective action in the Canadian system. The experience of the Association des entrepreneurs en construction du Québec, created in this manner, demonstrates the importance of this constraint.[37]

Labour and Agriculture

The system of consensual policy-making found in the smaller European democracies requires a capable voice representing the working classes. In some countries, like Sweden and Austria, strongly centralized and highly representative labour centrals with close ties to social democratic parties provide this voice. In other countries, such as Switzerland, labour is not well organized, nor is the social democratic party strong. In Canada, similar conditions prevail. The labour movement is divided at the national level among several labour confederations, including the Canadian Labour Congress (CLC), the Canadian Federation of Labour, and the Confederation of Canadian Unions. In addition, the influential Confederation of National Trade Unions in Quebec operates autonomously from all national-level organizations. The New Democratic Party (NDP), which is endorsed by one of these centrals, the CLC, has been a third party at the federal level until recently, the governing party or official opposition in the four western provinces, an opposition party in Ontario, and in the electoral wilderness east of Ontario.

It is unlikely that this weak position of labour organizations will change in the short run. The density of union organization is also rather low, which makes it difficult for labour centrals to speak for all of the working class. Yet labour and its concerns must be much better integrated into economic decision-making in Canada. The experience of the small European democracies suggests strongly that adapting a small, open economy to international competition in a liberal trading environment requires extensive *concertation* among major socioeconomic producer groups. Compensation for groups adversely affected by adjustments to international competition must be negotiated. Without greater co-operation and the cushion of a large domestic market, Canada will continue to experience economic difficulties, perhaps even more intensely than now.

Electoral reform offers one avenue to providing labour with more adequate political representation. Over the past decade, many have discussed proportional representation (PR). Traditionally, analysts have argued that such a system may not yield stable, majority governments. This argument is increasingly suspect. Majority governments have by no means been the norm in Canada at the federal level since 1945. In addition, the existing "first past the post" single-constituency system discriminates against traditionally smaller parties such as the NDP. The Task Force on Canadian Unity in its 1978 report noted that this electoral system also distorted regional representation by the two major parties and recommended the adoption of a partial PR system to remedy this problem.

PR gives a truer picture of party support in all regions of the country: if no party has majority support across the country, then it will not win a majority of seats in the House of Commons. The European experience shows, however, that such a result is hardly the catastrophe that many Canadians believe it to be. Coalitions are struck and compromises are made that allow governments to rule and accommodate the diverse interests represented. In short, such electoral systems foster the kind of bargaining and give and take required to manage the affairs of small, open economies operating in a liberal trading environment.

If the electoral system in the House is not changed, another, less satisfactory but potentially useful reform might involve the Senate. Since the late 1970s, demands for its reform have become more insistent. A number of individuals and groups have pushed for an elected Senate to strengthen regional voices in the national government. The Macdonald Commission recommended an elected Senate, with representation weighted in favour of the less populous regions. Members would be elected by PR in six-member constituencies.[38] Such a proposal would compensate for the under-representation of the NDP in Ottawa. A strengthened NDP caucus (House and Senate) could introduce more systematic consideration of labour's interests into the policy-making process. The proposed reforms to parliamentary committees, designed to de-emphasize divisions between government and opposition, and Senate PR would give more NDP parliamentarians a better opportunity to speak to the interests of labour as well as others represented by their party.

Reform of the policy process to improve Canada's position in international markets must consider agriculture. Agricultural exports, particularly of grains, account for an important part of Canada's international trade and could account for more. Two problems, however, beset the organizations representing agriculture and thus prevent farmers' more systematic involvement in the policy process. First, the dominant peak association, the Canadian Federation of Agriculture (CFA), has come close to collapsing since the early 1980s. Previously unable to accommodate divisions arising out of a divergence in interests between farmers and their successful commercial organizations, the CFA saw the National Farmers Union grow in stature in the 1970s. Disagreements between beef producers and farmers in other sectors as well as among grain producers over marketing plans and transportation kept the cattlemen and a minority of grain producers outside the CFA umbrella. Underlying both sets of problems were growing differences among farmers in basic philosophy, particularly on how best to stabilize their income and to involve themselves in the market-place. These divisions widened into chasms in the early 1980s, when the stakes became very high in the Crow debate. As we saw in chapter 6, these disputes resulted eventually in the disappearance of two provincial federations of the CFA, in Saskatchewan and Manitoba. These departures and others have left the CFA much weakened.

Second, agriculture has worked in Ottawa in a very traditional way. The Department of Agriculture has operated as a clientele department, seeing itself as representing farmers in government. Accordingly, the CFA has maintained very close relations with this department, lobbying it intensively and relying on it to represent agriculture in the cabinet and in the bureaucracy. Farmers have thus been less involved in other consultative forums and have seldom engaged in policy-making with other producer groups. Consequently, they have not had to take systematic account of the interests of other groups, nor have other groups been well briefed on the interests and concerns of agricultural producers.

While perhaps expedient for politicians and other groups in the short term, serious divisions within the organizations representing agriculture will hamper effective national economic policy. An integrated associational system sufficiently differentiated to represent various commodity and territorial interests is as necessary for farmers as for business. Assuming that these problems can be resolved over the medium term, the renewed organizations representing farmers should then be fully and directly integrated into the consultative process outlined above for business and labour. The exclusion of such a major group would undermine the very raison d'être of consultation.

DEMOCRACY AND BUSINESS

It is useful at this point to recall the definitions of two of the four types of policy networks discussed extensively in this book – clientele pluralism and co-optive pluralism. In both types of network, associations assume policy participation, that is, they are involved in a continuous, structured way in the making of policy. A one-on-one relationship predominates – the making of policy involves an agency or department working primarily with one interest association only. In the co-optive case, the group represents a sector that bears the costs of the policy. For example, if a policy sets out the regulations for the control and use of agricultural pesticides, a co-optive network might be composed of the relevant government agency and an association representing manufacturers of agricultural chemicals. These manufacturers are not the recipients of the policy output (effective or safe pesticides) but must bear some costs in providing the actual recipients, farmers and those in their environment, with this product. In a clientele network, the group represents a sector that receives the policy good. An obvious example is a policy designed to train workers in the automobile parts industry. A clientele network would be composed of a relevant state agency and an association representing manufacturers of automobile parts, which receive the policy good – trained workers.

These networks depart from the classical pluralist model in two important respects. First, in the classical model, groups are understood to operate outside the policy process and seek to influence what is going on within. In contrast, in the co-optive and clientele cases, the groups are incorporated directly into the making of policy itself. Second, the classical model speaks of a range of interests competing for the ear of the state, which then plays the role of a neutral arbiter weighing one demand against the other, seeking a common or even the public interest. The other two types are dominated by one group only, with the state showing a particular interest in that group. They become more likely when the state pursues policy objectives using regulatory or self-regulatory policy instruments. The state is likely to become dependent on a specific sectoral representative for information, or expertise, or support for and compliance with the regulations themselves. In an exchange relationship, the representative of the sector receives a say in the making of policy in return for its advice, its expertise, or its efforts to guarantee that the relevant firms comply with the regulations. The development of such networks is encouraged, Chubb adds, by the important sources of affinity between interest groups and bureaucratic agencies.[39] Both organizations tend to be specialists in the given policy area, and both are the most involved in the policy on a day-to-day basis. By virtue of their formal organization, they bring to the policy area greater expertise and permanence. "Theoretically they constitute the durable core of any policy arena."[40]

The analysis in this book has demonstrated that these two types of network are common in Canadian political life. They were present in virtually all the industries that we examined. In some cases, they were central to business-government relations: in forestry, securities underwriting, food processing, pharmaceuticals, occupational health and safety in mining, and so on. The presence of such networks becomes a matter of concern in any liberal democracy, for several reasons.

First, they accentuate the trend in the British parliamentary system towards what Pross calls "bureaucratic pluralism"[41] – the parcelling out of policy-making responsibility among various agencies and departments. In the process, these agencies gain considerable autonomy and thus freedom to make decisions. As this process becomes more and more common, it becomes increasingly difficult to coordinate policies and to avoid duplication. Even more disturbing, those responsible to the citizenry for the exercise of power, government members in the House of Commons, lose the ability to account adequately for the exercise of power. Their capacity to guard against the arbitrary application of public power or against favouritism towards the special interests of a select group of business firms becomes very weak indeed.

Consistent with the growth of bureaucratic pluralism is reliance on "delegated legislation." Such legislation sets out the general principles of a policy while delegating wide-ranging powers for specifying and implementing the law to a subordinate agency. Legislation flows to administrators without any guides, checks, or safeguards. At a time when the need for standards has increased, specific standards are disappearing from many laws. Without standards, Lowi writes,

the power of the democratic state is drained away; the system becomes one of legitimized privilege.[42]

The studies in this book have illustrated the widespread existence
(anticipated by Lindblom) of special privileges enjoyed by business
associations.[43] Through co-optive and clientele pluralist networks,
business has gained an immediate access to political power not often
possessed by other social classes and groups that also have a strong
interest in the given policy area. These comfortable nexuses of bureaucratic officialdom and association executives insulate themselves
from politicians and other interests alike by cloaking work in a technical, operational discourse. The problems then are several. Cabinet
members responsible for public policies to the House of Commons
and through it to the Canadian people cannot adequately account
for the decisions taken in their name. Other classes and groups that
might be affected by the policy do not have their demands and needs
considered on an equal basis with those of business; access to political
power is distributed unevenly. The business interest associations that
share in decision-making and hence in the exercise of public power
are not themselves accountable for their actions. They remain private
groups, speaking for a special sectional interest, accountable to their
own members only, business firms.

While these privileges have their roots in the position occupied by
business in a society with a market economy and a liberal democratic
polity, they are unacceptable. Business must be made more accountable to society at large for the exercise of its private and public power.
Improving the accountability of business will involve reforms to the
political process in Parliament, the procedures used by the bureaucracy, and the associational structures of business and other social
classes. Beginning with the political process, the role for parliamentary committees proposed by the Special Committee on Reform of
the House of Commons and echoed by the Macdonald Commission
– consultation and deliberation on legislation before first (or, in some
cases, second) reading – is a good one. By inviting and allowing a
range of individuals and groups to speak to a policy problem at these
early stages, the committees would force the policy process to become
more "other-regarding," that is, to consider interests and needs besides those of business. In addition, business associations would be
pressed to become more accountable to the public for the content
of their proposals.

The Special Committee's proposal that standing and special drafting committees play this consultation role and that new legislative
committees be struck to consider the details of legislation relates also
to its suggestions for resolving the problem of delegated legislation.[44]

The committee argued that the legislative committees should review, in particular, the enabling clauses in bills, delegating power to subordinate agencies and departments. It recommended further that the House of Commons adopt a mandatory procedure for affirming or disallowing delegated legislation and regulations. Finally, it advocated that all delegated legislation and accompanying regulations be referred to both the appropriate standing committee of the House and to the Joint Committee on Regulations and Other Statutory Instruments. These reforms would help Parliament control the use of power by bureaucratic agencies but would not have much impact unless governments define standards and basic values in the laws they propose to the Commons. MPs would have a most difficult job if the government failed to outline the values and principles upon which the definition of regulations rested.

If governments can improve on their directions to officials when they delegate power and on the resources they make available, agencies will be able to reform their procedures. Specifically, they need to carry out systematic consultation with all parties affected by the legislation they are planning to implement. An obvious tool is the "information letter." The agency draws up a proposal for a new policy or for a change to an existing policy and sends it out to the private sector for comment. Upon receiving comments, it revises its original proposals, sends out a further letter for comments, and then submits the revised proposals to the minister. Such an approach is used with some success in the Health Protection Branch of the Department of Health and Welfare and in the Department of Consumer and Corporate Affairs and could be adopted more widely. Government agencies must canvas classes and groups besides business. They should not solicit the opinion of only one association representing a given group unless that association is highly representative. Finally, they should consider bringing interested parties together to discuss proposed policies to provide guidance in finding a consensus and a better appreciation of the values and needs of the various affected parties.

These changes to parliamentary and bureaucratic procedure must be accompanied by changes in associational structures. The prescription for more encompassing, better integrated business associational systems outlined in the previous section is just as necessary for enhancing democracy in group-state relations as for managing the economy. More encompassing organizations alert business people to broader issues and to the consequences of narrow, self-serving behaviour.[45] Potentially, through suasion and indirect influence, they may even check the accumulation of co-optive and clientele privileges.

Even with these changes in business associative action, a fundamental problem remains: associations representing classes other than business are considerably weaker in resources and representativeness of their domains. Bureaucratic officials may simply not receive replies from consumers or labour or environmentalists when they solicit their opinions. The logic of collective action for business firms differs from that of labour, as Offe and Wiesenthal have shown,[46] and from that of public interest groups representing broad, diffuse constituencies such as consumers or environmentalists.[47] In comparison, business associations have greater resources – more funds and expertise and personnel more easily available from their membership. Serving on a committee in a business association may take 50 to 100 hours a year. The firm contributing its personnel often believes that this represents work on behalf of the firm itself. Normally, no one offers to continue the pay of people while they work for a consumers' organization. Serving in this capacity must be done in spare time or by people with wealth.

Solutions to these kinds of problems are neither obvious nor easy. Looking first at the organizations representing consumers, particularly the Consumers Association of Canada (CAC), the problem seems to be the reverse of that of business. Rather than a large number of very specialized, poorly integrated interest groups, there exists instead a large, diffuse, comprehensive organization that is poorly differentiated. With fewer resources than many of the larger business associations, the CAC is expected to represent the interests of consumers across a broad range of sectors. Each sector will have at least one special interest group representing business and able to overmatch the CAC's resources and effort. Public interest groups are more effective when they too are more specialized and can concentrate on a limited set of problems. Such organizations as Energy Probe and the Canadian Arctic Resources Committee illustrate these possibilities.

Strengthening the voices of consumers and other public interest advocates will require a strengthening of labour organizations. The system of trade unions already parallels better than any other system the differentiated pattern of business interest organization and has the best potential for matching one on one the special interest demands of business firms. Governments, particularly the bureaucracies that serve them, should seek to involve labour more systematically in consultation in policy-making. This will be possible only if other changes are made. Labour laws must be changed to encourage more workers to become organized, particularly the poorly paid and highly exploited, and to protect better existing trade union rights. Not only would labour organizations then become more representative of workers, they could also claim more legitimacy as participants in the policy process. Labour organizations must be encouraged to centralize their operations further so that they can speak more effectively for the general interests of workers and integrate better the special interests of workers in particular sectors with those more general interests. Strengthened in these ways, labour organizations will be able to obtain the resources and expertise to speak effectively for their members in the forums currently monopolized by business interest associations.

A strengthened system for representing the interests of workers will then become a natural rallying point for other groups wishing to counter the influence and privileges of business. Workers bear the brunt of policies that force high prices for goods or that allow for unsafe, sub-standard goods. They are least able to protect their health and safety in the face of environmental pollution. They experience more intensively the consequences of inadequate pay for women. A strengthened trade union sector will provide a forum for the discussion of these various concerns and their effect on the vital issue of employment. If these new organizations of labour can devise suggestions for accommodating conflict, they will become even more influential participants in the policy process.

CONCLUSIONS

The particular interpretation of Canada's economic position given here and the various changes suggested to the organization of business interests and the policy process are presented for the purposes of discussion. They should not be seen as the final word or dismissed out of hand. Yet the temptations to dismiss them will be strong. There is neither a tradition in Canada that compares the economy with the smaller European states nor much interest in these states. Canadians compare themselves with Americans or Britons, blinding themselves to the importance and the implications of possessing a small economy in a world where mass production of consumer goods is shifting rapidly to the newly industrializing countries of the Third World. Given their long experience with trading manufactured goods as small, open economies, the small European states merit some attention when alternative policies are considered in Canada. Nevertheless, the proposals presented in this chapter are likely to invite three major types of critical responses.

1. The proposals smack very much of corporatism. A corporatist system of governance is fundamentally antithetical to democracy, because it circumvents the usual mode for demand aggregation and articulation in a democracy – the political parties. In addition, corporatist structures are foreign to the parliamentary system.

The relationship between corporatism and democracy is indeed complex and worrying. The subject has received increasing attention in the past four or five years. Some, such as Schmitter, have analysed the relationship on a theoretical plane and argued that the liberal or "societal" corporatism found in many European states need not detract from democracy at all.[48] Others, such as Katzenstein, have explored empirically a range of states in Europe and shown that corporatist practices have merged well with liberal democratic principles. The consultation and joint decision-making forums found in these countries bear no resemblance to the régimes found in the Iberian dictatorships or in Mussolini's Italy. In short, both theoretical analysis and empirical research have shown that societal/liberal/social/neo- (the terms vary) corporatism and democracy are potentially compatible.

The extensive empirical research by Lehmbruch and Katzenstein in particular has shown that political parties and corporatist structures tend to coexist in relative harmony. Generally the two subsystems interpenetrate one another and are functionally specialized. The interest intermediation sub-system treats issues of economic and social policy that involve redistribution, particularly between business and labour. These issues normally pertain to the longer term, and the political élites involved prefer to keep them out of the partisan party system. When these issues cannot be resolved in the corporatist structures, they are debated by the parties, and further direction from the electorate is sought. The parties also deal with a range of issues involving policy areas other than social and economic redistribution and medium- and long-range economic planning.

The usurpation of party functions in Canada would not appear to be a problem given the brokerage party system. Many scholars have pointed out that the two major parties function as fluid coalitions of interests. They press towards the centre, trying to avoid definite stands on particular issues and problems, seeking only general mandates. In fact, it is debatable whether they ever receive a policy mandate in an election, as the title of a recent book on the subject suggests.[49] Political parties do not function well in Canada as aggregators and articulators of political demands; they exist more as latent organizations for fighting elections. In fact, Clarke et al argue that the development and articulation of policy innovations now fall outside the Canadian party system completely.[50] They see the bureaucracy and federal-provincial forums as the main sources for policy innovations. I would add only that bureaucracies tend to refine these innovations in consultation, often with business interest groups in particular. Interest groups themselves are important sources of political demands, and many possess organizations equipped to define political demands based on the needs of their members. They perform these functions in a way that helps business associations and that requires little accountability on the part of business. The proposals in this chapter designed to structure the dealings between interest groups and the Canadian state would increase accountability and perhaps, through reform of the electoral system or the Senate, make political parties more relevant participants in the policy process.

Finally, it is not immediately obvious why formalization of the structures in the interest intermediation system should pose a threat to a British-style parliamentary system. In fact, the increase in business's accountability for the use of its vast private economic power suggested here will draw on Parliament and its committees. The proposed reforms promise to strengthen Parliament by giving it a role in finding a consensus on economic policy among socioeconomic groups, including consumers. Parliament may provide a check against the abuses of bureaucratic discretion and interest group penetration of decision-making forums.

2. The proposed changes point to increased state interference with the actions of business, in particular, increased direct state intervention in the economy.

Indeed, it will be possible to enhance the accountability of business to the political community at large only with increased attention by the state to the actions of business firms and their representatives. The degree of intervention will depend on how responsible business turns out to be. If it continues to exploit clientele and co-optive relationships at the expense of other social classes, and if it refuses to provide itself with the organizational capability and sense of partnership needed to discuss economic policy with other major socioeconomic groups, then it should be prepared for calls for increased control over its activity. However, if it should move to increase its sense of social responsibility and its organizational capability, intervention would be less likely.

In addition, demands for decreased state involvement in managing the economy reflect a "head-in-the-sand" approach to the constraints and problems of the international market-place today. Canada, like all other Western nations, has been adjusting and rationalizing its manufacturing industries over the past two decades. This process will continue, probably at an even more frenzied pace over the next decade. The OECD, an organization noted for its economic orthodoxy and not for any sort of radicalism, has assessed the problems of managing structural change and made recommendations that reinforce this point. In view of the low growth and high unemployment that are likely to continue throughout this decade, the OECD asks member countries to consider policies that keep wage costs more in line with productivity trends.[51] It notes two ways for the state to proceed. The state can go ahead on its own and devise and implement the policies it feels to be necessary. Or it can draw labour and business into regular tripartite discussions of policies designed to achieve these economic results. In such a process, views can be exchanged and current conditions assessed in advance of events, helping perhaps to avoid crises. Such a strategy "enables the government to communicate in more detail its policy framework and policy options, and places the representatives of business and labour in a position to assess *a priori* the consequences of their alternative courses of action in an overall economic setting."[52]

It is apparent from the analysis in this book that business is not equipped for even this type of consultation. It lacks both the requisite openness to labour and organizational structures allowing it to participate in such discussions in a way true to the norms of a liberal democracy. When even an organization wed to established economic theory and analysis such as the OECD points to the advantages of *concertation* and consultation in facing current structural problems in the economy, it becomes even more difficult to listen to the tired refrain of the business community in Canada about the "freeing of enterprise." The laissez-faire state of the nineteenth century now sits on the museum shelf with child labour, the school strap, and the male-only franchise.

3. The proposed changes will only increase further the dominance of business over labour. They promise, if implemented, to co-opt labour, to the detriment of the conditions of life of members of the working class.

To say that such a scenario is not possible would be irresponsible. Relative to many other countries, the Canadian labour movement appears rather weak. Its organizations are highly decentralized and do not represent even a third of wage earners. The political party with which it enjoys close, formal ties has been a third, minor party in federal politics, although this may be changing. A more centralized, highly representative peak association structure speaking for business interests might dominate the policy process even more than business interests do now. Labour might become marginalized to an extent not known since the early twentieth century.

However, the thrust of this chapter has been directed at increasing the accountability and responsibility of business. In developing this theme, I have argued for more transparent relations between business and the state and for creation of formal forums where business might be held to account, not only by politicians but also by other social classes and groups, for its use of its private power. If necessary, the political system must compensate for the weakness of labour by adopting principles of equal representation and by counteracting the discrimination of the electoral system against the NDP. If a program cast along the lines suggested here were implemented, labour's position would be substantially improved over what it is today.

The stakes are high as Canadians consider whether to make changes. Simply put, failure to incorporate labour and other groups speaking for the disadvantaged will, in all probability, rule out the possibility of successful adaptation to the changed world economic context. The Canadian economy is too small and vulnerable to tolerate much longer insularity and closed minds. If business fails to use its private power responsibly, to recognize the rights of others to question and press for changes in this use from time to time, then society must consider other means for exercising that power. Not only the interests of business are at stake.

APPENDIX

Association Domains, 1867–1980

ISIC	Class	Business	Agricultural	Professional	Total
1110	Agricultural Products	3	82	1	86
1120	Agricultural Services		40	2	42
1200	Forestry General	2		1	3
1210	Forestry	5		4	9
1220	Logging	13			13
1300	Fishing General				
1301	Ocean Fishing				
1302	Fishing NEC*	1			1
2100	Coal Mining	7			7
2200	Petroleum, Natural Gas	11		1	12
2300	Metal Ore Mining	6		3	9
2301	Iron Ore Mining				
2302	Non-ferrous Metals	6			6
2900	Other Mining	1			1
2901	Stone Quarrying	2			2
2902	Mining NEC	1			1
3100	Food, Beverage, Tobacco Manufacturing	1			1
3110	Food Manufacturing	2			2
3111	Meat Processing	3			3
3112	Dairy Products	12	2		14
3113	Fruit, Vegetable Processing	3			3
3114	Fish Processing	8			8
3115	Vegetable Oils Processing	1			1
3116	Grain Mills	2			2

ISIC	Class	Business	Agricultural	Professional	Total
3117	Bakery Products	5			5
3118	Sugar Factories	1			1
3119	Confectionery	2			2
3121	Food NEC	6			6
3122	Animal Feed	2			2
3131	Distillers	1			1
3132	Wine Makers	4			4
3133	Malt Liquor	3			3
3134	Soft Drinks	4			4
3140	Tobacco Manufacturers	2			2
3200	Textiles and Clothing			1	1
3210	Textiles	5		1	6
3211	Spinning, Weaving	6			6
3212	Made Up Textiles	2			2
3213	Knitting Mills	1			1
3214	Carpets	2			2
3215	Cordage	1			1
3220	Clothing	24			24
3231	Tanneries	3			3
3232	Fur Dressing	2			2
3233	Leather Products	3			3
3240	Footwear	3			3
3300	Wood Products	2			2
3311	Sawmills	16			16
3312	Wooden Containers	1			1
3319	Wood NEC	1			1
3320	Furniture	5			5
3410	Paper Products	1			1
3411	Pulp and Paper	4			4
3412	Paper Boxes	6			6
3419	Paper NEC	1			1
3420	Printing, Publishing	21		4	25
3500	Chemicals				
3511	Industrial Chemicals	4			4
3512	Fertilizers	5			5
3513	Primary Plastics	2			2
3521	Paints	1			1
3522	Drugs and Medicines	5			5
3523	Soaps	2			2
3529	Chemicals NEC	5			5
3530	Petroleum Refineries	1			1

ISIC	Class	Business	Agricultural	Professional	Total
3540	Petroleum and Coal NEC	1			1
3559	Rubber NEC				
3560	Plastics Fabricating	2			2
3610	Pottery, China				
3620	Glass	2			2
3690	Other Non-metallic Products				
3691	Structural Clay	6			6
3699	Non-Metallic NEC	5			5
3700	Primary Metals	2			2
3710	Basic Iron and Steel	7			7
3720	Basic Non-Ferrous	2			2
3800	Fabricated Metals	1			1
3811	Cutlery, Hand Tools				
3812	Furniture	3			3
3813	Structural Metal	5			5
3819	Fabricated Metals NEC	1			1
3820	Machinery				
3821	Engines, Turbines	2			2
3822	Agricultural Machinery	1			1
3824	Special Industrial Machinery	1			1
3825	Office Machinery	2			2
3829	Machinery NEC	7			7
3830	Electrical	2			2
3831	Industrial Electrical	3			3
3832	Communications Equipment	2			2
3833	Appliances	1			1
3839	Electrical NEC				
3840	Transportation Equipment	1			1
3841	Shipbuilding	2			2
3842	Railroad Equipment	1			1
3843	Motor Vehicles	4			4
3844	Motorcycles	1			1
3845	Aircraft	3			3
3851	Professional Equipment				
3852	Cameras	1			1
3900	Other Manufacturing	2			2
3902	Musical Instruments	2			2
3903	Sporting Goods	2			2
3904	Manufacturing NEC	7			7
4101	Electrical Power Production	2			2

ISIC	Class	Business	Agricultural	Professional	Total
4102	Gas Distribution	1			1
4200	Water Works Utilities	2			2
5000	Construction	23		7	30
6100	Wholesale Trade	75			75
6200	Retail Trade	31			31
6300	Restaurants, Hotels	2			2
6310	Restaurants	1			1
6320	Hotels	2			2
6400	International Trade	1			1
7100	Transportation, Storage				
7110	Land Transport				
7111	Railway	6			6
7112	Urban Passenger	1			1
7114	Freight by Road	6			6
7115	Pipeline Transport	1			1
7116	Land Support	1			1
7120	Water Transport			2	2
7121	Ocean	1			1
7122	Inland	1			1
7123	Water Support	1			1
7130	Air Transport	1			1
7131	Air Carriers	2			2
7132	Air Support			1	1
7191	Incidental Transportation Services	3		3	6
7192	Storage	3			3
7200	Communication	5		1	6
8100	Financial	1		1	2
8101	Monetary Institutions	1			1
8102	Other Financial Institutions	9		5	14
8103	Financial Services	1		1	2
8200	Insurance	28			28
8300	Business Services	1		1	2
8310	Real Estate	5			5
8320	Other Services	1		1	2
8321	Legal			9	9
8322	Accounting	1		8	9
8323	Data Processing			1	1

ISIC	Class	Business	Agricultural	Professional	Total
8324	Engineering	2		25	27
8325	Advertising	9		10	19
8329	Services NEC	12		4	16
8300	Machinery Leasing	2			2
9100	Public Administration			31	31
9200	Sanitary Services	1			1
9310	Education Services	1		132	133
9320	Research Institutions	5		23	28
9331	Health Services	4		110	114
9332	Veterinary Services			1	1
9340	Welfare Services	1			1
9350	Association Services	4		13	17
9391	Religious Organizations			1	1
9399	Social Services NEC				
9410	Entertainment			4	4
9411	Film Production	6		3	9
9412	Film Distribution	6			6
9413	Broadcasting	10		7	17
9414	Theatre	3		5	8
9415	Artists	1		33	34
9420	Libraries, Museums	2		11	13
9490	Entertainment	4			4
9513	Auto Repair Services	5			5
9520	Laundries	1			1
9530	Domestic Services	1			1
9591	Barber, Beauty Shops				
9520	Photo Studios			1	1
9599	Other Personal	5		1	6
	Intersectoral	4			4
	NEC	14	1	10	25
	Overall totals	662	125	484	1,271

SOURCE: International Standard Industrial Classification.

*NEC: not elsewhere classified.

Notes

CHAPTER ONE

1 Ronald Manzer, *Public Policies and Political Development* (Toronto: University of Toronto Press 1985).
2 A. Przeworski and M. Wallerstein, "Democratic Capitalism at the Crossroads," *Democracy* (July 1982): 54.
3 C. Lindblom, *Politics and Markets* (New York: Basic Books 1977), 193ff.
4 Ibid.
5 Kenneth Dyson, "The Cultural, Ideological and Structural Context," in K. Dyson and S. Wilks, eds., *Industrial Crisis* (Oxford: Martin Robertson 1983), 25–66.
6 Carl E. Beigie and James K. Stewart, "Canada's Industrial Challenges and Business Government Relations: Toward Effective Collaboration," in V.V. Murray, ed., *Theories of Business-Government Relations* (Toronto: TransCanada Press 1985), 132.
7 D.H. Thain, "Improving Competence to Deal with Politics and Government: The Management Challenge of the 80s," *Business Quarterly* 45, No. 1 (1980): 31–45.
8 Wyn Grant, "Large Firms and Public Policy in Britain," *Journal of Public Policy* 4, No. 1 (1984): 9–13.
9 Ibid.
10 See Andrew Gollner, "Corporate Public Affairs in Canada: A Survey," paper prepared for the School of Community and Public Affairs, Concordia University, 1983, 21.
11 Ibid., 43.
12 James Gillies, *Where Business Fails* (Montreal: IRPP 1981), 34.
13 Ibid.
14 See Grant, "Large Firms," and W.T. Stanbury, *Business-Government Relations in Canada* (Toronto: Methuen 1986), chapter 5, for elaboration on this point.

15 Grant, "Large Firms," 7.
16 Thain, "Improving Competence."
17 Grant, "Large Firms," 7.
18 Michael Useem, *The Inner Circle: Large Corporations and the Rise of Business Political Activity in the u.s. and u.k.* (New York: Oxford University Press 1984).
19 William Carroll, *Corporate Power and Canadian Capitalism* (Vancouver: University of British Columbia Press 1986); Wallace Clement *The Canadian Corporate Elite* (Toronto: McClelland and Stewart 1975).
20 J.J. Richardson and A.G. Jordan, *Governing under Pressure: The Policy Process in Post Parliamentary Democracy* (Oxford: Martin Robertson 1979) 20ff.
21 A. Cawson, *Corporatism and Welfare: Social Policy and State Intervention in Britain* (London: Heinemann 1982) 30.
22 Richardson and Jordan, *Governing*, passim.
23 See ibid., 27 ff., and John Chubb, *Interest Groups and the Bureaucracy: The Politics of Energy* (Stanford: Stanford University Press 1983) 8–10.
24 W. Streeck, "Between Pluralism and Corporatism: German Business Associatons and the State," *Journal of Public Policy* 3, No. 3 (1983): 265–84.
25 A. Paul Pross, "Canadian Pressure Groups in the 1970s: Their Role and Their Relations with the Public Service," *Canadian Public Administration* 18, No. 1 (1975): 121–35.
26 D. Vogel, "The Power of Business in America: A Reappraisal," *British Journal of Political Science* 13, No. 1 (1983): 20.
27 sshrcc Research Grants 410–78–0716 and 410–80–0280.

CHAPTER TWO

1 Jack L. Walker, "The Origins and Maintenance of Interest Groups in America," *American Political Science Review* 77, No. 2 (1983): 391.
2 A. Paul Pross, "Canadian Pressure Groups in the 1970s: Their Role and Their Relations with the Public Service," *Canadian Public Administration* 18, No. 2 (1975): 125.
3 In particular, Robert Presthus, *Elite Accommodation in Canadian Politics* (Toronto: Macmillan 1974).
4 By nationally relevant, I mean an association that claims to represent an economic interest on the national plane. However, if the association is based in a region (group of provinces) or province that accounts for 35 per cent of the economic activity in the sector in Canada, it was also included. Finally, French-Canadian or Quebec-based associations set up to represent the interests of French Canadians in a sector parallel to a national-level English-Canadian association were also included.
5 See, for example, Douglas McCalla, "The Commercial Politics of the

Toronto Board of Trade, 1850–1860," *Canadian Historical Review* 50, No. 1 (1969): 51–67.

6 This number does not include trade union organizations.

7 Ben Forster, *A Conjunction of Interests: Business, Politics and Tariffs, 1825–1879* (Toronto: University of Toronto Press 1986) 35, 49.

8 This list of factors draws heavily on the influential study by Michael Bliss, *A Living Profit: Studies in the Social History of Canadian Business, 1883–1911* (Toronto: McClelland and Stewart 1974).

9 Ibid., 34–5.

10 Michael Bliss, "Another Anti-Trust Tradition: Canadian Anti-Combines Policy, 1887–1910" in G. Porter and R. Cuff, eds., *Enterprise and National Development* (Toronto: Hakkert 1973) 41–2.

11 Ibid., 47–8, and T. Naylor, *The History of Canadian Business*, Vol. II: *Industrial Development* (Toronto: Lorimer 1975), 162.

12 Naylor, *History*, 162.

13 S.D. Clark, *The Canadian Manufacturers' Association: A Study in Collective Bargaining and Political Pressure* (Toronto: University of Toronto Press 1938), 56.

14 T. Traves, *The State and Enterprise: Canadian Manufacturers and the Federal Government* (Toronto: University of Toronto Press 1979), 76.

15 Alvin Finkel, *Business and Social Reform in the Thirties* (Toronto: Lorimer 1979), 33–4.

16 Forster, *Conjunction of Interests*, 73.

17 Ibid., 109.

18 Ibid., 115.

19 Clark, *The CMA*, 8.

20 For a discussion of a split in the CMA over this issue, see Naylor, *History*, Vol. II, 206.

21 Clark, *The CMA*, 57.

22 J. Harvey Perry, "Origins of the Canadian Bankers' Association" *Canadian Banker* 74, No. 1 (1967): 103.

23 Ibid., 109.

24 Bliss, *Living Profit*, 36.

25 Naylor, *History*, Vol. I, 75.

26 Clark, *The CMA*, 26ff.

27 Ibid., 48, 50.

28 Ibid., 52.

29 See John Battye, "The Nine Hour Pioneers: The Genesis of the Canadian Labour Movement," *Labour/Le travailleur* No. 4 (1979): 46–7.

30 Bliss, *Living Profit*, 12.

31 Gregory S. Kealey and Bryan D. Palmer, *Dreaming of What Might Be: The Knights of Labour in Ontario, 1880–1900* (Cambridge: Cambridge University Press 1982), 90.

32 Bryan Palmer, *Working Class Experience: The Rise and Reconstitution of Canadian Labour, 1800–1900* (Toronto: Butterworths 1983), 99.
33 Clark, *The CMA*, 42.
34 Ibid., 79.
35 Bliss, *Living Profit*, 93.
36 Ibid., and Paul Craven, *'Impartial Umpire': Industrial Relations and the Canadian State 1900–1911* (Toronto: University of Toronto Press 1980).
37 The more ubiquitous BC organization representing smaller operations and prospectors, the B.C. and Yukon Chamber of Mines, was founded in 1912.
38 Earlier Albertan associations were the Central Alberta Oil and Gas Association (1925) and the Alberta Petroleum Association (1938).
39 Gordon Laxer, "Class, Nationality and the Roots of the Branch Plant Economy," *Studies in Political Economy* No. 21 (1986): 29.
40 Bliss, *Living Profit*, chapter 6.
41 Forster, *Conjunction of Interests*, 203.
42 Robert D. Cuff and J.L. Granatstein, *Ties That Bind*, 2nd edition (Toronto: Samuel Stevens 1977), 8.
43 O. Mary Hill, *Canada's Salesman to the World: The Department of Trade and Commerce, 1892–1939* (Montreal: McGill-Queen's 1977), 172. Examples cited are the Knit Goods Manufacturers' Association, the Canadian Shirt Manufacturers' Association, and the Canadian Clothing Manufacturers' Association.
44 Clark, *The CMA*, 47.
45 C.A. Curtis, "The Canadian Banks and War Finance," in E.P. Neufeld, ed., *Money and Banking in Canada* (Toronto: McClelland and Stewart 1964), 207.
46 See the discussion in R. Bothwell and W. Kilbourn, *C.D. Howe: A Biography* (Toronto: McClelland and Stewart 1979), chapter 11.
47 Henry Borden, "The Work of the Department of Munitions and Supply," in J.F. Parkinson, ed., *Canadian War Economics* (Toronto: University of Toronto Press 1941), 20.
48 J.F. McCracken, "The CLA Story, 1907–1977," typescript, 1977, 6–8 (manuscript provided to the author courtesy of the Canadian Lumbermen's Association).
49 R.W. James, *Wartime Economic Cooperation* (Toronto: Ryerson Press 1949), 299.
50 Ibid.
51 K.W. Taylor, "The War-Time Control of Prices," in Parkinson, ed., *Canadian War Economics*, 54.
52 C.R. Waddell, "The Wartime Prices and Trade Board: Price Control in Canada in World War II," PhD thesis, York University, 1981, 129.
53 Benjamin H. Higgins, *Canada's Financial System in War*, Occasional Paper 19, National Bureau of Economic Research (New York: NBER 1944), 15.

54 A.F.W. Plumptre, "Organizing the Canadian Economy for War," in Parkinson, ed., *Canadian War Economics*, 10.

55 Waddell, "Prices and Trade Board," 384.

56 See the discussion in Olga B. Bishop, *Publications of the Government of Ontario 1867–1900* (Toronto: Government of Ontario 1976), 124.

57 Government of Ontario, An Act for the Encouragement of Agriculture, Horticulture, Arts and Manufactures, 31 Vict. c. 29, s. 19.

58 H.A. Innis, ed., *The Dairy Industry in Canada* (Toronto: Ryerson 1937), 97.

59 See L.A. Wood, *A History of Farmers Movements in Canada* (Toronto: University of Toronto Press 1924), 202; and Gary Carlson, *Farm Voices* (Regina: Saskatchewan Federation of Labour 1981), 6.

60 Wood, *History*, 205ff.

61 This practice of combining association members with production co-operatives became a tradition with agricultural peak associations still follwed by the peak association in agriculture – the Canadian Federation of Agriculture – and most of its provincial federations.

62 Veronica McCormick, *A Hundred Years in the Dairy Industry* (Ottawa: Dairy Farmers of Canada 1968).

63 Carlson, *Farm Voices*, 59.

64 Finkel, *Business and Social Reform*, 57.

65 Philippe Schmitter and Wolfgang Streeck, "The Organization of Business Interests," Discussion Paper IIM/LMP 81–13 (Berlin: Wissenschaftszentrum Berlin 1981). Wyn Grant and I have shown how these properties may be used in the empirical analysis of business associations. See "Business Associations and Public Policy: A Comparison of Organisational Development in Britain and Canada," *Journal of Public Policy* 4, No. 3 (1984): 209–35.

66 The parameters of these two roles – advocacy and participation – are discussed at length in chapter 3.

67 For my definition of national relevance, see chapter 1.

68 By domain, I refer to the socioeconomic space from which the association draws its members as defined in its constitution. There are a number of dimensions to this space: branch of economic activity, territorial range, the membership unit (individual, firm, or association), the class status of the members, and the functional role assumed by the group.

69 These, it will be remembered, are associations based in a province or group of provinces with domains representing 35 per cent of the production in a given economic area or are French-Canadian associations paralleling an English-Canadian one.

70 These objectives were normally taken from the constitution or by-laws of the association. Failing this source, they were taken from brochures stating why the association existed.

71 Standards work was not mentioned so often by agricultural associations.

298 Notes to pages 35–43

A similar task in a functional sense was the maintenance and improvement of various animal breeds. Over half, 52.4 per cent, of agricultural associations mentioned this objective.

72 See D. Truman, *The Governmental Process* (New York: Knopf 1951), 112.

73 This scheme is a simplified version of the one devised by Wyn Grant and me in "Regional Differentiation of Business Interest Associations: A Comparison of Canada and the United Kingdom," *Canadian Journal of Political Science* 18, No. 1 (1985): 6–7.

74 Sometimes it was difficult to distinguish a confederal group from a federal one. In a confederal group, regional member associations usually ante-date the national organization. In addition, the names of the regional groups and the national body are not uniform. For example, in the Canadian Federation of Agriculture, a confederation, Alberta's group is named Unifarm, (former) Manitoba's, the Manitoba Farm Bureau, Quebec's, the Union des producteurs agricoles, and so on.

75 "Federalism and Interest Group Organization" in H. Bakvis and W. Chandler, eds., *Federalism and the Role of the State* (Toronto: University of Toronto Press 1987) 171–87.

76 For example, in 1982, the Canadian Chamber of Commerce and the Canadian Textiles Institute moved their operations from Montreal to Ottawa after a long history in the former centre.

77 I.A. Litvak, " 'The Ottawa Syndrome': Improving Business/Government Relations," *Business Quarterly* 44, No. 2 (1979): 22–9.

78 This skewness is indicated clearly by the standard deviations listed in Table 6. The spread in expenditures is particularly pronounced for the business associations.

79 The other mean expenditures are manufacturing ($210,000), construction ($273,000), trade ($228,000), transport ($360,000), and other services ($495,000).

80 Two larger manufacturing associations "service" associations on a contractual basis: the CMA and the Grocery Products Manufacturers of Canada. The CMA has used this as a means to support new associations in their early years.

81 Members who have completed the program may attach the letters CAE (certified association executive) to their name. The IAE is much less prominent in the agricultural sectors, where only 7.7 per cent of the associations reported IAE membership and no one reported having qualified as a CAE.

82 These coding decisions were eased by the useful classification practice in Brian Land's *Directory of Associations in Canada*. Land asks the associations whether they have an official name in both English and French and which of these is the primary one. While both names are given in

the directory, information on the association is listed under the primary name.

CHAPTER THREE

1 See in particular Grant McConnell, *Private Power and American Democracy* (New York: Knopf 1966), and Theodore Lowi, *The End of Liberalism*, 2nd edition (New York: Norton 1979).
2 S. Rokkan, "Norway: Numerical Democracy and Corporate Pluralism," in R.A. Dahl, ed., *Political Oppositions in Western Democracies* (New Haven: Yale University Press 1966), 70–115.
3 Keith Middlemas, *Politics in Industrial Society* (London: Andre Deutsch 1979).
4 For a relatively recent bibliography on the corporatism literature, see G. Lehmbruch and P. Schmitter, eds., *Patterns of Corporatist Policy-Making* (Beverly Hills: Sage 1982), 281–90.
5 For discussions of sectoral corporatism, see A.P. Wassenberg, "Neo-Corporatism and the Quest for Control: The Cuckoo Game," ibid., 83–108; A. Cawson, *Corporatism and Welfare* (London: Heinemann 1982); and A. Cawson, ed., *Organized Interests and the State: Studies in Meso Corporatism* (London: Sage 1985).
6 For an example, see M.M. Atkinson and W. Coleman, "Corporatism and Industrial Policy," in Cawson, ed., *Organized Interests*, 22–44.
7 R.H. Salisbury, "Interest Representation: The Dominance of Institutions," *American Political Science Review* 78, No. 1 (1984): 64–76.
8 See A.P. Pross, "Canadian Pressure Groups in the 1970s: Their Role and Their Relations with the Public Service," *Canadian Public Administration* 18, No. 2 (1975): 121–35; and A.J. McKichan, "Comments," in W.T. Stanbury, ed., *The Legislative Process in Canada* (Montreal: IRPP 1978), 219–24.
9 The development of central agencies has made this task even more difficult. See Pross, "Canadian Pressure Groups," passim.
10 The importance of timing here is noted by W.T. Stanbury, "Lobbying and Interest Group Representation in the Legislative Process," in Stanbury, ed., *The Legislative Process*, 167–207, and in Stanbury, *Business-Government Relations in Canada* (Toronto: Methuen 1986), chapter 7.
11 See Stanbury, *Business-Government Relations*, chapters 8 and 9, and Fred Thompson and W.T. Stanbury, *The Political Economy of Interest Groups in the Legislative Process in Canada* (Montreal: IRPP 1979).
12 See M.M. Atkinson and W. Coleman, "Bureaucrats and Politicians in Canada: An Examination of the Political Administration Model," *Comparative Political Studies* 18, No. 1 (1985): 58–80, and Colin Campbell, *Governments under Stress* (Toronto: University of Toronto Press 1983).

13 For the increasing importance of this activity, see Kay L. Schlozman and J.T. Tierney, "More of the Same: Washington Pressure Group Activity in a Decade of Change," *Journal of Politics* 45, No. 2 (1983): 357.

14 Mildred Schwartz, "The Group Basis of Politics," in J.H. Redekop, ed., *Approaches to Canadian Politics* (Scarborough: Prentice-Hall 1978), 326.

15 David B. Truman, *The Governmental Process* (New York: Knopf 1951), 112ff.

16 R.A. Bauer, I. de Sola Pool, and L.A. Dexter, *American Business and Public Policy: The Politics of Foreign Trade* (Chicago: Aldine-Atherton 1963), 331.

17 See James Q. Wilson, *Political Organizations* (New York: Basic 1973), chapter 3, and Terry Moe, *The Organization of Interests* (Chicago: University of Chicago Press 1980).

18 This point is emphasized strongly by McConnell. However, he uses the concept of autonomy to make this argument – a different usage than the one I have presented in this chapter. See McConnell, *Private Power*, particularly chapter 8.

19 In Canada, associations will sometimes have their chief lobbyist as the permanent president, supported by a corporate secretary, who runs the organization. An example is the Grocery Products Manufacturers of Canada. See W. Coleman, "The Political Organization of Business Interests in the Canadian Food Processing Industry," Discussion Paper IIM/LMP 84–6 (Berlin: Wissenschaftszentrum Berlin 1984).

20 This breakdown of tasks is borrowed from Frans van Waarden, "Bureaucracy around the State: Varieties of Collective Self-Regulation in the Dutch Dairy Industry," in W. Streeck and P. Schmitter, eds., *Private Interest Government* (London: Sage 1985).

21 This discussion of associational properties owes much to P. Schmitter and W. Streeck, "The Organization of Business Interests," Discussion Paper IIM/LMP 81–13 (Berlin: Wissenschaftszentrum Berlin 1981).

22 As Gerhard Lehmbruch has written: "This implies internal checks on the articulation of immediate, short range, and narrowly sectional intersts"; "Interest Intermediation in Capitalist and Socialist Systems: Some Structural and Functional Perspectives in Comparative Research," *International Political Science Review* 4, No. 2 (1983): 161.

23 W. Streeck and P. Schmitter, "Community, Market, State and Associations? The Prospective Contribution of Interest Governance to Social Order," in Streeck and Schmitter, eds., *Private Interest Government*, 1–29.

24 Ibid., 12.

25 Normally, if the association is for employers, the domain will contain some reference to the trade union(s) that constitute the domain of bargaining activity.

26 In using the term "system" here, I do not presuppose anything about the degree of integration of that system. This will be, in fact, one of our key variables, as will be shown shortly.

27 These properties are based on Schmitter and Streeck, "Business Interests," and Bernd Marin, "Organizing Interests by Interest Organizations: Associational Prerequisites of Corporatism in Austria," *International Political Science Review* 4, No. 2 (1983): 197–216.

28 The alternative possibility is that one association exists for each division and includes branches for each major sector, sector, and sub-sector.

29 Schmitter and Streeck, "Business Interests," 202ff.

30 The dimension of institutionalization is emphasized by A.P. Pross in "Pressure Groups: Adaptive Instruments of Political Communication," in Pross, ed., *Pressure Group Behaviour in Canadian Politics* (Toronto: McGraw Hill 1975), 1–22.

31 Schmitter and Streeck, "Business Interests," 49ff.

32 This dimension is also emphasized by Mancur Olson, *The Logic of Collective Action* (New York: Schocken Books 1968).

33 The role of such committees is discussed in more detail in W. Coleman and H. Jacek, "The Roles and Activities of Business Interest Associations in Canada," *Canadian Journal of Political Science* 16, No. 2 (1983): 257–80.

34 P.R. Lawrence and D. Dyer, *Renewing American Industry* (New York: Free Press 1983), especially chapter 1.

35 Ibid., 5–8.

36 Examples are the Business Council on National Issues, the Canadian Chamber of Commerce, the Canadian Federation of Independent Business, and the CMA.

37 On this point, see Bernd Marin, "Associationalism: Bureaucracies beyond Bureaucracy," paper presented to the Sixth Colloquium of the European Group for Organizational Studies, Florence, 1983.

38 See note 5, above.

39 This phenomenon is noted by Pross, "Adaptive Instruments," and is discussed at some length in I.A. Litvak, "Lobbying Strategies and Business Interest Groups," *Business Quarterly* 48, No. 2 (1983): 130–8.

40 These different roles are analysed further in chapter 7 and in W. Coleman, "The Political Organization of Business Interests in the Canadian Construction Industry," Discussion Paper IIM/LMP 84–11 (Berlin: Wissenschaftszentrum Berlin 1984).

CHAPTER FOUR

1 A good recent example in the Canadian context is A. Paul Pross, "Parliamentary Influence and the Diffusion of Power," *Canadian Journal of Political Science* 18, No. 2 (1985): 235–66.

2 For elaboration on this point, see Alfred Diamant, "Bureaucracy and Public Policy in Neocorporatist Settings," *Comparative Politics* 14, No. 1 (1981): 101–24.

3 On this transformation, see the introductory chapter by Alan Cawson in Cawson, ed., *Organized Interests and the State: Studies in Meso-corporatism* (London: Sage 1985), 1–21.

4 Theodore Lowi, "American Business, Public Policy, Case Studies and Political Theory," *World Politics* 16, No. 4 (1964): 688.

5 Peter Katzenstein, "Conclusion," in Katzenstein, ed., *Between Power and Plenty* (Madison: University of Wisconsin Press 1977).

6 These factors are defined based on the discussion in ibid.

7 Philippe Schmitter, " 'Neo Corporatism,' 'Consensus,' 'Governability,' and 'Democracy' in the Management of Crisis in Contemporary Advanced Industrial/Capitalist Societies," paper presented to the OECD Expert Group on Collective Bargaining and Economic Policies: Dialogue and Consensus Paris, July 1983, 13.

8 On the importance of this point, see Colin Crouch, "Pluralism and the New Corporatism: A Rejoinder," *Political Studies* 31, No. 3 (1983): 452–60.

9 Pross, "Diffusion of Power," passim.

10 This point is illustrated in R. Bauer, I. de Sola Pool, and L.A. Dexter, *American Business and Public Policy: The Politics of Foreign Trade* (Chicago: Aldine-Atherton 1963), 331.

11 The following discussion owes a great deal to John Chubb, *Interest Groups and the Bureaucracy* (Stanford: Stanford University Press 1983), part I.

12 For elaboration on this point, see W.D. Coleman, "The Capitalist Class and the State: Changing Roles of Business Interest Associations," *Studies in Political Economy* No. 20 (summer 1986): 135–60.

13 T. Lowi, *The End of Liberalism*, 2nd edition (New York: Norton 1979), especially part I; G. McConnell, *Private Power and American Democracy* (New York: Knopf 1966); A.P. Pross, "Pressure Groups: Adaptive Instruments of Political Communication," in Pross, ed., *Pressure Group Behaviour in Canadian Politics* (Toronto: McGraw Hill 1975) 1–15; Stein Rokkan, "Norway: Numerical Democracy and Corporate Puralism," in R. Dahl, ed., *Political Oppositions in Western Democracies* (New Haven: Yale University Press 1966), 70–115; and M.O. Heisler, "Corporate Pluralism Revisited: Where Is the Theory?," *Scandinavian Political Studies* 2, No. 3 (1979): 277–97.

14 McConnell, *Private Power*, 162.

15 Pross, "Adaptive Instruments."

16 Heisler, "Corporate Pluralism Revisted."

17 Ibid., 282.

18 Chubb, *Interest Groups*, 22–3.

19 Ibid., 22.

20 See Beat Hotz, *Politik zwischen Staat und Wirtschaft* (Zurich: Verlag Rüegger 1979), 370ff.; Lowi, *The End*, 6off.; and Pross, "Diffusion of Power."

21 For arguments developed along these lines, see McConnell, *Private Power*, and M. Olson, *The Rise and Decline of Nations* (New Haven: Yale University Press 1982).

22 Hotz, *Politik*, 38off.

23 Ibid., 375–8; W.T. Stanbury, "Lobbying and Interest Group Representation in the Legislative Process," in W. Neilson, ed., *The Legislative Process in Canada: The Need for Reform* (Montreal: IRPP 1978), 167–207.

24 See, in particular, W. Streeck, "Interessenverbände als Hindernisse und Vollzugsträger öffentlicher Politik," in M. Brockmann and F.W. Scharpf, eds., *Institutionelle Bedingungen der Arbeitsmarkt- und Beschäftigungs-Politik* (Frankfurt: Campus 1983) 179–98.

25 Lehmbruch presented the concept in "Consociational Democracy, Class Conflict and the New Corporatism," Schmitter in "Still the Century of Corporatism?," both reprinted in Schmitter and Lehmbruch, eds., *Trends toward Corporatist Intermediation* (Beverly Hills: Sage 1979), 53–62 and 7–52, respectively. Ray Pahl and Jack Winkler spoke of "The Coming Corporatism" in *New Society* 10 (October 1974).

26 K. von Beyme, "Neo Corporatism, A New Nut in an Old Shell," *International Political Science Review* 4, No. 2 (1983): 187. Cf. Panitch's definition: "a political structure within advanced capitalism which integrates organized socio-economic producer groups through a system of representation"; "The Development of Corporatism in Liberal Democracies," in Schmitter and Lehmbruch, eds., *Trends*, 123.

27 Philippe Schmitter, "Neo Corporatism and the State," European University Institute Working Paper No. 106 (Florence: European University Institute 1984), 7.

28 See M. Atkinson and W. Coleman, "Corporatism and Industrial Policy," in A. Cawson, ed., *Organized Interests and the State: Studies in Meso-corporatism* (London: Sage 1985) 22–44.

CHAPTER FIVE

1 I borrow the idea of these three poles of interest from Walter Simon, *Macht und Herrschaft der Unternehmerverbände: BDI, BDA und DIHT im ökonomischen und politischen System der BRD* (Cologne: Pahl Rugenstein Verlag 1976), 56, who makes a related point.

2 G. Lehmbruch, "Concertation and the Structure of Corporatist Networks," in J.H. Goldthorpe, ed., *Order and Conflict in Contemporary Capitalism* (Oxford: Clarendon 1984), 63–4.

3 Ibid., 64.

4 A. Rotstein, *Rebuilding from Within: Remedies for Canada's Ailing Economy* (Toronto: Lorimer 1984), 31.

5 This argument is made by Robert Reford in "The Business Council on

National Issues: Senior Voice of Business in Canada," *Canadian Business Management Developments* 2, No. 40 (1983): 373–7.

6 David Langille, "The Business Council on National Issues and the Canadian State," paper presented to the Annual Meeting of the Canadian Political Science Association, June 1985, 13–14.

7 Ibid., 15.

8 BCNI, *By-Laws Nos. 1 and 2* (Toronto: BCNI n.d.) 9–10.

9 Letter to the author, 18 October 1983.

10 This list is devised by comparing the membership roster of the BCNI to the 100 leading "industry" corporations in *The Financial Post 500* (Toronto: The Financial Post 1985).

11 Here I counted the first 100 companies in ibid., exclusive of public corporations.

12 The CSL group is represented indirectly again through Power Corporation.

13 Langille, "The Business Council," 11–15.

14 The Canadian Chamber of Commerce, the Canadian Manufacturers' Association, and the Conseil du Patronat du Québec are "associate members" of the council, and their chairmen serve ex officio on the Policy Committee. These associations are entitled to one vote, the same as a firm member. In the typical European case, associations are usually the only voting members of the peak association.

15 It is possible that Agropur and the Coopérative Fédérée are not eligible for membership because they are co-operatives. It depends on what the by-laws mean by "private business enterprises." None of the members of the BCNI in 1983 was a co-operative.

16 Task forces in 1986 included: National Finance, International Economy and Trade, Competition Policy, Social Policy and Retirement Income, Government Organization, Foreign Policy and Defence, and Taxation.

17 Letter to the author, 18 October 1983.

18 Quoted from a pamphlet printed by the council describing its operations.

19 Langille, "The Business Council," 39–41.

20 Quoted in a National Film Board production on the CFIB, "The Politics of Persuasion."

21 CFIB, *A Decade of Action for Independent Business* (Toronto: CFIB 1982), 17.

22 Letter to the author from the vice-president and director of communications, CFIB, 30 December 1985.

23 Taken from the association's financial statement for 1981, supplied to the author by the association.

24 Interview with Geoffrey Hale, policy director, COSB, 1982.

25 Ibid.

26 Marianne Tefft, "Small Business Helps Itself," *The Financial Post*, 10 April 1982.

27 The Board of Trade of Metropolitan Toronto, *By-Laws*, Revised July 1980, article II, section 1.

28 Letter to the author from the general manager of the board, 27 August 1980.
29 Roy Wilson, "Metro Board of Trade: A New Hand at the Throttle," *The Metropolitan Toronto Business Journal* 70, No. 7 (1980): 25–32.
30 Figures calculated based on a letter to the author from the manager, programming, Canadian Chamber of Commerce, 3 October 1983, and the Honourary Treasurer's Report to the Canadian Chamber of Commerce, 54th Annual Meeting, 1983, supplied to the author courtesy of the chamber.
31 La Chambre de Commerce de la Province de Québec, *Assemblée générale et Rapport annuel 1982* (Montreal: CCPQ 1982), 57.
32 Letter from the manager, programming, 3 October 1983.
33 This program was brought to my attention by Phil Nance, president of the Canadian Institute of Plumbing and Heating, who also supplied me with supporting documentation.
34 This process is illustrated well by A. Paul Pross in "Mobilizing Regional Concern: An Historical Review of the Maritime Freight Rates Issue," paper prepared for the Conference on the Regional Organization of Business Interests and Public Policy, McMaster University, 22–24 May 1985.
35 CPQ, *Répertoire des associations patronales québécoises, 1982* (Montreal: CPQ 1982), 5 (author's translation).
36 Ibid. (author's translation).
37 Quoted from a letter to the author from the vice-president, public affairs, Employers' Council of British Columbia, 28 October 1983.
38 The treatment of publicly owned corporations is a sensitive issue for Canadian business associations. As we have seen, the BCNI excludes them altogether. Most sector-specific trade associations accept them as members. The BCBC allows "government affiliate" members to participate in all activities of the council directed by the "industrial relations" division, including serving on committees; Employers' Council of British Columbia, *Constitution and By-Laws* (Vancouver: ECBC n.d.), 3.
39 In 1984–5, the board of governors of the council included the CEOs of Kelly Douglas and Co., Westcoast Transmission, Belkin Packaging, Placer Development, Weldwood of Canada, McGavin Foods, Johnston Terminals, Western Canada Steel, British Columbia Telephone, Chevron Canada, British Columbia Packers, Scott Paper, MacMillan Bloedel, Finning Tractor and Equipment, and Woodward Stores and vice-presidents of the Bank of Nova Scotia and CP Rail.
40 ECBC, *Standing Committees*, 28 October 1982; document supplied to the author courtesy of the council.
41 This definition of the Canadian party system and much of the paragraph below describing it are based on H. Clarke, J. Jenson, L. Leduc, and J. Pammett, *Absent Mandate* (Toronto: Gage 1984), 10ff.

CHAPTER SIX

1 Philippe Schmitter, "Reflections on Where the Theory of Neo-Corporatism Has Gone and Where the Praxis of Neo-Corporatism May Be Going," in G. Lehmbruch and P. Schmitter, eds., *Patterns of Corporatist Policy-Making* (London: Sage 1982), 259–79.

2 All the statistics on industry structure in the section, unless noted otherwise, are adapted from Statistics Canada, 1981 Census of Canada, *Agriculture*, Catalogue 96–901 (Ottawa 1983).

3 Agriculture Canada, *Orientation of Canadian Agriculture: A Task Force Report*, Volume I, Part A (Ottawa: Agriculture Canada 1977), 75–6.

4 Ibid., 209.

5 J.D. Forbes, *Institutions and Influence Groups in Canadian Farm and Food Policy* (Toronto: Institute of Public Administration of Canada 1985), 26.

6 Ibid., 60. See also Grace D. Skogstad, "Farmers' Political Belief Systems," PhD thesis, University of British Columbia, 1976.

7 For a history of the council, see L.R. Stephens, *The Canadian Horticultural Council: Fifty Years of Integrity, Leadership and Liaison* (Ottawa: CHC 1972).

8 The Coopérative fédérée is similar in this respect to the prairie wheat pools. It doubles as a firm and as an association representing farmers' producers' co-operatives in the province.

9 Western Agricultural Conference, *Constitution* (Regina: WAC 1974), 1.

10 A case in point is the Union des producteurs agricoles in Quebec, which groups commodities from each of the three major sectors. See J-P Kesteman with Guy Boisclair and J-M. Kerouac, *Histoire du syndicalisme agricole du Québec: UCC–UPA 1924–1984* (Montreal: Boréal 1984), Tableau 16, 276.

11 Grace Skogstad, "Interest Groups, Representation and Conflict Management in the Standing Committees of the House of Commons," *Canadian Journal of Political Science* 18, No. 4 (1985): 748.

12 J.D. Forbes, R.D. Hughes, and T.K. Warley, *Economic Intervention and Regulation in Canadian Agriculture* (Ottawa: Economic Council of Canada 1982), 74.

13 Grace Skogstad, *The Politics of Agricultural Policy-Making in Canada* (Toronto: University of Toronto Press 1987), 130.

14 Ibid., 131.

15 Ibid.

16 Interview with David Kirk, executive secretary of the CFA, 27 March 1985.

17 United Grain Growers, *Facts ... You Should Know about the United Grain Growers* (Winnipeg: UGG 1981), 1.

18 UGG, *77th Annual Report, 1983* (Winnipeg: UGG 1983), 3.

19 Quoted from the Annual Report of the Alberta Wheat Pool, 1980, 36.
20 Interested readers are referred to Skogstad, *Agricultural Policy-Making*, and to M.J. Laslovich, "Changing the Crow Rate: State-Societal Interaction," paper presented to the Annual General Meeting of the Canadian Political Science Association, Montreal 1985.
21 Skogstad, "Interest Groups," 766ff.
22 See CFA, *Report of the CFA Task Force* (Ottawa: CFA 1984). The task force was set up in 1984 to investigate the internal organizational problems of the federation.
23 Forbes et al, *Economic Intervention*, 86.
24 Ibid., 87.
25 Ibid., 133.
26 For this point, see Colin Crouch, "Pluralism and the New Corporatism: A Rejoinder," *Political Studies* 31, No. 3 (1983): 452–60.
27 Figures calculated on the basis of data supplied to the author by Statistics Canada.
28 For a history of the Canadian dairy industry, see Veronica McCormick, *A Hundred Years in the Dairy Industry* (Ottawa: Dairy Farmers of Canada 1968). A shorter yet useful summary may also be found in G.A. Hiscocks, "Review of the Canadian Dairy Commission: Background, Creation, Policy and Operations," Appendix 15, Commission of Inquiry into Certain Allegations Concerning Commercial Practices of the Canadian Dairy Commission, *Report* (Ottawa: Supply and Services Canada 1981).
29 Discussed in Hiscocks, "Review," 3.
30 See D. Peter Stonehouse, "Government Policies for the Canadian Dairy Industry," *Canadian Farm Economics* 14, Nos. 1–2 (1979): 1–11.
31 For information on the success of this aspect of the policy, see Richard Barichello, *The Economics of Canadian Dairy Industry Regulation* (Ottawa: Economic Council of Canada 1981).
32 Robert D. Anderson, "Government Regulation of the Canadian Dairy Processing, Distributing and Retailing Sector," Economic Council of Canada, Regulation Reference Working Paper No. 25 (Ottawa: ECC 1981) 28–9.
33 Stonehouse, "Government Policies," passim.
34 For a discussion of this constitutional arrangement, see Peter Hogg, *Constitutional Law of Canada*, 2nd edition (Toronto: Carswell 1985), 467–73.
35 Peter L. Arcus, *Broilers and Eggs* (Ottawa: Economic Council of Canada 1981), 37.
36 Interview, CPEPC, 15 January 1982.
37 For further discussion, see Skogstad, "Interest Groups," 759–64.
38 Kesteman, *Histoire*, 271–3.

39 CFA, *Report*, 7–8.

CHAPTER SEVEN

1 Joseph B. Rose, *Public Policy, Bargaining Structure and the Construction Industry* (Toronto: Butterworths 1980), 17.
2 P.R. Lawrence and D. Dyer, *Restructuring American Industry* (New York: Free Press 1982), chapter 6.
3 Canada, Royal Commission on Corporate Concentration, *Concentration Levels and Trends in the Canadian Economy, 1956–1973: A Technical Report* (Ottawa: Supply and Services Canada 1977), 56.
4 B.A. Keys and D.M. Caskie, *The Structure and Operation of the Construction Industry in Canada* (Ottawa: Economic Council of Canada 1975).
5 See Roger Miller, "Les formes d'organisation dans l'industrie de la construction," *Relations industrielles* 37, No. 2 (1982): 164–76.
6 Lawrence and Dyer, *Restructuring*, 9.
7 Why this should be the case is developed in W. Streeck, "Die Reform der beruflichen Bildung in der westdeutschen Bauwirtschaft 1969–1982," Discussion Paper IIM/LMP 83–23 (Berlin: Wissenschaftszentrum Berlin 1983).
8 See Lawrence and Dyer, *Restructuring*, chapter 1.
9 These sectors are defined based on the perception of the industry gained from interviews with associations. The sector defintions also correspond loosely to the classification of the industry developed by the Canadian government and the European Community.
10 An exception would be an industry like the pipeline contracting sector. The Pipeline Contractors Association of Canada is one of the few national-level, non-regionally differentiated associations in the industry. For a discussion, see W. Coleman and W. Grant, "Regional Differentiation of Business Interest Associations: A Comparison of Canada and the United Kingdom," *Canadian Journal of Political Science* 18, No. 1 (1985): 1–29.
11 Neil J. Lawrie, "The Canadian Construction Association: An Interest Group Organization and Its Environment," PhD thesis, University of Toronto, 1975, 60–5.
12 See Wyn Grant, "The Organization of Business Interests in the U.K. Construction Industry," Discussion Paper IIM/LMP 83–25 (Berlin: Wissenschaftszentrum Berlin 1983).
13 CCA, *Constitution and By-Laws* (Ottawa: CCA 1981), 2.
14 Lawrie, "The Canadian Construction Association," 93.
15 As we shall see below, the CCA has continued to be an important force in labour relations policy, although such policy is generally a provincial concern.

16 The Group of Eight is a loose coalition of leading associations in the British construction industry that has been chosen for longer-term policy discussions by the British government. Like the COCA, it has no constitution, no formal organization, and no staff. See Grant, "U.K. Construction Industry."

17 These figures are my own estimates based on analysis drawn from three Statistics Canada publications: *The Highway, Road, Street and Bridge Contracting Industry* (Cat. 64–206); *The Non-Residential General Building Industry* (Cat. 64–207); and *The Heavy Engineering Industry* (Cat. 64–209).

18 Paul Malles, *Employment Insecurity and Industrial Relations in the Canadian Construction Industry* (Ottawa: Economic Council of Canada 1975), 16.

19 C.H. Goldenberg and J. Crispo, *Construction Labour Relations* (Ottawa: CCA 1968).

20 Joseph B. Rose, "Employer Accreditation: A Retrospective," paper presented to the 1983 meetings of the Canadian Industrial Relations Association, 1.

21 Ibid., 2–3.

22 This case will be discussed below in more detail.

23 For a discussion, see Rose, *Public Policy*, 40–1.

24 Lawrie, "The Canadian Construction Association," 56.

25 Figures are drawn from Statistics Canada, *The Residential General Building Industry* (Cat. 64–208), and the catalogues noted above in note 17.

26 Figures calculated from the 1982 editions of the catalogues noted in notes 17 and 25.

27 Malles, *Employment Insecurity*, 16.

28 See W. Streeck, "Interessenverbände als Hindernisse und Vollzugsträger öffentlicher Politik," in F.W. Scharpf and M. Brockmann eds., *Institutionelle Bedingungen der Arbeitsmarkt- und Beschäftigungspolitik* (Frankfurt: Campus 1983) 179–99.

29 Robert F. Leggett, *Standards in Canada* (Ottawa: Economic Council of Canada 1971), 81.

30 These include: Use and Occupancy, Structural Design, Plumbing Services, Heating and Other Services, Construction Safety, Residential Design, Farm Buildings, and Standards for Handicapped Citizens; ibid.

31 Rose, *Public Policy*, 4.

32 Ibid., 5.

33 Based upon an estimate drawn from Construction Industry Development Council, *Report and Recommendations of the Task Force on Contracting Out* (Ottawa: CIDC 1980), 17.

34 An excellent discussion is available in Gérald Hébert, *Labour Relations in the Quebec Construction Industry. Part I: The System of Labour Relations* (Ottawa: Economic Council of Canada 1977).

35 Ibid., 5–8.

36 For the distinction between liberal (societal) and state corporatism, see P.C. Schmitter, "Still the Century of Corporatism?," in P.C. Schmitter and G. Lehmbruch, eds., *Trends toward Corporatist Intermediation* (Beverly Hills: Sage 1979): 7–52.

37 See Réal Mireault, "Les nouveaux défis de l'Office de la construction du Québec," *Relations industrielles* 31, No. 4 (1974): 553–65.

38 Quebec, Commission de l'enquête sur l'exercice de la liberté syndicale dans l'industrie de la construction, *Rapport* (Quebec: Editeur officiel du Québec 1974), 37 (author's translation).

39 Hébert, *Labour Relations*, 51.

40 Mancur Olson, *The Logic of Collective Action* (Cambridge, Mass.: Harvard University Press 1965).

41 Associational involvement in vocational training is not discussed extensively here. See the examination of the Pipeline Contractors Association of Canada and the Canadian Association of Oil Well Drilling Contractors in W. Coleman, "The Political Organization of Business Interests in the Canadian Construction Industry," Discussion Paper IIM/LMP 84–11 (Berlin: Wissenschaftszentrum Berlin 1984).

CHAPTER EIGHT

1 Jamie Swift, *Cut and Run: The Assault on Canada's Forests* (Toronto: Between the Lines 1983), 24.

2 Mining Association of Canada, *Mining in Canada: Facts and Figures* (Ottawa: MAC 1983), 33.

3 Ownership of a resource gives a province considerable power. Provincial governments can control exploitation, rate of production, degree of processing in the province, and, subject to market conditions, the price at which it is sold. See Peter Hogg, *Constitutional Law of Canada* (Toronto: Carswell 1985), chapter 25.

4 The primary sectors of fishing and hunting/trapping will not be studied intensively here. Given limitations on resources, I decided to concentrate on the forest and minerals sectors.

5 A possible alternative subject for study is the petroleum/natural gas sector. It also has an extensive regulatory apparatus. However, I decided to do the forests and metallic minerals in order to contrast a renewable and a non-renewable resource.

6 Ontario, Quebec, and the Maritimes have associations representing lumber manufacturers only: the Ontario Lumber Manufacturers Association, the Association des manufacturiers de bois de sciage du Québec, and the Maritime Lumber Bureau. The corresponding national association is the Canadian Lumbermen's Association. All four are members of the Canadian Wood Council.

7 However, the Log Operations Group, a sub-section of the Woodlands Section, has branches in the Maritimes, Quebec, Ontario, and the west.

8 Differentiation in British Columbia occurs within the Mining Association of B.C., which has a distinct Coal Mines Committee.

9 Quoted from a letter to the author from the MAC, 11 January 1984.

10 Economic Council of Canada, *Western Transition* (Ottawa: ECC 1984), 41.

11 COFI, "British Columbia Forest Industry Statistical Tables," typescript, Vancouver, COFI 1985.

12 Ibid.

13 ECC, *Western Transition*, 43.

14 Environment Canada, *A Forest Sector Strategy for Canada*, Discussion Paper (Ottawa: Supply and Services Canada 1981), 8.

15 COFI, "Tables."

16 Patricia Marchak, *Green Gold* (Vancouver: University of British Columbia Press 1983), 29.

17 Ibid.

18 See Table 4-1 in ibid., 84. Since Marchak wrote her book, B.C. Forest Products, which she listed as Canadian, has shifted to American control (Mead Corporation).

19 This problem is noted in Science Council of Canada, *Canada's Threatened Forests* (Ottawa: Science Council 1983), 6, as well as in EC, *Sector Strategy*, 3, and ECC, *Western Transition*.

20 See Marchak's discussion of the difference between allowable and actual cut; *Green Gold*, 77.

21 Information supplied to the author by COFI.

22 SCC, *Threatened Forests*, 14.

23 Ibid. Some would argue that these countries have logged their lands more than once while Canada has not and thus that this ratio will change when Canada reaches a similar position.

24 ECC, *Western Transition*, 40.

25 EC, *Sector Strategy*, 17.

26 For a breakdown of R&D expenditures, see EC, *Sector Strategy*, 18. The facilities of the CFS outside Ottawa are as follows: Maritimes Forest Research Centre (Fredericton), Laurentian Forest Research Centre (Quebec), Great Lakes Forest Research Centre (Sault Ste Marie), Northern Forest Research Centre (Edmonton), Pacific Forest Research Centre (Victoria), Forest Pest Management Institute (Sault Ste Marie), and Petawawa National Forestry Institute.

27 Ibid., 17.

28 Marchak, *Green Gold*, 29ff.

29 Ibid., 75.

30 SCC, *Threatened Forests*, 14–15.

31 ECC, *Western Transition*, 47.

32 Abridged from the ABCPF, *Constitution and By-Laws*, n.d.

33 Quoted from the President's Report to the 1979 Annual Meeting of the association and reprinted in ABCPF, *Annual Report 1979* (Vancouver: ABCPF 1979), 24.

34 Calculated based on materials supplied to the author by the association.

35 See Richard S. Lambert with Paul Pross, *Renewing Nature's Wealth: A Centennial History of the Public Management of Lands, Forests and Wildlife in Ontario, 1763–1967* (Toronto: Department of Lands and Forests 1967), chapter 10.

36 Information contained in materials sent to the author by the association.

37 Information drawn from the association's annual report for 1984 and from an associational brochure.

38 Support of the NFPA accounts for 32 per cent of the Wood Council's budget.

39 MAC, *Mining in Canada*, 6.

40 Ibid., 26.

41 Energy, Mines and Resources Canada, *Mineral Policy: A Discussion Paper* (Ottawa: EMR 1981), 12.

42 Ibid.

43 MAC, *Mining in Canada*, 24.

44 Elizabeth Urquhart, *The Canadian Nonferrous Metals Industry: An Industrial Organization Study*, Centre for Resource Studies (Kingston: CRS 1978), 102.

45 Statistics Canada, *Industrial Organization and Concentration in the Manufacturing, Mining and Logging Establishments in Canada*, Catalogue 31–402 (Ottawa: Statistics Canada 1979).

46 EMR, *Mineral Policy*, 69.

47 This analysis of the international market context is based on the discussion in EMR, *Canada's Non Ferrous Metals Industry: Nickel and Copper* (Ottawa: EMR 1984), chapter 1.

48 EMR, *Mineral Policy*, 69.

49 David Yudelman, *Canadian Mineral Policy Past and Present: The Ambiguous Legacy* (Kingston: CRS 1985).

50 Ibid., 127.

51 Ibid., 125. For a detailed history of CANMET, see A. Ignatieff, *A Canadian Research Heritage* (Ottawa 1981).

52 Yudelman, *Canadian Mineral Policy*, 126.

53 However, the Gold Institute and the Silver Institute, international associations listed in Table 15, promote their respective products. Their efforts appear to supplement those of the larger companies and, relative to those of COFI, are quite small.

54 See M. Bucovetsky, "The Mining Industry and the Great Tax Reform Debate," in A.P. Pross, ed., *Pressure Group Behaviour in Canadian Politics* (Toronto: McGraw-Hill 1975), 89–114.

55 W. Coleman and W. Grant, "Regional Differentiation of Business In-
terest Associations: A Comparison of Canada and the United Kingdom,"
Canadian Journal of Political Science 18, No. 1 (1985): 3–30. Also see
Schultz's description of this process as it affected the trucking industry
in R. Schultz, *Federalism, Bureaucracy and Public Policy: The Politics of
Highway Transport Regulation* (Montreal: McGill-Queen's 1980). Finally,
Glen Toner and G.B. Doern cover similar ground for the petroleum
industry in "The Two Energy Crises and Canadian Oil and Gas Interest
Groups: A Re-examination of Berry's Propositions," *Canadian Journal of
Political Science* 19, No. 3 (1986): 467–94.

56 David Yudelman, *Canadian Mineral Policy Formulation: A Case Study of the
Adversarial Process* (Kingston: CRS 1984), 63.

57 Yudelman, *Ambiguous Legacy*, 126–7.

58 Executive vice-president, Cominco; marketing manager, Esso Minerals;
assistant vice-president, marketing and sales, Falconbridge; manager
mineral economics and market research, Hudson Bay Mining and Smelting; senior vice-president, marketing, Inco; manager of marketing, Placer Development; senior vice-president, marketing, Kidd Creek Mines;
senior vice-president, copper division, Noranda; manager, metal marketing, Sherritt Gordon Mines; vice-president, marketing and sales, Teck
Corporation.

59 Other examples are the Federal Government/MAC Task Force on Mining,
which drew up detailed proposals concerning taxation; the MAC/De-
partment of Indian and Northern Affairs Consultative Committee for
the Joint Development of a Northern Mineral Strategy; and the MAC/
Environment Canada Work Group on Non Ferrous Smelters.

60 Response of the Forest Products Accident Prevention Association to a
discussion paper, "The Future of Accident Prevention Associations," by
the Advisory Council on Occupational Health and Safety; reprinted in
Second Annual Report of the Council, 1979–80 (Toronto: Government of
Ontario 1981), 322.

61 For this distinction, see David Easton, *A Systems Analysis of Political Life*
(New York: Wiley 1965).

62 Ronald Manzer, "Public Policy-Making as Practical Reasoning," *Canadian
Journal of Political Science* 17, No. 3 (1984): 577–96.

CHAPTER NINE

1 Ontario Task Force on Financial Institutions, *Final Report* (Toronto:
Government of Ontario 1985), 30.

2 Ibid.

3 Securities Industry Capital Markets Committee, "Submission to the
Standing Committee on Finance, Trade and Economic Affairs," 9 August
1985, 2–3.

4 Ibid., 3.

5 Canada, Department of Finance, *The Regulation of Canadian Financial Institutions: Proposals for Discussion* (Ottawa: Supply and Services Canada 1985), 51.

6 Ontario Task Force, *Final Report*, 30.

7 E.P. Neufeld, *The Financial System of Canada: Its Growth and Development* (New York: St. Martin's Press 1972), 51.

8 Department of Finance, *Regulation*, 8.

9 P. Nagy, *The International Business of Canadian Banks* (Montreal: Hec 1983), 159.

10 H.H. Binhammer, *Money, Banking and the Canadian Financial System*, 4th edition (Toronto: Methuen 1982), 102.

11 Department of Finance, *Regulation*, 65.

12 Nagy, *International Business*, 49.

13 Ibid., 38.

14 Ibid., 40.

15 Ibid.

16 Department of Finance, *Regulation*, 58.

17 The most spectacular recent controversy of this kind was the so-called Greymac Affair. Three trust companies, all closely held, bought 10,931 apartment and townhouse units in Toronto from Cadillac Fairview and then, through a series of resales, "flipped" those units to a series of numbered companies, virtually doubling their original purchase price. For a discussion, see T. Belford, *Trust: The Greymac Affair* (Toronto: 1983).

18 Department of Finance, *Regulation*, 67.

19 Neufeld, *Financial System*, 509–15.

20 See B. Critchley, "Underwriters under Pressure," *Financial Post*, 20 October 1984.

21 Ibid., 81.

22 Ibid., 98–9.

23 Ibid.

24 Ontario Task Force, *Final Report*, 32.

25 M. Moran, "Finance Capital and Pressure Group Politics in Britain," *British Journal of Political Science* 11, No. 4 (1981): 398.

26 A useful if somewhat polemicized description of the Bank's activities may be found in W. Stewart, *Towers of Gold, Feet of Clay* (Toronto: Totem Books 1983), chapter 10.

27 Binhammer, *Money*, 98.

28 The TCA has ten provincial sections but no regional offices. The IDAC has regional offices in Montreal, Vancouver, and Calgary, a head office in Toronto, and "District Councils" in each of the four western provinces, Ontario, Quebec, and the Atlantic region.

29 The reader will recall from chapter 2 the distinction between a federal and a confederal organization. In the former structure, members belong simultaneously to a provincial and a national organization. Both organizations have autonomy at their respective levels. In the latter case, members belong to a provincial association only and these associations are the "members" of a national umbrella group. The relationship between the Quebec association and the Life Underwriters Association is federal, whereas in the property-casualty field, the Canadian Federation of Insurance Agents and Brokers Associations is a confederation.

30 Letter to the author from the president of the IAO, 17 July 1980.

31 Hence the two branches of the organization, the Fire Underwriters' Investigation Bureau and the Canadian Automobile Theft Bureau.

32 For example, see the report on the FEIC's submission to the inquiry of the Ontario Securities Commission into the operation of the securities industry. The association argued that banks, trust companies, and insurers should be able to own up to 49 per cent of an investment dealer and to participate in the dealers' non-retail brokerage business. Barry Critchley, "More Key Issues under OSC Focus," *Financial Post*, 1 December 1984.

33 Ontario Task Force, *Final Report*, 37.

34 A general discussion of the inefficiency of the banks after 1910 may be found in Neufeld, *The Financial System*, 138ff. For a more recent analysis, see Jack M. Mintz, *The Measurement of Rates of Return in Canadian Banking* (Ottawa: Economic Council of Canada 1979).

35 Statement drawn from the announcement by the CBA of MacIntosh's appointment; *Canadian Banker* 87, No. 3 (1980): 13.

36 An Act to Incorporate the Canadian Bankers Association, Paragraph 8, as amended in 1980.

37 See R. McQueen, *The Moneyspinners* (Toronto: 1983), chapter 1.

38 Helen Sinclair, "Matters of Common Concern," *Canadian Banker* 89, No. 1 (1982): 19.

39 Letter to the author from the CBA, 15 November 1983.

40 The vice-president and chief economist of the Bank of Nova Scotia began serving a one-year appointment as adviser to Michael Wilson in November 1984. The former chief economist of the Toronto Dominion worked for Finance through the Executive Interchange Program. The former chief economist of the Bank of British Columbia began a term appointment with Finance in November 1984. "Bank Economists Making Moves," *Financial Post*, 3 November 1984.

41 From an interview with MacIntosh printed in the *Canadian Banker* 89, No. 5 (1982): 20–7.

42 "A Very Special Market," *Canadian Banker* 86, No. 5 (1979): 34–7.

43 A.B. Jamieson, *Chartered Banking in Canada* (Toronto: Ryerson 1953), 34.

44 See Gordon McCaffrey, "CPA could give banking rivals 'fair crack of the whip,' " *Globe and Mail*, 15 February 1982, 837.

45 For further discussion, see Binhammer, *Money*, 15.

46 Letter to the author from the CBA, 15 November 1983.

47 Neufeld, *Financial System*, 508–9.

48 For a detailed discussion of this history, see W. Coleman, "The Canadian Securities Industry: A Study in Self Regulation," paper presented to the European Consortium for Political Research, Amsterdam, 1987.

49 Ibid.

50 Securities Industry Capital Markets Committee, "Self Regulation in the Canadian Securities Industry," typescript, 2 October 1985.

51 The Securities Act, *Revised Statutes of Ontario, 1980*, s. 19.

52 IDAC, *Constitution*, By Law No. 19, 33–6.

53 Securities Industry Capital Markets Committee, "Self Regulation," 2.

54 A.G. Kniewasser, president of the IDAC, "Up against Queen's Park," address given at the University of Toronto, 26 March 1980, 4.

55 Quoted from a speech by the president of the IDAC to the Ontario Chamber of Commerce, 13 May 1980, reprinted in *IDA Report* (Spring 1980), 5–6.

CHAPTER TEN

1 William K. Carroll, *Corporate Power and Canadian Capitalism* (Vancouver: University of British Columbia Press 1986), 205.

2 Ibid., 204.

3 Roy A. Matthews with D.J. McCalla, *Structural Change and Industrial Policy: The Redeployment of Canadian Manufacturing, 1960–1980* (Ottawa: Economic Council of Canada 1985), 18.

4 Carroll, *Corporate Power*, 162.

5 The Canadian Manufacturers' Association, *Constitution and By-Law, 1981* (Toronto: CMA 1981) 5.

6 Information compiled by T.D. Thaler, "The Canadian Manufacturers' Association," honours essay, McMaster University, April 1980, 64.

7 Interview with Roy Philipps, former president of the CMA, April 1982.

8 See, for example, the document *A Future That Works*, published in September 1984.

9 For a discussion of the CBI, see chapter 11 below and W. Grant and D. Marsh, *The CBI* (London: Hodder and Stoughton 1977), and Keith Middlemas, *Politics in Industrial Society* (London: André Deutsch 1979).

10 See Wyn Grant, ed., *Business Interests, Organizational Development and Private Interest Government: A Study of the Food Processing Industry* (Berlin: de Gruyter 1987), especially chapters 1 and 2.

11 D.M. Prescott, *The Role of Marketing Boards in the Processed Tomato and Asparagus Industries* (Ottawa: Economic Council of Canada 1981), 11.

12 Marketing boards exist in several provinces for hogs. These boards do not have the power either to fix or negotiate prices or to manage supply. Rather, they operate as promotional bodies and as organizers for the sale of hogs. See J.C. Gilson, *Evolution of the Hog Marketing System in Canada* (Ottawa: Economic Council of Canada 1982).

13 Canada, Statistics Canada, *Domestic and Foreign Control of Manufacturing Establishments in Canada, 1976* (Ottawa: Supply and Services 1981), 13–15.

14 I refer here to the standard industrial classification system used by Statistics Canada and to a three-digit category.

15 Grocery Products Manufacturers of Canada, *By-Laws* (Toronto n.d.), 2.

16 By comparing the membership list of the GPMC to the list of the firms provided by Statistics Canada for a given industry, I estimate that, in 1981, the members of the GPMC represented 34 per cent of the employees in the red meat sub-sector, 23.4 per cent of the poultry sub-sector, 51.5 per cent of the fruit and vegetable sector, and only 8 per cent of the dairy sector.

17 For a more detailed description of these networks, see W.D. Coleman, "The Political Organization of Business Interests in the Canadian Food Processing Industry," Discussion Paper IIM/LMP 84–6 (Berlin: Wissenschaftszentrum Berlin 1984).

18 For further discussion of the industry, see T. Ilgen, "Better Living through Chemistry: The Chemical Industry in the World Economy," *Industrial Organization* 37, No. 4 (1983): 647–80.

19 Statistics Canada, *Foreign Control*, 35–7.

20 For greater detail, see W. Coleman, "The Political Organization of Business Interests in the Canadian Industrial Chemicals and Pharmaceuticals Industries," Discussion Paper IIM/LMP 84–9 (Berlin: Wissenschaftszentrum Berlin 1984), 29–33.

21 See ibid., 34–7.

22 For further discussion of the relationship between the CCPA and DRIE, see M.M. Atkinson and W.D. Coleman, *State and Industry: Growth and Decline in the Canadian Economy* (forthcoming), chapter 7.

23 For further discussion, see M.M. Atkinson and W. Coleman, "Corporatism and Industrial Policy," in A. Cawson, ed., *Organized Interests and the State: Studies in Meso-Corporatism* (London: Sage 1985), 22–44.

24 For a general treatment of this process of delegation, see Wolfgang Streeck, "Die Reform des beruflichen Bildung in der westdeutschen Bauwirtschaft 1969–1982: Eine Fallstudie über Verbände als Träger öffentlicher Politik," Discussion Paper IIM/LMP 83–23 (Berlin: Wissenschaftszentrum Berlin 1983).

25 Thomas L. Ilgen, "Between Europe and America, Ottawa and the Provinces: Regulating Toxic Substances in Canada," *Canadian Public Policy* 37, No. 4 (1985): 587.

26 Ibid.

27 Statistics Canada, *Manufacturing Industries of Canada: National and Provincial Areas, 1981,* Catalogue 31–203 (Ottawa: Supply and Services Canada 1984), 3.

28 Ibid., 7.

29 P.A. Victor and T.N. Burrell with J. Evans and C. Figueiredo, *Environmental Protection Regulation: Water Pollution and the Pulp and Paper Industry,* Technical Report 14 (Ottawa: Economic Council 1981), 1–3.

30 F.J. Anderson and W.C. Bonsor, *The Pulp and Paper Industry: A Regional Profitability Analysis* (Toronto: Ontario Economic Council 1985).

31 Letter to the author from the manager, Technical Section, CPPA, 26 August 1980.

32 Victor and Burrell, *Environmental Protection,* 3.

33 Ibid., 60–1.

34 Ibid., 88, 93.

35 Ibid., 35, 93, 106.

36 Quotation taken from a pamphlet put out by the PPRIC describing its role in the industry.

37 Statement based on budget figures given in the Annual Report of the Institute.

38 The interview was conducted by Kimberly Weslak with the Treasury deputy, in the fall of 1986. It is part of a larger research project on comprehensive business associations in Ontario that serves as the basis for her master's thesis at McMaster University.

39 Carroll, *Corporate Power,* 120ff.

CHAPTER ELEVEN

1 David Cameron, "Social Democracy, Corporatism, Labour Quiescence, and the Representation of Economic Interests in Advanced Capitalist Society," in John Goldthorpe, ed., *Order and Conflict in Contemporary Capitalism* (Oxford: Clarendon 1984), 143–78; G. Lehmbruch, "Concertation and the Structure of Corporatist Networks," in ibid., 60–80; Lehmbruch, "Introduction: Neo Corporatism in Comparative Perspective," in Lehmbruch and P.C. Schmitter, eds., *Patterns of Corporatist Policy-Making* (London: Sage 1982), 1–28; Schmitter, "Interest Intermediation and Regime Governability in Contemporary Western Europe and North America," in S. Berger, ed., *Organizing Interests in Western Europe* (Cambridge: Cambridge University Press 1981), 285–327.

2 Lehmbruch, "Concertation," 65–6.

3 Ibid.

4 Ibid., 68–9.
5 Peter Katzenstein, *Corporatism and Change: Austria, Switzerland and the Politics of Industry* (Ithaca: Cornell University Press 1984), 34.
6 Ibid., 15.
7 Ibid.
8 B. Marin, "Austria: The Paradigm Case of Liberal Corporatism?," in W. Grant, ed., *The Political Economy of Corporatism* (London: Macmillan 1985), 94.
9 Ibid., 95.
10 Katzenstein, *Corporatism*, 62–3.
11 Marin, "Paradigm Case," 97.
12 C. Offe and H. Wiesenthal, "Two Logics of Collective Action: Theoretical Notes on Social Class and Organizational Form," *Political Power and Social Theory* 1 (1980): 67–115.
13 Marin, "The Paradigm Case," 100.
14 Ibid.
15 Lehmbruch notes that in the "bourgeois" camp, there is normally stronger differentation between parties and associations than in the labour camp. There is also often more than one bourgeois party. See Lehmbruch, "Concertation," 75.
16 Marin, "Paradigm Case," 101.
17 Ibid.
18 Lehmbruch, "Concertation," 74ff.; Katzenstein, *Corporatism*, 74.
19 Katzenstein, *Corporatism*, 74.
20 Fritz Scharpf, "Economic and Institutional Constraints of Full Employment Strategies: Sweden, Austria and West Germany," in Goldthorpe, ed., *Order and Conflict*, 260.
21 For details, see Katzenstein, *Corporatism*, chapter 3.
22 Bernd Marin, *Die Paritätische Kommission: Aufgeklärter Technokorporatismus in Österreich* (Wien: Internationale Publikationen 1982), 29.
23 Ibid.
24 Katzenstein, *Corporatism*, 75ff.
25 Marin, *Paritätische Kommission*, 29.
26 Ibid., 15–16 (author's translation).
27 Katzenstein, *Corporatism*, 50.
28 Ibid.
29 The nationalized sector accounts for 28 per cent of the industrial workforce, compared to 28 per cent for foreign firms and 44 per cent for private Austrian firms; ibid.
30 K. Dyson, "Cultural, Ideological and Structural Context," in Dyson and S. Wilks, eds. *Industrial Crisis* (Oxford: Martin Robertson 1983), 45.
31 Ibid., 55–6.
32 John Zysman, *Governments, Markets and Growth* (Ithaca: Cornell University Press 1983).

33 Wyn Grant and David Marsh, *The Confederation of British Industry* (London: Hodder and Stoughton 1977), 32.

34 W. Grant, "Representing Capital: The First Fifteen Years of the CBI," paper presented to the British Sociological Association/Political Studies Association Political Sociology Group Conference on Capital, Ideology and Politics, University of Sheffield, 8–9 January 1981, 14.

35 Grant and Marsh, *The Confederation*, 81.

36 Ibid., 23.

37 Ibid., 74.

38 Ibid.

39 Grant, "Representing Capital," 11.

40 W. Grant, "The Business Lobby: Political Attitudes and Strategies," in H. Berrington, ed., *Change in British Politics* (London: Dent 1984), 173.

41 Grant and Marsh, *The Confederation*, 72.

42 Keith Middlemas, *Politics in Industrial Society* (London: André Deutsch 1979), 373.

43 Ibid., 379.

44 For further details, see W. Coleman and W. Grant, "Business Associations and Public Policy: A Comparison of Organisational Development in Britain and Canada," *Journal of Public Policy* 4, No. 3 (1984): 213–20.

45 Ibid., 216.

46 Ibid.

47 Ibid., 218–20.

48 Ibid., 220.

49 See ibid.

50 See W.D. Coleman and Wyn Grant, "Regional Differentiation of Business Interest Associations: A Comparison of Canada and the United Kingdom," *Canadian Journal of Political Science* 18, No. 1 (1985): 3–29.

51 Coleman and Grant, "Business Associations," 230–2.

52 W. Grant, "Large Firms and Public Policy in Britain," *Journal of Public Policy* 4, No. 1 (1984): 1–17.

53 Coleman and Grant, "Business Associations," 228.

54 Katzenstein, *Corporatism*, 31.

55 See, for example, the following papers presented at the Conference on the Regional Organization of Business and Public Policy, McMaster University, May 1985: W. Streeck, "The Organization of *Handwerk* in Germany," and Carlota Solé, "Business Organizations, Regionalism and Industrial Change: The Case of the Spanish Textile Industry."

CHAPTER TWELVE

1 Alan C. Cairns, "The Governments and Societies of Canadian Federalism," *Canadian Journal of Political Science* 10, No. 4 (1977): 695–725.

2 Ibid., 700.

3 Ibid., 706.

4 See ibid., 713–14, and David B. Truman, *The Governmental Process* (New York: Knopf 1951), 112; Helen J. Dawson, "National Pressure Groups and the Federal Government," in A. Paul Pross, ed., *Pressure Group Politics in Canada* (Toronto: McGraw-Hill 1975), 29–31; and David Kwavnick, "Interest Group Demands and the Federal Political System: Two Canadian Case Studies," in Pross, ed., *Pressure Group Politics*, 70–86.

5 Truman, *The Governmental Process*, 112.

6 Dawson, "National Pressure Groups," 29–31.

7 Ibid., 31.

8 For examples, see Richard J. Schultz, *Federalism, Bureaucracy and Public Policy: The Politics of Highway Transport Regulation* (Montreal: McGill-Queen's 1980), and Kwavnick, "Interest Group Demands."

9 For a good case study of this phenomenon, see Schultz, *Federalism*.

10 This argument is elaborated in Richard Simeon, *Federal-Provincial Diplomacy* (Toronto: University of Toronto Press 1972), 142, and in Hugh Thorburn, *Interest Groups in the Canadian Federal System*, Studies of the Royal Commission on the Economic Union and Development Prospects for Canada, Volume 69 (Toronto: University of Toronto Press 1985), 68–77.

11 A three-digit category corresponds usually to what Statistics Canada calls an industry, as opposed to a two-digit category, which is termed an industry group. For example, 37 refers to the group of chemical industries, and 374 to one industry in that group, drugs and medicines.

12 For further elaboration, see W. Coleman and W. Grant, "Regional Differentiation of Business Interest Associations: A Comparison of Canada and the United Kingdom," *Canadian Journal of Political Science* 18, No. 1 (1985): 7–9.

13 Stein Rokkan and Derek Urwin, *Economy, Territory, Identity: Politics of West European Peripheries* (London: Sage 1983), 181–7.

14 For elaboration, see Wyn Grant, "The Regional Organization of Business Interests and Public Policy in the U.K.," paper presented to Conference on the Regional Organization of Business Interests and Public Policy, McMaster University, May 1985.

15 Nevil Johnson, *Government in the Federal Republic of Germany: The Executive at Work* (New York: Pergammon 1973), 105.

16 Ibid., 86.

17 G.A. Codding, *The Federal Government of Switzerland* (Boston: Houghton Mifflin 1965), 43.

18 Jürg Steiner, *Amicable Agreement versus Majority Rule: Conflict Resolution in Switzerland* (Chapel Hill, NC: University of North Carolina Press 1974), 110.

19 Following the order of the sectors in Table 15–4 (food, machine tools, construction, chemicals), the associations selected for each country were as follows:

CANADA: Canadian Meat Council, National Dairy Council, Canadian Food Processors' Association, Grocery Products Manufacturers of Canada, Machinery and Equipment Manufacturers Association of Canada, Canadian Home Builders Association, Canadian Construction Association, Canadian Chemical Producers Association, Canadian Agricultural Chemicals Association, Society of the Plastics Industry of Canada, Canadian Fertilizer Institute, Pharmaceutical Manufacturers Association of Canada.

SWITZERLAND: Verband der schweizerischen Metzgermeister, Schweiz. Milchkäufervand, Vereinigung schweiz. Lebensmittelfabrikanten, Verein schweiz. Maschinenindustrieller, Schweiz. Baumeisterverband, Schweiz. Zimmermeisterverband, Schweiz. Gesellschaft für chemischen Industrie.

UNITED KINGDOM: Bacon and Meat Manufacturers' Association, Dairy Trade Federation, Food Manufacturers' Federation, Machine Tool Trades Association, Gauge and Tool Makers' Association, Engineering Employers Federation, Engineering Industries Association, Building Employers Confederation, Federation of Master Builders, Federation of Civil Engineering Contractors, Chemical Industries Association, and Association of the British Pharmaceuticals Industry.

WEST GERMANY: Deutscher Fleischerverband, Bundesverband der Fleischwarenindustrie, Verband des deutschen Milchwirtschaft, Bundesfachverband der Marktmolkereien, Bundesverband der privaten Milchwirtschaft, Deutscher Raiffeisenverband, Milchindustrieverband, Gemeinschaft der milchwirtschaftlichen Landersvereinigungen, Bundesverband des Obst- und Gemüseverarbeitenden Industrie, Bundesvereinigung des Deutschen Ernährungsindustrie, Verein deutscher metallindustriellen Arbeitgeberverbände, Verein deutscher Werkzeugmaschinenfabriken, Hauptverband der deutschen Bauindustrie, Zentralverband des deutschen Baugewerbes, Verband des chemischen Industrie, Bundesverband der pharmazeutischen Industrie.

Sources consulted included W. Grant, "The Organization of Business Interests in the U.K. Machine Tools Industry," Discussion Paper IIM/LMP 83–21 (Berlin: Wissenschaftszentrum Berlin 1983); Josef Hilbert "Verbände in produzierenden Ernährungsgewerbe der Bundesrepublik Deutschland," typescript, Bielefeld, 1983; Hanspeter Kriesi and Peter Farago, "The Regional Differentiation of Business Interest Associations in Switzerland," paper presented to Conference on the Regional Organization of Business Interests and Public Policy, McMaster University, May 1985; and Peter Farago, Heinz Ruf, and F. Wieder, "Wirtschaftsverbände in der schweizer Nahrungsmittelindustrie" (Zürich: Soziologisches Institut der Universität Zürich 1984).

20 See W. Coleman, "Federalism and Interest Group Organization," in H. Bakvis and W. Chandler, eds., *Federalism and the Role of the State* (Toronto: University of Toronto Press 1987), 171–87.

21 Kriesi and Farago, "Regional Differentiation," 11–12.

22 Thorburn, *Interest Groups*, 56.

23 The Conseil du Patronat (CPQ) is not a separate francophone business association, existing in parallel presumably to such national associations as the Business Council on National Issues and the CMA. The CPQ, it will be recalled from chapter 5, is an affiliate of the BCNI, and the Quebec Division of the CMA belongs to the CPQ! The Conseil was created at the instigation not of francophone business, but of big business in the province, French and mainly English. The chambers of commerce compete for francophone members. Similarly, the Chamber of Commerce in Quebec does not have a status any different than any other provincial chamber of commerce, also as noted in chapter 5. Its executive vice-president made this point forcefully in reply to a letter I sent to him on this matter.

24 Thorburn, *Interest Groups*, 56

25 See W. Coleman, "From Bill 22 to Bill 101: The Politics of Language under the Parti québécois," *Canadian Journal of Political Science* 14, No. 3 (1981): 459–86, and "The Class Bases of Language Policy in Canada," *Studies in Political Economy* No. 3 (1980): 93–118.

26 W. Coleman, *The Independence Movement in Quebec, 1945–1980* (Toronto: University of Toronto Press 1984).

27 See P. Fournier, "Les nouveaux paramètres de la bourgeoisie québécoise," in Fournier, ed., *Le capitalisme au Québec* (Montréal: Albert Martin 1978), 137–81. Fournier, in turn, is reacting to an alternative view proposed by J. Niosi, "The New French Canadian Bourgeoisie," *Studies in Political Economy* No. 1 (1979): 113–61.

28 A. Raynauld and F. Vaillancourt, *L'appartenance des entreprises: le cas du Québec en 1978* (Quebec: Editeur officiel du Québec 1984), 50ff. This work updates an earlier work by Raynauld, *La propriété des entreprises au Québec* (Montreal: Les Presses de l'Université de Montréal 1974), which drew on data from the 1961 census.

29 Raynauld and Vaillancourt, *L'appartenance*, 93.

30 Ibid., 107. The authors note that this figure represents progress for francophone firms: in 1961, they exported 22 per cent of their production.

31 Ibid., 118 (author's translation).

32 Ibid., 49.

33 Statistics Canada, *Sawmills and Planing Mills and Shingle Mills, 1982*, Catalogue 35–204 (Ottawa: Supply and Services Canada 1984), 4.

34 Letter to the author from the executive director, 28 May 1981.

35 This figure includes household furniture (416 establishments), office furniture (33), and miscellaneous furniture (166); Statistics Canada, *Furniture Manufacturers, 1982*, Catalogue 35–216 (Ottawa: Supply and Services Canada 1984), 12, 27, 36.

36 Letter to the author from the executive secretary, 15 August 1980.

37 This density figure is calculated using the list of establishments active in the sub-sector and their estimated level of employment published by Statistics Canada and the list of members supplied by the association. For a more detailed description of calculation procedures, see W. Coleman, "The Political Organization of Business Interests in the Canadian Food Processing Industry," Discussion Paper IIM/LMP 84–6 (Berlin: Wissenschaftszentrum Berlin 1984), 47–8.

38 The Association des entrepreneurs en construction du Québec is not discussed here. It is the compulsory employers' association (collective bargaining) in the province (see chapter 7).

39 By mixed association, I mean an association that has both direct firm members and association members.

40 At the time of writing, the CCA is moving towards abolition of the simple affiliate category.

41 For further elaboration of this argument, see Coleman, *The Independence Movement*, 103–29.

42 Sidbec is also a member of the Canadian Institute of Steel Construction.

43 Dyson, *The State Tradition in Western Europe* (Oxford: Martin Robertson 1980).

44 Ibid., 212.

45 Ibid., 66.

46 A.P. Pross, "Parliamentary Influence and the Diffusion of Power," *Canadian Journal of Political Science* 18, No. 2 (1985): 240.

47 Ibid., 251.

48 Pross, "Diffusion," 252.

49 Ibid., 255–63.

50 Colin Campbell, *Governments under Stress* (Toronto: University of Toronto Press 1983).

51 M.M. Atkinson and W. Coleman, "Bureaucrats and Politicians in Canada: An Examination of the Political Administration Model," *Comparative Political Studies* 18, No. 1 (1985): 66.

52 Ibid., 73.

CHAPTER THIRTEEN

1 Charles Lindblom, *Politics and Markets* (New York: Basic 1977).

2 Mancur Olson, *The Rise and Decline of Nations* (New Haven: Yale Uni-

versity Press 1982), 47–59.

3 John Zysman, *Governments, Markets, and Growth: Financial Systems and the Politics of Industrial Change* (Ithaca: Cornell University Press 1983), 78.

4 Based on calculations by the author using the publications by OECD, *Historical Statistics, 1960–1980* and *Historical Statistics, 1963–1984* respectively.

5 Gordon Laxer, "Foreign Ownership and Myths about Canadian Development," *Canadian Review of Sociology and Anthropology* 22, No. 3 (1985): 329.

6 Ibid., 330.

7 Roy A. Matthews, *Structural Change and Industrial Policy: The Redeployment of Canadian Manufacturing, 1960–1980* (Ottawa: Economic Council of Canada 1985), 18.

8 See ibid., 34, and J.H. Britton and J.M. Gilmour, *The Weakest Link: A Technological Perspective on Canadian Industrial Underdevelopment* (Ottawa: Science Council of Canada 1978).

9 For a discussion, see Richard French, *How Ottawa Decides* (Ottawa: Lorimer 1984), and Stephen Clarkson, *Canada and the Reagan Challenge* (Toronto: Lorimer 1985).

10 Peter Katzenstein, *Small States in World Markets: Industrial Policy in Europe* (Ithaca: Cornell University Press 1985), 86.

11 Ibid.

12 Calculations by the author drawn from Statistics Canada, *Science and Technology Indicators*, Catalogue 88–201 (Ottawa: Supply and Services Canada 1984), 188.

13 Katzenstein, *Small States*, 85–6.

14 Ibid., 59.

15 Zysman, *Governments, Markets and Growth*, conclusion.

16 Katzenstein, *Small States*, chapter 20.

17 Ibid.

18 This discussion is drawn from ibid., 30–4.

19 Katzenstein studied the following six countries intensively in ibid.: Belgium, Denmark, the Netherlands, Norway, Sweden, and Switzerland.

20 Ibid., 33.

21 G. Lehmbruch, "Interest Intermediation in Capitalist and Socialist Systems: Some Structural and Functional Perspectives in Comparative Research," *International Political Science Review* 4, No. 2 (1983): 153–72.

22 Matthews, *Structural Change*, 12.

23 Keith G. Banting, "The State and Economic Interests: An Introduction," in Banting, ed., *The State and Economic Interests*, Studies of the Royal Commission on the Economic Union and Development Prospects for Canada, Volume 32 (Toronto: University of Toronto Press 1986), 1–34.

24 G. Lehmbruch, "Neocorporatism in Western Europe: A Reassessment

of the Concept in Cross National Perspective," paper presented to the 13th World Congress of the International Political Science Association, Paris, 1985.

25 Royal Commission on the Economic Union and Development Prospects for Canada (Macdonald Commission), *Report*, Vol. III (Ottawa: Supply and Services Canada 1985), 54.

26 James Gillies, *Facing Reality: Consultation, Consensus and Making Economic Policy for the 21st Century* (Montreal: IRPP 1986).

27 Banting, "The State," 10.

28 Macdonald Commission, *Report*, III, 55.

29 The term "ambivalent" is borrowed from Keith Banting and his useful review of the Macdonald Commission's discussion of consultation. See his paper "Economic Consultation and the Macdonald Commission: Research and Recommendations," presented to the Symposium on the Consultative Process in Business-Government Relations, York University, 24–25 April 1986.

30 Macdonald Commission, *Report*, III, 63.

31 Ibid., 42

32 Special Committee on Reform of the House of Commons, *Report* (Ottawa: House of Commons 1985), 21–2.

33 Macdonald Commission, *Report*, III, 64–5.

34 Grace Skogstad, "Interest Groups, Representation and Conflict Management in the Standing Committees of the House of Commons," *Canadian Journal of Political Science* 18, No. 4 (1985): 770–2.

35 Charles Anderson, "Political Design and the Representation of Interests," in P.C. Schmitter and G. Lehmbruch, eds., *Trends toward Corporatist Intermediation* (London: Sage 1979), 290.

36 Canadian Manufacturers' Association, *A Future That Works* (Toronto: CMA 1984), 58.

37 For a discussion, see W. Coleman, "State Corporatism as a Sectoral Phenomenon," in Alan Cawson, ed., *Organized Interests and the State: Studies in Meso-Corporatism* (London: Sage 1985).

38 Macdonald Commission, *Report*, III, 463–4.

39 John E. Chubb, *Interest Groups and the Bureaucracy: The Politics of Energy* (Stanford: Stanford University Press 1983), 8–10.

40 Ibid., 10.

41 A. Paul Pross, "Parliamentary Influence and the Diffusion of Power," *Canadian Journal of Political Science* 18, No. 2 (1985): 235–66.

42 T.J. Lowi, *The End of Liberalism*, 2nd edition (New York: Norton 1979), 92ff.

43 Lindblom, *Politics and Markets*, chapter 13.

44 Special Committee on Reform of the House of Commons, *Report*, 35–6.

45 Olson, *The Rise*, passim.

46 Claus Offe and Helmut Wiesenthal, "Two Logics of Collective Action: Theoretical Notes on Social Class and Organizational Form," *Political and Social Theory* 1 (1980): 67–115.

47 See Jeffrey Berry, *Lobbying for the People* (Princeton: Princeton University Press 1977), and Jack L. Walker, "The Origins and Maintenance of Interest Groups in America," *American Political Science Review* 77, No. 2 (1983): 390–406.

48 See his two papers, "Democratic Theory and Neo-Corporatist Practice," European University Institute Working Paper No. 94 (Florence: EUI 1983); " 'Neo Corporatism,' 'Consensus,' 'Governability' and 'Democracy' in the Management of Crisis in Contemporary Advanced Industrial/ Capitalist Societies," paper presented to the OECD Expert Group on Collective Bargaining and Economic Policies: Dialogue and Consensus, Paris, 1983. Schmitter held a conference on this topic in May 1985 at the European University Institute, and a volume based on the papers will probably appear.

49 H.D. Clarke, J. Jenson, L. Leduc, and J.H. Pammett, *Absent Mandate: The Politics of Discontent in Canada* (Toronto: Gage 1984).

50 Ibid., 11–12.

51 OECD, *Positive Adjustment Policies: Managing Structural Change* (Paris: OECD 1983).

52 Ibid.

Index

198–203, 211, 213; compared to Britain, 233
Forbes, J.D., 105, 306n
Forest industry, 25, 144, 147, 154–6; regulation of, 157–8, 164
Forest industry associations, 147–50, 154, 212
Forster, Ben, 20, 24, 295n
Fournier, Pierre, 249, 253, 255

Germany (West), xii, 198, 206, 222, 236, 265; federalism, 244; territorial differentiation of associations, 244–9
Gillies, James, 10, 11, 270
Gollner, Andrew, 10
Government relations divisions, 9, 10, 11, 13, 208
Grain co-operatives, 107, 109, 112–13, 114
Grain transportation and handling system, 110–14
Grant, Wyn, xv, 9, 10, 231, 234, 246, 293n, 316n, 320n, 321n, 322n
Grocery Products Manufacturers of Canada (GPMC), 200–2, 203, 204, 298n, 300n

Health Protection Branch (HPB), 202, 203, 209, 279
Howe, C.D., 25

Independent Petroleum Association of Canada (IPAC), 23, 49, 151, 153, 255
Industrial policy, 7, 266, 268
Industry culture, 5, 264
Institute of Association Executives, 42–3
Investment Dealers Association of Canada (IDAC), xiii, 24, 174, 181,

187–90; and Canadian Securities Institute, 182, 189

Jacek, Henry J., xi, xii, xiv, 13
Jenson, Jane, 97
Jordan, A.G., 11, 294n

Katzenstein, Peter, 67, 68, 224, 226, 270, 282, 320n, 325n
Kealey, Gregory, 22
Kniewasser, Andrew, xiii, 316n
Knights of Labor, 22
Kriesi, Hanspeter, xiv, 246, 248, 322n
Kwavnick, David, 240

Labour, 13, 26, 83, 94, 219, 229, 269, 270, 284–5; and business associations, 22, 222–3, 271–2; and corporatism, 266–7; and political parties, 98, 267; fragmentation of, 273–4; in construction industry, 124, 132, 133, 138, 139–41, 142; strengthening organization of, 280–1
Langille, David, 83, 85, 86
Leduc, Lawrence, 97
Lehmbruch, Gerhard, 75, 82, 222, 269, 282, 300n, 319n, 325n
Lindblom, Charles, 4, 278, 293n
Litvak, Isaiah, 11, 38, 64
Lowi, Theodore, 67, 73, 74, 277, 299n

McConnell, Grant, 73, 299n, 300n, 303n
Macdonald Commission, 270, 271, 274
MacIntosh, R.M., 184, 186
Malles, Paul, 132, 135
Manufacturing associations, 31, 33, 38, 194; in chemicals, 203–10,